The Quiet Coup

The Quiet Coup

NEOLIBERALISM AND THE LOOTING OF AMERICA

Mehrsa Baradaran

W. W. NORTON & COMPANY
Independent Publishers Since 1923

For information about permission to reproduce selections from this book,
write to Permissions, W. W. Norton & Company, Inc., 500 Fifth Avenue,
New York, NY 10110

For information about special discounts for bulk purchases, please
contact W. W. Norton Special Sales at specialsales@wwnorton.com or
800-233-4830

Manufacturing by Lakeside Book Company
Book design by Brooke Koven
Production manager: Julia Druskin

ISBN 978-1-324-09116-5

W. W. Norton & Company, Inc., 500 Fifth Avenue, New York, N.Y. 10110
www.wwnorton.com

W. W. Norton & Company Ltd., 15 Carlisle Street, London W1D 3BS

1 2 3 4 5 6 7 8 9 0

To Cyra, Lucia, and Ramona, my candles in the dark.

Time catches up with kingdoms and crushes them, gets its teeth into doctrines and rends them; time reveals the foundations on which any kingdom rests, and eats at those foundations, and it destroys doctrines by proving them to be untrue.

—JAMES BALDWIN, *THE FIRE NEXT TIME* (1963)

Contents

Introduction

ON THE MORNING of November 8, 2018, the residents of Paradise, California, awoke to sirens announcing an emergency evacuation order. It was already too late. The wildfire was out of control and was spreading at a rate of eighty football fields a minute, closing off escape routes and melting asphalt faster than many of the town's elderly residents could leave their homes. One man abandoned his wheelchair and tried to crawl his way out of his house. Another elderly couple was found in their reclining chairs, holding their dogs and cats.[1] The Camp Fire raged for seventeen days, destroying three communities and one million acres, and killing eighty-four people.[2] Persistent droughts caused by climate change increased the threat of fire, but several investigations found that the catastrophic scale of the Camp Fire could have been prevented had the Pacific Gas and Electric Company (PG&E) made simple repairs to its outdated equipment. Such repairs would have cost money and hurt the company's bottom line with no financial upside, because PG&E is a state monopoly and does not compete for its customers. Instead, California taxpayers (that is, PG&E customers) had to shoulder the costs of the fire, which was among the deadliest, most destructive wildfires California had ever experienced.

Fires are often called "acts of God" in the anachronistic language of contract law, but a federal court exonerated God for the disaster and found PG&E criminally liable. The fire was ignited when winds knocked over a worn hook on a seventy-two-year-old PG&E tower, which the company's own internal reports had flagged as dangerous due to "severe wear." It was far from the first time the company's reckless disregard for customer safety had caused fires—since the state mandated PG&E to disclose its equipment failures in 2014, over fifteen hundred fires were blamed on it. The company even faced criminal charges for two subsequent catastrophic failures—the 2019 Kincade Fire and the 2020 Zogg Fire—but avoided prosecution both times.[3]

As the Camp Fire burned, a conservative activist in Georgia named Marjorie Taylor Greene took to Facebook to "ask some questions." The post was soon dubbed "the Jewish Space Laser theory," and it marked the beginning of Greene's rapid trajectory from CrossFit enthusiast to right-wing gadfly to one of the most prominent congressional Republicans.

Mimicking President Donald Trump's conspiratorial, "just asking questions" style, Greene's post tied together "coincidences" and facts out of context to insinuate that a cabal of California Democrats and bankers intentionally set the fire for profit. Her "evidence" included recent swings in PG&E stock, which plummeted during the fires but was sent soaring again when the California Public Utilities Commission (CPUC) signaled that it would bail out the firm if necessary.

For Greene, CPUC's announcement was just the latest bread crumb in a trail that implicated not only PG&E and California state officials, but Senator Dianne Feinstein, the clean-energy firm Solaren, and the Rothschilds, a Jewish banking family that once featured prominently in Nazi propaganda. Rather than state her views outright, Greene offered a series of "coincidences," hinting that the fires may have been part of a larger plot. "There are all these people," she wrote, who saw "lasers or blue beams of light causing the fires." After admitting, "I don't know anything about that," she said that she did "find it curious" that PG&E had partnered with Solaren in 2009 to pursue "space solar generation." (The enabling technology has yet to be developed, and Solaren has certainly built nothing like a blue light-beaming laser.)

The post landed Greene in the national spotlight. She was elected to Congress in 2020 after a campaign filled with even more incendiary accusations and hateful provocations, and her star kept rising. For several years, she has been one of the top five Republican fund-raisers and is also head of the Congressional Freedom Caucus, which is one of the most powerful blocs in Congress as of this writing.[4] While the money and fame reveal the nature of Greene's hustle, there remains the problem of why there is such a large market for what she is selling.

Greene's scientific absurdity and crude antisemitism quickly became the stuff of comedy: the hashtag #JewishSpaceLasers trended on Twitter and the cast of *Saturday Night Live* mocked her. Less amused commentators noted that Greene's insinuation of Rothschild collusion hinted that the story she was telling was much more sinister than one of quotidian corruption. They are right. The scapegoating of the Rothschilds may have been meaningless noise, an emanation from the internet's fever swamps, but what if it was the signal itself?

Adolf Hitler began spewing his conspiratorial lies in 1919 and they were denounced—he was jailed twice for his provocations and ignored by serious politicians until a majority of Germans voted for the Nazi party in 1933. What happened in the interim was economic crisis, inflation, and a growing resentment that the once great Germans were being taken advantage of by outsiders. There was some truth to the feeling.

John Maynard Keynes, a young British Treasury official, had attended the Versailles Peace Conference in 1919, when the British, French, and Americans met to determine Germany's war reparations. Instead of dealing fairly with the defeated Central Powers, Keynes explained, the Allies decided instead to take advantage of their defeated rival and take their pound of flesh in gold, which imposed a crushing debt on the German people. The Allied powers demanded 132 billion gold marks ($500 billion today) as restitution; it took Germany ninety-two years to pay the sum. The French proposed the scandalous deal and President Woodrow Wilson fatefully decided to agree to the much more punitive proposal, allegedly because he worried about congressional approval. Keynes resigned from the British economic team in protest, calling Wilson "the greatest fraud on earth."[5] Keynes explained the problem in *The Economic Consequences of the Peace*, published in 1919, pleading "if we aim at the impoverishment of Central Europe, vengeance, I dare say, will not limp." He explained that the reparations were unpayable and would lead to chaos and explained also that markets were not separate from politics and peace had as much to do with interest rates as with government. His warnings of the consequences of imposing this unfair deal must have seemed hysterical: "Nothing can then delay for very long the forces of Reaction and the despairing convulsions of Revolution," he wrote, "before which the horrors of the later German war will fade into nothing, and which will destroy, whoever is victor, the civilization and the progress of our generation."[6]

Rampant inequality is a threat to any system of power but most especially to democratic nations whose legitimacy is based on the consent of the governed. To insist on enforcement of property and contract rights while the state's legitimacy was under threat was to miss the full picture—it would be like showing up to a theater with a ticket and demanding to see the show while the theater was burning down. Or in real terms, it was like the European countries insisting that Germany pay full war reparations after World War I while ignoring the greater threat building inside the country, fascism.

Perhaps the analogy is off the mark and Greene is just a political sideshow, but it is hubris to assume that the atrocities that befell Germany could not happen here. It can, and it is already happening. The seeds of hate that Greene is constantly and recklessly spewing into the discourse have found fertile ground. Greene may be a canary in the coal mine or a real threat, but she is a clear symptom of the deep resentment-fueled cynicism in which many regular Americans have been marinating.

The discomforting truth is that if you look past the lies and the scapegoating, Greene's post is about political corruption—about deep-pocketed special interests, influence peddling, and regulatory capture that led to the fires. The basic thesis of the message is that something smells fishy; its emotion is moral outrage: "Someone is cheating and it's not fair." Change the message to "Some corporations are cheating and it's not fair" and it begins to harmonize with similar warnings from the left. But it is one thing to point out a corrupt system and quite another to begin naming names, blaming groups, and stoking resentments. Unfortunately, this phenomenon is not historically unusual—the fascist regimes of the twentieth century were spawned in a petri dish of state corruption and weaponized xenophobia. Across the globe, the conspiratorial right has risen to prominence in countries as different as India, Brazil, and Sweden. In each of these nations, and others, it has gained an audience by denouncing what is, in fact, a corrupt legal system.

Rule of law is essential to a thriving market; its absence is a harbinger of societal collapse. Yet the difference between a society where laws are generally followed and enforced and one where bribery, corruption, and violence are prevalent has much less to do with the laws on the books or their enforcement and is much more likely to come down to whether people *trust* that the laws are being enforced *fairly*. The distinction is invisible to the naked eye—but it makes all the difference in the world. Trust is a subjective experience—it must be felt. And like its kin feelings of fairness and freedom, it cannot be papered over with meaningless words if a society isn't actually fair or free.

A pervasive *sense* that a game is rigged will eventually destroy the game. Justice is a *feeling*, not a legal code. Faith in the just enforcement of laws is the Rubicon between order and chaos, and it is difficult to know how close any society is to the line where contracts and statutes are replaced by strongmen with guns. The United States has yet to cross this line, but one of the aims of this book is to convince the reader that we are close—and not because of the likes of Greene and Trump; they are the symptoms, the misfiring antibodies to a growing rot, a cancer in the body politic that began decades ago and can be seen across our legal system if one knows where to look.

This book tells the story of how an ideology called *neoliberalism* infected our politics, creating a complex and impenetrable network of laws and regulations that has created a system which is inherently unfair. Neoliberalism is an economic ideology that champions free markets as the sole guarantor of freedom and catalyst for prosperity while denouncing taxation and regulation as a threat to liberty. You may believe you've heard this story before. There have indeed been many brilliant books in recent years about the epochal changes to America's (and indeed the world's) political economy since the 1970s, covering everything from deindustrialization and financialization to the rise of "pink-collar" work and skyrocketing inequality, and more—and sometimes all at once. This book tells a revisionist story of neoliberalism that takes the conversation away from the realm of economics and focuses instead on the law. We've missed the root causes, the primary actors, and much of the (ongoing) harms of neoliberalism because we haven't looked closely at the role of law in shaping our society. Free markets aren't actually free, as many people now understand. They—and the ideology that supports them—have to be built and maintained. *The Quiet Coup* tells the story of how that has happened in America, and why it matters.

Specifically, this book focuses on how neoliberal ideologies justified subtle yet profound changes to the laws and institutions that govern the market. Neoliberalism did not make markets more free and government less interventionist as promised—they made both more complex, opaque, and unfair. These laws are still being enforced, of course, and the justice system works to put fraudsters, insider traders, and criminals in jail following appropriate procedures. But the system itself has been so perforated with loopholes and bogged down by opaque procedures and legal complexity that it has become almost impossible for the law to discipline corporations. Put simply, the laws that shape the market are not fair because they have been twisted to serve ends that are not *our* ends. This was no accident; the book will cover some of the key figures and milestones that shaped the course of legal change, weakening the legal system's power to regulate the market. It will only get worse if left unchecked, and the danger it poses to our democracy cannot be overstated. Corruption is a one-way ratchet that leads only to more corruption. The gap between justice and law is metastatic, and can only grow until it destroys what little remains of public trust in our government.

The 2018 Camp Fire is a good example of the rot of corruption burrowed deep inside the regulatory bureaucracy, which should have had many people asking questions. PG&E is a state utility monopoly that is also a publicly traded company—its legal mandate requires the firm to answer to the citizens of California while its bottom line has a different master: the capital markets. Specifically, shareholders who expect maximum return on investment (ROI). PG&E was privatized in the 1990s alongside other state utilities during the heyday of neoliberalism, but while its profit model oriented it toward Wall Street, it retained its status as a state utility with a monopoly over most of California's major cities.

This was typical of the neoliberal era, which promised one thing—free markets—but delivered its opposite—corruption and self-dealing.

After facing criminal charges for deaths caused by their malfeasance, the company pled guilty to criminal negligence and was mandated to pay $3.5 million in fines, a drop in the bucket compared with its annual revenues of $200 billion, which is why the company's stock price soared.[7] There would have been more fines, but the company promptly entered a Chapter 11 bankruptcy to head off future liabilities.[8] Part of PG&E's 2020 reorganization plan included a hedge fund loan of around $38 billion, which will come from PG&E customer profits over time. According to the legal code, the hedge fund loan takes priority over all other claims and liabilities, which includes the cost of updating the utility's fire-prone infrastructure.

After the company emerged from bankruptcy, it still did not update the faulty wires. Instead, PG&E chose the less costly alternative of shutting off power whenever its internal "fire potential forecasts" predicted a possible "ignition risk." In 2019, more than two million Californians had their power shut off for up to several days during the course of the year, causing hardship for the elderly and disabled in high fire-threat districts, which happen to be the most impoverished regions in the state.[9] To remedy the situation, which Governor Gavin Newsom described as an unacceptable burden "that no state in the twenty-first century should experience," the state budget included an additional $75 million to help the most vulnerable get help during the emergency shutoffs.[10] In other words, California taxpayers stepped in to protect the people who fell out of PG&E's cost-benefit analysis, thereby granting PG&E shareholders another taxpayer subsidy to help the bottom line. These so-called public safety shutoffs effectively passed the cost and inconvenience of preventing fires from the tortious arsonists to the past and future victims of the ruinous fires.

The point of bankruptcy—its *spirit*—is to offer flailing firms a second chance at survival by forgiving their debts. Yet, in a triumph of form over function, healthy corporations like PG&E and Purdue Pharma have taken advantage of the mercy offered by Chapter 11 protection to rid themselves of liabilities for their own malfeasance. For some businesses, filing for bankruptcy has become a routine maneuver enabling

them to reorganize their firms by ridding themselves of unwanted liabilities, including employee pensions and legal liabilities stemming from
their own wrongdoing. Even more troubling in the current state of the
field is that companies have the freedom to choose a lenient jurisdiction
and judge in a state far from their base of operations—all of Purdue
Pharma's present and future liabilities for fostering the opiate pandemic
were resolved in a small court in White Plains, New York, flanked by
a handful of Wall Street lawyers. PG&E filed for bankruptcy after the
Camp Fire fiasco, but it was the firm's second time through the process.
It had also filed in 2001. Both times, Wall Street rewarded the company
with surging stock prices and new investments after their liabilities were
"forgiven" by the bankruptcy court. As part of its restructuring, PG&E
handed 169 million shares of the company to a consortium of twenty
hedge funds in an equity-backstop deal, which resulted in $2 billion in
earnings for those hedge funds. It was a win-win for PG&E and Wall
Street, and the firm's CEO was rewarded with a pay raise.

The fact that PG&E can finance itself on the market and enjoy
monopoly status gives the firm the best of both worlds. The hitch is that
the firm has a dedicated state utility regulator, the CPUC, overseeing its
pricing and service requirements. The laws and rules that create the market are made not by legislatures, but by state or federal regulators who
have specialized knowledge and experience. On the federal scale, Congress has delegated practically all its market governance authority to a
group of regulatory bodies who have sole control over the industries they
oversee. The regulatory state was created and authorized after the Great
Depression to protect markets against malfeasance and excessive risk-
taking—since then, this government bureaucracy has grown in power,
authority, and complexity. These agencies are invisible to average people
and opaque even to the other branches of government on account of the
complexity and scale of the regulatory state and the markets they govern.
In the case of PG&E, the CPUC would have been the only legal entity
that could have mandated the repairs—in fact, the agency's explicit mission is to protect the safety of customers and to "serve the public interest."[11] The problem is, as is common across the regulatory state, an overlap
of personnel between PG&E executives and their regulators—the head

of the CPUC at the time was a former PG&E executive, a fact that Marjorie Taylor Greene managed to get right among her insinuations of collusion. Even the federal district judge overseeing the case noted the regulator's lackluster safety remediation efforts after a 2010 fire, noting that "it's a revolving door with PG&E over there."[12] Investigations called the relationship "too cozy," insinuating that the regulator may have been confused about whether it was protecting the people or PG&E. But these allegations do not violate the law, and in fact the offended regulator and PG&E both forcefully denied the insinuation of wrongdoing in court, and the judge who dared point out the revolving door formally apologized for making an unprovable (in a court of law) allegation.

State legislatures are another site of power that usually fly under the public's radar, and here it is important to note that PG&E is the largest political donor to California legislators. The firm's $10 million in lobbying funds to the state government should raise eyebrows for those concerned with democratic integrity. But for the bottom line, it's a no-brainer. Whether persuaded by donations or the revolving door, the CPUC did not force the upgrades and even issued a public statement promising to bail out the firm in the event of failure, which had the effect of reassuring markets and bolstering the stock price. The CPUC also generously waived $200 million in fees and fines it had levied for the malfeasance, in order to help the firm after its stock plummeted.[13] Even as it proceeded through the bankruptcy process, PG&E continued to spend millions on lobbying aimed at supporting policies "friendly" to its business model.

As far as PG&E's shareholders are concerned, spending money on lobbying yields the highest ROI—nothing else comes close. Although PG&E executives and shareholders are rewarded according to the terms of the competitive market, the firm has no market competition—its customers include all of California's residents who have no other option but to use PG&E.

Is it any wonder an average American unfamiliar with the legal intricacies of the law might *feel* that something untoward is going on? What can a frustrated PG&E customer do but throw up their hands and "vote the bastards out," as Greene urged? What to do with the pent-up rage and frustration born of powerlessness against untouchable megacorporations that run our lives? It is this feeling that fuels the resentment which Greene and Trump have taken advantage of—and that will only grow until it is addressed. The unseen currency of the complex market system is trust—the invisible hand is our democratic order: we the people, our fair and just legal order, and our democracy ensuring equal access to all, regardless of wealth. It is the "spirit of the law" whose absence is felt before it can be proved. When the fruits of the legal system are blatantly unfair, it is evident that the rot lies at the roots. And Americans are catching on.

One victim of the fire, who has been living in a trailer since losing her home, said of the revelations of the hedge fund sales: "I have zero doubt that Wall Street was behind this. The justice system thoroughly failed the survivors of these fires. They thoroughly failed us. That's a fact."[14]

It bears repeating that there were no conspiracies of the space laser variety behind the 2018 Camp Fire—the dots connected to something much more banal and insidious. Each entity did what it was incentivized to do: PG&E prioritized shareholder returns, the state legislators traded favorable treatment for donations, and investors skimmed more profits from public funds. It was just one instance among myriad others that have come to define the American economy. Nor is this an issue of left versus right, but rather decades of changes to the legal bureaucracy, sometimes called the *regulatory* or *administrative state*, that makes and enforces market rules. The revolving door between PG&E and its regulator, the direct line between lobbying funds and legal decision making, and the complexity of the entire regulatory infrastructure have created a situation where market laws resemble a gameboard, accessible only to those who know how to play. In other words, it was all perfectly legal and aboveboard—PG&E followed industry standards, technical procedures, and best practices to a T. But "legal" is not the same thing as "fair." And the underlying *unfairness,* the *sense* that something is wrong in the system, resonates with many Americans. Although it is hardly unique, the PG&E saga is emblematic of the larger threats to our legal system.

To many Americans, the game is rigged against the average person and in favor of a powerful, unseen force. YouTube videos and viral "news" stories promise to "expose the plot to destroy America." They blame the "deep state," Russian operatives, pedophile rings, "social justice warriors," immigrants, terrorists, Chinese scientists, "globalists," drug companies, the Fed, George Soros, Antifa, Black Lives Matter, "cultural Marxism," critical race theory, Anthony Fauci, and others. Protesters accuse school boards of racial indoctrination, "patriots" attack the Capitol to save America from traitors, and many denounce vaccines and masks as state tyranny.

The viral success of these conspiracy theories is not just a consequence of shameless politicians or of social media algorithms that have hooked us on sensationalism and lunacy. The declining trust in long-standing American institutions plays a role too, as does the notable disappearance of the so-called American dream, which promised success based on individual effort. We now wonder why college graduates are unable to achieve financial security like their parents or grandparents did. Why do pundits and politicians keep saying that the economy is doing great while the majority of Americans can barely make ends meet? Where have all the good jobs gone, and who has taken them? Why has the top 1 percent's net worth increased by $21 trillion over the last ten years, while the bottom 50 percent has lost $900 billion? Why are so many families paying student debt for two generations at once? Why don't bankers go to jail in a nation that still locks up low-level minority offenders at the highest rates in the world? And why do so many politicians keep voting for policies that enrich a minority of wealthy Americans?

In fact, the game *is* rigged toward the powerful—though not at all in the way the conspiracy mongers think. Indeed, many of the people who are complicit in the rigging are the same politicians and activists who speak in dark tones about all-powerful forces acting behind the scenes. Projection, the defense mechanism of blaming others for doing exactly what one is doing oneself, is all too common in modern politics. But while Big Pharma and Dr. Fauci didn't join forces to release a "plandemic" to sell us drugs that we didn't need, it's not outlandish to imagine drug companies covering up risk to extract more financial gain.[15] The 2020 election wasn't stolen from Trump—but Republican gerrymandering and attacks on voting rights, coupled with dark money

PAC donations, have greatly diminished the promise of "one person, one vote." There is no high-level, "deep state" surveillance apparatus run by Hillary Clinton, Bill Gates isn't surreptitiously inserting microchips into our bodies, and 5G towers aren't being used to impose social control—but the NSA spied on Americans, and tech companies routinely monitor our online behavior and exploit our data for profit. Space lasers didn't cause the Camp Fire—but fossil fuel companies have been using dark money for decades to sow doubt about the science of climate change. And obviously, pedophile rings are not pervasive in Washington or New York, but look at the root of the fear and one can see a set of real-world conditions, like social media firms' targeting of teenage girls in their relentless pursuit of engagement despite evidence that their algorithms drive addiction, depression, and psychological harm.

The harms are real and pervasive, and it is too easy to blame a secret confederacy of puppet masters behind the curtain rigging our economy. But the enemy is not a single person or entity. Instead, an ideological bug or virus has infected the law and has been manipulating it to serve its own ends. The bug is a doctrine of political economy whose proponents would call free market capitalism, that academics would call neoliberalism, but that bears an uncanny resemblance to just plain old corruption. From the beginning, neoliberalism was a hollow doctrine more useful as a rhetorical weapon than an actual economic policy.

As this book will explain, this ideology was embraced willingly at a transitionary stage in world history—the 1960s—to fulfill a specific job. Specifically, neoliberal dogmas justified the exploitative status quo of the world's former empires and undermined a global movement for justice and equality led by the formerly disenfranchised, colonized, and oppressed. One of the revisionist arguments of this book is that the ideology of neoliberalism is not the real problem, because it was a red herring from the start. The ideas at the core of the neoliberal project, which many describe as capitalism without state intervention, have long been debunked by scholars, volumes of research, and simple reality: rising tides don't lift all boats, free trade did not lead to world peace, and markets are not necessarily more efficient than governments. Debates about the virtue of markets versus state power miss the mark because they mistake what the ideology purports to do with what it does. For our current economy resembles capitalism as well as our political system resembles democracy—which is hardly at all.

From the beginning, neoliberalism was a Trojan horse. It promised market freedom but delivered its opposite: more laws, lawyers, subsidies, and the largest federal bureaucracy in our nation's history, consisting of over eleven million federal employees and a total government budget of six trillion dollars, which has ballooned in the decades since neoliberalism became state policy. What it did, in practice, was to invade and reshape the regulatory state, making the bureaucracy unintentionally complicit in its own slide toward delegitimization.

The neoliberal coup hardly even registered, because it originated deep within the bureaucracy. The revolutionaries were upstanding citizens—mostly white men in suits—who staffed an entire substructure outside of the regulatory state, including think tanks, academic centers, trade groups, and lobbying groups. This amorphous body is neither state nor market, but neoliberalism in action. It connects government to industry; it produces laws and regulations; it represents money alone. Not acknowledged under the principles of capitalism or democracy, it leaches the vibrancy from both. And the hundreds of thousands of (mostly) law-abiding lawyers, judges, regulators, politicians, and lobbyists engaged in it are guilty of nothing but doing the job the system pays them to do.

While neoliberal economists and politicians convinced the public that government intervention in markets was harmful and inefficient, successive neoliberal administrations that promised to repeal laws constraining the market actually reoriented the gears and levers of lawmaking away from the public they were meant to represent, and toward the industries they were supposed to oversee. Once industry became a key participant in the lawmaking process, laws became more specific, technical, and complex, which made public participation harder and lobbyist expertise more necessary to lawmaking. Under the guise of economic liberalism, a worm of corruption entered our institutions with the predictable result of widespread distrust. Less predictable is what the sense of shared distrust will do to our society. Because while Marjorie Taylor Greene's opinion is both wrong and dangerous, she and others like her are drawing attention to a very real disease in our democracy. Fact-checking and debunking conspiracy theories is easy but ineffective because it is either ignored or derided—and the worm remains.

Not only have neoliberal dogmas legitimized an unprecedented transfer of wealth and power from everyday people to a very small group of the superrich, they have concocted an alibi blaming the "looters," immigrants, our children's teachers, and even imaginary villains using technology that has yet to be invented. But the culprits are right there in plain sight: they are the laws, loopholes, and procedures that have hollowed out our judicial system from the inside, quietly draining the legitimacy from our institutions, the meaning from our rights, and the invisible yet essential substance underlying it all: our trust in our government and the confidence that "we the people" can choose *our* laws, how to use *our* money, and the shape of *our* economy.

IN MAY 2020, as worldwide anger and protest followed the murder of George Floyd, the satirical website *The Onion* published a piece with the headline "Protestors Criticized for Looting Businesses Without Forming Private Equity Firm First."[16] The quip resonated because financial firms have indeed caused much more harm to Americans' lives—from lost jobs and foreclosed homes to high-cost debt and the privatization of everything from hospitals to prisons—than have sporadic incidents of theft. The word "looting," similar to words like "terrorism" and "rioting," is preloaded with connotations beyond the crime itself. While looting a pair of sneakers from a store is theft, the systematic and routine looting of our democratic rights and privileges for private gain is just politics.

The looting of our society is an ongoing and orderly bureaucratic action that takes place in courtrooms and legislatures, public hearings, and agency rule-making. As agencies, judges, and laws became more specialized and fragmented, it became easier for well-resourced firms to choose their laws, judges, and regulators while the rest of us suffer under the illusion that we can choose anything. All seems to be fine from the outside—the law is still on the books—but its application is incoherent.

Upon closer inspection, though, the incoherency is not random. The laws apply to those without the resources to lobby for loopholes or hire lawyers to circumvent the law. The changes in each area of law have been difficult to see because they have occurred slowly and in siloed areas—such as slight changes to the bankruptcy code or new rules governing disclosures of securities—but their overall effect on the economy and society has been profound. And the trend of change has been in one direction: in favor of investor capital over community vibrancy, toward rescuing the market rather than people during crises, and protective of the rights of corporations over the rights of the people.

In case after case, law after law, corporations became monopolies that could donate unlimited funds to political parties, thus translating market power directly to political power. The subterranean changes in our law have resulted in lowered wages, crippled unions, and devastated communities. A handful of private tech companies control our culture, a few banks control our money, and large donors control our politics. Corporate lawyers found and exploited tax loopholes for their clients and fought laws that tried to close these loopholes. There is no single group of individuals or corporations responsible for the present problem, but they are playing by a rigged set of rules where the uber-wealthy don't pay their fair share to our nation's taxes while taking more than their fair share of our nation's treasures.

Our democracy, our society, our laws, and our prosperity are being pilfered through tax loopholes and offshore tax havens that enable corporations and wealthy individuals to evade their fair share of taxes. Instead of building trains or homes or public spaces, private equity firms use big pools of capital to privatize and monetize our public institutions, firing workers and cutting services in order to deliver unprecedented returns to wealthy investors. Despite paying virtually no taxes on their capital returns, these private equity firms are feeding off of the value of the institutions their workers and customers built. The industry controls our health care and our housing, and is squeezing our economy for even more. A mobile-home executive advised a resident on the brink of losing her home that she should consider donating her plasma to raise money. Investments in mobile homes and slumlike housing has yielded returns of more than 30 percent, seemingly all from increased rents combined with fewer services, leaching money from the poor and elderly who have no choice but to pay these firms more and more for basic shelter. And as another mobile-home executive told investors, "It doesn't matter for us who is president because poverty rates will continue to increase."[17] They can count on it—in part, because they use their lobbying powers to fight against tenant-friendly state and federal laws with great success. They are often joined by the payday-lending lobbyists—another industry owned by private equity—to lobby against minimum wage laws. There are also the private prison lobbyists who lobby for tougher criminal sanctions. And on and on. The big pools of money tend to favor and pass laws that favor big pools of money.

While our current problems do have an origin story and history, they are now driven by forces that operate on their own—some of which are so complex that even the people with the most power cannot see the whole. Beyond the individuals and political parties that shape culture, law, and markets, there is the invisible yet powerful force of *ideas* that become ubiquitous, ideologies transmitted automatically, like genes. The British biologist Richard Dawkins calls the process of self-reproducing ideas a *meme*. For one reason or another, an ideology hits a note of harmony in a particular society such that it—the meme— rides along, self-replicating in the minds and in the words of that society's members. Dawkins calls religion a meme because it can change the way you behave and thereby propagate itself through you; you become a meme replicator.

The historian Barbara Fields compared ideas about race to those about witchcraft, describing both as ideologies that need not be plausible let alone persuasive, but whose job is to help a society "make sense of the things they do and see—ritually, repetitively—on a daily basis." Ideology differs from doctrines, dogmas, and propaganda because the latter are imposed and taught, whereas ideology is performed in daily life and passed down without acknowledgment. "An ideology must be constantly created and verified in social life," notes Fields. "If it is not, it dies, even though it may seem to be safely embodied in a form that can be handed down." Ideologies like racial hierarchy come to resemble viral memes that self-propagate through the collective culture's consciousness without the knowledge or will of their human replicators.[18]

Ideologies that have developed memelike qualities, like race and religion, have been some of the most potent forces shaping human history, especially when they have fused with the law. Racial hierarchy began as ideology to justify plunder and slaughter—those who murdered unjustly, like the Spanish conquistadors or British slave traders, blamed their crimes on their victims' "inherent" inferiority and a meme was born in the world. Before the wholesale theft of indigenous land, the law justified it. In the early nineteenth century, Chief Justice John Marshall deemed that the indigenous tribes in America could not own or sell their land on account of their inherent "savagery." The law thereafter demarcated property rights as the exclusive domain of white men, paving the way for manifest destiny, the seizure of 1.5 billion acres of land for private ownership, and the genocide of millions of indigenous people. Marshall built his legal opinion on precedent and theory provided by the British philosopher John Locke, whose theory of property law was popular in Great Britain in the late 1600s at the height of the British slave trade. It was "natural" and just, noted Locke, that "the creator" had endowed only "the industrious and rational" white men with the right to own land and people. It was also expedient. Ideologies persist through replication exactly *because* they evade detection, and through the process of replication, they *evolve*. For example, the ideology of patriarchy once reinforced itself through property laws like coverture and primogeniture that prohibited women from owning property. Once an ideology is embedded in legal code, its silent perpetuation is guaranteed.

Patently immoral practices like colonial subjugation, slavery, land theft, Jim Crow, segregation, and forced labor lasted so long that the theories that once justified them—like divine decree—no longer did the job. Instead of addressing the injustices that racist ideologies had created, often, those with the most to lose went looking for new ideologies to justify their unfair position at the top: first, Christianity; then Darwinian science; then the pseudo-scientific babble of "human IQ" testing; then, as was the case at the end of the 1960s, economics.

As John Adams once wrote to Thomas Jefferson, "Power always sincerely, conscientiously . . . believes itself Right. Power always thinks it has a great Soul, and vast Views, beyond the Comprehension of the Weak; and that it is doing God's Service, when it is violating all his laws."[19] Such was the object of the neoliberal revolution in legal theory: to infuse raw power with a soul—and snuff out the discretion that is law's dynamic living heart.

The law is the most powerful engine through which ideologies can become self-replicating engines. John Locke's theory of property as the endowed right of white men to use and to produce worked like witchcraft—the natural world, which had sustained societies for thousands of years, could suddenly be taken by force, enclosed, and tilled for the sole profit of one man, with trespassers punished. The conversion of land into one person's permanent property was not permissible under the indigenous populations who had long occupied it, nor was such a thing permissible anywhere in the world except Europe—and even there, only after the enclosure movements of the 1600s. The brilliant and prolific philosopher Locke happened to be under the patronage of Anthony Ashley Cooper, one of the richest men in England (who later became the First Earl of Shaftesbury); he was first hired as Cooper's personal doctor, but as the earl entered politics to advocate for more property rights, Locke's star rose alongside his. And property laws were passed in legislatures and handed down over time, carrying memes from men long dead with ideas long denounced.

Law codified land into assets and has been extending the market into new frontiers ever since—from corporate shares and derivatives to NFTs—transforming abstract ideas into tradable assets. A similar alchemy transformed gold into money by smelting an image onto a coin, then transformed gold coins into bank notes emblazoned with the image of a king, queen, or president. Initially, it was gold's malleability that made it ideal for coinage. But with the rise of empire and Great Britain's dominance of the global trade in gold, the gold standard became yet another ideology to preserve power. Locke's theories about gold being the highest source of value on account of its scarcity have been as impossible to dislodge from monetary theories as his ideas about race have been from property laws. But Locke was wrong—gold was not valuable. Then, as now, money's value derived from the image on the coin. Money is a symbol of people's trust in the government that issued it. Gold's scarcity was not the source of its value, but it was one of the causes of hundreds of years of wars in Europe over the scarce metal. While empire based on the gold standard and justified by white supremacy fell to the global horror of World War II, the underlying logic of both lingered. Unaddressed and unexamined, these bad ideas continue to breed distrust in our societies and scarcity in our economies. The greatest villains of our modern times are rarely human beings but the zombie ideas of dead men that continue to shape our societies.

FAR FROM BEING a battle between capitalism and communism, as so many historians have painted the era's conflict, the global revolutions of the 1960s were the only world wars that involved the entire world. Truly, the world had turned upside down as a globe dominated by a handful of empires became a world with over a hundred independent nations—each demanding equal sovereignty on the world stage. The possibilities were breathtaking and the 1960s saw the first worldwide conversation between and among peoples speaking to one another. Neoliberalism was the successor ideology of empire. Gone were the gunboats, colonial governments, and talk of civilizing savages. Instead, development loans, sovereign debt markets, and transnational corporations became the face of power in the Global South. The guns did not disappear of course, but were traded on global markets from distributors to trade-friendly governments.

After decades of relentless activism by Black Americans across every legal domain, the American South's chokehold on the law finally broke and the Constitution's promise of equality was secured for all Americans. The last stages of the civil rights movement forced the quiet oppression of southern law to show its teeth and claws. Thanks to masterly coordination among activists and the courage of protesters—and the introduction of a television into every American home—a century of cruelty inscribed in law, procedure, and "the way things are done" norms was coaxed forth from the shadows. Americans of every race witnessed a moral standoff: Ruby Bridges, the brave Black girl walking into an all-white school, or George Wallace, the red-faced governor of Alabama standing at the schoolhouse door; kneeling marchers versus the clubs wielded by Bull Connor's police force in Birmingham; the men sitting at a counter and the menace of violence right at their backs; Rosa Parks's dignity and the routine humiliation of Jim Crow.

Yet no sooner had freedom fighters, equal rights marchers, and the newly sovereign former colonies achieved their aims of institutional recognition than the forces of reaction began a stealth campaign to erode the institutions of democracy from the inside. When forced to share "their" society and "their" democracy with nonwhite inferiors, a small group of radical elite activists staged a counterinsurgency to discredit and then demolish both society and democracy. Due to their efforts, the 1960s were an interregnum, not the birth of a new world.

Instead of fighting their uninspiring cause in the court of public opinion or even in a court of law, these counterinsurgents waged a subtle war of attrition that left, for instance, hard-won civil rights laws and cases intact to the unsuspecting public while changing the meaning of the words and rendering the laws practically meaningless. The neoliberal coup was perfectly legal because it was conducted *through* the law. The same courts and legal interpretations honed and argued by activists to bend the law toward justice were bent quietly back to protecting the powerful.

The hallowed revolutionary chant of freedom, its meaning clear and resonant across the world, soon came to mean something wholly different than it had before: market freedom. Instead of fighting the righteous demands of economic justice, the counterinsurgency theorized that any state "intervention" in markets would backfire and hurt the very people it was aimed to help. "Free speech," long the right protecting protesters against state tyranny, soon became a right granted to billionaires and corporations, allowing them to spend unlimited amounts of money on elections in secret. Using the tools of the moral crusaders and the civil rights heroes, these cynics and the wealthy donors who backed them co-opted and transformed the language of "freedom," "independence," and "equality" until the rights contained in those words lost their power—for all the public knew, civil rights had already been fought for and established. The coup occurred in plain sight, and yet was invisible to the naked eye. As George Orwell understood, the real struggle between freedom and tyranny in the modern era would be waged in the doublespeak of our shared language. If tyranny overtakes us, it will likely triumph under a flag proclaiming freedom.

Once neoliberalism made our courts, agencies, and legislatures porous to the influence of capital, it was capital—its needs and its priorities—that led the way. Except capital is not an institution, a person, or a thing. Capital is an abstraction created by another abstraction: the law. Not bound by the physical limits imposed by natural laws, capital's growth is exponential. The ideology of neoliberalism—the meme—is still embedded into the legal system, but capital has gained viral qualities and the legal system is no longer capable of restraining it.

The story of the neoliberal coup is much more complex than the one offered by conspiracy theorists because it has no single villain and no simple solution. The unseen forces that most affect us—from money to viruses and social media algorithms—are complex systems driven by a logic and rationality of their own, quite apart from human decision makers. Just as a virus "wants" to multiply itself, changing its human host in the process, so too does capital. It operates like artificial intelligence. Most laws are enforced automatically and without much flexibility while those with wealth or power can simply change the code to suit their needs. To see the neoliberal coup requires getting a handle on the big picture while also paying close attention to the nodes and sinews in the system, and especially to how small changes to laws enacted years ago can create systems that continue to self-replicate without human intervention. That phenomenon is the picture this book attempts to sketch out. It is a biography of an idea: when and why neoliberalism emerged, what problems it solved, and how it transformed America and the world.

Neoliberalism did not eviscerate regulations and free the market as its leading lights promised. In fact, neoliberalism has led to more and more complex laws, increased barriers to entry, less market competition in crucial markets like finance, and ballooning compliance departments. Neoliberal ideology delegitimized governance as inefficient and confiscatory with one hand while with the other it chipped away at the pillars of social trust sustaining our democracy. The result has been the pervasive distrust that has yielded conspiratorial explanations that continue to erode democracy. The remedy to neoliberalism is democracy and a free market, but stripped of the corrosive rot of dead dogmas.

Recognizing that markets are created by law, lawmakers and those who hope to influence them must be engaged in a debate about the values inscribed in legal tests and measures. In fact, it is more accurate to say on the question of policy that neoliberal dogma, hiding behind a mask of market freedom, forced the law to surrender its policy-making power. This book urges lawmakers to reclaim that power.

Standard accounts that take neoliberalism at its word as economic theory are fighting in the wrong arena. Understanding neoliberalism requires focusing on its outcomes as well as its theories—what it *did* and what it *said*. As the book will show, defeating the rot of corruption that neoliberal dogma embedded in the legal bureaucracy requires a holistic recounting of how justice was emptied out of the law—what can best be described as "the spirit of the law," along with its formal, rigid, counterpart, "the letter of the law." The sclerotic legal apparatus governing the market is no longer governed by ideology—it is a patchwork of legal forms and loopholes shorn of equity and reason.

Instead of continuing to add weight to the scale of justice, hoping that it will finally tip toward redistribution and equity, we must recalibrate the scale itself. We cannot achieve racial justice by engaging in a bureaucratic cost-benefit analysis, or argue for action on the climate crisis through an economic analysis. These metrics are preset toward a certain outcome, and that outcome will do little, if anything, to resolve the problems at hand. Even when laws are enforced, like the PG&E convictions for their negligence, another legal regime—bankruptcy— can provide an escape route from accountability. This game of legal evasion is not new and will continue indefinitely unless it is directly addressed—but it can no longer continue without causing significant damage to our society.

That is the concern—or fear—that drove this book. This book was very difficult for me to write—it took years longer than it should have and I wrote more words and read more books than could possibly fit into one narrative. Toward the end of the writing process, as my anxiety about the book matched my anxiety about the state of the world, I had a discomforting realization: Marjorie Taylor Greene and I are both doing the same thing—trying to use facts to explain a pervasive *feeling* of injustice. And that in this endeavor, she has the advantage—she could tell the whole story in one Facebook post. I needed several years, hundreds of books, and hundreds of thousands of words on the cutting room floor. And her story of conspiracies and devious Jewish bankers may be more salient and appealing for its simplicity. She is wrong about nearly every fact, but she is not wrong about identifying the feeling. So it has gone with every fascist regime throughout time, including the one that took over Iran the year I was born and filled my childhood with war, murder, and mass imprisonment of hundreds of thousands of regular Iranians. The fascists who took over my country occupied a government structure long rotted by corruption, which is why they were able to grab hold of state power in a matter of months. The United States differs from Iran in many significant ways and its democratic checks are more robust than Iran's then, but no nation is invincible to the cycle of corruption leading to distrust, leading to resentment, and ultimately to violence against its own people. Insofar as the *feeling* of injustice is sensed, people will seek to explain it and remedy it, using whatever means they can.

This book does not conclude with a list of policy proposals to reverse neoliberalism, because neoliberalism is not an economic policy or a clear ideology that can be debunked, but rather a cancer of corruption that must be plucked root and branch. It ends, rather, where it began—with an articulation of neoliberalism's future: a radical right-wing hunting for racial minorities on whom to pin America's many problems and an increasingly nonsensical market of FTX-like scams, repeated banking collapses followed quickly by government bailouts, a gutted middle class, and a market that rewards the above. Yet the book is not hopeless or resigned to the way things are. In fact, the difficult journey of researching and writing this book landed me—surprisingly, given my personality—into a place of optimism and hope that perhaps there is a silver lining to so much being broken. That perhaps the upside of nothing working is that everything is possible. Especially if we reformers who wish for justice and equity step out of the binary of market versus state to see if perhaps the market cannot be a route toward justice after all. I conclude by arguing that the market is far from being a bloodsucking vampire—rather, it is a big dumb machine incapable of the level of coordinated thinking that many on the left ascribe to it. Neoliberalism not only failed in promising that the market would deliver equity and justice, it failed to deliver even efficiency and productivity—our corporations are no longer thriving, our housing markets are broken, our economic ladders have disappeared, and everyone knows it. Neoliberalism promised that the market magic, in the words of President Ronald Reagan, would lift all boats and lead to global peace and freedom. The argument of this book is not that the market cannot do those things; it could have—had the Western nations taken the risk of trading with the newly "freed" sovereign nations and accepting the newly enfranchised racial minorities. There would have been risks, of course, in integrating all the world's people into the market and ensuring equality, but risk is the propulsion fuel driving market innovation. Contrary to the risk management regime of modern finance, risks cannot be managed because the future is the only unknown. And any risk that can be predicted and put neatly into a risk calculus is not the type of game-ending risk with which we should be concerned—such as global pandemics, nuclear bombs, authoritarian regimes, and climate crisis. None of these catastrophic risks can be dealt with by our fragmented and untrustworthy governments. We overcome them globally or we succumb to them—all of us.

The fundamental error of neoliberalism was its refusal to take seriously its own dogma of globalization. Instead of taking the risks attendant to a true global market with each nation's sovereignty as worthy of respect as any others', the strong Western powers, with the aid of neoliberal academics, continued the economic logic of empire and exploitation and called it a free market. It was hypocrisy from the start, rooted in fear and nihilism. Endless money for banks and austerity for the majority of the world's people is a program destined to produce exactly the world economy we inhabit—a capital market growing like a cancer while the human population is trapped underneath the capital empire with no way out except for whatever solutions the right-wing populists and would-be revolutionaries offer, including violence and a zero-sum division of resources. We are once again facing the same fundamental choice—we can either fight over microchip factories, supply chains, and food, increasing the gap between the haves and the have-nots and hoping for the best, or we can rationally calculate future risks and decide to spend our abundant money supply on something besides war.

A Note on Terminology

S O W H A T , E X A C T L Y , is the standard definition of neoliberalism? It depends on who you ask. According to the neoliberals themselves, like Milton Friedman, neoliberalism was a revival of classic liberal doctrines of individual liberty with an emphasis on maintaining "the competitive order," which would, in theory, require limited state intervention, including stable money, police power, limited social services to prevent abject poverty, and the prevention of monopolies in order to foster competition.[1] After Friedman's influential 1951 article "Neoliberalism and Its Prospects," a group of intellectuals called the Mont Pelerin Society (MPS) adopted the moniker.[2] Friedman helped define the MPS with his focus on strong property rights and free markets, but its members were not categorically laissez-faire fundamentalists. In fact, the policies espoused by the early neoliberals actually strengthened state power, deploying it to protect markets from the demands of democracy. The most successful neoliberal spokesmen, Friedman and Friedrich Hayek, spoke the language of economics and science, but the impetus of their movement and ideology was legal and political.

To the extent that popular culture talks about neoliberalism, it is used to signify a jumble of social conditions from the undesirable to the merely boring. The debate continues among scholars even as the term "neoliberalism" in popular media has approached parody, as in the depiction in the 2021 dark satire *The White Lotus* of two archetypal "woke" teens who dismiss their corporate mom's defense of Hillary Clinton as "neolib and neocon." Bo Burnham satirized neoliberalism in his 2021 Netflix special *Inside* with a sock puppet singing "private property's inherently theft, neoliberal fascists are destroying the left; and every politician, every cop on the street protects the interests of the pedophilic corporate elite." During the 2020 election, the label "neoliberal shill" was thrown indiscriminately at all Democratic candidates (other than Bernie Sanders), and pundits began to urge for more clarity around the term. *The New York Times*'s Ezra Klein has called neoliberalism "the most confusing phrase in political discourse today."[3] The left magazine *Dissent* convened an online forum called "The Uses and Abuses of 'Neoliberalism,'" about whether the term has been so misused in the discourse as to be left empty of meaning. The near ubiquity of the label as shorthand for all that ails society seems to indicate the actual demise of neoliberalism—or perhaps the reality that it is now the background music of our lives. Put simply, the term has come to mean both nothing and everything.

Despite these risks and pitfalls, I have chosen to use the label as an umbrella descriptor, for several practical and scholarly reasons. First, the term was used as a self-descriptor by the people who created the ideology, even as many neoliberal policies have strayed somewhat from what some early thinkers had in mind. Second, scholars across a range of disciplines have clearly articulated a shared if contested definition of the ideas, policies, and concepts of neoliberalism and are engaging in fruitful conversations organized by the term. Third, the fact that the term means nothing but can explain everything is exactly the point of the book. It was, for lack of a better term, bullshit from the start—incoherent as theory and just plain wrong empirically. Those are strong claims, but they aren't mine alone: there are libraries of studies and books debunking these theories. Brilliant scholars have worked hard to illuminate the errors and lies inherent in the basic assumptions of neoliberal dogma, calling it "zombie economics." In fact, the field of economics has even turned away from foundational neoliberal theories about markets as rational and efficient, through the field of behavioral economics; in addition, prominent economists have recently undercut many of the neoliberals' basic assumptions about the way markets work in what has been called "the credibility revolution," describing the field's turn back to the study of numbers, trends, and facts that can be proved rather than theorized. Yet neoliberalism lives on in policies; it is our zombie legal system that is, in the words of Keynes, "the slave to some defunct economist."[4] The salience of "neoliberalism" in the public consciousness, even as parody, is evidence that it is communicating *something* and that something may even be summarized as "some bullshit" ideology to which "serious" people are beholden. And this book is written for those serious people as a taxonomy of sorts of neoliberal myths, so that they can decide for themselves if neoliberalism is worth defending.

But the book was also written with a sense of urgency—based on my own reading of history, which shows, time and time again, that you can rig a system for only so long before it breaks. And once it does and trust is gone, fascism is not far off. And fascism is not a word I use lightly. Unlike neoliberalism, the ideology of fascism does not need theories to explain: it is the ideology of bullies whose solution to societal problems is violence. That is the alternative to neoliberalism: not free governments versus free markets, for we are being tyrannized by an unholy union of both. In other words, the time to squabble over words and theories has already passed; it is time for solutions because the fascists are at the door.

PART I

Freedom Fighters

CHAPTER 1

The Strange Career of Neoliberalism

The twilight zone that lies between living memory and written history is one of the favorite breeding places of mythology.... The process has been aided by the old prejudices, the deeply stirred emotions, and the sectional animosities that always distort history in any zone, however well illuminated by memory or research.

—C. VANN WOODWARD,

THE STRANGE CAREER OF JIM CROW (1955)

A s RICHARD NIXON was preparing for his second presidential campaign in September 1967, he received a memo titled "The Urban Riots of the 1960s," which contained advice to the candidate about the appropriate economic policies to address "racial strife."[1] The memo was written by his forty-one-year-old adviser on domestic policy, a whiz Wall Street market consultant named Alan Greenspan. A genius with numbers and statistics—a "quant" before the era of quants—Greenspan was renowned for his savantlike predictions of market movement.[2]

He was also very interested in politics. An avid supporter of and adviser to Arizona senator Barry Goldwater and a devotee of the author

Ayn Rand, Greenspan was an idealistic libertarian who, like Rand, held a quasi-religious belief in the free market as the sole guarantor of freedom and even of moral right. Although his libertarian orthodoxy would mellow over the years—by the time he was appointed to his first term as Federal Reserve chairman in 1987, he was a mainstream Republican—in 1967 he was still a true believer. He sounded just like his mentor Rand when he lamented the "creeping mediocrity" of American culture that no longer exalted "great wealth producers" of the past like J. P. Morgan and instead was surrendering to "the primordial morality of altruism."[3] (Greenspan himself was not immune to that primordial morality: he refused payment for his work on the Nixon campaign.)

Greenspan had originally been brought onto the campaign for his facility with statistics.[4] At the time, political campaigns' use of polling and data was still in its infancy. Although John F. Kennedy was the first president to use polling data, Nixon, thanks to Greenspan, would be the first candidate to deploy it methodologically to win the presidency. Greenspan was able to track the "mood" of American voters just as he had done with the stock and commodities markets: by looking for fluctuations in the numbers and then deciphering the underlying change that had occurred. This skill earned him nicknames like "the maestro of the market" and "the man who knew" from his later biographers.[5]

What Alan Greenspan did not know was anything about racial inequality. He had no experience or knowledge to draw upon, nor did he seem to care all that much about the cause of racial justice; prior to his work with the Nixon campaign, Greenspan had rarely discussed race or racism. Why then was he asked to provide policy recommendations to address the race riots? And how did it come to pass that Greenspan's free market fundamentalism would be jettisoned when it came to economic policy making, even as his ideas about racial justice would inspire the next fifty years of federal policy? The answers to these questions happen to tell us a great deal about the origins and nature of neoliberalism in America.

THE PRECIPITATING EVENT for Greenspan's memo was a July 1967 protest-turned-riot in Newark, New Jersey, sparked by the beating of a

Black cabdriver by white police.[6] Violence escalated after the National Guard and state troopers took over the city, leading to a four-day battle, and resulting in the death of a child hit by stray bullet and the shooting of a young mother whom troops mistook for a sniper as she leaned out of her window.[7] It was not the first time an American city looked like a war zone. Days after the passage of the Civil Rights Act of 1964, a white off-duty police officer shot a Harlem teenager, setting off a six-day rebellion in New York. On August 11, 1965, five days after the enactment of the Voting Rights Act, the police assaulted a Black driver in the Watts neighborhood of Los Angeles as a crowd looked on, leading to days of protests and violence. Even though Martin Luther King Jr.'s movement used nonviolent tactics, his allusions to the "coming storm," like the writer James Baldwin's to "the fire next time," were not mere provocations—violence was at the doorstep. King and Baldwin, among others, had warned that justice delayed would lead to a pent-up rage that might explode.

The riots were televised and covered by national and international news. Almost 70,000 troops were called out to quell the unrest in American cities in 1967 and 1968, and the riots resulted in a total of forty-six deaths, 2,600 serious injuries, 22,000 arrests, and $100 million in property loss.[8] Every Black leader was a suspect whenever a riot erupted. FBI director J. Edgar Hoover intensified his surveillance of civil rights leaders—including King, whom he wrongly suspected of Communist ties—and declared war against "black power" radical groups, which he considered the country's greatest domestic enemies.[9] Even Thurgood Marshall, a nominee to the Supreme Court during the summer of 1967, was blamed for those riots, and his confirmation hearing as the first Black justice was more contested than that of any previous Court appointee, with southern politicians accusing him of being "soft on crime."[10]

When the Kerner Commission, established by President Lyndon Johnson to study the cause of riots, issued its report, it summarized the violence as "the harvest of American racism." Although most of the riots were sparked by an incident of police violence, the commission found that police brutality wasn't the root problem; rather, police "often take the brunt of much hostility that might more logically be directed at the larger society and its less visible institutions." For the report's authors, the real culprit was "white society," which had established a system of American apartheid known as the ghetto; according to the report, "white institutions created it, white institutions maintain it, and white society condones it." The report urged a systemic answer to the endemic "unemployment and underemployment" (Black rates were double those of white rates), "inadequate housing" (due to a legacy of segregation), "discriminatory credit and consumer practices," and the concentrated poverty of the ghetto. Without comprehensive reforms, it warned, the nation would continue to break apart into two societies, "one black, one white—separate and unequal."[11]

The 426-page Kerner Commission Report became an unlikely blockbuster. The first edition sold 30,000 copies and was sold out in three days. Another 1.6 million copies were printed and sold between March and June 1968. There would be ten more printings in the next four years. The actor and activist Marlon Brando read aloud from the report on television. Perhaps the report struck a chord with the American public in providing a public airing of past wrongs, a penance, and a voicing of privately held white guilt over the treatment of blacks for three and a half centuries. *The New York Times* observed, "Reading it is an ugly experience, but one that brings, finally, something like the relief of beginning. What had to be said has been said at last, and by representatives of that white, moderate, responsible America that, alone, needed to say it." *Newsweek* reported, "Here was the formal ethic for action missing conspicuously from recent proclamations of the Congress and the President himself: an indictment of the System, by a top-level organ of the System, that might ring louder and clearer than all the thunder of the ghetto themselves." The Kerner Report was the closest the United States ever came to a public admission of wrongdoing, or a truth and reconciliation, though it was short on the latter. King called it a "physician's warning of approaching death, with a prescription for life."[12]

Much of white society, indulging in racist stereotypes and sequestered in segregated suburbs, resisted the prescription of a forced merger of black and white. Many were afraid of the scenes of violence and hardship they saw on the nightly news. They worried about removing any of the barriers, racial or otherwise, that kept their two societies—one safe and one unsafe—apart. Californians elected Ronald Reagan to the governorship in 1967, after he promised a never-ending "war on crime."[13] Earlier in the decade, polls had found that most Americans believed that nonviolent protests were unjustified and "hurt the negro cause."[14] If majorities of Americans believed that nonviolent protests were already too much, too fast, the riots that occurred *after* the passage of the historic Civil Rights Act of 1964 and the Voting Rights Act of 1965 set them off. Senators explained that their white voters were angry: "I'm getting mail from white people saying 'Wait a minute, we've got some rights too.'"

These were the exact voters whom Nixon needed to win the 1968 election, according to Greenspan's analysis of the polling data. The only viable path to clinch an electoral majority was through white backlash—Nixon needed to take the George Wallace voters and secure the southern states. Wallace, a Democrat who had summarized his racial policy in his 1963 inaugural address as Alabama's governor as "segregation now, segregation tomorrow, segregation forever," was running for president as an independent on an anti-civil-rights plank. He built his campaign on white Americans' fears of change, a fear that had hardened—thanks in part to his own efforts—into rage and resentment. Nixon had to attract Wallace's Dixiecrat voters without too much race-baiting, in order not to turn off his northern Republican base. Greenspan thus counseled Nixon to "be loud enough for the George Wallace leaners to hear us, yet protect ourselves from charges of distortion"—to denounce Wallace's "amateurism" and to avoid talk of matching violence with violence (which would scare "the housewife") but to go after the voters who sought "the emotional satisfaction" of seeing sheriffs "knocking heads" after every riot.[15]

The way to overcome the chaos of rebellion was to harness its energy. If Black Americans were angry about having been exploited for so long, well, so too was the "silent majority" of whites who was being overlooked and neglected because other groups were making so much noise. The Republican candidate in 1964, Barry Goldwater, subscribed to an austere libertarianism that was generally unpopular, and he lost to Lyndon Johnson by a wide margin. Yet, due to his opposition to civil rights, he had done something no Republican had ever done: win five Deep South states.

Pat Buchanan, the Nixon campaign's research director and media analyst, followed up in writing that it was "vital" that Nixon listen to Greenspan's polling data and to forget about ever getting "the Negro and Jewish vote." If these groups mattered at all, it was only because "the Negro loud-mouths are given access to the public communications media by a guilt-ridden establishment—and the Jews control the communications media." Greenspan, Jewish himself, was not privy to this correspondence.[16]

The idea to have Greenspan analyze the riots came from Buchanan, who would go on to a long career on the populist right fringe of the Republican Party stoking the "culture war" with his angry diatribes about immigrants and Black crime.[17] He pled with Nixon in a memo to consider bringing Greenspan on to "counsel on the negro thing" (Greenspan had initially been recruited to help with financial policy). But in 1967, Nixon did not have a coherent message on racial strife, which was one of the thorniest and most politically complex issues for the campaign. As Dwight Eisenhower's vice president, Nixon had worked with Congress to pass civil rights legislation, met with Martin Luther King, and in 1960 even gained the endorsement of the baseball great Jackie Robinson during his campaign against JFK. By the time Nixon became the Republican presidential candidate in 1968, his message about racial justice would be much clearer. As Robinson summarized it in a 1968 article revoking his support, "The Republican Party has told the black man to go to hell. I offer to them a similar invitation."[18]

Days after the July 1967 riot in Newark, Buchanan called Greenspan to request his advice on devising economic assistance programs that would deal with the race issue while also sounding fiscally responsible— that is, Buchanan (and Nixon) were seeking a politically palatable program of economic aid. However, the free market fundamentalist responded with a provocation: "The negro problem is not an economic problem and it is dangerous to think of its solution in financial terms."

He argued that *government aid*, rather than a solution to the problem of racial unrest, was in fact the problem. According to Greenspan, welfare and entitlements created dependency. He told the Nixon team that Black families were in fact relatively well off compared to, for example, Black populations in other regions in the world. What had created the anger that led to violence was not poverty but *antipoverty* programs that stoked racism and "class antagonism."[19]

The purity of this response would have made Rand proud; Rand had characterized the 1964 Civil Rights Act as "the worst breach of property rights in the sorry record of American history."[20] But it was a view far from the mainstream and far from what even Nixon or Buchanan had in mind.

GREENSPAN'S MEMO attacked the liberals who were demanding "some fundamental change in the system," calling any such claim "an attack upon America's system of free enterprise and individual rights." He urged Nixon not to capitulate. Instead, the candidate should pursue programs consistent with the free market, to "help Negroes help themselves." Greenspan argued that it would cost too much to raise Blacks to "the level of affluence of middle-class America," and so Nixon should shut down "anticapitalist" talk of reparations or remediation. Using government policy to address racial inequality would be, Greenspan warned, a "dangerous" harbinger of socialism, which would make "major inroads into this country" if the left got what it wanted. Greenspan's critiques of the "'Liberal' Hypothesis"—that it would lead to "horrendously expensive" poverty programs that were irrelevant to the fundamental problem—did not deal in numbers or economics, but rather in rhetoric and invective.

To Greenspan, the only solution to the riots was to stop the violence for the simple reason that violence was never justified. The "urban slums of our country" must be brought, continued Greenspan, toward "a civilized state." The uncivilized "riots" to which Greenspan referred were of a particular sort: those with Black Americans as the central actors. He had nothing to say about the white mobs opposing busing, the hollering masses blocking the desegregating schoolhouse door, or the vigilantes who threw bombs into churches, lobbed glass bottles at protesters, or burned crosses to terrorize.

The memo was similarly unconcerned with antiwar protesters, draft card burners, and activist students. It made clear that Greenspan's opposition to the left's agenda for economic justice was primarily based on its high cost. But Greenspan did include a section dissecting a core argument voiced by protesters and their government allies. "The critical question is, of course," he wrote, "whether the Negroes are correct in claiming that they have been exploited and that their violent reaction is the rational response." Greenspan acknowledged that "there can be little doubt that discrimination has been rampant," but he believed that the "distinction between discrimination and exploitation makes all the difference in the world." For Greenspan, the allegations that Blacks were being exploited was "clearly false." Just because scant few Black residents owned property did not mean that they were being exploited, he reasoned. He concluded that because exploitation wasn't apparent, the cries of "injustice" were "erroneous."[21]

Contemporary studies of and reports on the riots had already revealed, however, that acts of "looting" or "destruction of property" were not random but rather were directed at the many white-owned installment lenders and slumlords that proliferated in and profited off the ghettos. The riots—which were often actually planned protests or boycotts—demanded that these stores "burn the books" (that is, stop exploiting). In fact, the earliest seeds of the civil rights movement, in the 1940s and 1950s, were planned boycotts and protests in northern cities against usurious lenders who charged the highest rates in the country and whose default and repossession practices were held by courts to be predatory and unconscionable. These early actions had some success both in pressuring state legislatures to regulate interest rates and in garnering support from northern, liberal Republican lawmakers such as Nelson Rockefeller of New York and George Romney of Michigan (father of future Republican presidential candidate Mitt Romney). Romney had even compared the white suburbs to a "noose" choking the inner cities.

Greenspan's memo was historically ignorant in other ways, too. Jim

Crow laws enforcing racial segregation and the court-enforced racial covenants banning property sales to nonwhites were exactly the type of government coercion that dispossessed Black Americans in the first place. Racial ghettos had in fact been created by government subsidies to white homeowners, who used those subsidies to flee the city for the suburbs. Moreover, the urban riots were often in response to overpolicing, which was another form of government intervention that libertarian economists should theoretically decry.

But if the campaign was actually trying to understand the causes and solutions to urban violence, it would not have turned to Greenspan. Despite its tone of assertive confidence, the Greenspan memo contained no numbers, data, or cited studies. What Nixon, via Buchanan, wanted was not Greenspan's knowledge or expertise, but his ideology. And in that, he delivered.

The Wall Street whiz proposed that the candidate do *nothing* except stop the violence—to do nothing not out of indifference, not out of cruelty, but out of *principle*. Buchanan highlighted large portions of the memo and sent it to his boss, who was impressed. "I think I should have a talk with Greenspan," said Nixon. Shortly thereafter, Greenspan was brought onto the political strategy team and tasked with proposing an economic response to "racial strife." Greenspan helped the campaign adapt Wallace's resentful message on race—obstruction and denial—and present it as an embrace of capitalism and liberty.

But was predatory lending *exploitation* in the first place? Not to Greenspan. And his answer tells us a great deal about neoliberalism. As he explained in the same memo, the "profit rates in slum areas are doubtless distressingly low considering the risks."[22] This was partly true and here, in the world of debt and interest, Greenspan was finally on familiar ground. There were clearly profits to be made—otherwise, installment lenders would not be sending out door-to-door salesmen peddling everything from insurance to appliances on monthly contracts. However, federal subsidies that made lending so profitable and risk-free in the white suburbs had never crossed into the redlined ghettos, which led to higher costs: without Uncle Sam's credit guarantees, risk had to be priced into the cost for consumers.

The root cause of this disparity in risk and access was simple: segregation had created two economies, one subsidized by the state and available only to whites (or "Caucasians," per government standards and racial covenants), and one for the Black ghetto. Government subsidies for the white suburbanites kept interest rates low, which led to a virtuous cycle of low-cost credit that built intergenerational wealth, social capital, and even the low-cost college degree. In the ghetto, prices were whatever the free market could extract—which, given a vicious cycle of poverty, debt, and risk, was a lot more than many could bear. In fact, contrary to Greenspan's denunciations, zones of segregation were the only places where capitalism was unfettered. He was, in other words, technically right that high-interest lending in the ghetto wasn't simply price gouging, but that wasn't the whole picture.

It is unclear whether Greenspan had even a basic familiarity with the research being conducted on racial disparities—why would he? His expertise was in picking stocks and seeing market trends. His memo did not mention the multiple congressional hearings, agency studies, and volumes of economic data produced on this very issue of the price differential that had been made public in the preceding years. Neither did it mention the sociologist David Caplovitz's recently published study, *The Poor Pay More*, which in fact proved—through volumes of data and research—that consumers in segregated ghettos paid up to ten times more than white residents, a phenomenon Caplovitz called "exploitation of the poor."[23] Caplovitz was a professor at Columbia, where Greenspan was taking a few economics courses in pursuit of an economics PhD, which he would not finish (a decade later, the university would give him an honorary degree).

Even if exploitation wasn't exactly the correct concept, experts had revealed the distinct patterns of capital extraction that followed racial segregation, which resembled the dynamic of colonization and created a captive economy within a nation. In *An American Dilemma*, for example, the Swedish economist Gunnar Myrdal demonstrated the self-reinforcing trends that had kept segregated Black areas entrenched in poverty, a phenomenon he labeled a "backwash effect": a growing, capital-rich white community exerts a "strong, agglomerative pull, accelerating their rate of growth, and bringing increasing stagnation" to the capital-poor, but labor-rich, ghettos.

Myrdal's fifteen-hundred-page study, published in 1944, had taken on and debunked prevailing pseudo-scientific theories of biological racial hierarchy to show that the inequalities of health, wealth, and education observed between races were caused by segregation and racial oppression. When the Supreme Court's landmark 1954 decision in *Brown v. Board of Education* reversed school segregation, Myrdal's influential work was one of just three sources cited in the Court's opinion. In fact, if there was a contemporary foil to the neoliberals who would soon dominate economics, it was Myrdal, whose methods and outcomes would be challenged on every front in the coming years. Myrdal's study was not heavily mathematical or theoretical, but it was rich with data, statistics, and analyses. He had been commissioned to study race relations by the Carnegie Foundation, which had sought a non-American for the task because it wanted an unbiased study. Myrdal assembled a team of researchers led by Ralph Bunche, a Black political scientist and a key figure in the postwar decolonization process across the globe and the civil rights movement at home. Myrdal's study drew the very same conclusions the Kerner Commission would arrive at decades later: the "Negro problem" was a "white man's problem."

There were many other economists who, unlike Greenspan, had spent their careers researching the complex economic patterns created by segregation and discrimination and who would have disagreed vehemently with Greenspan if his memo for Buchanan and Nixon had been made public. Prominent among them was the Jamaican American scholar Donald J. Harris (father of future vice president Kamala Harris), who debunked the notion, articulated by Greenspan and other neoliberals, that discrimination was just a quirk of the dominant market. Rather, "the forms of discrimination" in segregated black ghettos were systemic, having little to do with what people felt about one another.[24] And contrary to what Greenspan surmised, the "slum landlord" was not only profitable but his profits were not based on the laws of supply and demand, just *laws*. The slumlords actively sought, said Harris, to "command the power of the state in making, implementing and enforcing legislation concerning rents, building codes, property taxes, etc." Due to his greater political power and influence, the (white) slumlord could "control and *exploit* his particular sphere of operation." It may not be the price gouging that Greenspan had dismissed, but it was nonetheless a form of high-level exploitation using the levers of state power to stack the deck in one's favor. In economics, this type of behavior is called *rent seeking*, which in this case could be read literally. White property owners were not losing money due to inefficient discrimination, as Greenspan and other neoliberals argued; they were making profits from the premium that white property earned on account of segregation.

Had Andrew Brimmer, a Harvard-trained economist who became the first Black governor of the Federal Reserve in 1966, been consulted on the issue, he too would have undercut the neoliberal assumptions underlying Greenspan's do-nothing thesis. Brimmer would become one of the most forceful opponents of Nixon's racial justice program—so-called Black capitalism—which he called "snake oil." If there was disagreement among the economists and activists who actually studied the unique economic environment created by racial segregation, it mostly hinged on solutions: Black separatists such as Malcolm X and Stokely Carmichael likened the ghetto to a colony and pushed for reparations or the creation of Black communities with sovereign governments. Brimmer, Harris, and others advocated programs that would integrate the Black and white economies, a solution that would require new government spending.

Even close confidants of Nixon who did read the memo were enraged by Greenspan's conclusions. Ray Price, a top Nixon aide and speechwriter, denounced Greenspan's "dogmatic rigidity" that set up a false binary between "government handouts" and "freedom of the individual." Freedom was not so easily cabined as market freedom. Yes, freedom from government tyranny was essential, but what about freedom from fear and deprivation, or freedom to develop one's talents? If every government program was seen as a handout, "we might as well give up on this old land of ours," he protested. Price's response represented the mainstream view at the time—not just on the left but among mainstream Republicans as well. Greenspan's theory that government aid *caused* poverty is now a common political sound bite, but it was controversial in the 1960s. Decades earlier, the statement would defy lived reality.[25]

From the Great Depression until the civil rights era, Americans and their elected leaders viewed poverty as caused by external conditions that could be alleviated with government aid. There were of course dissenters—those who warned of a slide toward communism or who were unhappy about the heavy tax burden they faced—but the majority of Americans had witnessed in their own families the positive effect of government programs: the New Deal's mortgage and student loan subsidies, social security, union wage protection, pensions, and the sheer number of well-paying jobs related to war production, space exploration, and research and technology.

The view of poverty as solvable was grounded in the dominant economics of the era. The leading thinker was still John Maynard Keynes, whose theories of stimulus spending were credited with reviving the U.S economy after the Great Depression and the European economies after the Second World War. There were certainly debates among economists in the years between the Great Depression and the late 1960s, but it was hard to argue against the pragmatic policies that had created the "mixed-state" economy which produced widespread prosperity in white America and curbed the spread of communism in Europe. Before the neoliberal era, the state and the commercial sector operated toward mutual advantages. Presidents Roosevelt, Truman, Eisenhower, Kennedy, and Johnson had all won decisive majorities against the likes of Robert Taft and Barry Goldwater, candidates who promised to cut government programs. Goldwater's ideological libertarianism failed to persuade at the polls in 1964. To the public and much of the business community, the government was a help, not a hindrance. Having ridden the boom spurred by government spending, most Americans had no appetite for free market extremists who threatened their social security, union wages, and federally subsidized mortgages.

The era between the New Deal and the rise of neoliberalism has come to be known as the "great leveling" for the historically low disparity between the wealthiest and poorest, but the shared prosperity was not shared by all. The size of the pie was expanded by government spending, and profits, assets, and taxes were distributed to a working population of white male breadwinners. White men were protected by unions that negotiated wage increases pegged to the strength of the economy and inflation. That arrangement would soon be detonated by neoliberals.

The era's exclusions and failures should not diminish its singular achievements. Before the rise of the neoliberal consensus, progressive lawmakers had already begun to extend the public franchise of credit to those left out. In the mid- to late 1960s, the economy was still booming and growing. There was no reason that federal policy could not continue to creatively spur the economy and lift all boats, including those helmed by Black Americans. The lesson of the New Deal–era mixed economy and Keynesian fiscal spending was that in order to reap the rewards of growth and production, the state had to sow by investing and spending. The civil rights laws of the 1960s had the potential to free up the channels of public spending to be assigned—potentially—to Black Americans and other nonwhite male breadwinners of nuclear families. (Women did not figure centrally in even progressive economists' analyses at the time.)

One obvious place to start would have been the inner cities. New York senator and former corporate attorney Jacob Javits and Texas senator John Tower, both Republicans, sponsored a 1968 piece of legislation, in conjunction with the activist Roy Innis, called the Community Self-Determination Bill, which Javits likened to a Marshall Plan for Black urban areas. Other options included giving the disenfranchised poor the same employment opportunities as the white poor, an idea proposed most forcefully by Martin Luther King's Poor People's Campaign; the development of a World Bank–style finance program for inner cities modeled on the self-funding Export-Import Bank; and housing integration, which was pushed by Republican presidential candidates like George Romney and by Johnson's Fair Housing Act. Fed Governor Andrew Brimmer had already proposed some notable (albeit minor) changes to Fed policy that could favor credit to low-income communities, and other groups had persuaded Congress to consider creative solutions via monetary policy. In fact, there were hundreds of proposals and plans introduced in Congress to reallocate credit fairly. As the sociologist Greta Krippner recounts in *Capitalizing on Crisis*, "Credit allocation schemes were continually on the legislative agenda from the mid-1960s to the mid-1970s, with nearly 100 separate bills under consideration in the 1974 legislative session alone." Although they varied in detail, notes Krippner, "the basic premise was the same: if government controls . . . were [already] distorting flows of credit in the economy, then government actions could be devised to counteract the distortion, directing scarce capital where it was needed."[26] America's recent history proved that public spending could spur a virtuous economic cycle and increase the size of the pie. In other words, there was no scarcity of government credit, no natural limits imposing austerity, no good economic reason not to extend economic opportunities to all and end America's system of racial apartheid. In fact, just the opposite was true—government credit had built America's wealth. Black communities were seeking the same kinds of jobs and mortgages that had created the white middle class. However, not only was this path not taken, but the very real possibility that the federal government would channel resources to Black communities resulted in a political backlash that eroded the political majorities which had voted for and benefited from the New Deal's mixed economy.

RACIAL RESENTMENT, more than budgetary constraints, killed the political consensus around the mixed economy. If the pie was not getting smaller for all Americans, many whites began to *feel* like it was. Perceptions of scarcity increased tensions between white and Black blue-collar workers. The reshaping of the electorate was not a natural phenomenon; it had to be directed. Nixon's "southern strategy" is so named not just for its regional focus but because the weaponization of white identity as a political class was an electoral strategy. To capture Wallace voters and win the election, Nixon's team stoked fears of Black violence, promising to impose "law and order" to end an impending race war, and primed white Americans to see their fellow Black Americans as moochers and takers of *their* resources rather than the rightful recipients of their overdue fair share. This was not the first time white identity politics was stoked as political strategy—Reconstruction failed when the southern plantation oligarchy split the interracial coalition of indebted sharecroppers by giving poor whites what W. E. B. Du Bois called "the wages of whiteness," instead of the actual wages the coalition sought through the democratic process.

To win the presidency, the uninspiring candidate Nixon used barely hidden dog whistles to create a new political bloc, which he referred to as "the silent majority," based on aggrieved white identity. No man on the moon or Great Society was in the offing if voters chose Nixon, but the candidate validated Americans' fears of societal change and promised to stop it by whatever means necessary. Long after the fact, either as a form of deathbed penitence or record correction, Nixon's former aides admitted that the administration had embraced race-baiting. John Ehrlichman, Nixon's domestic policy chief, revealed in a 1994 interview that, in the 1968 campaign, the Republican candidate had "two enemies: the antiwar left and black people. You understand what I'm saying? We knew we couldn't make it illegal to be either against the war or black," but what they could and did do was associate "hippies with marijuana" and "blacks with heroin"—and criminalize both. Law enforcement would then raid homes, break up meetings, and display the criminals on the nightly news. "Did we know we were lying about the drugs? Of course we did."[27]

In the 1960s, most Americans were not shopping in the marketplace of ideas for laissez-faire economics, and, indeed, Nixon wasn't pitching the free market—not exactly. What Nixon sold, and what a majority of Americans bought, was a stop to the protests, to riots, to busing, to minorities moving into white enclaves and (supposedly) taking white jobs, to an America that, in the view of its white majority, had gone haywire. And the way he sold it was via a new brand of economics.

DESPITE THE SUCCESS of Ayn Rand's novels, with their celebrations of heroic entrepreneurialism and send-ups of so-called planners, most Americans' aversion to socialism had more to do with fears of subversive outsiders who threatened to destroy the American way of life than with economic matters per se. For example, the same voters in Orange County, California, and Maricopa County, Arizona, who launched Goldwaterism into politics had benefited enormously from government contracts that had created their jobs in the war industry and their subsidized home mortgages. These voters hated Communists, loved America, but lacked the fortitude for pure capitalism; they did not want to go back to the old days before government mortgages, union wages, social security, and the GI Bill. So why, then, did a group of economists in thrall to a radical free market orthodoxy suddenly become influential in the halls of power? For the same reason that Goldwater's libertarian platform made inroads in the once solidly Democratic South in 1964: because those same voters did not want the "character" of their neighborhoods to change. It was the same reason Greenspan was an adviser on race policy and not economic policy: voters wanted unfettered capitalism for others, but not for themselves.

A few economists of the emerging neoliberal school, like Greenspan, applied their theories directly to the issues of race. Among the first to do so was Gary Becker. Trained at the University of Chicago, which was and remains the intellectual center of neoliberalism in the United States, Becker devoted his PhD dissertation to an analysis of racism, and it was published in book form in 1957 as *The Economics of Discrimination*.

Becker's theory of employment discrimination was that it was a matter of personal taste—or, rather, distaste. And because it was a matter of taste—rather than the product of a careful weighing of alternatives— discrimination was both irrational and inefficient. In a free market, an employer who refused to hire Black employees would have to pay more for white employees and would therefore face a competitive disadvantage. Applying the simple law of supply and demand to a vexed social issue, Becker concluded that discrimination would die out naturally in a competitive market because it created excess costs for the discriminatory white employer. Becker believed that the answer to discrimination was more market competition, rather than government intervention. Unsurprisingly, this view led him to oppose civil rights laws. The implication of Becker's theory of racism as inefficient market preference, a foundational premise in subsequent neoliberal theorizing on race, was that the answer to racism was always more markets. In other words, do nothing.

Becker's mentor at the University of Chicago, Milton Friedman, shared his suspicion of civil rights legislation. In his 1962 book *Capitalism and Freedom*, Friedman lamented discrimination as distasteful and yet opposed civil rights laws on the grounds that they were an "interference with the freedom of individuals to enter into voluntary contracts with one another." He even compared civil rights laws prohibiting racial discrimination with Hitler's Nuremberg laws, which rendered German Jews second-class citizens in the 1930s. Friedman could not see a meaningful difference. "If it is appropriate for the state to say that individuals may not discriminate in employment because of color or race or religion," he explained, "then it is equally appropriate for the state, provided a majority can be found to vote that way, to say that individuals must discriminate in employment on the basis of color, race or religion."[28]

For Friedman, as for Becker, the answer to discrimination was the free market: it would root out inefficient practices like discrimination and favor color-blindness simply because the latter was more profitable. Because discrimination was costly to whites, Friedman opined, they would soon stop doing it: "The man who objects to buying from or working alongside a Negro" was expressing an inefficient preference and would therefore "pay a higher price for what he buys."

Of course, these analyses were wrong, both as description and as prediction. Discrimination was not costly—especially to whites who had long been beneficiaries of racial discrimination through the exclusion of Blacks from unions, from white suburbs, and from higher-paying jobs. Becker's and Friedman's economic models simply were not based in the reality of the 1960s (or any earlier era, for that matter); rather, as with so much of what their profession produced, they assumed a theoretical society where markets are efficient and all trade was based on price. In *theory*, it was costly for homeowners, merchants, or employers to refuse to employ or sell to Blacks insofar as Black people were willing to pay market price; but in *reality*, homes were worth *more*, not less, when they came with racial covenants prohibiting nonwhites from occupying them, and merchants and bankers who served an exclusively white clientele were *more*, not less, profitable than those who served Black customers. In fact, Black customers and borrowers paid more for the same (if not inferior) goods and services than did white customers. That clear race-based disparity was exactly what the Montgomery bus boycott in 1955, one of the first major episodes in the civil rights movement, sought to demonstrate. The laws of supply and demand had not ended disparities in the hundred years since Emancipation. Only federal laws, enforced by federal troops, had put an end to them—the same laws that Friedman and Becker had denounced as unnecessary, undoubtedly while shaking their heads at those backward white southerners ignorant of the nuances of macroeconomics.

Moreover, even if discrimination did suddenly disappear, the *effects* of discrimination would not. Discrimination had created market forces that were now operating on their own. Since the end of legal discrimination in the mid-1960s, the racial wealth gap has only increased, not decreased. Housing and school segregation have also increased, despite repeated promises that the free market would eliminate racism. In theory, credit, capital, and money do not discriminate and everyone is judged by their own skills and hard work. In American history, capitalism *did* discriminate. Black men and women were held *as capital* for hundreds of years; when freed, their property rights were not consistently enforced and they were routinely denied the basic legal protections essential for participation in capitalism. Their property was not protected by law; rather, it was vulnerable to constant conversion—that is, theft—by white majorities who could also breach contracts with impunity. When Black communities or individuals were more successful than white majorities, resentment would sometimes lead to riots or even massacres, as Tulsa, Wilmington, and various other places revealed. White lynch mobs, consisting predominantly of local residents but occasionally including outsiders, were frequently encountered, along with incidents of explosives being planted in homes sold to Black families residing in northern regions. This history of violence and exclusion was not free market capitalism but the opposite: a systematic sabotage of Black prosperity conducted by the state through law. The U.S. economy, despite its claim of being a free market, has not effectively ensured equal opportunities for all. In other words, Becker's and Friedman's—and Greenspan's—theories were nothing more than a fantasy.

It was good politics, however. The new neoliberal theories advanced by Greenspan and the Chicago anti-Keynesian economists gave right-wing southerners cover by coding their racist preferences, such as opposition to civil rights laws and school desegregation, as simple fidelity to the free market. Compared to George Wallace's rabid racism, the economists' views allowed for the genteel maintenance of the status quo.

Still, sometimes the mask slipped to reveal that perhaps there was more than just love of markets driving neoliberal theories and the solutions that followed from them. In 1962 George Stigler, the head of the Chicago economics department and a future Nobel Prize winner, penned a column on the Black protests entitled "The Problem of the Negro." His thesis was that Black people needed to stop blaming white people for their problems—that they should stop demanding antidiscrimination laws. The issue they faced wasn't discrimination, Stigler reasoned; rather, it was with Black people themselves. Sure, the Black worker may be discriminated against in some places, "but he is excluded from more occupations by his own inferiority as a worker." According to Stigler, Blacks weren't being hired because they were "lacking education, lacking a tenacity of purpose, lacking a willingness to work hard." He asked why Black leaders weren't "fostering the ancient virtues of diligence and honesty and loyalty?" and answered his own question: "It is so much easier to seek quotas."[29]

Stigler's treatise didn't stop with discrimination in the labor market; he also had thoughts about housing segregation. Instead of inveighing against the racial covenants, redlining, and other race exclusions that had created American apartheid, Stigler suggested that Black people should look inward and ponder why they were "repelled and avoided by the white man." His own view was that it was not prejudice, but that "the Negro family is, on average, a loose, morally lax, group, and brings with its presence a rapid rise in crime and vandalism." And because these traits were inherent in Black Americans, restitutionary laws wouldn't solve the problem: "As if," he quipped, "individual responsibility could be bought with a thousand dollars a year."

Stigler concluded by suggesting that the Black community take to heart the lessons of Jewish immigrants, who brought to America "precisely the virtues that should be instilled in the Negro: a veneration and irrepressible desire for learning; frugality; and respect for the civilizations of the western world." In fact, thanks to these virtues, Jews were "in a rapid process of losing their identity," such that, in a few generations, "we shall all have a little, but only a little, Jewish blood." For Stigler, this kind of erasure was a worthy goal.

Stigler and Greenspan were saying essentially the same thing that all opponents of progress have always said: that inequality was not created by *injustice* but by *inferiority* and was therefore either deserved or, in any case, not "our problem." The idea of neoliberalism itself wasn't groundbreaking—what was new were the clothes that an old idea was now wearing.

Usually, the development of any discipline proceeds in fits and starts over time, as researchers add brick by brick to a wall of knowledge, moving along under the current paradigm until a new discovery or theory—germ theory, quantum physics—revolutionizes the field and a new wall begins to be built. Sometimes, change happens very slowly, a reality that led the German physicist Max Planck to conclude that, in fact, science advances one funeral at a time. In a famous, oft cited example, when cholera was spreading through London in the mid-nineteenth century, scientists blamed it on "bad air," the miasma theory. The disease continued to spread until a physician named John Snow mapped the outbreak and found a single water pump from which cholera was infecting people. Germ theory was born, as was the modern science of epidemiology, which was refined by new data and tests. The old guard resisted Snow's theory, but that theory stopped the spread of cholera and, epidemic by epidemic, it became the reigning one. It replaced the old one because it worked. The scientific method demands that each discovery can be tested (or replicated) and falsified.

Neoliberal economics did not appear through such a process. There was no economic problem vexing researchers at the time—in fact, neoliberalism made inroads in American politics amid a period of phenomenal and unprecedented economic output. Events would pose challenges to Keynesian principles in the coming years—"stagflation," for example—whose resolutions would divide economists. But those problems, still years away, were not the reason Greenspan was advising Nixon as he was. In 1968, the issue was an old one: how to maintain and justify a racially segregated society in a democracy. How to do nothing instead of something.

NIXON'S AIDES, including Buchanan and Greenspan, traveled with the candidate to the Republican National Convention in Miami in August 1968. Buchanan had lobbied to bring Greenspan, the savvy numbers guy, to a Hilton hotel, where the campaign had barricaded itself on the top four floors. Greenspan was squeezed into a room with another staffer. His presence set off warning bells. Profiling Nixon's new economic adviser at the convention, *The Washington Post* quipped: "It is strange to find a man somewhat to the right of [William] McKinley as a key economic adviser to the new Nixon. Or is it?"[30] The article focused on Greenspan's advocacy of the gold standard, his opposition to antitrust, and his comment about the welfare state being "nothing more than a mechanism by which governments confiscate the wealth of the productive members of a society," which placed him far outside the Republican mainstream in that era.

The convention was Nixon's fourth as a nominee for national office, the second time for president. Party conventions at the time were dynamic events where votes were still up for grabs, and the platform and ticket were still being finalized. Nixon and his aides were busy behind the scenes trying to stay on top of the vote totals, with Greenspan calculating the votes in real time. The main drama at the convention was the split between the party's right flank and its center. When the party's new right had chosen Goldwater in 1964, most moderate Republicans refused to endorse him—except for Nixon. In 1968, Nelson Rockefeller stood for the moderates, the pro-business so-called Eisenhower Republicans who refused to debase themselves for the southern vote. George Romney had already gaffed himself out of the running earlier in the race when he said that he'd been "brainwashed" into supporting the Vietnam War. Standing for the right was Ronald Reagan, whose surprising—at least to the establishment—third-place finish at the convention would foretell the party's future. Nixon was considered by many to be in the moderate camp—he had been Eisenhower's vice president, after all—and his policies generally moved to wherever the party's base was. As his team calculated the changing tallies, his advisers, Greenspan in particular, instructed the boss on talking points and promises. The team had already surmised that Nixon could win only if he got out of the moderate's camp and became a bridge to the right. In public, Nixon was careful to signal to the right without offending the moderates. Behind closed doors, he was more direct, promising southern Republicans that he would "lay off pro-Negro crap" if elected president.[31]

Once Nixon clinched the nomination, his acceptance speech sanitized that message for the rest of the party. Nixon vowed "not [to] overpromise" on reforms. "Black Americans, no more than white Americans, do not want more government programs which perpetuate dependency. They don't want to be a colony in a nation." And so, the candidate said that "instead of government jobs, and government housing, and government welfare," he would use government tax and credit policy to "enlist in this battle the greatest engine of progress ever developed in the history of man: American private enterprise." He believed that it was time to see what "private enterprise and individuals" could do to "provide hope" and "reconciliation."[32]

Nixon seemed to have a natural talent for stoking fear in voters and yet keeping above the fray. In an early campaign speech titled "Human Dignity," he had explained that the country needed to "go beyond civil rights." In fact, in the first draft of the written speech, which can be found in Nixon's presidential files, the phrase was "forget civil rights," but Nixon himself had crossed it out and replaced it with the softer final wording.[33] The speech asserted that "civil rights is no longer an issue," because Jim Crow was over. As for the unfinished business of achieving actual equality, Nixon promised that integration of the races must proceed, "but in order for it to come on sound and equal basis, the black community has to build from within." What did this mean?

His campaign used advertising to get the point across, in particular the series of ads that outlined his signature race program, "Black capitalism." A campaign ad called "The Wrong Road" displayed the unhappy faces of minorities and then cut to a store sign that read "Government Checks Cashed Here." Nixon's voice-over explained, "For the past five years we've been deluged by programs for the unemployed—programs for the cities—programs for the poor. And we have reaped from these programs an ugly harvest of frustration, violence, and failure across the land." The ad was a subtle subversion of the Kerner Commission's conclusion that the urban rebellions of the decade were the harvest of racism. Nixon's message, which echoed Becker, Friedman, Stigler, and Greenspan, was that it was government intervention in the free market that had stifled true racial progress. The solution was to get off "the wrong road." The ad continued with upbeat music as the camera panned across images of construction sites, a factory line, and a shipyard while Nixon said, "We should enlist private enterprise to solve the problems of America."[34]

Ironically, Nixon sold Black capitalism to the Black community as a companion, of sorts, to the Black power movement, claiming that his plan was in sync with black nationalism. Nixon pressed for "more black ownership, black pride, black jobs, black opportunity, and yes, black power, in the best, the constructive sense of that often-misapplied term." While Nixon was using the language of the Black power movement, law enforcement snuffed out the movement itself. Nixon's adoption of the slogan was pouring salt on the wound.[35]

Black capitalism was a hit, especially with the press. *The Wall Street Journal* and *Time* magazine called the proposals "thoughtful" and "promising." His fellow Republicans embraced Black capitalism wholeheartedly. When the AFL-CIO denounced Nixon's ideas as apartheidlike, the conservative intellectual William F. Buckley offered a forceful rejoinder in the *National Review*, flipping the criticism on its head: "The call for special efforts to help the black people especially develop may be anti-democratic in the sense that it imposes special burdens on the white community." But Buckley believed that Black capitalism would be beneficial to "black power."[36]

Back in 1957, Buckley had argued in an editorial called "Why the South Must Prevail" that southerners should take "whatever measures are necessary" to prevent Black people from voting. Summoning the "dramatic choice" faced by the British in Kenya, a choice "between civilization and barbarism," Buckley likened the question facing "the White community" to "whether the claims of civilization supersede those of universal suffrage" and concluded that "sometimes" the numerical minority (of whites) had to take whatever action necessary, even violence, rather than "bow to the demands" of the majority of Blacks.[37] The same community that Buckley had dismissed as "backwards" he now wished to empower through capitalism. In his *National Review* piece about Nixon's program, he praised the "spirit" of "militant black leaders who have been preaching black initiative, black capitalism, and yes, black power." Buckley saw Black capitalism as aligning with his libertarian small government philosophy, and he proposed that the program need not reach every African American, because "scattered success can give universal hope." This was key: the government did not need to underwrite Black businesses—just the community's *hope* in and for Black businesses.[38] Ehrlichman, Nixon's top aide, explained that with "a relatively small budget impact, this is one program which can put the Administration in good light with Blacks without carrying a severe negative impact on the majority community, as is often the case with civil rights issues."[39]

Hubert Humphrey, the Democratic nominee in 1968, called his opponent's Black capitalism plan "double talk." When Nixon promised voters that his program would cost little, Humphrey retorted, "Of course it will take money. Talking about black capitalism without capital is just kiting political checks."[40] Humphrey was right. But Nixon still won.

GREENSPAN WOULD NOT be Nixon's Treasury secretary, the position he wanted above any other. Although one day, as Federal Reserve chair, Greenspan would be known for his gravitas, he was still a little too frank with reporters for a major public-facing role. He had made an embarrassing gaffe during the campaign, telling a journalist that Nixon "would be willing to take slightly more unemployment in the short run" to avoid inflation. This was likely true, but not the sort of thing you told the public. Greenspan's mentor, Columbia professor Arthur Burns (whom Nixon would appoint as Fed chairman late in 1969), intervened to deny that the statement reflected Nixon's position.[41] Additionally, and much to Greenspan's consternation, Nixon had no intent to practice fiscal restraint while in office. Greenspan, who was head of the New York–based economic consulting firm Townsend-Greenspan from 1954 to 1974, wasn't completely powerless, however. Toward the end of Nixon's tenure (though he didn't know it), the President asked Greenspan to lead his economic policy as chairman of the Council on Economic Affairs. Greenspan accepted, but by the time he was confirmed in 1974, he was serving under a new president, owing to the Watergate scandal and Nixon's resignation. Greenspan remained part of the inner circle of advisers for every subsequent presidential administration, except for Jimmy Carter's. By the time he left office in 2006, he held more power over world markets than any of the presidents he served.

Greenspan's legacy as Fed chairman was a financial system so reliant on Fed support that it is near impossible today to delineate where government monetary policy ends and financial markets begin. In crisis after crisis, Greenspan's policy "stabilized" the market, which led banks to take risks with confidence that the Fed would step in to save them, if necessary. The libertarian economist who once convinced Nixon that the only solution to America's racial apartheid regime was "to help the Negro help themselves" took a much more "helpful" stance toward the market. Each time a crisis loomed, Greenspan plied banks with loans, bought distressed assets to place on the Fed's balance sheets, lowered interest rates, purchased Treasury bonds to boost bank profits, and promised any "backstops" necessary to return banks to profitability. These measures were so common that they came to be called "the Greenspan put." In response to the "urban crisis," Greenspan urged *nothing*, but in response to turbulence in the market, Greenspan hurried to do or say *something* even before a crisis loomed. Wall Street profits were insured against loss by the public fisc, a transfer of wealth from the bottom of the population to the very top and a commensurate transfer of risk from the top to the bottom.

NEOLIBERALISM STILL has not yielded a free market. But it has prevented any meaningful remedy to racial injustice even as the government has continued to grow and its tentacles have penetrated ever deeper into the market. The difference between the "free market" state of our neoliberal era and the "mixed economy" of the New Deal era is that what was explicit in the past is hidden in the present. The neoliberal state would keep its management of the market behind a curtain of complex bureaucracy. Before neoliberalism, the people—or at least a certain subset of the people—were party to a social contract. Under neoliberalism, the people were cut out of the deal entirely.

Thus to cast neoliberalism as an economic theory and event, as most historians and other scholars have, is to miss its core function. Neoliberalism as state policy did not begin as a response to communism; nor were Americans persuaded to throw away Keynesianism after reading Cold War blockbusters like *The Road to Serfdom*, Friedrich Hayek's 1944 bestselling treatise, or *The Fountainhead*, Ayn Rand's 1943 novel. Neoliberalism began as political propaganda with Nixon as aided by the useful punditry of Greenspan and the Chicago School. While pure neoliberal ideas such as Gary Becker's did represent something new, neoliberalism was not a revolution led by ideas. It was not the supply of theories that led to their demand, but rather the other way around.

Free market zealotry and antigovernment libertarianism have always been present in American politics; the Gilded Age of the late nineteenth century witnessed the triumph of unfettered capitalism, including violent clashes between workers demanding better conditions and industrialists using state power to silence protest. Neoliberalism represented something different from the historical contest of power between a wealthy minority who controlled capital and production and a majority who worked the field or the machine. It did not emerge to resolve a conflict between labor and capital—its aim was not to free the market but to maintain the status quo against claims leveled by long marginalized groups. Its roots were not in the United States, even though America was most warped by it and, as the most powerful nation in the world, did the most to spread it. Neoliberalism would overspread much of the globe. As the next chapter shows, free market capitalism, as rhetoric, did the work of maintaining the power of Western nations in the face of widespread anticolonial and racial uprisings around the world.

Nixon's commitment to neoliberalism was haphazard and surface level. It was not free market capitalism he wanted as economic policy, but Black capitalism as racial policy. He increased the size of the federal government, installed price controls, ended the gold standard, and violated almost every tenet held dear by neoliberals. Nixon was not a true believer in the free market or likely anything else; rather he was a connoisseur of détente and decoy, and he spotted in free market economics a politically savvy, data-backed passage through a political thicket. Neoliberalism was based on a myth. As economic policy, it was unpopular and impractical, but it would become state policy as it transformed law and culture in reaction to the tense interregnum of the civil rights era.

In *The Strange Career of Jim Crow,* the historian of the American South C. Vann Woodward lamented the long-lasting effects of Jim Crow, which destroyed the soul and character of the South for generations. It tainted every aspect of southern life and recruited every southern institution to serve its malign purpose. Neoliberalism, like Jim Crow, rose during a political crisis when coalitions were in flux and power was contested. Once inscribed across southern law and enforced by every institution, Jim Crow became much more than a political slogan; it became a way of life. Neoliberalism has had the same effect on the entire nation. It sank its teeth into the law, and consumed everything.

CHAPTER 2

Empire's New Clothes

*People in Western societies ... have begun to realize
that the difficulties confronting us are moral problems,
and that the attempts to answer them by a policy of
piling up nuclear arms or by economic "competition" is
achieving little.*

— CARL JUNG, *MAN AND HIS SYMBOLS* (1964)

T O WIN A Nobel Prize is to have reached the pinnacle of one's
profession: to be recognized for making uncommonly significant contributions to society. Usually the winner is thrilled
and humbled. Not so with the Economics Nobel in 1974. Instead, its
two winners were angry—not because they had to share the prize, but
over whom they had to share the prize with. Gunnar Myrdal and Friedrich A. Hayek harbored no personal animosity for each other; Hayek
had in fact translated Myrdal's first book into German. But their world-
views were in direct opposition—condoning one meant condemning
the other. And their disagreement was not the typical pettiness of rival
scholars, but rather about the future of the world economy. Specifically,
whether the former empires in the Global North had a duty to alleviate the economic distress of their former colonies in the Global South

(Myrdal), or whether they did not (Hayek). With stakes so high and perspectives so polarized, the Nobel committee had decided to split the baby. It is no wonder both winners were offended.

Myrdal was a Keynesian before even Keynes himself, and his biographer wondered whether the Keynesian revolution in macroeconomics would have been called the "Myrdalian revolution" had Myrdal's book *Monetary Equilibrium* been available in English before 1936.[1] Myrdal was a champion of the welfare state and an advocate for the global redistribution of resources. His work was more empirical than Hayek's, but each attempted the kind of cross-disciplinary, big-picture project that was increasingly out of fashion in economics. Both were more interested in essentially political questions, about society and the survival of democracy, and as such, both were more concerned with policy and government than pure economics.

Coincidentally, both Myrdal and Hayek had published their best-known books to wide readerships in America in 1944. To Myrdal, whose *An American Dilemma* helped inspire the Supreme Court's *Brown v. Board of Ed* decision, "America's greatest and most conspicuous scandal" was that its laws were racist and sexist and violated its own ideals of egalitarianism—which he called the "American creed." To Hayek, the dilemma for America and the world in 1944—or in 1974—was socialism and redistribution, which posed grave threats to liberty and freedom. As Hayek saw it, Myrdal's message that wealthy nations had a moral duty to lift up the global community was the kind of seductive and seemingly harmless "collectivism" that he warned would lead society down the "road to serfdom." Myrdal had spent the years after *An American Dilemma* addressing the dire poverty of the Global South, which could be remedied only through wealth redistribution. It was not an easy fight. As for Hayek, in the thirty years since he first rose to prominence, his then prescient warning of the Soviet menace and its collectivist hypocrisies had receded in urgency and his star had dimmed as he retreated from the limelight. By 1974, he was primarily concerned with writing about law and governance.

Neither prize winner had lost any of his truculence when it came to defending his convictions, especially against what each construed as the other's dangerous heresies. Myrdal reported a few years after the Nobel ceremony that he regretted accepting the prize at all, but that he'd received the call from the committee "very early in the morning in New York, when I was totally off my guard." Hayek disavowed the prize during his acceptance speech itself: "I must confess that if I had been consulted whether to establish a Nobel Prize in economics, I should have decidedly advised against it."[2]

Their skepticism was warranted. The Nobel Prize in Economics is not a real Nobel Prize. Rather, it's an award sponsored by the Bank of Sweden; its official name is the Bank of Sweden Prize in Economic Sciences in Memory of Alfred Nobel. From the very start, the Nobel in economics has been politicized; and it has had as much to do with bolstering neoliberal ideology as neoliberal ideology has had in bolstering it.[3] The prize was the innovation of the neoliberal-led Swedish central bank to counter the socially democratic Swedish parliament's social spending. The prize did much more for Hayek and the worldview he represented than it did for Myrdal, the Swedes' hometown economist, who was the safe and obvious choice for the Nobel committee. He was the policy wonk next door whose ideas shaped their own country, based on the same Keynesian playbook read by many policy makers.

Myrdal was the shock-absorbing element that allowed the committee to select Hayek. As one analysis of the Nobel reveals, there were several other potential choices, like John Kenneth Galbraith and Joan Robinson, whose Keynesian stars shone brighter than did Myrdal's but whose post-Keynesian theories were not state policy as his were in Sweden. Hayek, meanwhile, was revered by few, controversial to some, and unknown to most.

The 1974 prize was awarded at a moment when Keynesianism—as theory if not as practice—was still king. Richard Nixon, upon imposing top-down price controls in 1971, told reporters that he was "now a Keynesian in economics."[4] At the time, Hayek's reactionary economics was increasingly seen as a response to a threat that no longer existed. But with the Nobel came renewed interest. Despite Hayek's misgivings, the prize helped transfer power from Keynes (who had died in 1946) to himself; he was soon to become the omniscient economist of the future. Just a few years later, British prime minister Margaret Thatcher would reach into her handbag amid a debate with her fellow Conservative Party leaders to retrieve her copy of Hayek's *Constitution of Liberty*, slamming it on the table while declaring, "This is what we believe." But the transition from Keynes to Hayek had less to do with the content of their theories than with the world events.

IF THE PERIOD from the mid-1960s to mid-1970s was an era of flux in the United States—a tense interregnum between political ideologies—it was exponentially more so worldwide. Although many Americans view the postwar decades through the lens of the Cold War standoff, this ignores the other half of the world, the Global South, home to many former colonies. These nations and peoples differed from one another culturally and politically, but many shared a common goal of independence.

For the preceding five hundred years, much of the world had been colonized and fought over by seven European nations: Portugal, Spain, the United Kingdom, France, Belgium, the Netherlands, and Germany. In a few short decades in the middle of the twentieth century, the tottering European empires lost practically all their colonial holdings, as almost ninety former colonies gained their independence. The era of empire building through violence was ending—and ended in a final frenzy of violence. The Third Reich had brought the logic of European imperialism to Europe itself, using the myth of racial supremacy that had justified colonization to commit mass murder with the most advanced modern technology, and thereby helping discredit ideas of European superiority. The horrors of the Nazis' Final Solution, according to Hitler's speeches and writings, was a justified extension of European and American conquests of "inferior" peoples. Centuries of rationalizing the brutality of colonization had made Europe, in the words of postcolonial theorist Aimé Césaire, "sick with colonization."[5]

Yet empire—and European supremacy—would not die easily. Colonialism had carved up the world to suit its own ends, transforming land, people, and culture along the way. The European empires were themselves transformed as they justified their dominion over the world. In

The Origins of Totalitarianism, Hannah Arendt's exploration of how free European societies succumbed so quickly to totalitarian regimes in the twentieth century, she concluded that they were primed by the mentality and practice of colonialism. European nations developed the "economic logic" of endless growth through violence during the "scramble for Africa." The logic and practice of empire that justified hundreds of years of ruthless exploitation abroad until it became "a permanent, supreme aim of politics" was eventually—inevitably—imported back to Europe, a phenomenon Arendt called "the imperial boomerang." It was colonialism, Arendt believed, that was the "true origins of totalitarianism."[6]

The era of empire thus fell at the hands of its own logic. The racial myths that justified the slaughter and enslavement of people based on nothing more than phenotypes had become embedded into law, thanks in part to John Locke's theories that held that God had granted the "wild" and "uncultivated" blank land "to the use of the Industrious and Rational," which were white men like him. This hierarchy was "natural" and thereby fixed. After industrial cultivation, aided by the slave trade, bore new fortunes in cotton, sugar, tobacco, and rubber, the rational and the industrious did what was rational and industrious. In the words of a character from Joseph Conrad's *Heart of Darkness*, they seized more of the "many blank spaces on the earth."[7]

Empire based on white supremacy had extended this logic across the globe and Nazism was its end point. "Never has our future been more unpredictable," said Arendt, "never have we depended so much on political forces that cannot be trusted to follow the rules of common sense and self-interest—forces that look like sheer insanity, if judged by the standards of other centuries." The Nazi Party had given Germans a unifying national myth "that claimed to explain whole trends of history" and that took root in disorienting and unpredictable times. The hubris of social Darwinism ended with the efficient and scientific mass murder of Jews and other undesirables by the "superior race." So much savagery disguised as progress. After the Allied victory, pseudo-scientific racism and state-supported eugenics programs, which were British and American innovations, were abandoned without fanfare. The steady self-assured rise of Western Europe gave way to destruction and vertigo. How had the "rational" and "civilized" men of Locke's imagination turned away so dramatically from Enlightenment ideals toward totalitarianism? While intellectuals searched for answers in the rubble of their fallen myths, statesmen and their economists worried about practicalities.

If the violent hypocrisy of the Second World War had shorn the myth of imperialism of its allure, it only strengthened the economic case for imperialism. In both world wars, victory in battle hinged on control over resources, supply lines, and trading routes. The victors in each were those who dominated colonial imports. Oil reserves, minerals, and food supplies were secured along the periphery of the main theater of war through the occupation of neutral countries. In fact, war among the European empires had begun just as soon as the first colonial spoils were taken back to the homeland. Hundreds of years of colonial exploitation were mirrored by hundreds of years of war among the great powers over those resources. Europe needed those imports to maintain its standard of living. Though European powers now renounced war, they also understood that maintaining peace in societies built on colonial wealth required exclusive access to cheap and abundant resources from former colonies.

Transnational corporations, backed by gunboats, had built fortunes extracting colonial wealth. It was these companies that were, practically speaking, the successors of empire. To compete economically on the world stage, the former colonies would need to develop their own economies, imposing taxes, fostering homegrown corporations, exporting goods, or allowing free exchange, but based on the dictates of their own people and not foreign entities. European nations and the United States had long imposed a mercantilist system of trade barriers involving high taxes and fees on imports in order to protect their economies from foreign competition. But if the former colonies did the same, Western economies would feel the pinch of higher prices, lower profits, and less government revenue through taxation.

Empire had created a worldwide economic system with Europe pulling in resources from the orbiting colonies. Although the empires formally lost their colonies, they did not lose their vast reserves of wealth and their relative economic strength. This strength stemmed, in part, from how colonialism had stunted and suppressed the economic development of resource-rich nations. Imperialism created a centripetal force that pulled resources into Europe, making the colonies akin to satellites whose purpose was to supply key resources at a fixed and predictable rate. Countries with rich histories and diverse economies came to be seen primarily as "oil exporters" or "copper mines," with their populations flattened into "labor" or obstacles to production. In some colonies, like India or Algeria, European empires effectively maintained their rule after independence. Few nations evaded direct colonial control, but those that did maintain their sovereignty during the imperial era—like Iran, Afghanistan, Thailand, Bhutan, and Nepal—were either controlled through vassal leaders, devoid of valuable resources, or, like Afghanistan, a continual war zone.

For the former colonies to reach a state of equilibrium and equity after the Second World War required them to transition from their forced status as exporters of monocrops or cheap commodities while European nations weaned themselves from imports. The United States faced no such dilemma; it had become the world's dominant economy due to its vast native resources, including oil, steel, and lumber, combined with its wartime ramp-up of manufacturing capacities. Yet while the United States did not need former colonies for imports, many American companies were transnational corporations with a significant foreign presence, such as Kennecott copper in Chile, Chevron oil in Iran, and Chase Bank everywhere. American weapons companies feeding the military industrial complex relied on overseas mining and labor for their corporate revenues. These firms, too, could have transitioned their businesses, although not without some financial losses. For the former colonies to get their fair share of the world's wealth, the powerful would have to lose their special rights and privileges. The accumulated wealth had gone one way during colonization—from south to north; from nonwhite to white; and from poor to rich. Attempts to stop or even reverse the flow would be met with resistance from onetime occupiers.

Either the age of empire and colonization would end, or the dominion of the Global North would be reasserted in a different form. That was the question that the 1974 Nobel committee had tried to avoid answering. In his acceptance speech, Myrdal called the decolonization movement that "swept over the globe like a hurricane" the most important issue facing Western nations, because they bore a responsibility to alleviate the "morally disturbing" poverty of the Global South. Myrdal condemned those Western nations and urged aid for former colonies as a matter of "human solidarity and compassion for the needy." By contrast, Hayek rejected the very notion of "moral obligations" rooted in solidarity, calling exhortations about "the greater good" or "social justice" a "mirage" hiding some form or other of tyranny. Hayek insisted that the state's only moral obligation was to ensure each person the "freedom to order our own conduct.... Once you admit that the individual is merely a means to serve the ends of the higher entity called society or the nation, most of those features of totalitarian regimes which horrify us follow of necessity." Hayek's radical individualism denounced any state obligations to remedy historic wrongs while Myrdal's economics demanded it. It was either Hayek's world or it was Myrdal's. It could not be both.[8]

THE AMERICAN SOCIOLOGIST Daniel Bell declared in 1960 that society had reached the "end of ideology." Like Francis Fukuyama heralding "the end of history," Bell spoke much too soon. In fact, 1960 was the beginning of a renaissance of ideologies from people not previously recognized as thinkers by the Western world. The Second World War had pushed science to reveal its unimaginable potential to destroy and to save—the atom bomb and chemical weapons were invented alongside vaccines, antibiotics, the Pill, and the modern computer. The television, radio, and copy machine allowed for the quick distribution of advertisements as well as revolutionary tracts. By 1955, average Americans could fly anywhere in the world on a commercial airline—including Martin Luther King, who traveled to India to meet Mahatma Gandhi's family; Malcolm X, who made a hajj to Mecca; and W. E. B. Du Bois, who self-exiled to Ghana. Meanwhile, the poets and intellectuals of the Global South traveled to Europe and America and across to other nations to discuss a world after empire. It was the greatest cross-pollination of ideas from the widest range of perspectives since before the era of colonial conquest, when the Silk Road trade route connected thinkers from Africa to China. The most urgent issue by 1960 was how to fairly integrate the former colonies into a European-led economy built on looting resources from the colonies.

Decolonization was not a uniform process, with each former colony following its own path. Yet if the story of decolonization is told as a single narrative, it could accurately be described as another "world war," not over territory but over sovereignty and economic control. Between the Second World War and the end of 1960, forty countries won their independence, including most of Southeast Asia, the Middle East, and Africa. Between 1961 and 1971, another fifty other countries broke free of imperial control. The Algerian revolution led to a political crisis in France and the sudden withdrawal from fourteen of its other African colonies. The year 1960 saw Britain's loss of Somalia and Nigeria and Belgium's loss of the Congo. In March 1960, Nelson Mandela was arrested for his role in leading the Sharpeville uprising, which began the decades-long fight against apartheid, prompting political scientist Ralph Bunche to call 1960 "the Year of Africa" for the "explosive rapidity with which the people in Africa are emerging from colonialism." Other African countries soon ejected their colonizers, including Kenya, Malawi, Uganda, and Mozambique. Meanwhile, China experienced a decade of tumult with the Cultural Revolution beginning in 1966 and the Middle East was upended by the Six-Day War in Israel in 1967. The Indo-Pakistani War broke out in 1965, and several countries, including Turkey, South Korea, Brazil, Iraq, Libya, Saudi Arabia, and Yemen, grappled with military coups or civil conflicts as part of the decolonization process.

The revolts spread to the United States, as Black activists linked their struggle with the worldwide fight against colonialism. Malcolm X, Martin Luther King, W. E. B. Du Bois, and, most provocatively, the Black Panthers viewed their activism as part of the new world war. "A revolutionary wants land so he can set up his own nation, an independent nation," said Malcolm in 1963. King called the 1964 Civil Rights

Act "the child of a storm" and "a component of a world era of change," and he compared northern ghettos to a "colonial area...powerless because all important decisions affecting the community were made from the outside."[9] Du Bois, who died in 1963, was active in the anti-colonial struggle, joining United Nations committees and coordinating declarations of peace and disarmament alongside his old friend Gunnar Myrdal and Myrdal's wife, Alva, herself a future Nobel laureate. At a 1949 peace conference in Paris, Du Bois lamented that his "own native land built by my father's toil and blood, the United States" had become "drunk with power... and [was] leading the world to hell in a new colonialism with the same old human slavery which once ruined us; and to a third World War which will ruin the world."[10]

Back in the eighteenth century, Thomas Paine's widely circulated pamphlet *Common Sense* provocatively denounced the evil myth of monarchy and "hereditary succession," persuading colonists to challenge the bogus idea that "a race of men came into the world so exalted above the rest" and distinguished themselves like "some new species."[11] The empire had divided the world into "two species," wrote the Algerian revolutionary Frantz Fanon, the Thomas Paine of the anticolonial struggle, in 1961.[12] His polemic *The Wretched of the Earth* urged the subjugated populations ("the wretched") to challenge the false racial hierarchy of empire. For Paine, it was "common sense" that "all men being originally equals, no one by birth could have a right to set up his own family in perpetual preference to all others forever."[13]

In the contest for imperial power, the Europeans had drawn lines around their territorial "holdings" and imposed racial categories and hierarchies foreign to the civilizations they conquered. Though empire was initially justified by theories of divine right, its defenders proved to be ideologically adaptable. Communities with different customs, beliefs, and ways of life were lumped together as "Mongoloid," "Oriental," "Negro," or "Caucasoid," categories supplemented by charts and skull measurements that appeared scientific and seemed to prove that race was essential and "natural," and therefore incontestable. Pseudo-Darwinian race science coincidentally showed the citizens of the conquering nations to be the most highly evolved species of men, neatly justifying the brutal savagery required to "civilize" the natives. "Africans were made to believe that they were savages" in need of civilization, said the Iranian revolutionary intellectual and Fanon acolyte Ali Shariati, and Middle Easterners that they were "Barbarians" needing "reformation," which resulted in both groups being "Europeanized through export and exchange."

As Fanon saw it, "The peoples of the Third World are in the process of shattering their chains." Revolutionaries across the world adopted European racial categories to link themselves together in a common cause. "The cause is the effect: You are rich because you are white, you are white because you are rich." The threat of race war loomed. Fanon did not equivocate: "Decolonization is always a violent event." Fanon himself fought in the Algerian war. In his introduction to *The Wretched of the Earth*, Jean-Paul Sartre wrote, "What then has happened? Quite simply this: we were the subjects of history, and now we are the objects. The power struggle has been reversed." To Sartre, all the French could do was delay the inevitable.

As with the mainstream reaction to uprisings in American cities, global white fears of violence far exceeded the reality. But in the United States and elsewhere, the violence was disordered and chaotic. Outmatched by professional armies, some rebels used extralegal tactics, like suicide bombings or assassinations of political figures, blurring the lines of war and recruiting unwilling civilians into the turmoil. Revolutionary "freedom fighters" from the Irish Republican Army (IRA), the Palestine Liberation Organization (PLO), the African National Congress (ANC), and the Jammu Kashmir Liberation Front often treated violence as spectacle or threat. Most paramilitary groups relied on a much larger group of civilians sympathetic to their cause. The IRA and ANC depended on support and solidarity from large swaths of the population who were willing to shelter and feed those directly engaged in the conflict. To be sure, the violence of the revolutionaries paled in comparison to the violence of empire or the European wars, but it was not the orderly violence of battle or the routine, bureaucratic brutality of repression or enslavement. Guerrilla warfare, suicide bombs, and homemade explosives—the new face of violence was shocking and destabilizing.

Without help from the main arms-producing nations of the world, few rebel groups could achieve their aims through violence alone. Those that did—in Algeria and Cuba, for instance—were the exception. Influenced by Mohandas Gandhi's successful resistance movement against the British, Martin Luther King Jr. chose nonviolence as his strategy of resistance. As he noted, attempting to use violence against the U.S. government would have ended in certain failure. The reason resistance worked at all was that the world had changed. King and Gandhi rejected violence because it was a moral failure perpetuated by white supremacy. The ideology of empire and the myths that sustained it no longer prevailed.

If Europe was "sick with colonization," as Césaire had put it, it was also sick with war. After the concentration camp, the gulag, and the nuclear bomb, Europeans tried to end war once and for all. The Nuremberg trials prosecuted Nazis for "crimes against humanity," while the Geneva Convention refined the codes against "war crimes" to try to prevent atrocities like torture and genocide. The United Nations was founded in 1945, and in 1948, it released a Universal Declaration of Human Rights that recognized "barbarous acts" as the "disregard and contempt" for human rights, decreeing "the inherent dignity [and] equal and inalienable rights of all members of the human family" as "the foundation of freedom, justice and peace in the world." The idea of "the international community" was forged and nations swore off colonial wars of aggression. As the Second World War was ending, world leaders met in Paris, Bretton Woods (New Hampshire), Vienna, and Geneva to establish or empower international governing bodies: not only the United Nations, but also the International Monetary Fund (IMF), World Bank, North Atlantic Treaty Organization (NATO), International Joint Commission, and World Health Organization, in addition to scores of treaties and compacts. The ideals—if not the reality—of equal rights for all the world's people was a direct rebuke to the logic of colonization. Of course, many world leaders rejected the notion of racial equality and many more paid mere lip service, but if one nation was going to assert dominion over another, it could no longer rely on the old myths of inherent superiority. The notion of equal rights, foundational to the American creed as put forth in the Declaration of Independence, was now adopted around much of the globe.

As European nations gathered to swear off empire and war, their former colonies forged alliances around their own common aims. In 1955, twenty-nine newly independent states from Africa and Asia met in Bandung, Indonesia, to declare "Five Principles of Peaceful Coexistence" and a ten-point "declaration of world peace and cooperation," denouncing colonization in all its manifestations. The conference attendees demanded "the equality of all races and the equality of all nations large and small," and the "abstention from intervention in the internal affairs of another country." As the Indonesian leader Sukarno said, they were united "by a common detestation of colonialism," "a common detestation of racialism," and a desire for peace.[14] These nations declared themselves to be not formally aligned with any of the great powers and came to be called the nonaligned movement; they asked to be left out of other people's wars and promised to leave other nations alone. The following year, Black writers and intellectuals from across the world met at the Sorbonne in Paris to address colonialism, slavery, and racism under the banner of "Pan-Africanism." In attendance were Césaire, Fanon, and Baldwin. The eighty-eight-year-old Du Bois, who had predicted in 1903 that "the problem of the Twentieth Century is the problem of color line," had been banned from traveling abroad by the U.S. government. Artists and activists from across the globe were aligning along the color line—a reflection and also rejection of the course of empire.

Not only was strength in numbers a necessity, but a window of hope had opened that the future would be shaped by diplomacy and cooperation rather than coercion and bloodshed. Tensions and conflict among and within former colonies continued; the power vacuum created by rapid decolonization had spurred civil wars and unleashed long-standing animosities between rural peasants and educated elites, complicating attempts to forge solidarity within and across territorial boundaries. Still, the era witnessed the birth of a cooperative spirit and an ambitious vision of equality put forward on the world stage. The joint declarations by the newly independent nations fostered a sense of utopian possibility, as world leaders came together to produce documents calling for "mutual respect," "solidarity," cooperation, coexistence, equality, and world peace. Constitutions were being written and rights defined. The demands were practical, but the aspirations were lofty.

"We choose to go to the moon," said President Kennedy in 1962, and NASA did it in 1969. Why not choose to see this planet's inhabitants as equal? In a time when the unimaginable had already happened and the future was up for grabs, poets and thinkers began to speak to one another about freedom and equality. The sense of possibility was not unlike the American Revolutionary War—the empire was retreating and a movement for freedom was being advanced through ideas.

AMONG THE international institutions founded in the aftermath of the Second World War, the Mont Pelerin Society (MPS) didn't attract the same fanfare as the United Nations or NATO, yet its impact on the era's decolonial movements—indeed, on world history—has been as significant as that of the better-known organizations, if not more so.

Established in 1947 by Hayek and named for the Swiss mountain town where its inaugural meeting was held, the MPS's purpose was to counteract creeping "collectivism" in Europe and attacks on liberalism worldwide—to defend the "central values of civilization" by shoring up the "belief in private property and the competitive market; for without the diffused power and initiative associated with these institutions it is difficult to imagine a society in which freedom may be effectively preserved."[15]

Most of the attendees at the first meeting were economists, but a smattering of political philosophers, journalists, and business leaders participated, too. The group addressed topics including state power, international politics, and specifically how Western nations could preserve market freedom against rising political threats. The MPS issued a "statement of aims" that, in contrast to the Third World declarations envisioning a future of peaceful coexistence, lamented a bygone era: "over large stretches of the Earth's surface the essential condition of human dignity and freedom have already disappeared." The MPS would attempt to preserve and defend.

The first meeting of the MPS is usually presented as the origin point for neoliberalism. And from its genesis, the movement born in the Swiss mountains was about political power rather than economic theory, specifically how the levers of state policy could be used to counter the global revolt against Western corporations. An exchange among Milton Friedman, George Stigler, and Friedrich Hayek in a subsequent meeting is illustrative. Friedman argued that states should enact "automatic stabilizers" to return the market to equilibrium in the event of disruption, to which Hayek (more astutely, perhaps, than he realized) responded: "How can monetary policy be automatic and outside the range of politics?" Both economists were staking out their positions early on—for Friedman, all economic questions could be simplified into a formula, while Hayek realized that these were fundamentally political issues. Hayek consistently argued that "the work of men like ourselves create the political climate in which the politicians of our time must move." Stigler also voiced opposition to Friedman's argument: "Can we agree that the first step [for monetary stability] should be to bring all money-making institutions under the control of the state?"[16] There was no clear consensus at the first meeting, but thanks to the men in the room, monetary policy would soon be brought under state control.

Disagreement also erupted with respect to unemployment, and specifically how much unemployment states should create to spur a competitive market. These were discussions about politics and policy—about who should control the levers of money creation in a democracy, and whether and how to impose order and predictability, even automaticity, given the inevitability of political change, if not upheaval.

In the late 1940s, none of these MPS members had any role in government. They were academics—well-connected ones, to be sure, but no one in power was asking them to resolve issues of money and employment. The U.S. economy was humming along, and while the country was dealing with various domestic and international challenges, those concerns were not economic. Yet decades later, members of the MPS and their acolytes would be designing state policy across the globe, including in the United States, the United Kingdom, and across the Global South. Their ambitions to take control of monetary policy away from sovereign nations and remove constraints on global capital would become state policy forty years after their initial meeting. Though it typically takes time for academic ideas to shape public policy, the lag between MPS's theories and MPS's influence on state policy was unusually long. More curiously, given the group's stated aims and preoccupations, the problem the MPS was formed to confront (creeping socialism) was not the one that its slate of policies was eventually employed against. That problem—the revolt of the Global South—had not yet emerged when the MPS first met. But when it did, it threatened to destabilize the historical balance of winners and losers. In response, empire's new clothes would be stitched out of the MPS program, a socioeconomic philosophy that, after Friedman's influential 1951 article "Neo-liberalism and Its Prospects," came to be known as neoliberalism.

The obstacle former colonies faced on their way to realizing equality was similar to that faced by Black communities in America: freedom was meaningless without the power to use it. Achieving independence required not just political sovereignty but economic sovereignty, too. Without "money, property, nor friends," said Frederick Douglass of the freedman after Emancipation, "he was free from the individual master, but the slave of society." Former colonies sought power through alliances ("friends"), but they found themselves "slaves" to the world economy. The former empires had to give up their exclusive claims to resources and some of their privileges in world trade so that former colonies could develop their economies. But formal "freedom" meant nothing if transnational corporations had power over resources. As Gunnar Myrdal emphasized in his Nobel speech and italicized in the written version, "the blunt truth is that without rather radical changes in the consumption patterns in the rich countries, any pious talk about a new world economic order is humbug."[17] Despite formal decolonization, resources and profits continued to flow predominantly from the Global South to the Global North.

It would be the attempts by former colonies to achieve economic independence that truly shocked and enraged the former empires of the Global North. Any resource-rich nation was only provisionally free if it could be cut off from international trade. At Bandung and at the U.N. General Assembly, nations joined together to promise to support one another's sovereignty and to fight back against the so-called seven sisters, a group of major multinational oil companies—Anglo-Iranian Oil Company (later renamed British Petroleum or BP), Gulf Oil Corporation, Royal Dutch Shell, Chevron Corporation, Exxon, Mobil Oil (later merged with Exxon to form ExxonMobil), and Texaco (later merged with Chevron)—that wielded significant influence and held substantial control over oil production, distribution, and pricing. As the Iranian parliamentarian Djalal Abdoh told the U.N. General Assembly, "Certain industrialized countries would have to realize" that exploitation of other people's resources was not part of "the modern world." In the early 1950s, Iran's democratically elected prime minister, Mohammad Mossadegh, asserted the nation's sovereignty and ended the British occupation of its oil fields. Although this legal change has been described as nationalization, Mossadegh was clear that foreign firms were welcome to remain in Iran and purchase the oil, but that Iran would sell its oil on the international market based on market prices. The Anglo-Iranian Oil Company (AIOC) had previously held a monopoly over Iran's oil and enjoyed privileged rights under a concession agreement. Mossadegh's move was met with opposition from foreign powers, particularly the United States and Britain, who perceived it as a threat to their interests and regional influence. The AIOC and its Western supporters regarded the nationalization as a violation of contractual rights and economic interests. Amid these events, various voices emerged in support of Iran's right to nationalize its oil industry.

Eleanor Roosevelt invited Abdoh on her NBC television show and, addressing its American audience, he repeated the message that Iran had "legal" and "legislative right" to nationalize oil, emphasizing the lawful nature of Mossadegh's actions as Iran "exercising an indisputable sovereign right." This argument spurred other legislators across the Middle East to plead their case to the international community under the terms of law and legal contract.[18]

In response to oil price cuts imposed by the seven sisters, as well as U.S. government import caps that depressed prices of foreign oil in the 1950s, five oil-producing states—Iran, Iraq, Kuwait, Saudi Arabia, and Venezuela—met in Baghdad in 1960 to form the Organization of the

Petroleum Exporting Countries (OPEC), with the Shah of Iran joining in solidarity with the other nations in an anticolonial agreement
and message. The OPEC documents alerted the seven sisters that the
oil-producing countries had an inalienable right to permanent sovereignty over their natural resources in the interest of their national development. OPEC's legal director, Hasan Zakaria, a graduate of Harvard
Law School, argued against the Western legal tradition's presumption of
"natural law," the Lockean principle at the foundation of Western common law that upheld formal contract and property rights as divinely
endowed and therefore fixed and unchanging. By demanding "a slavish
adherence to precedent," Western nations held their counterparties to
contract terms "negotiated," if at all, under coercion. Law must evolve to
match recent developments.

The colonies were taken by force and held by the power of legal codes,
contracts, and corporate charters—these "rights" to other people's natural resources were the contested domain of the Third World revolt.
Even after formal empire ended, some European and American corporations insisted on maintaining control of their holdings abroad, based
on the fact that they had legally inscribed those rights in contracts. In
an earlier era, Keynes had denounced the "absolutists of contract" who
insisted on the preservation of their property rights at all costs as "the
real parents of revolution." Third World intellectuals argued that these
old contracts were now invalid because of changed conditions. Contract
rights were not sacrosanct and eternal, but were contingent on higher
order laws, specifically international law, which "owed its existence to
the moral conscience" of the world population. The core dispute was
over which order of law—corporate contracts or international treaties—
was of higher importance. Insisting on legal formality was a red herring; the issue was power. To increase their relative power against the
still dominant armies of the former empires, the resource nations joined
together. OPEC was one of the many coalitions of the colonized to push
back against transnational companies and former empires. What Henry
Kissinger, Nixon's secretary of state, later derided as "an unholy alliance
between OPEC and the Third World" was to its Third World architects an expression of a legal right to economic independence. As the

president of the Arab League, Abdul Khalek Hassouna, noted in Bandung, "Economic sovereignty [is] the basis of political sovereignty."[19]

Through treaties and declarations, the nations of the Global South tried to nurture and protect their nascent export economies with tariff protections and capital controls. As more countries joined the United Nations, it became another site where leaders from the Global South forged alliances. In 1960, Bunche's "Year of Africa," the United Nations added seventeen newly independent countries to the General Assembly. The formerly colonized could plead for justice in the United Nations. At the meeting of the General Assembly in New York that December, Asian and African countries introduced a proposal for a full vote by the assembly, declaring that the "subjection of peoples to alien subjugation, dominion and exploitation constitutes a denial of fundamental rights" and is contrary to the U.N. Charter promoting "world peace and cooperation." Soviet premier Nikita Khrushchev introduced a counterproposal urging the assembly to "place the subject of colonialism in next year's agenda," but it was rejected. When the assembly voted on this proposal for a "Declaration on the Granting of Independence to Colonial Countries and People," it passed, yet not without controversy. A few nations abstained from the vote, including Britain, France, Belgium, Portugal, South Africa, and the United States.

At the 1964 U.N. General Assembly in Vienna, a coalition of seventy-seven nations from the Global South formed a group called the G-77 and issued a joint declaration proclaiming a "new world order," which aimed to raise the living standards of people in developing countries. The declaration pushed back against the IMF and World Bank's insistence that developing nations be open to international trade, which, the G-77 believed, did not take into account the distinct needs of the developing world to foster its own economies to close "the trade gap." The thrust of the G-77's demands was that the powerful nations honor the sovereignty and national borders of the developing ones. The G-77 also demanded that when trade deals were made, or when the United Nations, IMF, or World Bank determined issues of global economic policy, these bodies give "cardinal importance to democratic procedures which afford *no position of privilege*" economically, financially, or politically. In other words, international decisions should be made democratically, "one country, one vote." The G-77 issued another declaration in 1967, the "Charter of Algiers," inveighing against South Africa's apartheid regime and calling for a global disarmament.

In 1970, the G-77 unveiled its plan for a "New International Economic Order," which advocated for self-determination for each country and the fair distribution of world resources. Among other things, the G-77, OPEC, and other coalitions of the Global South demanded autonomy to sell—or not to sell—to transnational corporations that had become permanent fixtures in their nations and in their politics. The proposals included imposing trade barriers to keep foreign investors out, a practice that was routine among most of the Western nations, including the United States during the era of Bretton Woods. Small nations could not build their economies without tariffs and capital controls, which allowed native industries to grow without having to compete with better-resourced nations. Their main area of concern was with the power of transnational corporations, including the multinational coal, copper, and diamond miners, and their political influence.

The dilemma for Western nations after the age of formal empire was ideological and material. They could not maintain economic dominance if former colonies became sovereign democratic nations, and they couldn't use brute force to maintain that dominance without abandoning their democratic principles. It was this challenge, not Keynesianism or communism, whose ideal solution was neoliberalism.

CONTROLLING THE resources of former colonies in the absence of political domination was a delicate diplomatic maneuver—one that the members of the MPS were well equipped to handle. In the 1950s and 1960s, MPS debates started focusing on such issues as the uneasy relationship between national sovereignty and international trade and the growing threat that revolt represented. At the 1957 meeting, Arthur Shenfield, a British economist who would soon become president of the society, explained that it was very difficult for the "liberal" to oppose democracy, but that it was sometimes necessary. Western leaders and the international business community did not have to concede to the demands of each national democracy and "allow the claim of dependent peoples to choose to misrule themselves," though this was, admittedly, a difficult position to justify. Another MPS member, Fritz Machlup, lamented that "the cost of democracy is rather high" because it "makes it impossible to do what ought to be done" and forces "one to do what not ought to be done, in the public interest." Or, as he would put it more bluntly, "there can be no liberty for 'savages'": democracy "may not be the most suitable system of government" for people who were "politically and intellectually immature."[20]

Although neoliberalism became American policy, although the movement was funded mainly by American interests, and although the ideology was exported primarily by American economists, its focus was European. This was little surprise, given its origins. The United States had emerged from the Second World War as the leading power in the world, and the MPS members' early speeches and writings during the 1950s and 1960s reveal a sense of paranoia and desperation over Europe's loss of status. The rise of the Global South was all but inevitable, and Europe's decline in living standards and wealth would be commensurate. There was also a fear of a different kind of boomerang—that what the colonizers had meted out on the colonies, they would now suffer at the hands of their former subalterns, a situation one founding MPS member called "black imperialism."[21]

Just as the leaders representing the "wretched of the earth" were uniting along shared interests, so too were the blessed of the earth. In 1967, Martin Luther King warned that when "profit motives and property rights are considered more important than people, the giant triplets of racism, extreme materialism, and militarism are incapable of being conquered."[22] While it is tempting, given neoliberalism's success in quelling the Global South revolutions in a relatively short amount of time, to assume coordinated planning and design, the reality was messy and unpredictable. The neoliberals were no Machiavellian architects of the future; the truth was far less inspiring. Their ferocity and diligence in plotting a long-term and ultimately successful defense against democratic power was most likely fueled by the urgency of certain loss.

While the Global South imagined a future different from the past, the neoliberals worked painstakingly toward a future that was similar to the past—or as close as possible. The basic feature of that plan was to counteract rising national power of the former colonies by undercutting the power of *all* states to regulate corporations. Neoliberal intellectuals began fighting against the very idea of sovereignty itself. Speaking at The Hague about the future of international law in 1955, founding MPS member Wilhelm Röpke noted that "to diminish national sovereignty is most emphatically one of the urgent needs of our time."[23] The neoliberals sought a new international economic order, one very different from the G-77's bid for a flattening of the trade hierarchy among nations; this neoliberal world order would instead seek to augment the power of corporations and capital over that of national governments.

In *Globalists*, historian Quinn Slobodian traces the lineage of neoliberalism to a group of European intellectuals called the Geneva School, whose peak era of influence came immediately after the fall of empire. The group, including Röpke, Ludwig von Mises, Michael Heilperin, and Hayek, were the first intellectuals to envision and plan for an economic order after empire. Their goal, according to Slobodian, was "to inoculate capitalism against the threat of democracy [and] to create a framework to contain often-irrational human behavior."[24]

The Geneva School's model was inspired by the Nazi jurist Carl Schmitt's theory that the world was divided into two overlapping spheres, which he called *imperium* and *dominium*. Both covered the entire globe, but *imperium* was the world divided up territorially by sovereign nations, while *dominium* was the world of money and capital ruled by market forces. "Over, under and beside the state, political borders of what appeared to be a purely political international law between states," wrote Schmitt, "spread a free, i.e. non-state, sphere of economy permeating everything: a global economy."[25] For Schmitt, the goal was to increase the power of *imperium* over *dominium*, whereas the Geneva neoliberals sought just the opposite: to empower the free movement of money and capital, and thus to weaken state power. Their goal was attractive to postimperial European nations, because it would allow them to persist in their control over resources like oil and copper even after the nations that held those resources had become sovereign. *Dominium* would do what *imperium* could no longer.

Before neoliberalism could be exported, it had to be cleansed of the stain of colonialism and racism. Maintaining imperial resource extraction without empire would take some trial and error. MPS founder William Hutt, an English economist, was among the first to articulate the developing neoliberal consensus. Hutt's academic work until the 1960s had denounced unions as harmful to the economy and characterized collective bargaining actions such as strikes as unlawful, paramilitary-like violence. In *The Economics of the Colour Bar*, published in 1964, Hutt, who was then living in South Africa, attacked the apartheid regime there as a restraint on market freedom. Hutt began the book by quoting a long passage from Milton Friedman's *Capitalism and Freedom* about capitalism being the antidote to racial discrimination. Hutt blamed the imposition of the color bar, which maintained the dominant status of white Afrikaners, on collectivist tendencies and "socialist and labour union pressures." Hutt's remedy? *Black capitalism*: "Private property and capitalism have been a major source of opportunity for Negroes and have permitted them to make greater progress than they otherwise could have made."[26]

Although the neoliberals would continue to hone their response to issues of race, the basic steps were already apparent in Hutt's book. First, racism is bad; second, racial disparities were actually created by unions, collectivists, or the left; finally, capitalism was the only remedy.

Hutt's earlier writings defended the large mining companies in South Africa, stating that "the cheapness of African labour [was] not 'exploitation.'" Quite the opposite. The mines had actually been "the greatest single uplifting factor" for the poorer races and classes in South Africa. To blame the mining companies for paying Africans lower wages than whites was to "blame a mitigating factor and not a cause." Hutt believed it was the "backwardness" of "primitive races" that was part of the reason for the lower wages, as well as market interventions by whites. The economist also defended British colonization. He wrote that "the current, almost world-wide disapproval of colonialism is derived from the idea that the colonizing nations have held or are holding the colonized peoples in some sort of subjection."[27] They hadn't, and weren't. Hutt also argued that racism could not be an explanation for economic disparities between Africans and whites because of the relative success of the "educated and responsible non-Whites" compared to those complaining of "injustice."

As for democracy, Hutt argued against the idea of political representation, noting that "universal suffrage would merely mean the transfer of power to a new political majority, with no constitutional limitations to prevent retaliatory abuse."[28] Nelson Mandela had been in prison for two years when Hutt published *The Economics of the Colour Bar*, and he would remain in prison for the next twenty-six years—neither he nor his political party, the ANC, is mentioned in Hutt's book, even though it was entirely about South Africa. The intended audience was clear. In his concluding chapter, Hutt wrote: "The white intelligentsia are thinking more and more in terms of how to avoid black supremacy (a mere turning of the tables)."[29] He urged the white minority in South Africa against fixating on democracy and to unleash "entrepreneurs" and "consumers" instead, because "competition liberates minorities" and only "the market is colour-blind." The idea of "one man, one vote," Hutt believed, "created wholly justifiable fears" on the part of the whites. Hutt's exalted, color-blind market could only be built by tipping "democracy" in favor of the votes of the white and wealthy against the black and poor.[30]

If apartheid South Africa was a central example for neoliberals' ideas on race and democracy, postcolonial South America provided a laboratory in which to try out their full slate of economic policies without the inconvenience of political dissent. Funded by an international NGO, Milton Friedman and a group of University of Chicago economists he called "the Chicago Boys" went to Chile beginning in 1957 to implement a formal "program of technical assistance and development aid." Their work started to shape government policy after Augusto Pinochet's 1973 coup, which saw the democratically elected president, Salvador Allende, either commit suicide or be killed during the uprising.

The coup was aided by a long anti-Allende propaganda campaign, which records reveal was either wholly manufactured by the CIA, or at least stoked and abetted by it. Allende had moved to nationalize Chile's resources and impose restrictions on foreign companies, foremost among them the American mining companies Anaconda Copper and Kennecott and the communications firm International Telephone and Telegraph. When the coup was met with condemnation from American newspapers, Henry Kissinger, then Nixon's national security adviser, complained in a phone call to the President that, if it had still been the Eisenhower era, they'd be considered "heroes" for overthrowing a "Communist" government. Nixon replied, "Well, we didn't—as you know—our hand doesn't show on this one."[31] It was an example of the dilemma former empires faced in the postimperial era, when actions against other nations on behalf of domestic corporations often had to be carried out clandestinely.

The Chicago Boys would soon make their mark as well. Their program of economic "shock treatment," which they called *El Ladrillo* (the brick), consisted of severe budget cuts, as well as the far-reaching macroeconomic reorganization of the Chilean economy toward privatization, world trade, and exports. The real shock came later, when their much heralded plan of transformation came under attack after the international community "discovered" that the Pinochet regime had murdered and tortured tens of thousands of Chileans—thirty thousand in 1973 alone, when the Chicago Boys were embedded across government offices.[32] In subsequent years, two hundred thousand Chileans were forced into exile and the country descended into poverty.

Nevertheless, the Chicago Boys' program spread across the region, including to Peru, Argentina, and Mexico, despite local protests. Even though the Chicago Boys were largely discredited at the time, their economic ideas and tactics found widespread adoption, resulting in the implementation of market liberalization programs across much of the world. To date, the International Finance Corporation, World Bank, and IMF have launched countless "technical assistance" programs around the globe, which have included loans, official trainings, wholesale takeovers of government functions, and more. A Latin American joke has it that "people have to go to jail so prices can remain free."

* * *

DESPITE EMPIRE'S new look and tools, it was not hard to see that the old ideas were just under the surface. Wilhelm Röpke once responded to press criticism for his support of the apartheid regime in South Africa by noting that the left "will not be satisfied until they let a real cannibal speak." Röpke and his fellow MPS members often used the word "cannibal" in their discourse. As they saw it, such talk was justified by the cultural—if not racial—superiority of the rich countries.

Evidence that empire was still alive and well could be found in the United States, too. In his 1964 *Suicide of the West*—another common utterance in neoliberal discourse—conservative intellectual James Burnham warned of the danger posed by Third World revolutions and domestic racial uprisings that, in his view, sought to destroy the classical liberal ideals of the West, such as free market capitalism. He wrote of the civil rights movement as "the jungle now spreading within our own society, in particular in our great cities," and of "the explosive population growth and political activization" of the "world's backward areas," primarily among the "non-white masses."[33]

Burnham's *National Review* compatriot William F. Buckley was beholden to the old myths too—until he wasn't. In 1957, as we saw in chapter 1, Buckley stated that he had been vehemently opposed to extending the vote to Black people because whites were the "advanced race." In 1960, the *National Review* editorial board wrote, regarding apartheid, that "the whites are entitled, we believe, to pre-eminence in South Africa." In 1963, Buckley defended apartheid as the rightful prerogative of white South Africans to protect their civilization. But by 1969, Buckley was *opposing* apartheid, noting in the pages of the *National Review* that "what makes apartheid objectionable is not that it is anti-democratic, but that it is compulsory." Buckley, like a great many other right-wing reactionaries, began the decade as a racist and ended it as a free-marketeer.

In 1968, the English politician Enoch Powell gave two notable speeches. One was to a Conservative Association Meeting in Birmingham, in which he infamously argued for a ban on all nonwhite immigrants, predicting that, "in fifteen or twenty years' time, the Black man will have his whip hand over the white man" and England's rivers would "[foam] with much blood." The other was an address to the MPS, at the invitation of Friedrich Hayek, a longtime admirer, arguing for tighter monetary policy aimed at choking off public spending. Powell was dismissed from his position as shadow defense minister after this "Rivers of Blood" speech caused an uproar, but he would get his immigration ban in 1971. Having spent his career as an intelligence and military officer in various colonial outposts, even aspiring to be viceroy of India, Powell had been devastated by Indian independence in 1947 and Britain's loss of its empire. Neoliberalism is often seen as entailing the free movement of people across national borders. But in fact, many neoliberals combined anti-immigrant animus with market fundamentalism. Powell, as he showed in 1968, was a good example of this tendency.[34]

Beginning in the 1960s, Powell began his campaign to shut down "the unlimited role of the state," which had been giving in to calls for redistribution. In his 1968 speech to the MPS, he repeated the "doctrine of the market," which opposed public ownership, social security, the National Health Service, and public benefits. Powell also attacked unions, accusing them of "fascism" and "mob rule," echoing Hutt. "It seems all our hopes for England rest now on Enoch Powell," said Hayek.[35] His hopes would soon be surpassed. The neoliberal revolution was just beginning, but it would be fully realized when Margaret Thatcher, Hayek's book tucked in her purse, finished what Powell had begun.

Powell also joined with other MPS members, notably Milton Friedman, to push for an end to the Bretton Woods Agreement, the Keynesian postwar pact to stabilize the world economy. Bretton Woods, in restricting the mobility of capital investments between nations for speculative, investment, or sheltering purposes, bolstered the authority of national governments, particularly in affluent countries like the United States and the United Kingdom. These governments could impose substantial taxes on corporate profits, allowing them to allocate more funds toward their welfare states. The barriers kept capital and businesses from leaving their home countries to pursue more lucrative investments, lower taxes, or lower costs by offshoring jobs and production. In the United States, the barriers were a boon to government investments not just in the welfare state, but in infrastructure and research, too. Such protections enabled American automakers like Ford and General Motors to pay union wages, build factories across the country, and make record profits year after year. The Bretton Woods Agreement also helped limit national debts through the implementation of fixed exchange rates among currencies. The fixed rates promoted stability and mitigated the likelihood of currency devaluation. As a result, countries were discouraged from adopting internal policies that would lead to volatility in worldwide currency markets, which favored global interdependence rather than currency competition. Bretton Woods, indeed, was in part inspired by the social and political havoc national debt from the First World War had caused in Germany, with grave consequences for the entire world.[36]

The wealth of Western nations still depended on resources from the Global South. But decolonization had led to a nightmare scenario for Powell in which his beloved former colony of India would keep control of its resources while sending its *people* to England. Immigrants would "swarm" the British welfare state. To extend British resources to these immigrants, as he warned during his 1968 MPS speech, would surely lead to the British pound's debasement through inflation. A somewhat similar fear ran under the surface of his "Rivers of Blood" speech, which was not about monetary policy or economics at all, but warned that the "inflow of some fifty thousand *unmarried* dependents" would lead inevitably to race mixing, creating a largely "immigrant-descended population," surely a debasement of the nation's racial purity. "Color is the uniform," he said, which signals "a separate and strange population."

Powell and the MPS proposed building a (legal) wall against the immigrants while tearing down the (legal) wall surrounding capital. The free movement of capital would achieve two of the group's major aims. First, it would deplete the coffers of European and American governments by allowing large corporations and the wealthiest citizens to escape the state's taxation regime—both by actually taking the capital out of the country and by *threatening* to take it out of the country, thereby pressuring lawmakers to lower taxes. This is in fact what has occurred, in the United Kingdom and elsewhere. Second, without the ability to prohibit capital investments in their nations, weaker states would perpetually be vulnerable—as Allende found out in Chile—to the intrigues and corruptions of powerful multinationals. Nations could impose barriers to foreign corporations and foreign investors, as China, Iran, and a few other "rogue" states have done, but most countries needed foreign investments to develop their economies. Typically, the funds that are traditionally received from foreign corporations flow through institutions such as the World Bank, IMF, and the financialized sovereign debt market. Capital and debt would replace empire and colony, respectively.

But there were many obstacles to achieving these aims, including national politics, existing laws, and popular opinion. That is, what about the citizens of Western nations? Ending the system that had produced good jobs, free education, subsidized homes, and health-care benefits would be unpopular. The Labour Party and its social welfare program were popular in Britain, and Americans had resoundingly voted against Barry Goldwater and for Lyndon Johnson's Great Society. Those who could vote chose Myrdal and Keynes, not Hayek. Once Black voters in America were permitted to vote and former colonies were free to design their economies, they too chose government power over financial power. That is why MPS members grumbled about democracies that "would not do what ought to be done." The major obstacle to neoliberalism's worldwide adoption, in other words, was the people. Yet the MPS would find ways to circumvent the voting public in order to dismantle European welfare states and the American mixed economy. The neoliberals' revolt against democratic majorities changed not only the Global South but the former empires themselves.

THERE WERE two options for the Western states. They could accept that formerly colonized people were human beings no less worthy than they were, who deserved their fair share of the world's resources. The

West would not have to live without oil or copper, but would have to pay the market rate, which might have had the added benefit of lowering demand for costly fossil fuels. Less oil would have meant lower profits for Chevron, but the free market would have forced innovation and perhaps Chevron would have gone the way of Xerox. Making this choice would have required a renewed Bretton Woods Agreement, allowing developing economies the same national powers that Western nations had until the "trade gap" was gone. This was exactly the plan proposed by Gunnar Myrdal during his Nobel speech.

The other option, coincidentally, was Hayek's. To Hayek, all state action, especially toward "international cooperation," was indistinguishable from serfdom. He favored the total privatization of industry, removing Bretton Woods barriers, and—although MPS members disagreed vehemently on this last part—a new monetary order, which would be based on either purely private money or a floating exchange rate of currencies. Hayek's system would free capital to be invested worldwide, weakening state social safety-net spending but maintaining the economic strength of the Global North, given its vast capital advantage. If the new "sovereign" nations wished to build their native industries, they could apply for a "development loan" from the IMF and World Bank. Experts from these NGOs would then offer "technical assistance" to the new governments to help them tighten their budgets and promote trade.

Just as politicians in the United States adopted neoliberal ideas to perpetuate the domestic racial order, the Western powers overall adopted neoliberal ideas to tame independence movements and launder their own efforts to continue subjugating the Global South. Even Western nations that practiced Myrdalian social democracy at home exported Hayekian capitalism abroad, because it allowed them to maintain their imperial privileges. Not capitalism, but *Black capitalism*. Free trade for thee but not for me. Yet to call it "free trade" is to engage in Orwellian doublespeak—free trade was, in fact, what Mossadegh, the G-77, and OPEC were after. In other words, market prices for all. What the corporations of empire wanted was not free trade, but the continuation of their exclusive rights to *all* of Chile's copper, Iran's oil, and Africa's diamonds.

One of the promises the United States had made at Bretton Woods in order to stabilize world trade was to always stand ready to exchange other countries' currencies for gold, America having the most gold of any nation. The dollar thus became the world's currency; one French official spoke of America's "exorbitant privilege." But the system would fall apart in the early 1970s when Nixon decided to end the U.S. involvement. The event marks a significant pivot in the world's monetary history and has been much discussed along those lines, but it was also an important shift in how the United States would overcome colonial attempts at collective action. The crisis began when American military spending in Vietnam led to the devaluation of the dollar on the world market. For oil-producing countries whose contracts were pegged to the dollar, the crisis became acute as they began losing money even as they were pumping and exporting more oil. Meeting in Tehran in February 1971, the OPEC countries decided to respond to the sinking dollar by posting prices only in gold, which intensified the dollar's slide downward. An irate Kissinger, who had helped ply the Iranian monarch with billions of dollars worth of weapons, urged the President to break up OPEC, presumably using the same covert CIA tactics that had broken the Mossadegh coalition back in the 1950s and would soon be used to break up the Allende coalition.

During the interregnum era before neoliberalism took hold, U.S. foreign policy revealed a contemptuous disregard for the political complexity of other countries, not to mention the lives of many thousands of innocent people murdered. The CIA was complicit in coups and upheavals across the Global South—often replacing an elected leader with one more favorable to foreign corporate interests. The "Nixinger" stance toward the world can be and has been described as hard-nosed realpolitik, in contrast to the idealism of "freedom fighting" ideologues or naïve U.N. diplomats wishing for world peace in a world of evil. Indeed, the duo's iron-fisted "management" of other countries revealed a willful disregard of principles of right and wrong. Still, war demanded justification and when forced to produce them, Nixinger spoke of order, freedom, and liberation from the clutches of tyrants with just as much panache as the freedom fighters did. Nixon and Kissinger, too, were fighting for freedom, they claimed. The confusion of colonial wars helped. There were no simple lines between sides, and there were many interests and factions within each country. But war had to be justified in a democracy. And this is where Nixon faltered; his secret bombing of Cambodia was leaked in the Pentagon Papers, which led to congressional investigations. These in turn began the unraveling of the President's other secret schemes, including Watergate, which would end in his resignation in the summer of 1974.

On Friday, August 13, 1971, a desperate Nixon held an emergency meeting at Camp David to discuss ending the United States' international obligations under Bretton Woods. The group included Treasury Secretary John Connally, Fed Chairman Arthur Burns, Treasury Undersecretary Paul Volcker, and George Shultz, the director of the Office of Management and Budget. Burns, the supposedly independent representative of the Fed, should not have been there. Nixon had a bad habit of pressuring Burns to bring down inflation, which was the purpose of the meeting. Connally, who had no prior experience with or knowledge of international finance before being named Treasury secretary earlier that year, proposed the radical idea of revoking the accord. Reflecting on his proposal later on, Connally said, "I want to screw the foreigners before they screw us." Ending the accord temporarily halted inflation during the subsequent presidential campaign, allowing Nixon to win reelection, but it did nothing to fix the underlying problem. For that, Nixon imposed wage and price controls for ninety days to force prices down by government mandate. This type of top-down central planning should have been shut down immediately by any self-respecting capitalist, like those in the room at Camp David. The decision was called "the Nixon shock" for its effects on the world economy. The President announced the decision to the public, stating that "the effect of this action, in other words, will be to stabilize the dollar." In November, at a meeting of the G-10, a consortium of the leading Western powers, in Rome, Connally told the finance ministers and central bank governors: "The dollar is our currency, but it's your problem."[37]

Ending Bretton Woods was one step in the transformation of monetary policy that neoliberals had long sought: taking monetary policy out of the people's hands and delivering it to the experts. Hayek had challenged Friedman at the first MPS meeting because he was skeptical that "monetary policy [could] be automatic and outside the range of politics," but he underestimated his own exhortation that "the work of men like ourselves" would change "the political climate" and move politics toward their aims.

Although other works of his are better known, Milton Friedman's most influential treatise is *A Monetary History of the United States, 1867–1960* (coauthored with Anna Schwartz). In this 1963 book, Friedman offers a novel interpretation of the Great Depression: through the meticulous analysis of data, he argues that the crisis was exacerbated by misdirected government monetary policy. The theory that emerged from this analysis—dubbed *monetarism*—effectively revived the fixed-money standard and updated it for the neoliberal era. The very basic idea of the theory was that the quantity of money in the economy affected conditions and that inflation "is always and everywhere a monetary phenomenon."

Just as Locke's theories of natural law and monetary scarcity were being challenged by the expansionary economics demanded by the new world order, they were revived through monetarism, which was based on the theory that even without gold reserves, there was a fixed and natural rate of currency that was necessarily outside of any state's ability to control it. Friedman proposed a "commodity money" with a fixed rate that had a "real" basis for value pegged to the "natural" economy and that replaced "irresponsible governmental tinkering."[38] Monetarism described money and its creation as highly technical and rule-bound and warned of the perils of departing from the natural and right equilibrium for money. Thus, according to the theory, decisions about money should be made by technical experts who did not bend to the wishes of interest.

In 1975, future Nobel laureate Franco Modigliani and future Greek prime minister Lucas Papademos elaborated on the "natural rate" theory to propose an equation called non-accelerating inflation rate of unemployment (NAIRU), which has since become a core feature of monetary policy. Based on NAIRU and the Phillips curve, a model devised by the British-based economist William Phillips, neoliberal economists predicted a direct correlation between unemployment and monetary inflation. Based on these theories, which remain contested, neoliberal economists proposed that the remedy to inflation was to drive up unemployment. If inflation was high, they speculated, it was because wages and employment opportunities were too high and needed to be brought down. The effects of this unproven "scientific" formula as a stand-in for policy were profound—especially in suppressing employment and wage growth. Policy makers who adopted NAIRU as an oracle of natural law believed that the remedy to inflation was to suppress employment and wage growth. Incidentally, high unemployment and lower wages strengthened the hiring power of corporations and simultaneously weakened labor unions.

Milton Friedman won the Nobel Prize in 1976, two years after his friend and mentor, Hayek. Friedman dedicated his speech to rebutting his predecessor who had denounced the prize because of his conviction that economics was not a science. Friedman was pragmatic and flexible compared with his purist colleague, Hayek, which made Friedman the more influential of the two. The American had a knack for simplifying economic principles and using tidy examples to illustrate his point. In his Nobel speech, Friedman discussed his own scientific thesis about the "natural rate" of unemployment, which extended his monetarist theory affixing money to a scientific formula to employment. If economics was a science resembling natural sciences like physics or chemistry, as Friedman insisted it was, then it followed that economists like himself were just measuring and theorizing toward discovering some preexisting truth about the state of the world. Just as planets in orbit followed Newton's laws of gravity, earthly phenomena like unemployment and inequality could not resist the Phillips curve. The distribution of wealth and poverty among the nations of the world could not be altered by man-made laws, but only measured, studied, and explained by trained economists. Except, unlike the laws of motion studied by physicists, man-made policies like European social welfare programs or American mortgage subsidies had in fact changed the form, shape, and motion of the economy. Not without significant harm to the ideal state of the economy, according to Friedman, who blamed the various economic slumps, collapses, and diverse tribulations affecting nations on their ignorance of economics.

Also unlike the natural laws studied by physicists, which operated the same way regardless of human understanding, economic laws demanded strict obedience from policy makers whose failure to learn the science of economics could result in disaster. To Friedman, the rampant misuse of economic resources, high unemployment, and even the "suppression of human freedom" stemmed not from "evil men" or even "difference in values among citizens," but to simple "errors" of understanding economics as a positive science—errors that could be corrected by economists like him. His tone was condescending and acerbic, especially when he was explaining the "errors" of governments around the world that destroyed their economies by their rigid adherence to Keynesian policies. To Friedman, it was all very simple: "Leave your economic decisions to the experts." He concluded the Nobel speech by excusing those who had erred—they had not messed up because of bad ideology or evil intent, but insufficient scientific understanding.[39]

Although monetarism was a theory that could not be proved or disproved in real life, it affected Fed policy nonetheless. Friedman joked once about replacing the Fed chair with a computer algorithm.[40]

The problem with placing the mantle of "science" on economics, a discipline that does not follow the scientific process, noted Hayek during his Nobel Prize acceptance speech, is that it "confers on an individual an authority which in economics no man ought to possess."[41] Despite the warning, the insistence on the scientific nature of these laws has been a constant refrain of the neoliberals. Friedman even claimed that he had "introduced a version of the natural-science laboratory" to economic study at the University of Chicago. The patina of science, rigor, and technicality was in fact one of the most effective ways in which a shroud was pulled over law and policy during the heyday of neoliberalism. By converting moneymaking into a scientific enterprise worthy only of the highest priests of macroeconomic theory, the public is procedurally and practically cut out of one of the most important decisions affecting their lives. While monetary policy had been up for discussion at the very genesis of the MPS, it took forty years to realize the dream of both taking power away from the people and placing it in the state while, also, making monetary policy (seem) automatic.

The role of monetarism in neoliberal market orthodoxy was important, but obscured. This was due to its own success—monetarism hid the levers that control credit and money supply behind a curtain of "data-based scientific measurement." Out of sight were the New Deal–era credit programs, subsidies, and the entire system of credit and money—and, most important, the trust that undergirded it was created by federal government power. The dollar became the world's currency and its control was handed over to neoliberal economic theories, ensuring monetary scarcity and maintaining the advantages of the already wealthy nations. Without the flexibility to expand their economies according to their own economic programs, the Global South would have to rely on "development loans." In fact, the dollar became the United States' most valuable export.

At the time Friedman's monetarism was introduced, it was widely denounced by everyone from mainstream economists like Paul Samuelson to even Hayek. It could not be proved or debunked in a real economy and without exact measures of monetary supply. But it would become the policy of the Federal Reserve, especially when Ronald Reagan appointed Alan Greenspan to lead the Fed in 1987. Monetarism did not rise on account of its explanatory or predictive powers. Even Friedman had to apologize for so confidently predicting a recession that never came based on monetarist principles. He admitted, "I was wrong, absolutely wrong. And I have no good explanation as to why I was wrong."[42] As William Poole, a former Fed executive, summarized monetarism, "Those of us who have developed strong theories tried to fit the world into the theory rather than the other way round."[43] Wrong as Friedman was, the "science" of monetarism reshaped the world economy—and that process started during the 1960s interregnum.

The road to taking monetary policy out of the public's hands began at the first meeting of the MPS, was fully theorized by Friedman in 1963, backed by Enoch Powell in 1968 for Great Britain, first made into policy at Camp David in 1971, was validated by the Nobel committee in 1976, and was ready to become state policy by the stagflationary crisis of the late 1970s. To lay out the events in order of occurrence is not to suggest causality. In fact, there were various complex and chaotic changes to the economy in the 1970s that were not only unplanned but completely unanticipated.

To TELL a history of neoliberalism that moves straight from Hayek and Friedman to Reagan's and Thatcher's deregulatory actions is to miss the political shifts that occurred in the 1960s and 1970s, and it is to narrowly focus on words rather than deeds.

Neoliberalism did not simply untether markets—it reshaped them in a particular way. The movement's leaders gained prominence only once they proved themselves useful politically in providing leaders the ideological armor they needed to fight back the justice movements in America and abroad. Undoubtedly, there were true believers among the neoliberals who were committed to racial equality and believed that the free market would indeed remedy racial disparities, but these zealots mixed with politicians whose aims were much more cynical. It was a cynicism bred from fear, which voters would likely have rejected if they had truly understood what they were losing, which was their democracies.

Neoliberalism was not a reaction to socialism abroad or Keynesianism at home, as standard accounts have it, but rather a rhetorical tactic in forestalling a racial reckoning. Neoliberalism was not a good economic idea—the basics of neoliberal economics are hardly decipherable from basic theories of free markets going back centuries. What made neoliberalism attractive in certain quarters of the Western world was that it provided a race-neutral program for maintaining the former empire's tentacles of extraction in place with an updated race-neutral rhetoric. For hundreds of years, a handful of European nations relied on colonial imports for everything from food and lumber to oil and gas.

They justified violent dominion of these nations through the ideology of racial supremacy—the world wars ended the ideology of empire, but not the reality of Europe's reliance on its colonies.

From the very first time a group of self-described neoliberals met as the Mont Pelerin Society in 1947 until neoliberalism became official state dogma under the Reagan and Thatcher regimes in the 1980s, the economics of neoliberalism was secondary to its political agenda, which was to weaken state power while augmenting the liberty of corporations. While standard accounts of neoliberalism describe it as an ideology prioritizing the "free market" over government control, neoliberalism in action was in fact a prioritization of corporate rights over democratic rights. The context and timing of neoliberalism's rise is relevant to understanding its function. Neoliberalism did not take hold of government while Keynesianism reigned or amid the Cold War or even after the MPS meeting; instead, neoliberalism leapt from obscurity into global dogma amid a global revolt that threatened to reorder the world economy. Its primary function abroad was not to increase freedom or liberty for the earth's people, but the opposite: to undermine the demands of coalitions of former colonies and disenfranchised minorities for an equal voice in deciding the world's future. It was past time to share the world's resources equally, but corporations wanted to continue their extraction without paying market prices. The greatest beneficiaries of neoliberalism were the very global corporations, the miners and drillers, who had been the extractive arms of empire. The wealthy heirs of these legacy corporations also happened to be the philanthropists who funded the state infrastructure of neoliberalism. The neoliberal coup had to be quiet because it was propelled by the new world's losers, the profitable corporations unwilling to let go of their control over other people's wealth and autonomy. Once the ideology of empire fell, the wealthy and powerful investors who had the most to lose from a just and equal world went shopping for a new ideology and found neoliberalism.

Neoliberalism succeeded in the job it was recruited to do, but it has been a total failure as economics. None of its promises—of peace through trade, freedom through markets, and shared prosperity—have materialized. In fact, neoliberalism's myriad hypocrisies have sown worldwide distrust in governments and corporations such that many countries, including Western nations, have renounced these ideals altogether and ideologies long thought dead, like fascism and white supremacy, are resurgent among voters. It is tragic to imagine the road not taken during the interregnum—the pause after the nuclear bomb showed humanity its own world-changing power—to consider actually working together. Had global leaders heeded the vision of Myrdal and Keynes and Du Bois and Gandhi, our world would look much different than it does today.

Not just abroad, but at home too because what was done abroad was also done at home. "Injustice anywhere is a threat to justice everywhere," noted Martin Luther King, and so the evasion of international treaties and sovereign rights abroad led to the same erosion of rights at home. Undoing Bretton Woods and unleashing capital to blow through national borders via a murky financial system affected not just the former colonies, but everyone, including Americans. It would take decades before the global debt markets came for the average American's mortgage loan, but the road was paved by the economists promising freedom while delivering its opposite. Rather than trade with new nations, which would certainly entail risks of loss, of change, of intermixing, of "devaluing" their currency and, for some, their racial purity, the countries of the Global North chose neoliberalism. In doing so, they fixed the world in a trap of financial austerity that still beggars us all. Ending Bretton Woods officially ended the gold standard, which meant that the world's monetary system was—and is—based on nothing more than belief, or trust. Yet at the crucial interregnum after empire, Western nations chose the path of distrust and separation, a decision that, in time, would boomerang back to the homeland.

Had the nonaligned nations, the utopians, or the freedom fighters of the era succeeded in their purest intentions, trust between nations would have been a renewable resource. Money is among the few human innovations that has enabled abundance and cooperation where none was possible. The 1960s presented the world's nations with an opportunity to level up their economies, to trade, and to build together. This is not a naïve view possible only in retrospect—there were certainly scarcities that would have had to be dealt with through cooperation, but as the economist Oded Galor shows in his comprehensive historical account of humanity's race against the Malthusian limit, innovation has historically allowed populations to surpass resource constraints, insofar as we have been willing to work together. Instead of welcoming newly freed nations into global trade, a group of influential Western interests held on to their interests and twisted our laws and our democracies to do it. The nihilism was baked in from the outset. Instead of abundant money and free trade, they chose scarcity and secret deals. They fought to privatize our national treasures, empty the public fiscs, and hollow out our democracies—all under the guise of "freedom." Instead of making the pie a little bigger and accepting the common sense that no race of people deserved more than another, they continued the same poisonous myths of white supremacy that had not only shaped the colonies but destroyed the European homeland. "Social justice" was a mirage, said Hayek, and he made it so. The Austrian economist and MPS leading light Ludwig von Mises explained the logic: "If it is right for the British to nationalize the British coal mines, it cannot be wrong for the Iranians to nationalize the Iranian oil industry."[44] Mises was not arguing that Iranians should have control over their resources; rather, he was saying the British should lose theirs. Biting off the nose to spite the face.

Call it geopolitical karma, or the latest version of the colonial "boomerang," but once the logic and methodology of empire was reasserted through covert violence and finance, it was bound to erode the legal infrastructure back home as well.

As the following chapters of the book will show, a small collection of powerful interests have carried out a silent coup within the legal system sustaining American democracy, empowering financial interests and silencing the will of voters. The legal coup kicked into gear when the nations of the Global South tried to enforce U.N. declarations, OPEC treaties, and Bretton Woods, and U.S. policy makers responded by choosing the needs of capital over the laws enacted by other sovereign nations. Once the American government began undermining democratic governments abroad, the worm of hypocrisy began to eat away at our own democracy. When a mob attempted a coup at the U.S. Capitol on January 6, 2021, with the aid of a deposed autocrat, many Americans expressed shock, saying that this was the sort of thing that happened only in Third World countries. But the logic of the coup—its disrespect for democracy and rule of law and its dismissal of the will of majorities (not to mention the xenophobia of its perpetrators)—is best understood as an echo of this nation's own policies abroad. Once American policy makers justified overturning other people's democracies, their own became vulnerable. Such was the lesson of empire—that evil done abroad would eventualy, inevitably, find its way back home.

At the end of the radical decade of the 1960s, the revolutions that looked to be remaking the basic power structure of the world had all but fizzled out. By the end of the 1970s, freedom fighters and racial conflicts were, with a few exceptions, a relic of the past. Some of these revolutions were stifled by the CIA or FBI, which replaced revolutionaries with dictators friendly to American, and indeed Western, interests. But the mythology of free market capitalism as proposed by the intellectuals of the neoliberal movement also played a role by providing the ideological cover for establishing a new world order that had an uncanny resemblance to the fallen world order. In response to global revolts, the neoliberals turned to debt and free capital flows. Instead of gunboats, interest rates would keep the flow of resources from going in mostly one direction, from Global South to Global North. With few exceptions, the interregnum of the 1960s and 1970s ended with a reimposition of Western (economic) empire.

CHAPTER 3

Corporate Guerrilla Warfare

A corporation is an artificial being, invisible, intangible, and existing only in contemplation of law. Being the mere creature of law, it possesses only those properties which the charter of its creation confers upon it, either expressly or as incidental to its very existence.

—JOHN MARSHALL (1819)

IN THE WINTER of 1970, James Roche, the chairman of the board of directors of General Motors, included an unusual addendum to the annual shareholder report of year-end results. Roche relayed that GM had hired a total of 97,150 minority workers, a category he defined as "Negroes, Orientals, Indians or Spanish Americans." In fact, Roche revealed that the majority of minorities hired at GM—60 percent—had been brought on since 1965. He was quick, though, to address concerns of "special treatment." He assured shareholders that management had applied, and would continue to apply, "to our minority employees the same standards we apply to others." While GM was "willing to go the extra mile to help," he continued, "we do a man no favor when we hire him for a job he cannot master, or promote him to a job beyond his capabilities."[1]

The impetus for this curious annex to the standard financial data was affirmative action.[2] Title VII of the 1964 Civil Rights Act had established the Equal Employment Opportunity Commission to take "affirmative action" to stop employment discrimination. Black leaders and activists had coordinated protests against rampant discrimination in hiring and in union membership for years, culminating in the March on Washington for Jobs and Freedom in 1963, which led to monumental legal reforms making discrimination based on race and gender illegal for the first time in our nation's history. Neoliberal economists had denounced the laws as antithetical to capitalism and unnecessary because racism was inefficient. Having lost the fight against the passage of the law, neoliberal economists pivoted to making lemonade out of lemons.

Affirmative action became the political juggernaut it is today thanks to the Chicago economist George Shultz, who made it a key pillar of Nixon's Black capitalism. A close friend and ally of Milton Friedman and George Stigler, Shultz was so valuable an asset to Nixon that he held three different positions in the administration. He started out as secretary of labor, went on to be the founding director of the newly created Office of Management and Budget, a key agency in the neoliberal takeover of the administrative state, and would become Nixon's third, but not last, Treasury secretary. While serving as secretary of labor, Shultz proposed that instead of prosecuting employers for discrimination, the administration should urge companies to hire a certain threshold of minority workers. Much better to be a corporate hero like Roche announcing new jobs than being called a racist by the government. This so-called Philadelphia Plan of 1969 imposed quotas on federal government hiring and inaugurated a program of minority business procurement—or "set asides"—to "help ethnic groups" start businesses. If affirmative action's aim was to integrate the workforce, the minority business programs that made up the rest of Black capitalism aimed at maintaining geographic segregation by boosting Black-owned businesses in the segregated ghetto economy. Both programs were ineffective yet controversial. Nixon placed the Black capitalism programs in the Commerce Department and forgot about them.

The Philadelphia Plan was the result neither of a particular demand by civil rights groups nor an altruistic streak in the Nixon administration; rather, it was a cheaper alternative than the redistributive proposals made by activists, all of which would have required capital, actual or political, to be spent on enriching Black communities. Nevertheless, the plan would soon come under fire, most notably from white union workers. Unionized blue-collar workers were among the New Deal Democrats whom the Nixon administration's clever weaponization of race turned into free market libertarians. Affirmative action was a political sword to cleanly sever the two key Democratic constituencies—blue-collar workers and minorities—from each other, which, according to some historians of the Nixon era, may have been its intended consequence.[3] As John Ehrlichman wrote in his memoirs, "Shultz had shown great style in constructing a political dilemma for the labor leaders and civil rights groups."[4]

Nixon's Black capitalism began and died with the Philadelphia Plan—though the notion of quotas would continue to haunt the agencies and programs of every administration that followed. After almost two centuries of enabling racial discrimination, followed by the largest racial uprisings in the nation's history in the 1960s, the federal government scuttled any paths toward meaningful reforms with the red herring of affirmative action. Even so, affirmative action became the focal point of a white backlash, animated by accusations of "reverse discrimination."

The mandates had the doubly pernicious effect of providing nothing of substance to the intended recipients while giving the impression that special treatment was being granted on account of race. A perfect score on cost-benefit analysis, affirmative action cost the administration nothing, but gave it so much—in just a few years it would even be said to have *caused* "polarization and racial segregation."[5] "It is a paradox," said a 1975 House Appropriations Committee report, that an agency charged with helping minorities "should follow essentially the same practices" that had created the problem, which was that the contract recipients "were picked mostly on the basis of race."[6] In an administration unwilling to change America's racial order, Black capitalism became a surprising success—not for what it did for Black communities, but for what it did for Nixon's activation of white resentment. Affirmative action created a façade of special treatment that hid the administration's actual policy on race, which (as Nixon's southern strategy dictated) was to preserve America's racial hierarchy while silencing dissenters of that hierarchy. The federal government's role in affirmative action ended shortly after the initial 1969 push for minority hiring, but it has enjoyed a long afterlife as a renewable source of energy fueling the culture war.[7]

GM, HOWEVER—as its 1969 annual report indicates—bought into the principles of Black capitalism more than most corporations. In promoting the program publicly, Roche called on other companies to join in, stating that it was the responsibility of businesses "who have worked within and gained from the free enterprise system to help others share in it."

GM's adoption of Black capitalism may have had something to do with its unique role in American society. At the time, it was the most profitable corporation in the country. It had benefited from $4 billion in defense contracts over the preceding decade. Its 794,000 employees were part of the most influential unions in the United States, and its 1950 "Treaty of Detroit" bargain with those unions shaped the expectations of a generation of American workers. GM and other American automakers helped create thriving communities across the Midwest. During the Second World War, GM had helped produce "the arsenal of democracy," making a staggering "119,562,000 shells, 206,000 aircraft engines, 97,000 bombers, 301,000 aircraft propellers, 198,000 diesel engines, 1,900,000 machine guns, 854,000 military trucks, Cadillac tanks, Oldsmobile bullets, Buick airplane engines," according to *Car and Driver*, which dubbed GM "the largest military contractor on earth."[8]

GM was so closely identified with the military that President Eisenhower appointed former General Motors president Charles E. Wilson as his secretary of defense. Wilson, called "Engine Charlie," had transformed the company for war production and rode the Cold War boom in government spending. At its peak in the late 1940s and early 1950s, GM sold more than three million cars annually. Asked during his Senate confirmation hearing about whether his holdings of $2.5 million in GM stock would present a conflict of interest in his new role, Wilson responded honestly, "I cannot conceive of one, because for years I thought what was good for our country was good for General Motors and vice versa. The difference did not exist. Our company is too big. It goes with the welfare of the country."[9]

In fact, if there was a conflict, it was because the company was too big. In the 1950s, GM was so large and so powerful that it was dominant in several sectors, and Eisenhower's Department of Justice (DOJ) began investigating it under its antitrust authority. George Romney, then the CEO of American Motors, testified in favor of a breakup, stating that there wasn't enough competition among carmakers. "Like boxing champions who lack suitable opponents, companies will become soft and flabby," Romney said.[10] The DOJ investigated GM eighteen times for violations of antitrust laws, which led to fines and consent decrees, but none made more than a dent. By 1967, GM's market share had climbed to 49 percent, yet President Johnson rejected his DOJ's pleas to break up the firm. GM was the country's largest taxpayer and government supplier. Having evaded antitrust enforcement and benefited enormously from government contracts, GM executives had every reason to volunteer to lead the White House's Black capitalism program.

However, for some shareholders, GM's efforts to hire employees of color were insufficient, given the scale and type of changes they saw as necessary. Calling themselves Campaign GM, these "activist shareholders" (before the term was coined) were organized by a group of young lawyers affiliated with Ralph Nader. Nader, whose 1965 book *Unsafe at Any Speed* accused the automakers of recklessly endangering drivers, was already familiar to the GM leadership, which had been spying on him for a few years, attempting to find some controversy with which to smear the rabble-rousing corporate crusader. By 1970, Nader was a trailblazer of public interest law, and his Nader's Raiders were all graduates of top law schools. (At one point, notes the historian Paul Sabin, a full third of Harvard Law's graduating class applied to work at Nader's advocacy group, Public Citizen.)

The Raiders' activities ran the gamut: sometimes the goal was to win a lawsuit, sometimes to change the law, sometimes just to stage a public action to bring attention to an issue. Legal maneuvers could create a public spectacle, and thereby pressure firms to make changes. Nader was an outside agitator from the start and often criticized his natural allies, including unions and government agencies, decrying the "fecklessness of regulation and the narrowness of labor union concerns." American citizens had a choice, Nader wrote, "between increasing predation or increasing accountability of corporate power to the people." Nader's myopic focus on the law as the site of legal change would backfire phenomenally as he brought a string of cases to federal courts in the throes of neoliberal backlash, but Campaign GM was a relative success.

Campaign GM was part of a groundswell of shareholder unrest across corporate America. In the spring of 1970, a scant few weeks after Roche issued his report on minority hiring, dissent began roiling corporate shareholder meetings, mirroring the broader upheaval in the United States over racism, the Vietnam War, and environmental concerns. Beginning in March, at the annual meeting of Bank of America, and continuing through May, dissident shareholders disrupted the annual meetings of United Aircraft, AT&T, CBS, GE, Union Carbide, Commonwealth Edison, Gulf Oil, and Honeywell.[11] Executives were asked to account for their company's social impact rather than just its quarterly earnings. A *Detroit Free Press* reporter dubbed 1970 the year of the "corporate guerrilla fighter."[12]

For GM, matters would come to a head on May 23, 1970, at the company's annual meeting. For five hours, Roche squared off with Campaign GM—identifiable by their "Tame GM" buttons—over the company's social initiatives. *The New York Times* described the rebels as including everyone from "housewives dressed in bright flowered print dresses" and "students with long hair and peace buttons" to "ministers, businessmen, college professors, and presidents." Stuart Mott, the son of Charles Mott—the oldest member of GM's board—is reported to have said that GM had a responsibility to speak out "about the disastrous directions of our nation's military policies." When a young Detroit student rose to nominate a friend to the board and asked Roche, "How are you doing today?" Roche responded lightly, "Seen better," which momentarily broke the tension in the hall. A UCLA law student named

Barbara Williams skipped the pleasantries and asked a direct question: "Mr. Roche, why are there no blacks on the board?" Roche answered that it was because "none had been nominated and none elected." She replied, "You have failed not only the shareholders but the country."[13]

The activists had three demands. First, they wanted three people added to the board of directors: consumer advocate and former actress Betty Furness; Channing Phillips, a civil rights leader and divinity professor at Howard University; and René Dubos, an author and academic biologist who was credited with the dictum "think globally, act locally." Second, they wanted GM to pledge not to undertake any activity that "is detrimental to the health, safety, or welfare of the citizens of the United States."[14] Third, they sought to establish a shareholders committee for corporate responsibility that would have access to the company's files.[15] These shareholder activists focused on GM because it was the largest and most powerful firm in the country; they focused on board seats and corporate procedures because they believed that the company's board of directors was not representing the interests of shareholders or the broader public, noting specifically that the several board members with significant ties to oil and gas companies could not be objective about proposals to transition the firm away from "internal combustion engines" toward cleaner cars.[16]

Campaign GM's resolutions failed to win a majority of shareholder support, but the effort showed how a sophisticated group of lawyers armed with rigorous proxy voting documents and a mastery of corporate law could bring the revolution to American corporations. Campaign GM was employing the same playbook as the group of civil rights lawyers who paved the way for equal rights, establishing precedent using carefully selected cases and, building on that legal precedent, strategically marshaling time and patience to transform the energy of the movement into enduring structural change. It was the same strategy that Third World diplomats employed at the United Nations through the drafting of charters and proposing votes. These lawyers were just one small part of broader social movements at the time, but they played a critical role in harnessing the energy of the moment and channeling it into corporate law. *The New York Times* even sent a reporter who observed that "the campaign may not have won many votes, but it may have captured the high moral ground and the fight may just be the beginning."[17] It sure was. These so-called guerrilla tactics would be adopted and enhanced by the neoliberals in defense of corporate profits.

ON AUGUST 31, 1970, three months after Campaign GM's shareholder vote, GM announced that it had named five new outside directors and that they would be tasked with representing "the public interest." It also dedicated five pages of its newest annual report to environmental issues, "aid to minorities," and product safety.[18] These developments were likely helped along by letters from some of the corporation's largest investors writing in support of Campaign GM's proposals. In one letter, a Harvard trustee and GM shareholder who had voted no on those proposals said, "From an investment point of view the Committee is concerned that if General Motors does not move to discharge its full public responsibility as rapidly as possible, the public will begin to withdraw the premier acceptance which it has accorded the company's products in the past." The letter stated that this was justified even if "such costs *impinge on profits.*"[19] The Rockefeller and Carnegie Foundations wrote that, while they hadn't supported the "unwieldy and impractical" proposals of Campaign GM, their investment goals were to "serve the well-being of mankind, [which] requires us to recognize that more is at stake than our role as stockholder." Jay Rockefeller, the thirty-three-year-old great-grandson of Standard Oil founder John D. Rockefeller, noted that "next time around it may be different."[20]

After the announcement of the new outside directors, there was no protest from shareholders or anyone at the company, and even Campaign GM seemed pleased. Roche, the target of the activist's ire, was conciliatory, noting that although the company had earned the confidence of the majority of shareholders, "it was not a victory" in his eyes. "When even a small fraction of our stockholders—even if only one—is not convinced of our record of responsibility, then we are concerned."[21]

Two weeks after GM made its announcement, *The New York Times Magazine* ran an article titled "A Friedman Doctrine: The Social

Responsibility of Business Is to Increase Its Profits." On the page opposite Milton Friedman's words, the *Times* placed a picture of James Roche
at a podium under GM's logo, with a caption explaining that Roche was
replying "to members of Campaign GM." Although no one could have
known it at the time, Friedman's article would be the first salvo of the
neoliberal revolution that would transform corporate law.

IN THE ERA between the New Deal and 1970, the dominant corporate
law text was Adolf Berle and Gardiner Means's *The Modern Corporation and Private Property,* first published in 1932. It held that shareholders are the "true owners" of a corporation, with executives and
corporate directors authorized only to act on behalf of shareholders,
that is, as their "agent." According to Berle and Means, shareholders
made up a kind of legislative body in a microdemocracy with the power
to elect the board, determine executive salaries, approve mergers, hire
managers, change the direction of the company, or fundamentally
restructure the firm. Corporations are chartered for a certain purpose
(for example, to sell books, make sneakers, or drill for oil) and to enable
people with some extra money to invest through purchasing stock in
that project for (hopefully) profit. Those holding common stock are
allowed one vote per share.

Berle and Means extrapolated from this model a requirement of
thorough transparency and disclosure on the part of the directors—
for, in order to vote, shareholders must have all relevant information.
In this, they were reacting to the recent stock market crash and subsequent economic turmoil. Whereas a not insignificant portion of
Americans urged the abolition of the capital markets and private
finance altogether—to be replaced by central planning—and certain
businessmen fought against any reform at all, Berle and Means staked
out a moderate position of saving capital markets by reforming them.
"Modern conditions," said Berle and Means, "require that corporations
acknowledge and discharge social as well as private responsibilities as
members of the communities in which they operate."[22]

Of the two authors, Berle would have the more lasting impact. A child prodigy who matriculated at Harvard at the age of fourteen, earned his law degree at Harvard Law School at twenty-one, and joined Columbia Law School's faculty in 1927, Berle would soon enough become a member of the famed "brain trust," a group of advisers who played a significant role in shaping the policies and programs of the Roosevelt administration during the Great Depression. Instead of working to diminish corporate power—as many of the progressives in FDR's administration wanted—Berle advocated making corporations more accountable to their shareholders and to the rest of society. With socialist central planning as the alternative to capitalism, Berle preferred to "transform the system rather than abolish it." He summarized his view of the economy in a 1963 book, *The American Republic*: "An economic system is not an end in itself. It exists to serve men. When it ceases to do that, it ceases to be acceptable . . . [and it] requires curing."

Corporations are legal constructs created through social agreements enforced by state law. However, once established, their power to channel and increase capital becomes a self-propagating force for driving social transformation. Corporate charters were first granted in America exclusively for companies tasked with public duties such as building railroads, canals, or water infrastructure. The Constitution granted the states ultimate power over chartering and regulating their corporations, a power they still hold. However, unlike other state law matters—and due to a curious history of state-by-state competition—corporate law has been dominated by one state: Delaware. Today, most of the nation's corporations are chartered in Delaware and governed by the five justices of the Delaware Chancery Court, who are appointed by the governor to serve twelve-year terms.

Corporations have duties to the public not just because they have benefited so handsomely from government investments, contracts, and trade protections, but because their legal charters mandate such duties. In 1969, no less an authority than Manuel F. Cohen, the chairman of the Securities and Exchange Commission, alerted corporate America that their inaction on racial inequality had "created smoldering resentments which explode into violence," warning that because they had "so much power and influence in society . . . they had a responsibility to meet the needs of the nation as a whole."[23] To Berle and the capitalists of his day, including the executives at companies like Ford and GM, corporations were like the military in their relationship to society. They ran according to their own internal management and objectives, but their existence was related to—if not entirely premised on—serving society. Occupying a space between the public and the government, corporate leaders, like military generals, should view themselves as humble and trustworthy public servants responsible for creating an honorable corporate culture. This was always an aspirational goal, but it was one that Roche and others took seriously.

Courts widely recognized that corporations had an obligation to address social problems and contribute to the overall well-being of society, which went beyond prioritizing profit-seeking motives. For example, a study of Delaware Chancery Court decisions concerning corporate social responsibility, specifically cases related to "the solution of ghetto, minority group and other social problems," found that the court repeatedly ruled that corporate social responsibility was in the best interests of a business, even when firms sacrificed profits to increase salaries, reduce pollution, or hire and train more Black workers. As one judge remarked, shareholders—who, in this case, were the ones bringing suit *against* these programs—could not "thwart the long-visioned corporate action in recognizing and voluntarily discharging its high obligations as a constituent of our modern social structure."[24]

That the Delaware courts subscribed to this view had a profound effect on corporate behavior as well as society at large. The law being what it was, corporate directors were seen as agents acting on behalf of shareholders first—and communities and society a close second. The majority of shareholders, the same study reported, had rightfully concluded that these corporate programs were good *business* decisions exactly because of "the depth of social needs." What was good for society was good for business—because businesses, big ones included, were "members" of society.

The culture of corporation-as-community-member could be seen across the economy: in the more reasonable gap between CEO and employee salaries (at least compared to today), in the somewhat equal balance of power between directors and the rest of the company, and in the relative modesty of profits (again, compared to the present). The general attitude was also reflected in the popular business books of the postwar era, from economist Howard Bowen's 1953 book *The Social Responsibilities of the Businessman* to Morrell Heald's *The Social Responsibilities of Business, Company, and Community, 1900–1960*, published in 1970.[25] Notably, Bowen's book proposing that free enterprise was justified only if it could achieve economic justice for all of society, not just owners, was sponsored by a consortium of Christian evangelical groups, the Churches of Christ in America.

MILTON FRIEDMAN'S *New York Times* article responding to Campaign GM did not cite any corporate law cases or scholars. Rather, the economist launched a tirade against corporate leaders, those businessmen who "speak eloquently about 'social responsibilities of business in a free enterprise system,'" who believe they are "defending free enterprise when they declaim that business is not concerned 'merely' with profit but also with promoting desirable 'social' ends." According to Friedman, they were not defenders of the market: "In fact they are—or would be if they or any one else took them seriously—preaching pure and unadulterated socialism." These business leaders were actually the "unwitting puppets of the intellectual forces that have been undermining the basis of a free society."

Friedman moved from one insult to another. He dismissed the "social responsibility of business," a phrase he continually put inside quotation marks despite its clear meaning in the law and the business community, as empty "nonsense," faddish and unscientific, "lacking in rigor." Friedman believed that "influential and prestigious businessmen" who gave speeches using the "cloak of social responsibility, and the nonsense spoken in its name"—he was presumably referring to Roche—were "clearly harm[ing] the foundations of a free society." These leaders were getting "kudos in the short run," but ultimately engaging in what Friedman saw as a "suicidal impulse." Once this view took hold, he warned hyperbolically, "the pontificating executives" would no longer be in charge, but rather, it would be "the iron fist of Government bureaucrats."

According to Friedman, "only people can have responsibilities." For a corporate manager to decide, "at the expense of corporate profits, to hire 'hard core' unemployed instead of better qualified available workmen to contribute to the social objective of reducing poverty" was irresponsible, unlawful, socialist thinking. (This was a reference to the language used by GM and the Nixon administration, whose Black hiring programs were designed, in part, "to train and employ the hardcore unemployed.") As when Alan Greenspan wrote to Nixon arguing against reparations programs, and as when the MPS argued against trade restrictions enacted by the developing world, Friedman warned that accepting "social responsibility" was equivalent to submitting to the inevitable tyranny of collectivism. The doctrine of "social responsibility ... *does not differ* in philosophy from the most explicitly collectivist doctrine." To acknowledge any collective morality, or any responsibility besides profits, was a "socialist view," because it subverted the "market mechanism," which to Friedman was the only acceptable way to allocate resources.

The logic of Friedman's argument followed from Berle and Means's model of the corporation, enshrined in corporate common law, that shareholders were the "real owners" of a company—the "principal" in corporate law terms—and managers their "agents." From this uncontroversial principle, which he called "shareholder supremacy," Friedman arrived at a far more extreme and controversial conclusion: that "corporations have no higher purpose than *maximizing profits* for their shareholders." To Friedman, the only legitimate interest of shareholders was the bottom line.

Friedman's gift for simplifying complex issues was on full display in the article, but there was a flaw at the heart of his argument, especially as it regarded GM. For it was not the directors or managers like Roche who was pushing "social responsibility"; rather, it was a group of shareholders. Friedman addressed Campaign GM in a parenthetical, calling "the recent GM crusade" a "newer phenomenon" that was misguided because "some stockholders were trying to get other stockholders ... to

contribute *against their will* to 'social' causes favored by the activists."
Unlike corporate law's democratic orientation toward shareholders as
akin to the voting public, Friedman's shareholder supremacy doctrine
recognized only one kind of shareholder: the self-interested rationalist
of the neoliberal imagination whose sole goal was to maximize short-
term profits. This theory contradicted corporate law at the time as
understood by a majority of corporate lawyers, scholars, and judges, but
as neoliberalism began to invade the law, so too would Friedman's radical new doctrine. Shareholder supremacy took hold of the Delaware
courts over the next decades, as we will see.

FRIEDMAN WAS not alone in his crusade against corporate responsibility. The same month that GM attorney Donald Schwartz was encour-
aging the business community to use its great power to embrace social
change, another corporate lawyer, Lewis Powell, was circulating march-
ing orders to wage war *against* that change.

Powell's 1971 memo, "Attack on American Free Enterprise System,"
was addressed to his friend Eugene Sydnor, the chairman of the U.S.
Chamber of Commerce's education committee. It was sent to all the
members of the chamber, which comprised (and still comprises) top
business leaders across the country, and was leaked to the press a year
later. The seven-page memo struck a reactionary tone akin to Friedman's,
but it was also full of practical strategies covering a range of issues, making it one of the most significant documents of the neoliberal revolution
in America. Its importance flows not from its originality—many of the
ideas within it were already common talking points on the right—but
from its clairvoyance. Schwartz's law review article conveying the mainstream view of the time seems, in retrospect, to be wildly idealistic; Powell's memo, however, circulated in secret and stirring controversy when
leaked, predicted the world we live in today. The future was forged by
those who fought hardest against progress.

"No thoughtful person can question that the American economic
system is under broad attack," Powell began, citing Milton Friedman
for support. The victim of the attack? "Truly the 'forgotten man,'"

according to Powell, was "the American business executive." Powell confidently asserted that it is "crystal clear that the foundations of our free society are under wide-ranging and powerful attack." The precise nature of the attack was left unspecified, but given the riots, strikes, and protests of the previous years, Powell may not have felt the need to elaborate beyond mentioning the "ideological war against western society." Nor did he identify the attackers—with one notable exception. Rather, he wrote that the business executives were being besieged by sources "varied and diffuse" coming from "perfectly respectable elements of society," including colleges, churches, media, and politicians. The exception to Powell's generalities was Ralph Nader, who was "the single most effective *antagonist* of American business," turned into a "legend" by the media whose aim was to smash corporate power. Not just free enterprise and the forgotten businessman but *economics* must be protected from Nader's "economic illiteracy," which was "confusing the public" with nonsense about tax "loopholes" that would "benefit only the rich" or "big companies." Like Friedman had done with the "social responsibility," Powell put quotation marks around the words "rich" and "poor," as if to deny such things existed. "Setting the so-called 'rich' against the 'poor,' of business against the people," warned Powell, "is the cheapest and most dangerous kind of politics."

In his day job, Powell had experience defending a variety of corporations against activists (he might have said zealots) like Nader. Among his other activities, like helping the state of Virginia block school integration orders, Powell served as a director at the cigarette company Phillip Morris from 1964 to 1971, and along with his close friend, CEO Gordon Crenshaw, helped the firm cast doubt on the link between cigarettes and cancer.[26] They utilized academic research, changed the narrative, fought in court, and lobbied legislatures—all strategies that he was advising other businesses to employ to defeat the so-called defenders of the "poor." Powell warned business leaders that unless they learned to cultivate and wield political power aggressively without "embarrassment" or "reluctance," they would lose not just free enterprise but also Western culture overall. Powell claimed that the fight would require "careful long-range planning" and consistent action over "an indefinite period of years." In

order to secure the "scale of financing" and the "political power" necessary to beat back the college kids and the Naderites attacking free enterprise, they had to create organizations dedicated to their cause. The costs
would be great, said Powell, and businesses would have to be "far more
generous" and patient than they had been previously. He was calling for
nothing less than a counterrevolution in defense of free enterprise.

Powell advocated a pair of approaches to counteracting democratic
claims made on corporations. One, a long-term plan to change hearts
and minds conducted through the universities and the media; and two,
the quiet accumulation of political power through legal change hidden
from public view. If public opinion eventually aligned with the business
community's interests, the secret strategy to subvert democracy could
eventually come out into the open without repercussions.

In pursuit of the first goal, Powell urged corporations to fund scholars who would push the new party line and establish beachheads at elite
institutions that he believed to be "graduating scores of bright young
men . . . who despise the American political and economic system." Yale
was a particular bogeyman of the aggrieved right—it is mentioned three
times in Powell's memo. Fighting against the ideas of the bright young
men of Yale would not be easy, but with time and limitless money, anything was possible. To be credible, the faculty corporations funded must
be "attractive, articulate, and well-informed." Instead of resorting to
"improper pressure" to influence administrators and hiring committees,
the business community should insist on "balance, fairness, and truth."
He urged corporate funders to "aggressively insist upon 'equal time'"
because universities could not refuse to hear "'diverse' views."

Powell's program for ideological warfare didn't stop there. He suggested that all academic textbooks be evaluated to ensure that they
include the "accomplishments" of free enterprise and its "relationship to
individual rights and freedoms." Just as the "the civil rights movement
insists on re-writing" curriculums, he grumbled, so should corporate
America. It should also publish its own scholarly journals, books, and
pamphlets to advertise "our side" to compete with the likes of Eldridge
Cleaver, the prominent Black Panther leader, "for reader attention."
It was time for American businesses to "enlighten" the public, to stop

being "the favorite whipping-boy [of] politicians," and to "assume a broader and more vigorous role in the public arena."

As to the other goal, that of effecting legal change, the business community had to take back the Supreme Court from the "activist-minded" courts, by which he meant the Warren Court.[27] Powell called the judiciary "the most important instrument for social, economic and political change." And he believed that the civil rights groups, public interest law firms, and labor unions had seized it (in fact, those groups had won only a modest number of victories in the prior decades). Business groups must hire and train "highly competent" lawyers to write amicus briefs at the Court and engage in strategic litigation to fight back against the gains made by the left in the law. This is what Powell had done in defending Phillip Morris against scientific evidence. In fact, he would soon become the highly competent lawyer tasked with taking back the Supreme Court back from the "activists."

It is difficult to know whether the Powell memo caused the surge of corporate activism that followed or was merely reflective of it, but it is clear that what Powell said should happen *did* happen. The Chamber of Commerce formed a task force of forty executives from top firms to carry out the measures outlined in the memo, and, according to the historian Kim Phillips-Fein, "many who read the memo cited it afterward as inspiration for their political choices."[28] Reading the Powell memo led Richard Scaife, the Pittsburgh-based billionaire and supporter of anti-Clinton movements, to begin funding right-wing foundations, the cause to which he would devote the rest of his life and fortune. He joined Joseph Coors, the youngest grandson of the beer magnate Adolph Coors, to establish the Heritage Foundation in 1973.[29] Coors had been radicalized against the left when his son became a hippie while attending the University of Colorado, but unlike other disappointed parents, Coors was a regent of the university and tried to bar left-wing speakers from the school and require faculty to take a loyalty oath to America. When his efforts to get rid of faculty, whom he referred to in a commencement address as "pleasure-minded parasites living off the state dole," failed, he turned his money and rage into a think tank.[30]

In 1972, the CEOs of Alcoa, GE, U.S. Steel, and other top firms created the Business Roundtable to represent the country's largest corporations on Capitol Hill. From 1974 to 1980, the membership of the Chamber of Commerce doubled while its budget tripled.[31] And after 1971, a number of conservative family foundations began to fund think tanks and academics. Among the donors, in addition to Scaife and Coors, were the Koch brothers (sons of Fred Koch and heirs to an oil empire), John Olin (son of a weapons and mining magnate), and the Bradleys (heirs to Allen-Bradley, a family-owned factory-automation company).[32] Ironically, capitalism's most ardent defenders happened to be the heirs and scions of family fortunes whose experience with capitalism in practice was likely limited.

In 1966, based on new legal prohibitions on discrimination, a group of female employees had sued Allen-Bradley for paying them less than male employees. Then in 1968, the federal government began investigating Allen-Bradley for racially discriminatory hiring policies to which the company responded as had GM, through an affirmative action program. The Bradley brothers felt persecuted by both the federal government and their ungrateful employees, which led them to political activism.[33] They used their father's fortune to support a right-wing, anti-government ideological program in universities, dedicating more than $370 million to right-wing groups, including the Federalist Society, that have had a significant effect on law and policy. The Bradley Foundation's eponymous prize gives $250,000 yearly to individuals whose ideas "advance freedom." Past winners include Fox News Chairman Roger Ailes; John Bolton, who served briefly as Trump's National Security Adviser; race IQ proponent Charles Murray; and neoliberal economists Gary Becker, Thomas Sowell, and Richard Epstein.[34]

John Olin was apparently appalled by the Black student protests in 1969 at his alma mater, Cornell University, which spurred him to direct his foundation's philanthropy to fight the alleged liberal takeover of universities. According to his authorized biography, John Olin "saw very clearly that students at Cornell, like those at most major universities, were hostile to businessmen and to business enterprise, and indeed had begun to question the ideals of the nation itself."[35] John's father, Franklin Olin, had made a fortune selling gunpowder, ammunition, and blasting powder for mines. The company's colorful history went well beyond the weapons manufacturing that, coinciding with the world wars, became extremely lucrative. According to the journalist Jane Mayer, between 1958 and 1966, the Olin Foundation "served as a bank for the CIA," laundering $1.95 million that went toward anti-Communist intellectuals and work.[36] After Lewis Powell wrote his memo, John Olin began directing funds to groups like the American Enterprise Institute (AEI), the Hoover Institution, and the Heritage Foundation. He may also have had a financial interest in weakening government regulation. In the 1970s, the Olin Corporation was caught up in various environmental lawsuits resulting from its blast mining and burying toxic waste in an upstate New York landfill called Love Canal, the first place the Environmental Protection Agency designated as a superfund site. Olin also became the first company charged for violating the arms embargo of 1963 due to its continued sale of weapons to South Africa's apartheid regime.

Much of the Olin Foundation's funding was spread across top universities and law schools, making John Olin one of the most generous—and most powerful—donors in the academic world. Olin began focusing heavily on funding law schools at the urging of his close friend, William Simon, a partner at the investment bank Salomon Brothers and Nixon's former energy czar and fourth, and last, Treasury secretary. Olin chose Simon as president of his foundation in 1977 because, as he noted, "his thinking is identical to mine." Indeed, both men had summer homes in East Hampton, New York, were heirs to family fortunes, and felt that the country was in danger of "careening toward collectivism" and were dedicated to fighting that threat.

Simon's goal was to create a "counter-intelligentsia" that would use "ideas as weapons." He urged foundations to "give grants, grants, and more grants in exchange for books, books, and more books."[37] The Olin Foundation contributed financially to everything from William F. Buckley's show *Firing Line* to Allan Bloom's book decrying progressivism on college campuses, *The Closing of the American Mind*, as well as to Dinesh D'Souza's book *Illiberal Education*, which railed against "political correctness." The foundation also supported the conservative philosopher Harvey Mansfield, the political scientist Samuel Huntington, and the law scholar John Yoo, who would author the notorious torture memos leaked during the second Iraq war.

The Law and Economics movement—the subject of chapter 5—owes its existence to the Olin Foundation, which endowed almost all of the top Law and Economics programs in the country until it ran out of money in 2005. After leading Olin, Simon returned to Wall Street just in time to help pioneer the leveraged buyout. He launched his own private equity firm, and made around $300 million in less than a decade.[38]

The founding of the MPS itself had to do with another heir turned philanthropist. When William Volker, a wealthy German immigrant, was alive, his nickname was "Mr. Anonymous," owing to his anonymous charitable donations to the needy and his modest house. After he died in 1947, however, his nephew Harold Luhnow became president of the William Volker Fund. Luhnow brought Friedrich Hayek to the University of Chicago, financed the publication of Hayek's *The Road to Serfdom* in America, and funded the initial MPS meeting.[39] He paid Ludwig von Mises's salary at NYU, funded the lectures by Milton and Rose Friedman that became *Capitalism and Freedom,* and supported the Foundation for Economic Education, which became a model for the right-wing think tanks that followed.

Many of neoliberalism's early boosters also emerged from the industries most threatened by changing market conditions, like oil and gas, tobacco, and weapons. These motivated billionaires were the silent forces propelling the spread of neoliberal theories like shareholder supremacy through the channels of idea dissemination like the academy, think tanks, and media, until they became conventional wisdom.

Other think tanks and lobbying groups that formed after the Powell memo included the American Legislative Exchange Council (ALEC) in 1973, the Cato Institute in 1977, and the Manhattan Institute in 1978. Lobbying firms grew from a total of 175 in 1971 to more than 2,500 a decade later (these figures include many groups that were not identified with neoliberalism). Political action committees, organizations that pool financial contributions to support or oppose issues or candidates, increased in number from fewer than 300 to over 1,200. Already existing groups like the AEI, the Foundation for Economic Education, and the

Hoover Institution transformed themselves from small nonpartisan think tanks to well-funded neoliberal powerhouses. In Great Britain, the neoliberal Institute of Economic Affairs (IEA), which calls itself an "educational institute," was formed in 1955 to "educate" the public to defund the National Health Service. (The IEA was Enoch Powell's chosen home after his "Rivers of Blood" speech got him demoted from public-facing politics.)

There were so many think tanks and nonprofits created to advocate for free markets that coordinating them all required an umbrella nonprofit. The Atlas Economic Research Foundation, subsequently called the Atlas Network, was formed by Sir Antony Fisher, a British entrepreneur, MPS member, and Hayek acolyte who founded the IEA, the Manhattan Institute, and the Pacific Research Institute in the 1970s. The Atlas Network lists more than five hundred members worldwide, including think tanks across the Global South, all dedicated to orienting government policy toward free markets. As a group of health-care policy researchers found, the Atlas Economic Foundation's think tanks "acted as a strategic ally to the tobacco industry" with 37 percent of its partner foundations receiving funding from the tobacco industry, primarily Lewis Powell's company, Phillip Morris.[40]

Most of these think tanks worked together to coordinate a "defense of free enterprise." Their influence extended into academic scholarship, college campuses, Congress, and administrative agencies—anywhere public opinion is shaped or legal battles are waged. And their impact has also extended, and increased, into the present. Although they vary in focus, they do not waver in their opposition to taxation, redistribution, or public services of any kind, especially public schools. Some of these organizations, like ALEC, specialize in writing legislation for state legislatures and Congress on a range of issues, not all directly related to economics, from deregulating payday lenders to opposing gender-neutral bathrooms and tightening voting requirements. Others, like the Hoover Institution, have kept their distance from shaping the lawmaking process, focusing instead on supporting high-profile fellows, among them Milton Friedman, Gary Becker, Henry Kissinger, and former Speaker of the House Newt Gingrich. Honorary fellows at Hoover have included Margaret Thatcher, Ronald Reagan, and Hayek.

The benefits these organizations offer to the billionaires who fund them are manifold. All of the foundations, think tanks, university centers, and policy outlets are 501(c)(3)s—meaning any money flowing into them is considered a tax-free charitable donation. Instead of giving to charities that feed the poor or shelter the homeless, billionaires donate considerable resources to right-wing foundations, which churn out white papers and "studies" blaming the poor for their condition and comparing estate taxes to socialism. Money multiplying into more money. Over time, the transaction—hard cash for laws benefiting the wealthy—was made shorter and smoother by many of these same groups.

The white papers of the numerous new institutions of the neoliberal right were circulated to presidential administrations, journalists, and the public. On the "glut of papers" produced by right-wing think tanks and pundits, journalist Lewis Lapham commented in *Harper's*, "I could find no unifying or fundamental principle except a certain belief that money was good for rich people and bad for poor people. It was the only point on which all the authorities agreed."

THE LONG STRUGGLE toward civil rights had required bold experimentation, including tactics coordinated across institutions and types of institutions, such as unions, federal courts, and activist groups. There was disagreement among leaders and organizations about strategy and much else. They tried and erred and changed tack, learning from one another and the opposing force of the status quo. It was the same with the forces of backlash. Like the civil rights movement, the neoliberal movement was loosely coordinated, but coordinated nonetheless.

One significant difference—among many—is that the neoliberal movement was fundamentally an elite creation and an elite movement. It had no natural base of voters, because until voters were "educated" by Lewis Powell's army, they had no taste for pure market capitalism. But neoliberals had endless funds and a plan of attack targeting every cultural and political institution. With assistance from the Federal Communications Commission's fairness doctrine, which mandated all media to present "both sides" of controversial issues, the message got out.

Powell's media strategy of deploying articulate defenders of the free market found its man easily enough. He was the obvious choice: Milton Friedman took the neoliberal cause to the public in a ten-part PBS series called *Free to Choose*, released alongside a book of the same title in 1980. The series covered topics including "The Power of the Market," "What's Wrong with Our Schools?" and "The Tyranny of Control." In the episode directly about race, "Created Equal," Friedman begins, "A myth has grown up that free market capitalism increases such inequalities that the rich benefit at the expense of the poor. Nothing could be further from the truth." In this he was seconded by Thomas Sowell, the Chicago-trained Black economist who appeared on the show: "I would disagree violently with the notion that the people are stirring," Sowell begins, referring to protests among the Black community. "A very small handful of intellectuals have generated an enormous amount of noise." In fact, he noted, "most Blacks in the United States do not take any strong position in favor of equality of results." As he then said, "Most polls that I've seen of blacks put them . . . very well to the right of most intellectuals on most of these social issues. It is not the people who are stirring, it is a handful of intellectuals."

AT HOME and abroad, the rise of neoliberalism was not an economic response to various challenges but a way of preserving existing power structures and preventing significant societal changes. Just as Third World intellectuals were sharing ideas and revolutionary tactics, the intellectuals of the Western powers were also waging a counterrevolution over ideology. If Fanon, Mandela, Gandhi, King, and other intellectuals inspired resistance movements and revolutions through new theories and ideals, so too did Hayek, Friedman, Stigler, Goldwater, and the others justifying the old power structure. It was an era of intellectual entrepreneurialism and a worldwide competition over whose ideas would rule the future. It was a struggle over narrative, history, and power. The global struggle only grew in heat and urgency over the course of the 1960s, linked to uprisings for Black freedom and antiwar protests in the United States. The reason this worldwide anticolonial struggle has not already been identified as a central theme in the story of neoliberalism is that neoliberalism was so successful in moving the conversation away from freedom against empire toward freedom against state power of any kind.

More than anything else, neoliberal economic theory gave the Nixon administration the linguistic cover for their cynical strategy of race-baiting the voting public. Segregated Black neighborhoods formerly called "the ghetto" were now called "enterprise zones" while the former colonies of the Global South became "developing countries," "emerging markets," or "export nations." Nixon, Lewis Powell, and the wealthy heirs who helped birth the neoliberal state were not hard-core capitalists. Rather, capitalism, as described by neoliberals, provided a useful explanatory paradigm that incidentally justified the maintenance of the already existing social hierarchy in the face of revolution.

As older myths of social and global hierarchy frayed and failed, neoliberalism slowly filled the void. Part of its success is owed to the fact that it did not overtly challenge the global rise in demand for freedom. Nevertheless, the result was the same. By employing the language of economics, neoliberalism maintained and reinforced empire and racial subjugation. The ideology was especially potent because it disguised itself as a neutral statement of economics rather than just another theory.

In the United States, neoliberalism entrenched itself through three institutional pivots from the civil rights era. The first was the Black capitalism programs that bureaucratized and nullified the economic demands of the civil rights movement. The second was replacing democratic choice with technocracy, such as designating decisions over crucial economic matters like monetary policy to the exclusive domain of specialists in government agencies. The final pivot was the strategy proposed in the Powell memo: the ideological capture of law and legal doctrine in order to resist and roll back progressive victories won by the civil rights and environmental rights movements of the 1960s. Each of these strategies was born out of backlash to actual or threatened societal change and each would be successful and long-lasting. The third pivot, the turn toward the law, was perhaps the most consequential, and is the focus of part II.

PART II

Revolution

CHAPTER 4

Blind Justice

The process of democracy is one of change. Our laws are not frozen into immutable form, they are constantly in the process of revision in response to the need of a changing society.

—JUSTICE THURGOOD MARSHALL (1974)

AMONG THE VARIOUS attractions for visitors to the Supreme Court Building in Washington, D.C., is a statue named *Contemplation of Justice*. Situated to the left of the main exterior staircase, it depicts a woman draped in a robe, one arm resting on an ornately bound tome. In her other hand she holds a figurine: a blindfolded woman cradling a sword and scale to her breast. This, we know, is Justice.

Justice's blindness implies her impartiality, the requirement that judges ignore status or power in pursuit of truth, but the blindfold had a different meaning when it first appeared on Lady Justice in 1497 in a satirical cartoon by the German printmaker Albrecht Dürer. A crook places a blindfold on Justice so she can ignore the corruption and abuse of the law on display right in front of her—so she can enact corruption while feigning objectivity. To facilitate the unbiased pursuit of justice and to insulate them from the influence of politics or mammon, the American Founders gave Supreme Court justices lifetime appointments and guaranteed salaries. With "no influence over either the sword or the purse; no direction either of the strength or of the wealth of the society," said Alexander Hamilton in the Federalist Papers, "the general liberty of the people can never be endangered from that quarter." The absolute independence of the judiciary made the Court the "citadel of the public justice and the public security," wrote Hamilton. "It may truly be said to have neither force nor will, but merely judgment."[1]

Hamilton's paean to the judiciary belies the reality, then and now. And there are few better examples of the Supreme Court's political character than Richard Nixon's process for selecting his third and fourth appointees (despite his second term being truncated, he was unusually fortunate in judicial retirements and deaths). Having already appointed two justices—Warren Burger as Chief Justice Earl Warren's replacement in 1969, and Harry Blackmun as associate justice in 1970, replacing Justice Abe Fortas, who resigned—Nixon was presented with two more positions to fill in 1972. Nixon was determined to get a southerner on the bench who was "a strict constructionist," a coded term his campaign often used to signify the opposite of "judicial activist," their label for the Brown-deciding Warren Court. He also toyed with appointing a woman. Yet when the American Bar Association (ABA) determined that his proposed nominee, Appellate Judge Mildred Lillie, wasn't qualified, Nixon responded gleefully. Speaking to an aide named Dick Moore, he gloated, "The Bar has, incidentally,... played right into our hands... exactly what we wanted."[2] Nixon was able to dispense with the female nominee he didn't really want and hang it on the ABA.

Nixon had two requirements for his appointee. "First, I don't want the guy to be a racist." But at the same time, he did not want "a fellow who is going to go hog-wild on... integration, [attacking] de facto segregation." He warned, "That would just be dynamite."[3] In other words, he needed someone who could "be loud enough for the George Wallace leaners to hear us," as Alan Greenspan had advised, yet who was not an outspoken racist. Henry Kissinger, the national security adviser, was the first to propose William Rehnquist, and when White

House Chief of Staff H. R. Haldeman sought assurance that he was conservative enough, Kissinger said: "He's way to the right of [Pat] Buchanan."[4] Nixon did not know Rehnquist well, despite his serving as an assistant attorney general. Yet the President picked him, and told Attorney General John Mitchell to "make sure to emphasize to all the Southerners that Rehnquist is a reactionary bastard, which I hope to Christ he is."[5]

Prior to his role as assistant attorney general for the Office of Legal Counsel, Rehnquist had served as a clerk to Justice Robert Jackson and had articulated his views in several memos written about cases the Court considered. "It is about time the Court faced the fact that the white people of the south do not like the colored people," Rehnquist wrote Justice Jackson in a memo about a 1953 voter disenfranchisement case. As Rehnquist saw it, the Court must not act because the Constitution "most assuredly did not appoint the Court as a sociological watchdog to rear up every time private discrimination raises its admittedly ugly head."[6] Calling racism "admittedly ugly" was apparently all one needed to evade the charge of being a racist. On the decision that most concerned southern voters, *Brown v. Board of Education*, Rehnquist had urged Justice Jackson to blind his eyes to the persuasions of "sociological views," "'liberal' colleagues," and public opinion that derided segregation as "unpopular and unhumanitarian." Racial segregation was settled law; overturning it, to Rehnquist, would be a violation of property rights. "To those who would argue that 'personal' rights are more sacrosanct than 'property' rights,'" he said, "the short answer is that the Constitution makes no such distinction."[7] In other words, he concluded, "I think *Plessy* v. *Ferguson* was right and should be re-affirmed." Justice Jackson ignored Rehnquist and joined the other justices in overturning *Plessy*, the 1896 case in which the Court upheld segregation. When questioned about this memo during his confirmation hearing in 1972, Rehnquist denied that he had ever opposed the decision; the memo itself was only made available through government archives in 2012, years after his death.

In addition to *Brown v. Board of Education*, the Warren Court (1953–1969) had extended free speech rights to protect the press from charges of libel in *New York Times Co. v. Sullivan* and war protesters from sanctions in *United States v. O'Brien*; guaranteed contraception access in *Griswold v. Connecticut*; extended the Sixth Amendment's right to counsel through publicly funded defense lawyers in *Gideon v. Wainwright*; and required arresting officers to inform suspects of their rights in *Miranda v. Arizona*. The Warren Court also decided *Loving v. Virginia,* which decriminalized interracial marriage. It struck down poll taxes and racial covenants. It made real and actionable the abstract rights to speech, due process, equal protection, and voting, and it upheld the separation of church and state as well as prohibitions on cruel and unusual punishment. Not all of its jurisprudence resulted in progressive outcomes—the justices were all elite white men, and most were Republican appointees. However, much of the Court's decisions have become so rooted in Americans' understandings of rights that they seem inevitable. To conservatives, it was a time of rapid change, especially given the other upheavals taking place at home and across the world.

The Warren Court's judicial philosophy of jurisprudence was *legal realism*, which held that the law should be based on scientific evidence, empirical data, sociological reality, and observations about how the world works. In other words, justice should *not* be blind: it should open its eyes to how power, money, race, and gender affected the law. Removing the blindfold to see how money determined a criminal defendant's "right to an attorney" led the Court to hold that an abstract right to an attorney was not real if someone could not actually pay for a lawyer. Seeing that "separate but equal" was a legal fiction in a world where race and wealth were entwined led the Court to overturn statutory segregation.

The period between 1897 and the dawn of legal realism in 1937 has been called the "Lochner era," after a crucial case that pitted the rights of workers against the rights of business owners; in that 1905 case, the Court ruled that New York State's statutory limit on the amount of hours a baker could work per week violated bakers' rights to contract. The Lochner court, in contrast to the realists, insisted on a "formalist" interpretation of law, which held to a standard of absolute contractual liberty and property rights rather than the legislature's right to pass laws that balance among a variety of rights and freedoms. The Industrial

Revolution had brought a boom in factory production and wage labor that transformed American society. By the turn of the twentieth century, labor tensions had escalated into violence, but the Lochner court refused to budge from its formalist interpretation of contract laws—that even legislation could not override the enforcement of valid contracts—forged in an era of small merchants with equal bargaining power in making contracts. Yet legal realists like Robert Hale, a law professor at Columbia University, argued that freedom of contract could not be assumed in the real world, which was already riven by inequalities of wealth. Because laws forbid the worker from taking food and shelter to survive or factory equipment to produce their own goods, it is "the law of property which coerces people to work for factory owners"; labor contracts made out of the necessity of survival were not like contracts made with equal bargaining power and thus could be deemed coercive.[8] Realists thus argued against the formalist Lochner court's blindness to reality. Just "because courts can do nothing to revise the underlying pattern of market relationships," said Hale, did not mean that "courts should, in the name of liberty and equality, thwart [legislative] attempts to equalize the economic liberty of the weak."[9]

Between 1897 and 1937, the formalist Lochner court struck down more than two hundred state laws as violations of "economic liberty."[10] During the 1930s, four justices on the Court—the so-called four horsemen—stood in the way of Roosevelt's New Deal. The Lochner era ended with the 1937 case *West Coast Hotel Co. v. Parrish*, in which the Court upheld a state's right to impose minimum wage laws. The change had as much to do with FDR's threat to pack the Court as it did with a change in judicial philosophy. One of the horsemen, Justice Owen Roberts, joined the majority's holding that "the Constitution does not speak of the freedom of contract," effectively dropping the curtain on legal formalism.[11] Labor laws and regulations replaced the law of contract.

WHILE NO ONE wanted a return to Lochner, Nixon hoped, with Rehnquist, to curb the legal realist instincts that had led to *Brown* and the vicious backlash it spurred on the right. So too with his second pick: Lewis Powell, the same Lewis Powell who had written the 1971 memo to the Chamber of Commerce, and whose paper trail was even cleaner than Rehnquist's. Not only was Powell a well-connected and highly respected corporate-lawyer-cum-political-strategist, he was also, as Nixon put it, strong on "law enforcement" and like-minded on "civil rights."[12] In fact, Powell had proved his southern reactionary bona fides on the front lines after *Brown*. He was a member, and then chairman, of the Richmond School Board from 1951 to 1961, during the time the integration orders took effect, and his legal ingenuity enabled the district to comply with the technical orders while avoiding integrating schools through consolidating district boundaries.

Powell stayed out of the controversy over segregation, eschewing the public spectacle that surrounded politicians like Wallace. Powell's tactic as a member of the Richmond School Board after *Brown* was to remain "steadfastly silent," according to his biographer.[13] He would not openly defy the Court's orders, as the proponents of massive resistance, a strategy Virginia politicians designed to prevent school desegregation, had urged, taking a more measured tone that focused on practicalities and timing rather than obstipant refusal to integrate. Powell wrote a memo on behalf of the attorney general of Virginia opposing school integration plans, arguing that they imposed the "stigma of legal apartheid" on the South. Instead of pushing for integration "now," which Powell believed would accelerate white flight and diminish the quality of schools, the Court should wait until residential segregation simply petered out.[14]

Yet Powell's diplomatic and genteel resistance reached the same results without the controversy, presaging his tenure on the Court. Rather than oppose the desegregation orders, he found a route around them through a series of legal procedures that drew district lines using neighborhood maps which were conveniently racially segregated, ensuring that Richmond schools remained segregated "within legal bounds."[15] By the time he stepped down from the school board, he had avoided any real protests, and "only 2 of 23,000 black children in Richmond attended schools with whites."[16] Powell remained steadfastly opposed to school integration through busing and worked—including during his time on the Court—to place all decision-making power in the hands of local school boards.

Despite his age—he was sixty-five when he was appointed and therefore too old to really take advantage of lifetime tenure—Powell was Nixon's ideal candidate. As the President put it on a call with Attorney General Mitchell, "I'd say that two years of Powell is worth twenty of somebody else, and that's the damn truth."[17] While Nixon was worried about the young and relatively unknown Rehnquist—was he a "playboy?" or did he have a "jackass record?"—he was sure that Powell, whom he called a "distinguished looking gentleman," had an "outstanding record."[18] Like Nixon's strategy of détente through diversions like Black capitalism, Powell was a reactionary operating behind a genteel façade. Both men were gifted strategists who could patiently await long-term results, and both preferred to maneuver behind the scenes, taking great care—especially in their public pronouncements—to moderate their language in order to avoid controversy and confrontation. Before his appointment, Powell had publicly spoken about civil rights only once, when he had given a speech denouncing Martin Luther King and the lawlessness of civil rights protesters. Mitchell assured the President that this speech was not "too rabid" and primarily focused on "civil disobedience."[19] Nixon responded that he had himself spoken about protests in the same way, and that they represented "a legitimate thing" to talk about.

The only issue with the candidate was that he didn't want the job. Powell had already turned Nixon down when he had first offered him a seat on the Supreme Court in 1969. Powell's corporate law practice was lucrative and his power, which was always used in private, was sufficient. Nixon and Mitchell finally persuaded Powell to join the highest court in the nation, despite the significant pay cut, by appealing to his conscience and a duty to "rehabilitate the Court in the eyes of the South."[20]

Nixon was very pleased when Powell accepted. "I think he'll do a fine job." Powell's friends at Phillip Morris thought so too; when the Virginia Chamber of Commerce threw a formal dinner to celebrate Powell's appointment to the Court, his close friends at the tobacco company presented him with a robe.[21] They might as well have handed him a blindfold.

Once confirmed and seated, Powell began a long-term campaign to quietly transform the law. Race and the free market were joined together in the neoliberal worldview. What Powell did was help infuse the law with neoliberal principles—empowering corporations while curtailing state power to right historic wrongs. Rehnquist is the more famous (or infamous) of the two late Nixon nominees due to his conservative bomb throwing; he was a reliable dissent in cases recognizing greater liberties, including *two* separate dissenting opinions in *Roe v. Wade*. But Powell's impact on the law has been both more profound and more damaging.

To be sure, the Supreme Court was never a "Powell Court"; it was Chief Justice Burger's. And the Burger Court's reputation, if it has one, is as a kind of oddity, producing unconventional pluralities of liberals and conservatives rather than clear binaries. Because of the Burger Court's lack of definition and Powell's careful lawyering around controversial cases, Powell and the Burger Court are remembered as moderate compared to the Rehnquist Court's rightward turn. For instance, Powell sided with the majority in *Roe v. Wade* and saved affirmative action in *Regents of the University of California v. Bakke*. But his reasoning, even in opinions where he joined the liberal justices, paved the way for some of the major legal and political changes of our era. The dramatic rightward shift seen in today's Supreme Court opinions can be seen as just the belated detonation of the explosives planted during Powell's tenure.

THE FIRST CASE in Powell's personal legal revolution emerged from his home state of Virginia and involved the person he had called "the single most effective antagonist of American business": Ralph Nader.[22] In *Virginia State Board of Pharmacy v. Virginia Citizens Consumer Council, Inc.* (1976), Nader's consumer group had challenged a Virginia law prohibiting pharmacies from advertising drug prices. The ostensible purpose of the state law was to maintain the professionalism of pharmacies and prevent "aggressive" marketing. Nader and fellow public interest attorney Alan Morrison, the lead lawyer on the case, argued that unlisted prices were harmful to consumers who could not seek better alternatives. The plaintiffs bringing the case were sympathetic and their cause was just—sick people relying on lifesaving drugs could not get any pharmacies to quote them their prices. Nader and Morrison decided to argue the plaintiff's case on First Amendment grounds, but because they were representing consumers and not the pharmacy, they creatively argued that the prices were information that the public had a right to hear, and thus should be protected by the free speech. They didn't directly argue that corporations should have the right to free speech, but they did ask the Court to determine that prices (that is, corporate speech) are protected by the First Amendment. They did not realize they were handing the Court the rope with which to hang them. Until that point, the First Amendment had belonged to the left and there was no reason to fear its expansion. Beginning with a pivotal 1919 Supreme Court ruling protecting antiwar protest from state censure, each expansion of the First Amendment had yielded more protection for civil disobedience, protest, and speech. In that earlier case, *Abrams v. United States*, Justice Oliver Wendell Holmes famously framed the First Amendment as fostering a "marketplace of ideas," a notion the Naderites now used themselves.

The Court decided the case in favor of Nader and the pharmacy customers on First Amendment grounds, with Justice Blackmun writing for the majority in consultation with fellow conservatives, Powell and Burger. The majority of justices signed on to the opinion that, at least in this case, it was "too simplistic" to differentiate between an individual's right to protest and a company's rights to speech. In doing so, they unwittingly opened a legal door through which Justice Powell would maneuver First Amendment jurisprudence toward the elimination of any distinctions between corporate speech and individual speech. Like Powell's refusal in his 1971 memo to see the difference between "rich" and "poor," his aim was to blindfold the court from seeing disparities in power. It would have likely given Powell some satisfaction to deliver a loss to Nader, but ultimately, it was better to sacrifice a pawn now to win the game in the end.

In a move that might surprise, given his reputation today, Rehnquist refused to wear the blindfold that obscured the obvious difference between people and corporations, and wrote an outraged dissent. He argued not only that the conservatives on the Court, against type, had *extended* rather than *limited* the First Amendment but also that the right to regulate businesses' speech belonged to the states. Rehnquist warned, all too presciently, that the Court was in danger of returning to the Lochner era's laissez-faire fundamentalism. "There is certainly nothing in the United States Constitution which requires the Virginia Legislature to hew to the teachings of Adam Smith in its legislative decisions regulating the pharmacy profession," Rehnquist wrote.[23]

"Great cases, like hard cases, make bad law," Justice Oliver Wendell Holmes once said, and *Virginia Pharmacy* fit the description. The facts of the case—sympathetic victims, a straightforward demand for price information, and the unusual alignment of Nader and Powell—meant it was an easy case. And that should have alerted the justices to the danger of building a new interpretation of a crucial constitutional right with it. Only Rehnquist the reactionary saw the decision as a harbinger of change, and raised the crucial issue of exactly how far the ruling extended. He pointed out the many state laws placing limits on advertising of products considered "vices," like alcohol, pornography, and cigarettes. Was the Court willing to extend the First Amendment's protection of speech to these commonly restricted ads?

The answer was yes. In 2001, the Court's majority would uphold First Amendment protection in tobacco advertising in *Lorillard Tobacco Co. v. Reilly*. This was the slippery slope Rehnquist foresaw, but there were many other repercussions of *Virginia Pharmacy* that even a hyperbolic alarmist like him could not have predicted. For example, the increasing direct-to-consumer marketing of prescription pills, including highly addictive prescription pills like OxyContin, was just a bit further down the slope. In 2011, the Roberts Court even struck down a Vermont law prohibiting data mining companies from selling individual health information, for the use of direct marketing of prescription drugs, without patient or doctor consent. Building directly on *Virginia Pharmacy*, the Court protected the free speech rights of "pharmaceutical companies and data miners" to profit from information gathered without consumer consent and to their detriment.[24] Great cases led to bad law.

In the same 1976 term as *Virginia Pharmacy*, the Court decided a case about campaign donations, *Buckley v. Valeo*, which was also uncontroversial both on the Court and to the public. The issue in *Buckley* concerned whether and how much Congress could regulate campaign donations without running afoul of First Amendment protections. The question was not whether the First Amendment applied to political donations—that was settled law—but the degree to which limits on spending could be opposed. The case did not deal with corporate "speech," but with limits on spending by the wealthy on elections. In 1974, after a series of scandals had come to light during Nixon's second term, including Watergate and "suitcase-gate" (the Nixon campaign solicited suitcases full of cash from donors in order to avoid disclosure mandates), Congress amended the Federal Election Campaign Act (FECA) to impose stricter disclosure rules and limits on donations from individuals and corporations. New York senator James Buckley, brother of *National Review* founder William F. Buckley, challenged the law on several grounds, including by arguing that campaign donations were political speech that was protected under the First Amendment.

The case was not a straightforwardly partisan issue. President Gerald Ford sent his solicitor general, Robert Bork, to fight FECA's mandate before the Court, but the administration took no official position. (Incidentally, Nixon had promised Bork a seat on the Supreme Court because of his loyalty to the President during the infamous Saturday Night Massacre—Bork was the Justice Department official who carried out the President's order to fire Watergate Special Prosecutor Archibald Cox.) Bork now unironically denounced the anticorruption law as unconstitutional. He was joined by the Libertarian Party and the ACLU, both hawkish on the First Amendment. The two main national political parties did not mobilize around the case. Nor was there any public debate. The case was not then viewed as a significant change, likely because few could have anticipated just how much money was being mobilized by right-wing groups and that would soon pour into American politics.

A five-justice majority (Burger, Powell, Rehnquist, William J. Brennan Jr., and Potter Stewart) wrote a 150-page opinion, one of the longest written opinions in the Court's history and one of its most complicated. Despite so many words, the Court upheld the majority of FECA's mandates, including limits on campaign contributions, mandatory disclosures, limits on expenses by a campaign, and a provision allowing candidates to use government funds rather than soliciting donations. On the other hand, the majority struck down limits on individual spending by the candidate, independent expenses (campaign-related expenditures made by those outside of the candidate or their campaign, such as research, polling, issue advocacy, or advertising), and on total campaign spending. A person or group, including the candidate, could spend as much money as they wanted on a campaign.

As is often true of Supreme Court opinions, the reasoning buried in the opinion ended up being critical. The majority wrote that limits on spending were fine, but only when they were based on the government's concern about actual or perceived corruption. FECA was certainly a response to corruption, but Congress also described the law's stated aim as "equaliz[ing] as far as practicable the relative ability of all voters to affect electoral choices."[25] The lower court that already ruled before the case reached the Supreme Court had upheld the law based on the importance of protecting elections from "the corrosive influence of money," so that democratic participation was not determined by "disparities in wealth." The Supreme Court's majority, however, waved away the government's interest in "equalizing" democratic participation as "ancillary," and in any case determined that motive unconstitutional: "The concept that government may restrict the speech of some elements of our society in order to enhance the relative voice of others," proclaimed the majority, "is wholly foreign to the First Amendment."[26] The fact that *some* and *the others* were not arbitrary distinctions but based on relative wealth hardly mattered.

Justices Thurgood Marshall and Byron White refused to wear that particular blindfold. Writing about the "widespread evasion" of the law's purpose that the majority's opinion enabled, they warned in their dissent that limitless spending would result in candidates being forced onto an endless treadmill "of raising increasingly large sums of money."

Marshall also argued that even the appearance that the political arena was "the exclusive providence of the wealthy" was a valid government concern. Not so after *Buckley*, which began aligning the interests of the wealthy with those of the government. Soon Congress and the presidency would be filled with the best candidates money could buy.

As with many of the Court's decisions, *Buckley* and *Virginia Pharmacy* had an amplifying effect when combined. The two 1976 cases hardly seemed to be related—*Buckley* was about money in politics, *Virginia Pharmacy* about the right of consumers to information—but it would not take long for the first signs of convergence to appear.

The 1977 case *First National Bank of Boston v. Bellotti* featured another corporation pleading First Amendment speech protection. This time, a Boston bank was challenging the constitutionality of a long-standing Massachusetts law prohibiting corporate spending on ballot initiatives that were unrelated to the company's business. The bank wished to spend money to defeat a proposed state tax increase, but was prohibited from lobbying against it as a corporate entity. The Massachusetts court had upheld the state law prohibiting corporate spending and the bank was now appealing to the Supreme Court to overturn the law as an unconstitutional violation of their free speech rights.

Unlike *Virginia Pharmacy,* this case divided the justices and led to heated debate. To the liberal justices, this case was a far cry from their decision to apply the First Amendment to *Virginia Pharmacy* to protect the poor and sick from hidden drug prices; it was another matter altogether to protect bank lobbyists from limits imposed on them by state legislators. When Chief Justice Burger tried to assign the majority opinion to Justice Brennan, he was surprised when Brennan demurred, writing in a court memo that he did not agree with the majority in the case. Powell, who saw no difference between this case and *Virginia Pharmacy*, responded to Brennan's memo by writing "Wow!" on the margin. Brennan, who had been appointed by Republican president Dwight Eisenhower but who often sided with the liberals in court decisions, reasoned that corporations were creatures of state law and as such could be regulated by the states; therefore, the majority's decision to overturn the Massachusetts law would be disruptive to a majority of states.

Liberal justices White and Marshall also refused to stretch the *Virginia Pharmacy* ruling to undercut state law. Although they maintained that corporate speech was "within the scope of the First Amendment," the speech at issue in the case was not the type of speech the First Amendment was meant to protect. Massachusetts law prohibiting political spending was about "preventing institutions which have been permitted to amass wealth as a result of special advantages extended by the state for certain economic purposes from using that wealth to acquire an unfair advantage in the political process." In other words, the state had a right to regulate an entity it had created in the first place. The state need not "permit its own creation to consume it."[27]

Rehnquist, for his part, having already raised red flags in his *Virginia Pharmacy* dissent, raised them again, this time with feeling. Not only was the Court returning to the bad old days of Lochner, but it was encroaching on states' rights. Thirty other state legislatures had passed similar laws. Was it not the height of judicial activism for the Court to wave away the people's laws? The Court had gone too far, in his view, in breaking with a consensus of the majority of so many state and federal governments that had restricted such speech. For good measure, Rehnquist also quoted the influential Chief Justice John Marshall, who had clearly distinguished the First Amendment rights of corporations from those of "natural persons."

In response to the hand-wringing of his colleagues, an unconcerned Powell demurred: too late! In a memo circulated among the justices before opinions were written, he wrote that, after the decision in *Virginia Pharmacy*, it was "too late to hold that persons who elect to do business in the corporate form may not express opinions through the corporation." If the Court turned back now, it "would be a most serious infringement of First Amendment rights."[28] In his memo, Powell wrote that corporations were the real victims of the changes in American culture; he had come to the Court to fight for them, and his colleagues had given him an opening in *Virginia*

Pharmacy. It was a checkmate case for Powell, on a strategy that went beyond just the facts of the case. Powell wrote the majority opinion, joined by Burger, Stewart, Blackmun, and the newest associate justice, John Paul Stevens. Powell argued that the question in the case wasn't whether corporations had First Amendment rights—on this score, he stated explicitly, there was "no question"—but rather how far those rights extended. Powell's response was: pretty far. Citing his argument in *Buckley* that the distinction between corporations and people was "*wholly foreign*" to the First Amendment, Powell wrote that the speech at issue in the case "is at the heart of the First Amendment."[29] In other words, not only was a bank's political donation to defeat a state tax protected by the First Amendment, it was the *express purpose* of the First Amendment.

Three years later, in *Central Hudson Gas and Electric Co. v. Public Service Commission of New York* (1980), Powell had yet another chance to drag the Court further down the path of corporate free speech. The case concerned a state ban on ads promoting electricity use, which was imposed amid the oil shocks that had sent prices soaring and after President Jimmy Carter's request that Americans reduce consumption. Central Hudson Gas challenged the ban as a violation of its right to free speech. The Court took the case, Burger assigned the opinion to Powell, and despite heavy criticism from his colleagues on the bench, moved the Court, the law, and the nation closer toward an interpretation of the First Amendment as a shield for corporations to protect against state laws. Powell's opinion stated that the "First Amendment's concern for commercial speech is based on the informational function of advertising."[30] This was the framework that had been used by Nader and Morrison in *Virginia Pharmacy.*

Rehnquist again strongly dissented, reiterating many of his prior warnings: that the Court had unlocked a Pandora's box by "elevating" commercial speech to the level of traditional political speech; and that by accepting and codifying market supremacy, the Court had "gone far to resurrect the discredited doctrine of cases such as *Lochner.*" Rehnquist reminded the Court that "in a democracy, the economy is subordinate to the political, a lesson that our ancestors learned long ago, and that our descendants will undoubtedly have to relearn for many years hence."[31]

What Powell knew—and what Rehnquist would soon learn—was that the economic *was* political. As Powell had said in his 1971 memo to the Chamber of Commerce, the judiciary is the "most important instrument for social, economic and political change," and he had come to change it.[32] The Court's corporate speech decisions would allow a minority of Americans to use their wealth to shape democracy, even as the authors of those decisions, who sat in the "citadel of the public justice and the public security," purported to serve the majority.[33]

The effects were not immediate, but gradually elections became fund-raising contests in which the wealthiest Americans exerted immense power. After *Buckley v. Valeo*, the total amount spent on presidential campaigns rose precipitously: from $20 million total in 1960 to $107 million in 1980, $186 million in 1992, $300 million in 2000, and $696 million in 2004. In 2008, Barack Obama and John McCain spent $1 billion combined, which paled in comparison to 2016 (over $2 billion between the two candidates), which itself paled in comparison to 2020, when a ludicrous $14.4 billion was spent between the two candidates.[34] These staggering numbers for presidential races (and just for the two candidates who won the major parties' primaries) do not account for Senate, House, or state legislature races, or for the many corporate-sponsored ballot initiatives across the country. And these figures do not include undisclosed donations, or "dark money," which are technically—thanks to the Supreme Court's 2010 decision in *Citizens United v. Federal Election Commission*—not part of the official campaign. The stratospheric rise in spending has undoubtedly changed the American political system.

With one hand the Court cleared away all constraints on political spending by wealthy donors and groups (*Buckley*); with the other, it extended free speech protection to corporations (*Virginia Pharmacy, Bellotti, Central Hudson Gas,* and *Citizens United*). Given the rightward drift of the Court and the precedents set by Powell, the decision in *Citizens United*, which eliminated the last barriers safeguarding our democracy from the corrupting influence of money, was an inevitability. Thereafter, American politics would witness the rise of not only dark money, but "soft money" (funds used for general party-building or issue advocacy rather than supporting a candidate directly, and not subject to the same regulations as "hard money") and corporation-funded and -sponsored laws. When Oliver Wendell Holmes had explained the value of free speech to our democracy by invoking the "marketplace of ideas," he was deploying a metaphor. Now, it is the actual market that decides what ideas shape our democracy.

Opening the spigot of political donations by corporations and the wealthy has naturally increased their influence on elections, but it has also, perhaps less predictably, increased the influence of corporations and the wealthy on the Supreme Court itself. In 2014, Harvard Law professor John Coates analyzed every Supreme Court decision involving a corporation and a right to speech, assembly, or press from 1946 to 2014. He found that before *Virginia Pharmacy,* businesses only won 20 percent of First Amendment cases; afterward, they won 55 percent.[35] Even more important, all the cases before *Virginia Pharmacy* were about "expressive speech," such as opinions or views expressed in newspapers and in media; after the decision, the speech protected by the First Amendment was primarily "nonexpressive"—or commercial—speech. According to Coates, the use of the First Amendment to protect this kind of speech was "not simply a New Lochnerism," as Rehnquist had it; rather, by employing the First Amendment to achieve deregulatory goals, the Court was doing "what economists call 'rent seeking,' or in more legal language, socially wasteful transfers, or in ordinary language, theft, waste and graft."[36] Just as the Powell era did not merely revive Lochnerism, the neoliberal era was not merely a revival of neoclassical economics (a broad theory centered on production and consumption), as is sometimes claimed. Whereas laissez-faire doctrine of the Gilded Age essentially meant government nonintervention, neoliberalism was defined by extreme intervention on behalf of business. As corporate lawyer Powell instructed in his 1971 memo and Justice Powell demonstrated, the Court would be deployed to protect business from activist courts.

Projecting fears of judicial activism, President Nixon appointed a revolutionary to the Court.

Such was Powell's legacy. In his chamber memo he urged his readers to fight for the real victim, the forgotten businessman, and to do so "without embarrassment and without reluctance."[37] On the Court, he was showing them how it was done.

UNDER THE BURGER COURT, the free speech protections of the First Amendment were remade into a shield for corporations with long-lasting repercussions. Yet it was in the equal protection cases where Powell's covert jurisprudence was in full display. The Court took racial discrimination cases purporting to determine the parameters of the right to equal protection, but in each instance, the spirit of the law was slowly gutted and replaced with mere formality. Powell worked with a scalpel in these cases to make civil rights laws moot by making the Constitution color-blind for the first time in the nation's history.

In 1971, before Powell and Rehnquist joined, the Burger Court had decided a challenge to Title VII of the Civil Rights Act prohibiting employment discrimination in *Griggs v. Duke Power Co.* Black employees accused North Carolina–based Duke Power of discrimination. The company had ninety-five employees, fourteen of whom were Black. All the Black employees worked in the "labor" division of the company, where the highest salary was lower than the lowest salary in any of the other four divisions. On July 3, 1964, the day after Title VII was passed, Duke Power instituted a new policy: Only employees who passed a variety of "aptitude" and "IQ" tests could work in a department other than the labor unit. White employees passed the tests at a rate ten times that of Black employees.

Proving intentional racism in a court of law is, in general, incredibly difficult. The Black employees would have needed to show a statement of intent or an articulated policy that only white employees could be hired at positions above a certain salary. Given the suspicious timing and the company's past discriminatory policies, it was obvious to anyone willing to admit it that the tests were a pretense. The lower courts agreed that this was clear discrimination.

The nine justices of the Supreme Court sided with the employees, too. In a unanimous ruling, the Court held that the Civil Rights Act prohibited actions that created a "disparate impact" on minorities even if the action was racially neutral. The decision was authored by Burger, who opined that, because of the country's history of racism, exclusion, and segregated schooling, there were certain metrics and requirements that would have an "adverse impact" on minority applicants and were therefore unconstitutional despite the purported neutrality of the requirement. "Good intent or absence of discriminatory intent" did not redeem procedures that operated as "built-in headwinds for minority groups."[38] Rather than mandating equal treatment of all parties, civil rights laws recognizing this history of inequality allowed business to seek "equal results" instead. Recognizing that historic discrimination had created present-day inequalities at the "starting line," the Court decided that institutions would have to take account of race until equality was achieved.

The Burger Court's *Griggs* ruling—which was also applied to school segregation cases—became very useful in challenging the most pernicious kind of discrimination, the "race-neutral" policies that disproportionately harmed African Americans. It should not be surprising, then, that Powell, who had employed such policies himself when he was on the Virginia school board, had *Griggs* in his sights when he joined the Court a few years later.

The case that would give him his chance was *Washington v. Davis* in 1976. Black applicants sued the Washington, D.C., police department for discrimination based on aptitude tests that Blacks failed at a rate four times higher than whites. The U.S. Court of Appeals, following the *Griggs* precedent, ruled in favor of the Black defendants. The police department appealed to the Supreme Court. In the federal judicial system, appellants aren't able to appeal to the Supreme Court as a matter of right; rather, the prospective appellant has to file a petition with the Court. If four members of the Court believe a lower court decision warrants review, the Court grants a writ of certiorari ("cert"), teeing up briefs, oral argument, and an eventual ruling. Otherwise, it allows the lower court decision to stand.

Because *Griggs* was such a recent precedent, overturning the appellate court decision based on a new constitutional interpretation of equal protection would be widely denounced as judicial activism. The "pool memo"—a summary of the potential cases before the Court that helps make their selection or denial by the justices easier—described the *Washington* case as "arguably consistent with some of *Griggs*," but noted that perhaps the police department had a better case than Duke Power because the tests in question were verbal, and "everyone seems to admit that verbal skills are job related in nature."[39] (This pool memo happened to be written by a Burger clerk named Kenneth W. Starr, whose Starr Report led to President Clinton's impeachment two decades later.) The Court decided to hear arguments in *Washington v. Davis* in 1976, with the conservative justices surely hoping to somehow limit *Griggs*.

Powell found a way to go much further. Or, rather, one of his clerks, Christina B. Whitman—now a professor of law at the University of Michigan—did, figuring out a technical end run around *Griggs* that would limit it to a narrow set of cases. Because the *Washington* case had appeared in the District of Columbia before Congress had applied Title VII to local governments, the discrimination claim arose under the Fourteenth Amendment's equal protection guarantee. *Griggs* was a Title VII case—so, technically, the Court was not bound by *Griggs* when considering *Washington*. Whitman suggested remanding the case back to the lower court to be argued based on Title VII rather than "constitutionalize *Griggs* and Title VII *sub silentio*," noting that this was "a drastic move."[40] Powell wrote "yes" in the margin of the memo. It was drastic because it meant that the case would have to be retried starting at the trial court level, which would be expensive and time-consuming. It was drastic because everyone assumed that *Griggs* had been decided on equal protection grounds, and that it was about how racial discrimination could be proved according to the Constitution and not just in a tiny sliver of Title VII employment cases. It was drastic because it was such a small technicality—the case would have been a Title VII case but for the unique status of the District of Columbia as a local government.

No one—not Starr, not the justices who wrote *Griggs*, not plaintiffs nor defendants or lower courts—had even considered that *Griggs* applied only to Title VII cases and not to any discrimination claim brought under the Fourteenth Amendment. Justice Blackmun had even written the justices after oral arguments that the case was "not difficult" and "not important" because there was no issue, meaning that they had already decided the issue in *Griggs*.

For his part, Justice Brennan told his colleagues what they already knew—that there is "no difference between Equal Protection" and Title VII. But Powell had found a difference—a minor, technical loophole—that would affect all future plaintiffs trying to prove discrimination without a smoking gun.

The fact that the Court was determining an issue that no one had brought up at trial, but that had been concocted by Powell, was no obstacle. The Court waved away the procedural question by arguing that it was correcting an error by the lower court, which is usually reserved for egregious mistakes. The majority determined, in *Washington*, that disparate impact did not apply to cases brought under the Fourteenth Amendment while acknowledging that "there are some indications to the contrary in our cases." From that point forward, plaintiffs could not show, for example, how facially neutral policies caused disparate impact in death penalty cases, prisoner disenfranchisement, or any other place where racism lived on. When a lawyer named Clarence Thomas became the chairman of the Equal Employment Opportunity Commission during the Reagan administration, he would even attack the use of disparate impact in Title VII cases of employment discrimination. The Court would finally overrule *Griggs* once Thomas took Thurgood Marshall's seat on the Court after the latter's retirement.

Although it would prove to have far-reaching consequences, *Washington v. Davis* wasn't Powell's first opportunity to short-circuit antidiscrimination laws. In 1973, during Powell's first year as a justice, the Burger Court heard a series of school desegregation cases. At issue in the first, *Keyes v. School District No.1*, was whether the city of Denver's "placement testing" plan—which had been imposed to keep schools segregated—was in violation of *Brown*. The key question for the Court was: Was *Brown* limited to de jure segregation or did it invalidate de facto segregation, too?

While de jure segregation (laws explicitly designating schools white or Black, which had all but disappeared by the 1970s) was clearly prohibited by *Brown*, de facto segregation (laws, tests, or practices that were on their face neutral but that led to segregation) was easy to design for districts that wished to resist the spirit of *Brown*. In *Keyes,* the Court ruled that de facto segregation also violated equal protection, but it evaded the issue of busing—the practice of forcing students to take transportation either within or outside of their district to diversify schools. Powell, who preferred to persuade his colleagues behind closed doors rather than throw bombs in solo-authored dissents like Rehnquist did, joined the majority after failing to convince them in this case. He did, however, write a separate opinion expressing "profound misgivings" with "large-scale or long-distance transportation of students in . . . metropolitan school districts."

In *Milliken v. Bradley*, decided in 1974, Solicitor General Robert Bork defended the state of Michigan's redistricting plan as compliant with *Brown*. The NAACP had challenged the state's desegregation program for fifty-three segregated schools, which, it argued, had in fact *increased* segregation. Bork argued that judicial "disruption" in "local affairs" was unwarranted because there was no intent to segregate.[41] Like *Keyes*, the case hinged on questions of de jure versus de facto segregation.

The Court now ruled that de facto segregation was not unconstitutional, with Powell casting the deciding vote for the majority. Although Powell hoped to be assigned to the opinion, Burger decided to write it himself. Nevertheless, Powell was able to exert his influence on its reasoning. Whereas Burger wished to focus on the goal of achieving "racial balance," Powell insisted that the Court take Bork's position: that any remedy must be limited to the de jure constitutional violation. Powell got what he wanted—which meant no busing, no state responsibility for segregation, and complete local control. He was keenly aware that his position would be controversial. His papers reveal the great effort he took to draft a "scholarly, restrained, and carefully crafted" opinion so as not to be attacked by the "eastern media."[42] By "eastern media," Powell likely meant "the public," or at least that portion of it that had cheered the *Brown* decision.

Powell's majority in *Milliken* gave Nixon exactly what he'd hoped for when the now disgraced former president had selected the Virginian. The Court effectively halted busing programs by ruling that *Brown* did not require "any particular racial balance in each school district." Justice Marshall's dissent called the ruling "a giant step backward" that denied "our children, whatever their race," the right to "an equal start in life and to an equal opportunity to reach their full potential as citizens." Marshall's dissent apparently "infuriated Powell."[43] Perhaps it was because, despite the careful effort Powell made to couch his reactionary position in a technical and scholarly opinion, Marshall saw through it, calling the holding "a reflection of a perceived public mood that we have gone far enough in enforcing the Constitution's guarantee of equal justice than it is the product of neutral principles of law."[44] The upshot of *Milliken* was a hamstrung school integration movement. Redlining and white flight had created residential segregation—and, thus, de facto school segregation. *Milliken* foreclosed remedies to address this type of inequity.

Powell's most consequential ruling was in 1973, through *San Antonio Independent School District v. Rodriguez*, where he once again cast the crucial swing vote. The case was brought by a group of parents who argued that the state of Texas's unequal allocation of funds between neighboring schools violated the Fourteenth Amendment's equal protection clause. The lower courts had determined that the funding disparities were wide—one school spent almost $400 more per pupil than the other. These disparities resulted in dilapidated conditions for the school serving poorer, predominantly minority students while the majority white school had more teachers, books, equipment, and facilities.

The latter school was located in the wealthy Alamo Heights neighborhood, which had home values eight times those in the Edgewood district, which was served by the majority minority school. (Despite the elevated values of their homes, the white residents paid significantly *less* in property tax than minority homeowners in Edgewood, thanks to the state's property tax scheme linking tax liabilities to the number of children in schools—Alamo Heights had 5,000 children compared to Edgewood's 22,000.) Edgewood parents had urged their district to levy more taxes and had attempted to raise money for their schools through issuing bonds, but lower home values and incomes in Edgewood translated to higher interest bonds, yet another example of de facto harm or disparate impact, bolstering their case for a remedy.

Powell's reasoning in *San Antonio* tracked with neoliberal theories of poor people in the ghetto and the Global South. Which is to say, it was built on abstract ideas of capitalism and competition that bore no resemblance to the real world. Sure, in theory Edgewood parents could "innovate" (a word Powell actually used) and move toward improving the school district, but the bond market would always see what the economic theorists would not: that Edgewood families were poor, which meant they would have to pay higher interest, which meant costlier loans. It was a vicious cycle that was connected to a legacy of racist laws. From 1934 to 1968, between 96 and 99 percent of all home mortgages were guaranteed by the Federal Housing Administration, which imposed de jure racial segregation across America. To ensure that neighborhoods would stay homogeneously white, most home sales included racial covenants, legal mandates that attached to the property itself and that mandated that the home could not be sold to nonwhite persons. Covenants were another instance of de jure segregation, which led to the supposedly de facto all-white neighborhoods marked by wealth borne of housing subsidies, as well as minority neighborhoods with underfunded schools and depressed housing markets. And although the 1968 Fair Housing Act had finally prohibited de jure racial segregation in housing, it persisted thanks to *Village of Euclid v. Ambler Realty Co.* (1926). "Euclidean" zoning continues to allow cities to maintain de facto segregation by, for example, demarcating zones restricted to single-family homes from the "nuisance" of multidwelling buildings and apartment buildings.[45] The long legacy of legally enforced segregation could not be remedied without considering the actual effects of segregation. For the *San Antonio* plaintiffs or any of the other communities living in segregated and underfunded communities, a remedy would have to include actual considerations of the effects of segregation—it was impossible to cure de jure segregation without de facto remedies. It was hairsplitting nonsense to even distinguish between cause (de jure) and effect (de facto), but that is exactly the kind of analysis that had earned Powell his place on the court. This absolute formal adherence to the text would become a foundational pillar of the Federalist Society (that organization will be discussed in the next chapter), but it was innovated in decisions like *San Antonio* to evade the purpose of *Brown* without technically overturning it. Powell's jurisprudence on segregation was a master class in using the letter of the law to defeat its spirit. The false division between de jure and de facto in the law, which still stands in the way of economic equality, is the Burger Court's legacy.

Powell persuaded four justices to join him and to pivot away from their prior rulings, which looked to the de facto outcome or "disparate impact," and to focus instead on abstract rights. Powell of course understood how de facto segregation could achieve the same effects as de jure segregation and had arguably earned his place on the Court for his ingenuity in crafting just such a plan in Richmond. He also understood that wealth translated directly to educational outcomes. In his *Keyes* opinion and in his briefs opposing busing and school integration, Powell had reasoned that "the socioeconomic status of children (white or black) is the single most relevant factor in determining the success of schools," which, he stated, meant that "mixing the races in schools" would not have "any significant effect" on education quality.[46] The Edgewood parents effectively agreed with Powell and proposed that, instead of busing or integrating kids, the city "integrate" its tax dollars. Yet Powell conveniently ignored what he knew about these dynamics.

Powell's majority opinion held that, first, there was no constitutional right to education, and, second, equal protection did not apply to disparities that had to do with wealth, even when there were clear racial dimensions to the disparity. Ignoring the facts of the case, his own previous arguments, and the reality that race and wealth inequality were often linked together, Powell resorted to abstractions. He argued for the benefits of "local control" that would provide "the freedom to devote more money to the education of one's children." He urged the poor parents to "innovate" and "compete" for "educational excellence," conveniently overlooking the facts the parents presented showing their multiple efforts at competing and innovating for more funds. Texas had not "purposefully segregated" schools, mused Powell, but had devised "an enlightened approach" to a problem that had "no perfect solution."[47]

The case, whose outcome would have been very different without Powell's interventions, shaped the future of public education in America, conferring constitutionality on school disparities pegged to residential segregation and barring claims based on socioeconomic status from constitutional attention. In the years since *San Antonio,* not only has school segregation *increased*, but so have the disparities in home values. By ignoring the reality of racism in economic and educational inequality, Powell cut out the substance of the *Brown* decision without alerting the "eastern media" that *Brown* had basically been overturned.

POWELL CREATED another constitutional shield in *Bakke* in 1978. The case, which concerned affirmative action, was brought by a white candidate who had been rejected from the UC Davis medical school, which reserved sixteen places each year for members of a "minority group" and the "economically disadvantaged." Four members of the Court—Brennan, Marshall, White, and Blackmun—would have upheld affirmative action while Burger, Rehnquist, Stewart, and Stevens would have found it illegal. Powell was the swing justice who determined the case—and the future of affirmative action. The case resulted in eight separate opinions, with Powell writing for two different majorities. He joined the conservatives in holding that affirmative action violated the equal protection clause of the Constitution because only a "compelling state interest" justified "discrimination" based on race, and affirmative action didn't meet that bar. In the other majority, Powell joined the liberals in upholding the affirmative action program but in a way quite different from what anyone, including UC Davis, his colleagues, or even former president Nixon, had contemplated. He decided that universities had a right to "educational diversity valued by the First Amendment"; they could not use quotas and must treat "each applicant as an individual," but they could use race and other "plus" factors to achieve "beneficial educational pluralism."[48]

Powell's decision has been frequently characterized as an exception to the Burger Court's retrenchment on civil rights. Even critics have championed *Bakke* as "a Solomonic decision," which, according to Anthony Lewis of *The New York Times,* proved the "unique quality" of the Burger Court. The decision appeared to be a victory for liberals, enough so that Bork, whom Reagan would nominate for Powell's seat upon the latter's retirement, called the justices supporting UC Davis's affirmative action scheme "hard-core racists of reverse discrimination."[49]

But in splitting the baby in *Bakke,* Powell gutted the purpose of affirmative action while leaving most people thinking he hadn't. Like the other rulings in Powell's quietly devastating oeuvre, his decision in *Bakke* undercut progress by holding that remedying past discrimination violated the Constitution's mandate of equal protection. In so ruling, Powell undermined the bedrock principle on which all racial justice programs—however weak or limited—had been built.

John Marshall, the longest reigning chief justice of the Court, had stripped indigenous tribes of all property rights, reasoning in the 1823 case *Johnson v. McIntosh* that they were "savages . . . with whom it was impossible to mix." The Constitution was clear, said Chief Justice Roger Taney thirty-four years later in *Dred Scott v. Sandford*: "the enslaved African race were not intended to be included." To Powell, this history was irrelevant. There was, according to him, "no principled basis for deciding which groups would merit" judicial scrutiny. He found it illogical that "those whose societal injury is thought to exceed some arbitrary level of tolerability then would be entitled to preferential classifications at the expense of individuals belonging to other groups." Just as "rich" and "poor" were meaningless, and there was no basis to distinguish between corporate commercial speech and human speech, the difference between Black and white in America was arbitrary. In his opinion with the conservatives, Powell even floated the novel idea that whites could also be minorities. He stated that the "white majority" is made up of various ethnicities that, if divided out based on nationality, would in fact yield "a new minority of white Anglo-Saxon Protestants."

In *Bakke*, Powell not only made it exceptionally difficult for any law seeking to remedy historic discrimination to pass muster. He also took a swipe at the kind of evidence that had been used by the Warren Court to reverse Jim Crow. In a clear reference to the Court's reliance on academic studies in the *Brown* decision, Powell decried laws based on the "kind of *variable* sociological and political analysis necessary to produce such rankings." Blinded to race, ignorant of social science, Powell urged plurality and diversity.[50]

As a lawyer for the NAACP, Thurgood Marshall had worked for decades to persuade the Supreme Court to overturn the *Plessy v. Ferguson* precedent sanctioning the inhumane legal segregation of Jim Crow. As a colleague of Powell on the Supreme Court, Marshall witnessed firsthand as those hard-won civil rights were eviscerated. Marshall explained that the "legacy of years of slavery and of years of second-class citizenship in the wake of emancipation could not be so easily eliminated." It had only been a decade since the passage of the civil rights laws and, still, too little had changed. "Measured by any benchmark of comfort or achievement, meaningful equality remains a distant dream for the Negro." All of this, as Powell himself knew, was on account of economic disadvantage, which was, Marshall said, an "inevitable consequence of centuries of unequal treatment.... For it must be remembered that, during most of the past 200 years, the Constitution as interpreted by this Court did not prohibit the most ingenious and pervasive forms of discrimination against the Negro." He noted the irony and cynicism of the *Bakke* decision: "now, when a state acts to remedy the effects of that legacy of discrimination, I cannot believe that this same Constitution stands as a barrier."[51]

THE JUSTICES who had decided unanimously in *Brown* were derided as "judicial activists" by the reactionary right, yet those same critics were strangely quiet as the Burger Court radically transformed the meaning of the Constitution. In just two Court terms, Nixon's justices had put on blindfolds and managed to effectively overturn *Brown*. Powell and his colleagues' deliberate ignorance of racism and inequality prevented the Court from hearing the demands of justice.

The long fight to end race-based discrimination had begun during the Reconstruction era. Almost a hundred years and many fights later, the Court, in *Brown*, had finally made good on the Fourteenth Amendment. Although Nixon's own four horsemen—Warren Burger, Harry Blackman, William Rehnquist, and Lewis Powell—left the formal laws standing, they challenged their meaning, the history on which they were built, and their effects on the world. The programs that remained, like affirmative action, were rerationalized using formalistic arguments based on a neutral, race-blind doctrine that amounted, effectively, to a sentiment not unlike "All Rights Matter."

Many of the cases on racial inequality the Burger Court selected to hear were pleas from white "victims" of racial injustice. Not only that, but the conservative majority used the same amendments and constitutional provisions that had secured gains for Black Americans to claw those gains back. For the Burger Court, equal protection meant interpreting the Constitution as color-blind for the first time in American history, effectively cutting off legal remedies to past wrongs. If war protesters had free speech protections, that meant corporations did, too. If Black students got special attention, so too should whites. Nixon's "strict constructionists" slipped a straitjacket over the Court's ability to see the difference between rich and poor, corporation and human, justice and law.

Just as the macroeconomic models of Milton Friedman and Gary Becker erased the actual history of racism, so too did the ideals of equal protection and free speech ignore actual differences in power. Lewis Powell tilted the scales of justice imperceptibly but surely toward the powerful by building a case law with allegiance to an abstract and idealized Constitution that bore a striking resemblance to the abstract and idealized market of economic theories. By blinding justice to the reality of discrimination and wealth disparity, the Court's power not only left those inequalities unremedied, but amplified them.

CHAPTER 5

The Legal Coup

*God hath made us ministers not of the letter, but of the
spirit. For the letter killeth, but the spirit giveth life.*
—2 CORINTHIANS 3:6

MANY OF THE pillars of neoliberal economics—the theories developed and promulgated by members of the Mont Pelerin Society—have been discredited by events, primary among them the 2008 financial crisis (which I discuss in detail below). Yet neoliberal ideas refuse to die, a phenomenon commentators have called *zombie economics*. Among these undead ideas are the standard neoclassical economic models: the efficient market hypothesis, trickle-down economics, deregulation, and privatization. According to critics of zombie economics, these ideas need to be replaced with new and better "living ideas," like democratic socialism, progressive taxation, and Keynesian fiscal stimulus. But, as this chapter argues, the zombie that walks and stalks the land is not in fact neoclassical economics, but rather the law. Specifically, by dint of the neoliberal capture of the American legal system, Americans are beholden to a dead Constitution, one that is continually being mobilized against its own intended aims.

As progressive reformers faced off against the Lochner court's formalism, President Woodrow Wilson warned of the tyranny of a petrified Constitution. The Constitution must evolve to deal with changing in times, said Wilson, in "recognition of the fact that a nation is a living thing and not a machine." The pragmatistic and progressive strain of Supreme Court jurisprudence, which extends from Oliver Wendell Holmes in the Progressive Era to the Warren Court, has been called *living constitutionalism*, a reference to these jurists' dynamic and adaptive interpretation of the Constitution.

With the neoliberal legal revolution, however, came a new dominant interpretive paradigm: a revival of the formalist natural law that placed the discretion inherent in judicial decision making outside of the law, either to the coded meaning inherent to the text (*textualism*) as or to the invisible hand of the market (Law and Economics).

Formalism can indeed yield consistency and uniformity and scientific precision, but justice requires something more. To evade the law is to reject its demands, but to use the law against justice is to empty it of meaning. Justice requires discretion or judgment, ineffable qualities that cannot be made into staid categories. Prudence, wisdom, and common sense are fuzzy values, unscientific and hard to prove, which can make courts vulnerable to accusations of bias and subjectivity. The allure of textualism and Law and Economics was their false promise of consistency and objectivity. But justice requires something beyond categorical knowledge—something closer to *wisdom*.

As this chapter will show, the purported neutrality of formalist doctrines like textualism and Law and Economics was how the right was able to transform the law during the neoliberal revolution. Formalism promises simplicity of use and consistency in application—a holy grail of sorts for the judicial system. However, just like the fantasy of pure market capitalism, it is a mirage. Not only have formalist legal doctrines not been used consistently, their cumulative effect has been to turn the law into an empty husk: all words and no meaning. This transformation of the law was nothing short of a revolution, but it was not fought in the arena of democracy; rather, it was a coup led by a small group of interested parties, without juries or votes. Regime change occurred quietly, though not in secret: over the last three decades, hundreds of law professors, lawyers, judges, and regulators slowly shifted the tectonic plates on which American society sits.

This chapter discusses two branches of neoliberal legal theory, originalism/textualism and efficiency/cost-benefit analysis, advanced by two distinct but overlapping networks of legal scholars, the Federalist Society and the Law and Economics network. These legal theories constitute the intellectual foundation of the neoliberal revolution in the law. Introduced at the top of the legal food chain—by legal scholars at elite law schools—these purportedly neutral doctrines have trickled down into textbooks, political debates, and court decisions, becoming the invisible substructure of U.S. jurisprudence. By seeping into the fulcrum of justice—the scale where laws are balanced—and tipping it toward a certain outcome, neoliberalism has achieved a legal coup.

Legal theory, or *jurisprudence*, refers to the underlying philosophy guiding decisions in the law. As between two interpretations of a given law, how should a court choose? Many law students are taught the importance of legal theory through a hypothetical scenario about a law mandating "no vehicles in the park"; they are asked to consider an ambiguity: Would the law prohibit, for example, a motorcycle, an ambulance, a hoverboard, or a parade float? When a law is susceptible to different meanings and interpretations and a judge has discretion, what arguments can be used to tip the scale on the balance? What "framework," "procedure," "method," or "rubric" can a jurist or a lawyer use in making their case? Should a court decide whether a vehicle is permitted using polls about how the population defines a vehicle or should a court use only a dictionary in deciding? Does it matter what the lawmakers had in mind when prohibiting vehicles from the park in the first place? Should an *economic* argument about the efficiency of allowing motorcycles in parks matter to a court? In other words, when it comes to arguing cases, what are the rules of the game?

Such questions are the domain of legal theory. Legal theories are the abstract ideas and philosophies that shape judicial decisions, the *ideologies* that influence the fulcrum that tips the scales of justice. The "vehicle in the park" hypothetical was in fact the hypothetical issue at the center of a series of influential exchanges beginning in 1958 between two of the most prominent legal theorists of the twentieth century, H. L. A. Hart and Lon L. Fuller. Hart used the hypothetical situation of a tricycle in the park to demonstrate that in many cases, the words of the law were enough for a judge to make a decision. There was no need to look to the intent of the law, its history, or its theoretical underpinnings; all one had to do was look at the plain meaning of the law to decide that a tricycle was not a vehicle. Laws could be valid and clear regardless of their provenance. But the choice of hypothetical can shift the debate. Fuller did not like the tricycle example, so he changed the scenario, using a different kind of vehicle: in his hypothetical, a group of war protesters mounting a military truck passed through the park as part of their demonstration. According to Fuller, it *did* matter whether the park had issued the law to prevent this act of free speech, which in his view would make the law prohibiting vehicles invalid because it violated a greater principle. Fuller's point was that law had to be rooted in morality and when it wasn't, even those provisions of the law that seemed neutral were invalid. Morality had to be the higher-order principle legitimatizing the law; immoral laws were invalid laws.

Hart and Fuller weren't really talking about vehicles. In fact, the debate emerged from a much more pressing political and moral issue: the validity of Nazi laws. The actual case that led Hart to propose the vehicle hypothetical concerned a German woman who was having an affair but was inconveniently married at the time. Per Nazi antisedition laws, she turned her husband in for his privately made comments disparaging Hitler, a crime punishable by death. The Nazis did not kill the husband but sent him to fight in the war. Upon his return, and understandably angry, he wished to have his wife charged with a crime of "illegally depriving another of his freedom," a law that was in effect when the "crime" occurred but was not a Nazi law. Did the wife commit a crime by following a code of law imposed by an immoral regime? The court said yes and convicted the woman because, although the Nazi laws were valid, they were immoral, or "contrary to the sound of conscience and the sense of justice of all decent human beings." Both Hart and Fuller believed the Nazi laws to be immoral and invalid, but if that was the case and the wife was committing a crime while following an immoral law, how far could that principle extend? And who is to decide? The choice of hypothetical matters. While it's one thing to dismiss all Nazi laws as invalid, what about laws that are not so straightforwardly immoral like a ban on vehicles in the park? What if a justice believes abortion—or taxes—to be immoral? Pull at the thread of law's legitimacy and watch the edifice of rule of law in a modern democracy crumble.

In fact, it is likely that the existential moral and legal crisis underlying the debate was a case decided much closer to home a year before the Hart/Fuller debate: *Brown v. Board of Education*, decided just a few years before the Hart/Fuller debate, involved a similar existential challenge to rule of law. "No Black students in white schools" was a clear law similar to "no vehicles in the park" and many southern jurists were inflamed by the Supreme Court's clear flouting of their long-standing laws. Was an immoral law to be followed just for the sake of precedent? The Warren Court invalidated the entire Jim Crow legal order by deeming it harmful in a triumph of living constitutionalism over formalism. The legal realists of the Warren Court refused to grant the formal law authority if it did not suit society. Although the Warren Court did not analogize to Nazi law, the precedent was in the ether. In fact, Jim Crow laws in America provided a blueprint for the Nazis in drafting the Nuremberg laws.[1] As the proponents of *Brown* saw it, the American legal system had justified a string of moral wrongs that could no longer be tolerated regardless of their validity as formal law. The nation's system of value had evolved, and its laws must follow that evolution.

Those who oppose changes to long-standing laws, including racial segregation, often find refuge in a fixed set of unchangeable formal laws whose violations, they warn, will inevitably lead to cultural decay. The Marshall and Taney Courts, which lasted from 1801 to 1864, held to "universal" principles of rights to deny property rights to nonwhites. These universal rights stemmed from John Locke's theory of natural rights emanating from a fixed source—the Creator, or Reason, or some other unchanging moral principle. The Black person's enslavement was not up to him, Chief Justice Taney explained in the 1957 *Dred Scott* decision, because Black people "had *no rights* which the white man was bound to respect." Because of this fixed and natural law, Blacks were "*justly* and *lawfully* reduced to slavery *for his benefit.*" White men's rights to land, women, and all the world's people and resources were "natural," "endowed by their creator"—universal and immutable.

Yet time rends all doctrines. The law oppressed and enslaved because men in power, beholden to racist ideologies, wrote those laws—or so said abolitionists and prominent legal realists like Oliver Wendell Holmes and Louis Brandeis. "The common law is not a brooding omnipresence in the sky," said Holmes, "but the articulate voice of some sovereign . . . *that can be identified.*" The legal realist challenge to formalism was existential; legal realists rejected the law's claims to neutrality and objectivity, but also morality. Laws, by virtue of being laws, had no intrinsic moral value. Rather, laws reflect the politics, biases, values, and circumstances of the people and societies that make them. This does not invalidate the laws that were made, but it does mean that if society could be made better by changing the laws, judges should do it.

The Great Depression—in addition to the obstruction of New Deal reforms by the Lochner court—was the critical juncture that caused the final pillars of formalism to fall. Realist jurists like Holmes and Brandeis steered the law away from the Lochner court's insistence on property and liberty as "natural rights." Instead, they approached the law contextually, recognizing that the law should reflect reality and balance property rights, for example, with equality concerns. It was legal realism that made the progressive reforms of the New Deal possible.

Of course, as historical and contingent actors, legal realists too are susceptible to the biases of their time. Justice Holmes, for instance, spoke for the Supreme Court when he determined that eugenics was in the interest of "public welfare." The case, *Buck v. Bell*, concerned a destitute young woman who was sterilized against her will. In his opinion, Holmes announced that "it is better for all the world, if instead of waiting to execute degenerate offspring for crime, or to let them starve for their imbecility, society can prevent those who are manifestly unfit from continuing their kind." He concluded coolly, "Three generations of imbeciles are enough." All but one Supreme Court Justice, the lone Catholic on the Court, joined the decision.

In the aftermath of *Buck v. Bell*, several states imposed mandatory sterilizations of women deemed unfit to reproduce, a practice that was stopped only once these practices were adopted, almost wholesale, into the Third Reich's Nuremberg codes. The pseudo-scientific, "biologically based" racism that had justified eugenics and more was slowly abandoned. Though eugenics was the *law,* that did not mean eugenics was *moral*; this was the realists' point. The law was made by men, not God or some other infallible source—if the case was wrong, it should be overturned.

But if laws are made by men, and judges can modify or overrule laws based on their own proclivities—their ideas about fairness, their moods, their personal or cultural biases—then how can the fairness of the system in toto be guaranteed? Such was the gravamen of the critics of legal realism, who sought to retether legal reasoning to some fixed and unmovable principle. "We are governed by laws, not by the intentions of legislators," said Supreme Court Justice Antonin Scalia, alluding to realist judges looking for a law's meaning. "The text is the law, and it is the text that must be observed."[2] To Ronald Coase, a British-born economist who taught at the University of Chicago's law school, allocations of property rights by judges were "deviations" from the market's "spontaneous order" (in Hayek's terminology) of the market, and therefore unjustified. For these critics, the radical relativism opened up by legal realism was unacceptable and had to be challenged.

The new legal theories that arose to meet realism were textualism—which appealed to the sanctity of the legal text itself—and Law and Economics, which appealed to the new "science" of economics to ground its interpretations. Textualism and Law and Economics were two fronts of the reactionary right's battle against living constitutionalism, constraining the law against the forces of evolution through a revived formalism.

Originalism and its companion doctrine, textualism, root constitutional law to the "intent of the founders" and lesser laws to the "plain meaning of the text." For Scalia, arguably textualism's most sophisticated exponent, clearing up legal ambiguities was very simple: look "vehicle" up in the dictionary and then ask whether the "thing" in question—a skateboard, a tank, etc.—is a vehicle. In his own rendition of the famous hypothetical, Scalia chose the example of an ambulance. And because an ambulance is quite clearly a vehicle based on the dictionary definition of "vehicle," Scalia concluded the ambulance is prohibited. For Scalia, for whom every hard or complicated problem in the law had a simple, incontrovertible solution, the text is the law and no other argument can alter the written text. "Textualism, in its purest form," he wrote, "begins and ends with what the text says and fairly implies."[3] The same principle applies to the interpretation of the Constitution: jurists are to interpret the Constitution only as it was originally understood (hence the name "originalism").

Law and Economics is a legal theory that interprets legal ambiguities using market logic. For example, a Law and Economics analysis of our hypothetical would begin with the question "What is the definition of 'vehicle' that will produce the most economically *efficient* outcomes?" Because the market is always more efficient than government regulation, Law and Economics urges that statutes should be interpreted narrowly to allow the free market to work. "The utility of economics in statutory interpretation," writes the conservative jurist Richard Posner in his *Economic Analysis of Law*, is to remind "judges to watch out for interest groups" and to "not assume" that "every word in a statute" has a "distinct function."[4] Law and Economics is deeply skeptical of the process of democratic lawmaking, preferring instead the simple math of a cost-benefit analysis.

More than anything, Law and Economics resembled a revival of formalist property rights and liberty to contract, not because those natural "rights" were granted by the "creator," but because the laws of supply and demand were wiser and more knowing than human-led courts and interest-group-dominated legislators. Originalism and textualism, on the other hand, make idols of the writers of the Constitution, imbuing their dated words with authority above and beyond present conditions.

By locating the true meaning of a law either in an abstract principle or inert text, courts beholden to these doctrines can enact injustice while pointing to some object *other* than their own necessary judgment. Law was not being made and remade by a living and evolving society, but existed beyond human control, fixed and dead.

Though textualism and Law and Economics might seem to come from divergent presuppositions—textualists focus on meaning of the text itself while Law and Economics jurists treat the text as irredeemably compromised by interest-group politics—both approaches are the fruit of the right-wing strategy to infiltrate the legal academy with business-friendly ideas and scholars. Both theories restrict judicial discretion by forcing the law to submit to a higher authority—not morality but a fixed text or an unproven economic theory. Lewis Powell began to dismantle the Warren Court's jurisprudence haphazardly, but the law school takeover his memo inspired would do so methodically and would go much further in advancing the cause of protecting powerful corporate interests—Powell's "forgotten man"—against the justice system.

THE LEGAL COUP was accomplished largely by two institutions: the Federalist Society and the Law and Economics network, which promote textualism (originalism) and economic analysis, respectively. Both insist they are nonideological and that they exist simply to engender debate and scholarship, but their claims are undermined by their origins and funding and the consistency with which their pet methods produce right-wing outcomes.

Because both organizations are focused primarily on the legal academy and tend to gravitate toward elite law schools, their endeavor differs from that of right-wing lobbyists and think tanks. Rather than directly pushing policies and funding campaigns, their role is to legitimize right-wing ideas and disseminate them across the elite precincts—the judiciary and the regulatory state—that exercise legal and political power. These ideas move horizontally, among legal scholars or between economics departments and law schools, and vertically, from scholars to judges and regulators. Both the Federalist Society and Law and Economics host academic conferences, award young-scholars prizes, and work across institutions and disciplines. Scholars who are "affiliated" with the Federalist Society are independently employed by their institution and owe no allegiance to the society, but the affiliation can pay off when lists of "Federalist Society–approved scholars" for federal judgeships are presented to Republican presidents. Law and Economics is a more diffuse network of legal scholars that entails no membership or affiliation, but only the use of certain theoretical language stemming for economics. Yet it has become the dominant methodology used by legal scholars of corporations, finance, and bankruptcy. These institutional legal networks, while outwardly uncontroversial, seemingly focused on technical aspects of law that no non-lawyers would ever want to contemplate, have in fact made radical changes to American society. As such, they wield outsized power in the United States and drive the neoliberal movement even more than the economists who began it.

THE FEDERALIST SOCIETY can best be described as a marketplace of ideas for the right, with legal scholars as the merchants, federal judges as the purchasers, and lawyers—especially public interest lawyers—as middlemen, packaging and distributing ideas in legal briefs and arguments. The best public interest lawyers, like Ken Starr or Theodore Olson, spot an opportunity in the "market" to change a law and seize it by selecting the perfect plaintiff to effect the change. Progressive lawyers also use this tactic, but the difference is that the Federalist Society is a closed market where buyers and sellers are unusually aligned ideologically and where competition is restricted.

From its post-Powell-memo origins at Yale Law School in 1982 to the present, the Federalist Society has defined itself as a fortress for freethinkers to safely discuss their dissenting views from the dominant liberal orthodoxy at elite law schools. Its first conference brought together a soon-to-be-legendary group of conservative lawyers and scholars, among them Steven Calabresi, Richard Posner, and Olson.[5] Looking back on the event, an official statement of the society explained: "At a time when the nation's law schools are staffed largely by professors who dream of regulating from their cloistered offices every minute detail of our lives, the Federalists met—and proclaimed the virtues of individual freedom and of limited government."

With no sense of its future import, *The New York Times* covered the inaugural Federalist Society meeting in 1982 under the headline "Yale Is a Host to Two Meetings About Politics," noting that "two historically divergent groups" held simultaneous inaugural meetings. The other meeting, "Under the Color of Law," was the first annual conference of Yale

Law's Black alumni. Whereas "Under the Color of Law" was attended by about forty students and took place in the biology building a few blocks away from the law school, the Federalist Society meeting—which was keynoted by Robert Bork, then a Yale law professor—drew two hundred students from across the country. The *Times* reported that the Federalist Society had raised $24,000 from the Olin Foundation, then led by William Simon, and other donors. In contrast, a participant in the Black alumni conference quipped, "This is a poor people's conference."[6]

Within a decade, the Federalist Society was a force; within four decades, its members would dominate the nation's judiciary at the highest level, holding a majority of seats on the Supreme Court and on federal appellate courts. Yet, despite the society's deep pockets and judicial successes, the original tone of reactionary aggrievement has remained unchanged. "Law schools and the legal profession are currently strongly dominated by a form of orthodox liberal ideology which advocates a centralized and uniform society," states the group's website as of this writing. "While some members of the academic community have dissented from these views, by and large they are taught simultaneously with (and indeed as if they were) the law." Although the Federalist Society still advocates debate and dialogue, the group's stated long-term aim is "reordering priorities within the legal system to place a premium on individual liberty, traditional values, and the rule of law."[7]

Bork was the patron saint of the Federalist Society, and its first and only judicial martyr. After serving in the Nixon and Ford administrations, he became a prolific legal scholar whose influence spanned the various aspects of the neoliberal enterprise. He was among the first scholars to advance the theory of originalism in constitutional law, and he served as a mentor to the Yale Law students who founded the Federalist Society.

Unlike a jurist such as William Rehnquist, who sometimes deviated from expectations, Bork's views were consistent and predictable. The 1964 Civil Rights Act? "Unsurpassed ugliness."[8] *Griswold's* granting of a right to contraception? "Utterly specious," "unprincipled," and "intellectually empty."[9] A right to privacy for a Navy SEAL discharged for "homosexual activity"? "The effects of homosexual conduct within a naval or military unit are almost certain to be harmful to morale and discipline."[10] As the title of his book *Slouching Toward Gomorrah: Modern Liberalism and American Decline* suggested, Bork believed "Western culture" was in a state of collapse due to the gamut of conservative bugaboos: affirmative action, pornography, abortion, feminism, secularism, and more, all attributed to the influence of liberals and the left.

As was the case with neoliberal economists, what made Bork's scholarship so influential was the language and delivery of his arguments. His prolificness and prominence only further enhanced his project: any scholar in his subject areas was compelled to read him and cite him, even if to disagree.

Bork was also influential because he used the language of theory. As postmodernism and its esoteric theoretical paradigms, including structuralism, deconstructionism, and poststructuralism—and in the law, critical legal theory—began to dominate elite academia, reactionaries who could formulate theoretical responses held great sway. In his 1982 Nobel Prize lecture, George Stigler pronounced the "fundamental rule of scientific combat: it takes a theory to beat a theory," a dictate he and his fellow Chicago economists followed scrupulously.[11] The aphorism was repeated by Justice Antonin Scalia in promoting originalism, legal scholar Richard Epstein in proposing antiunion common law, and by Milton Friedman and Richard Posner. It became a slogan of sorts for the Federalist Society.[12] Bork not only spoke theory, but spoke it well and across the spectrum of neoliberal concerns.

Originalism, a trademark theory of Federalist Society greats like Bork and Scalia, refers to the approach which posits that the Constitution should be interpreted by focusing on the initial intentions of the Framers. Through the medium of Scalia, Bork's mentee, originalism would eventually determine some of the most important Supreme Court cases in American history. Despite the breadth and depth of his academic influence, Bork's most enduring legacy was in the economic domain—or, rather, in his skillful merger of economic analysis with textualism, which we will get to below.

President Ronald Reagan appointed Bork to the D.C. Court of Appeals in 1982 and nominated him for the Supreme Court in 1987 to fill the position vacated by none other than Lewis Powell. However, Bork faced stiff opposition from Democrats, who called him "an ideological extremist." Senator Edward Kennedy famously took to the Senate floor to level a strong condemnation:

> Robert Bork's America is a land in which women would be forced into back-alley abortions, blacks would sit at segregated lunch counters, rogue police could break down citizens' doors in midnight raids, schoolchildren could not be taught about evolution, writers and artists could be censored at the whim of the Government, and the doors of the Federal courts would be shut on the fingers of millions of citizens for whom the judiciary is—and is often the only—protector of the individual rights that are the heart of our democracy.[13]

This was hyperbole, but it was not baseless. Bork had opposed the civil rights laws, the *Griswold* ruling prohibiting contraceptives, and *Roe*. (And yet, placed among the six conservative justices on the Supreme Court in 2023, Bork would be one of the most moderate.)

The rejection of such a prominent figure outraged Republicans, who vowed never to be "borked" again. Bork, for his part, resigned from the Court of Appeals in protest and took a job teaching at the George Mason University School of Law. (In 2016, the law school received a $30 million donation to rename itself after Antonin Scalia, with $10 million coming from the Charles Koch Foundation and the other $20 million coming from an anonymous donor, who was later reported as Barre Seid, a businessman known for philanthropy to conservative causes.) Bork was also appointed a senior fellow at the American Enterprise Institute, the right-wing think tank. Bork's most important legacy was as a bridge between the radical right wing and legal academia, fulfilling the Powell memo's mandate of placing "articulate defenders of the free market" in the academy. And he had pierced the legal academy at its prestigious heart—Yale—whose "takeover" by the left had been decried by a diverse cast of intellectuals ever since William F. Buckley's diatribe *God and Man at Yale* had become a hit among reactionary conservative elites. Under the banner of "intellectual diversity," the radical right established a toehold in the legal academy that lent credibility to their political endeavors, credibility siphoned from an institution whose mission was truth seeking. The toehold would only grow thanks to right-wing funding. Bork's ideas would also proliferate until he became one of the most influential legal scholars of all time. You cannot learn the law today in any law school without learning Bork's theories, which are now considered "foundational" in a variety of subjects.

THE FEDERALIST SOCIETY'S influence is in large part a function of its membership network, which funnels conservative students into prestigious clerkships and conservative scholars into nominations to the federal bench. Even in the norm-breaking and chaotic administration of Donald Trump, every Supreme Court nominee came from the Federalist Society's list of judges, all of whom are hand-selected and vetted to ensure compliance with a standard set of pro-business imperatives.

The last time a Republican president attempted to nominate a non-Federalist Society member was in 2005, when George W. Bush tapped Harriet Miers. Bush was swiftly chastised by none other than Bork. Appearing on Tucker Carlson's MSNBC show *The Situation with Tucker Carlson*, Bork called the nomination "a disaster on every level" and "a slap in the face to the conservatives who've been building up a conservative legal movement for the last twenty years." He mentioned Miers's lack of qualifications and experience—the standard set of critiques lobbed at every female candidate—but he focused on a charge that distinguishes the Federalist Society from a simple partisan outfit. According to Bork, Miers had "no constitutional philosophy," and without one, she would "be influenced by factors, such as personal sympathies and so forth, that she shouldn't be influenced by." Bork was articulating what would soon become a litmus test for Republican nominees to the judiciary—allegiance to originalism, which he called the "judicial philosophy of the right." Bush learned his lesson and asked Miers to withdraw her nomination. Samuel Alito, a committed originalist and a member of the Federalist Society, was appointed instead.

The Federalist Society is first and foremost a powerful networking group in the law—and not just the conservative movement. It is affirmative action for conservative legal scholars to reach the top of the legal field, as scholars, judges, or top government officials. Law students and young scholars are groomed through clerkships, fellowships, and social events with powerful people in the network. Young scholars who are articulate in making originalist arguments or supporting a pillar of conservative orthodoxy are rewarded with prizes and lifted even higher in the ranks.

Federal judges enjoy lifetime tenure and decide hundreds of thousands of cases each year; the appellate courts, which are the end point for most federal cases, hear about fifty thousand cases per year, according to their own tallies.[14] Today, there are roughly seventy thousand members of the Federalist Society, in chapters at every law school and including alumni practitioners and judges. The society's annual revenue of $20 million comes from member donations as well as long-standing support from right-wing supporters, including the Scaifes, the Mercers, the Kochs, and corporate donors like Google, Chevron, and Facebook.

The Federalist Society nevertheless maintains that it is not a partisan group. Its commitment to "debate" has shielded the group from the accusation that it is a mouthpiece for its right-wing donors. Indeed, the group today makes more money from its members than donors; but its success is due, in large part, to the decisions made by the early donors, who were willing to support, as Lewis Powell urged, an academic society that could build an ideological movement rather than worry about producing short-term results. This has allowed the society to shape the contours of legal reasoning over a period of decades.

Instead of bringing cases or donating to candidates, the group provided theories of legal change that could be debated, honed, and distributed.[15] These legal theories hewed closely to a "neutral" principle of law, meaning that they focused on frameworks or concepts like textualism rather than on specific laws or cases. The Federalist Society preferred to persuade courts indirectly and over time rather than to wage a full-frontal assault. For example, instead of arguing that abortion was morally wrong, it took no official position on abortion, training its energies instead on undercutting the claim that the right to abortion stemmed from privacy rights the Framers intended to include in the Constitution.

The Federalist Society proposed strict constructionism (i.e., originalism/textualism) as the the antidote to "judicial activism" (i.e., the Warren Court and legal realists who upended settled laws like *Lochner* or Jim Crow). The so-called judicial activists were not blamed for the outcome of their decisions—for example, overturning *Lochner* and *Plessy*—but for the jurists' faulty *methodology*. The realists had "muddied" the Constitution; their theory of living constitutionalism (that the Constitution could evolve and adapt over time) was, in fact, unconstitutional. The only way of interpreting the Constitution was originalism. The Federalist Society critiqued the realists not on the basis of results but on the basis of ideas—more specifically, strategically useful ideas that cloaked reactionary dogma in neutral principles.

These debates were hardly of interest to anyone beyond constitutional law scholars, which was a key part of the neoliberal coup's success. As American law has become more technical, specialized, and complex, it has become an exclusive realm populated by a select few. The average American isn't paying attention to the esoteric arguments taking place in the conference halls and classrooms of the nation's law schools. And yet it is in those conference halls and classrooms that profound changes to the law—and thus to society—are first proposed and developed.

ALTHOUGH FEDERALIST SOCIETY scholars have advanced a myriad of legal theories, their most distinct and consistent have been the doctrines of originalism and textualism, as well as an overall commitment to "judicial restraint," which Chief Justice John Roberts has described artfully: "If it is not necessary to decide more to dispose of a case, then it is necessary not to decide more." Not all Federalist Society judges are originalists and not all originalist judges are Federalist

Society members, but what is unambiguous is that originalism is a doctrine of the neoliberal right.

Much like other neoliberal principles, originalism was a reaction to perceived liberal overreach. Originalism doesn't go back to the founding, as its name might suggest. In fact, the origins of originalism can be found in *Brown v. Board of Education*—or, rather, the backlash to *Brown*. After oral arguments in the case, Justice Felix Frankfurter worried that his colleagues on the Court would decide to desegregate schools. As Alexander Bickel, one of the justice's clerks that term and a future Yale Law professor, recounted, Frankfurter asked the Department of Justice to brief the history of the Fourteenth Amendment, specifically to answer the question: "Did the framers of the Fourteenth Amendment intend or contemplate school desegregation to fall within the scope of the equal protection clause?"

According to the historian Calvin TerBeek, the plaintiffs addressed this question during the oral arguments with a deep historical excavation of the Reconstruction amendments as well as of the "founders' intent." The state of Kansas filed a brief stating that the "framers did not intend" desegregation while the NAACP briefed the court that the *Plessy* standard of "separate but equal" was not in line with the "intent of the framers."[16] In deciding the controversial case, Chief Justice Warren not only dismissed the evidence presented by the parties with regard to intent as "inconclusive," but also waved away the idea that the Court should "turn back the clock to 1868," the year the Fourteenth Amendment was ratified, in resolving the modern dispute. Casting off the dead hands of the past and the binds of precedent, Justice Warren and the Court made their historic, unanimous decision based on changed circumstances and new realities. *Brown* breathed life back into the Constitution. Citing Gunnar Myrdal's research that discrimination and not biological race differences had created racially unequal outcomes, as well as the psychologist Kenneth Clark's experiment documenting Black children picking white dolls over Black ones as a psychological effect of segregation, the Court chose function over form, the spirit of the law over its letter. It was not judicial restraint, but it was justice.

Brown terrified conservatives, especially when federal troops were deployed to enforce the Court's ruling. James Kilpatrick, a prominent Virginia journalist who urged state judges to mount a "massive resistance" to integration, wrote to William F. Buckley to opine that in "constitutional cases clocks must always be turned back," and that Americans must take "the Constitution as we find it."[17] Over the decades from there, leading conservatives like Kilpatrick, Buckley, Bork, Edwin Meese, and even Barry Goldwater began to talk about the "original intent" of the Founders as the proper way for courts to interpret the Constitution.

Originalism was thus inaugurated as a response to *Brown*—an attempt to turn back the clock, to forbid the judiciary from looking to the future, to tie the hands of progress to the merciless dogmas of the unchangeable past. According to Loren A. Smith, a federal judge and longtime Federalist Society member, "The more basic formulation [of originalism] was the result of some of the actions of the courts . . . of the fifties and sixties and seventies where the judge was making the decision based on what the judge's view of social policy was." He continued, "It was important to democracy to follow the text as [the] controlling principle that controls judges from going off and doing whatever they want."[18]

No one is more associated with the doctrine of textualism and originalism than Antonin Scalia, who explained his allegiance to textualism as an antidote to what he saw as a judicial obsession with finding the *meaning* of laws through a search for legislative intent. Scalia, who was appointed to the Supreme Court in 1986, got grumpier about that search over time, noting in the 1993 case *Conry v. Aniskoff* that "the greatest defect of legislative history is its illegitimacy. We are governed by laws, not by the intentions of legislators." By this he meant the actual words of the law.

Scalia's hard-line textualism held that the "text is the law, and it is the text that must be observed." Contrary to conservative belief, judges were indeed using the text before the advent of originalism; it was just that they were weighing the text of the law among other factors. This, according to Scalia, opened the door to subjective rulings and unpredictable outcomes. Textualism was thus supposed to restrain judges from enacting their ideology. Scalia insisted that "following the text" would prevent judges from "doing whatever they want."

However, textualism's supposed restraints proved illusory, especially in the hands of a master of the craft like Scalia himself. Time and time again, Scalia was able to use originalism to reach outcomes consistent with his political goals. With wit and an abrasive certainty in his beliefs and capacity as a scholar and a jurist, Scalia brought originalism from the extreme margins of legal thought to its current position as the leading standard in judicial review.

Yet the result of originalism has been not less but *more* disagreement about the text, especially in issues of constitutional interpretation. In theory, originalism and textualism yield consistent and predictable results, just as, in theory, markets eliminate racism and corporate speech is the same as any other speech. The judge is a mere practitioner and translator—the text speaks for itself or on behalf of the Founders. Like the formalism of the natural law that the Founders subscribed to, textualism and originalism assume that there is a fixed meaning to words and that all judges can decipher it mechanically or automatically once trained in the technique. Yet the devil is in the application.

The first-order dilemma is whether it is a good idea to apply the original meaning of the text of the Constitution to modern-day issues the Founders did not and could not have envisioned, like data privacy or the regulation of an AR15 (leaving aside the question whether the Founders themselves would have *wanted* the Constitution to be a sacrosanct and unchanging document, a notion their own writings seem to rebut). But if, for the sake of argument, we grant that it *is* a good idea, that still leaves the most important requirement of any legal theory, especially one whose entire purpose is its consistent applicability: whether it reaches the basic threshold of justice, or whether it can be bent to justify any outcome desired by a judge.

The 2004 Supreme Court case *District of Columbia v. Heller* is instructive. The case was brought against the District of Columbia by Dick Anthony Heller, a D.C. special police officer who claimed that regulations against licensing for personal firearms violated the Second Amendment. The Court ruled 5–4 (along partisan lines) in favor of Heller, finding that the District's ban on registering handguns and its requiring firearms in the home to be nonfunctional were unconstitutional. In his opinion for the majority, Scalia, borrowing from Federalist Society member and legal scholar Randy Barnett's originalist interpretation of the Second Amendment, read the "plain meaning" of the text as guaranteeing an individual right to bear arms, despite a century of Court opinions and legal statutes that allowed cities and states to regulate and limit gun rights. This reading was "off the wall," in the words of the law professor Jack Balkin, in that it advanced an argument that most of the legal academy would find clearly wrong. However, thanks to the tireless efforts of the Federalist Society, that argument had found its way into the mainstream of legal discourse.

Dissenting from Scalia's *Heller* opinion, Justice John Paul Stevens, not himself of the originalist faith, used originalism to call out the majority's hypocrisy. The Second Amendment, wrote Stevens, was clearly a protection of a "well-regulated militia" as opposed to a grant of unlimited rights to personal gun ownership. He called the *Heller* decision "a twin failure—first, the misreading of the intended meaning of the Second Amendment, and second, the failure to respect settled precedent." In another, more recent Second Amendment case, *New York State Rifle and Pistol Association v. Bruen*, in which Justice Clarence Thomas, an originalist, interpreted the amendment to prohibit any state's restrictions on individual gun ownership, Justice Stephen Breyer criticized the sloppy "law office history" of the opinion: "Some of the laws . . . are too old. But others are too recent. Still others did not last long enough. Some applied to too few people. Some were enacted for the wrong reasons. Some may have been based on a constitutional rationale that is now impossible to identify. Some arose in historically unique circumstances. And some are not sufficiently analogous to the licensing regime at issue here."[19] In short, historical context is inescapable, and originalism is merely a ploy for arriving at the decision one seeks.

*   *   *

AS SCHOLARS have found and as Supreme Court opinions amply demonstrate, the flow of ideas between the Court's right wing and Federalist Society panelists and scholars goes both ways. Prominent scholars on the right provide justices with innovative originalist arguments that can be used flexibly in upcoming cases, while practitioners hear from judges themselves what types of arguments will be persuasive. In an iterative process, judicial decisions that push the boundaries of interpretation can be built on and expanded even further.

While the Federalist Society network provides the Court with fodder for argumentation, it also serves as a brake on the Court. According to founding member Steven Calabresi, the justices are "absolutely" "kept in check" by the Federalist Society: "When one tries to think about what kinds of checks exist on officials as powerful as Supreme Court Justices, I think the check of criticism by law schools, journalists, and conservative think tanks like the Federalist Society, criticism from those quarters is something that they notice."[20]

The Federalist Society learned relatively early on that it needed to keep its judges in line. Justices John Paul Stevens, Anthony Kennedy, and David Souter—all nominated by Republican presidents—drifted to the middle or even the left over their years on the Court, a phenomenon the society has dubbed the "Greenhouse effect" (after, in their eyes, the liberal *New York Times* reporter Linda Greenhouse). To counteract the Greenhouse effect, the Federalist Society uses the pressure of its network of law clerks and prominent right-wing social elites to keep conservative justices firmly tethered to the right's judicial orthodoxy. The audience that matters to these hand-selected justices is the subset of right-wing elites, foundations, and donors who control the judicial pipeline and maintain a watchful eye lest the justices move toward the desires of the majority of the American public.

Given the succession of "betrayals" by conservatives who migrated to the moderate center—examples also include William Brennan and Sandra Day O'Connor—the Federalist Society decided to take the risk out of the selection process. By nurturing hard-liners from the cradle of law school to postgraduate fellowships at right-wing institutions and judicial clerkships with conservative Supreme Court judges, the Federalist Society places nominees on a "track" to the federal judiciary.

The Federalist Society's reach and capacity can be seen in some of the landmark legal transformations of the neoliberal era, including one of the most pivotal triumphs of the right: *Citizens United v. Federal Election Commission*. This decision found that corporate political donations are protected under the free speech protections of the First Amendment and thus restrictions on these donations are unconstitutional and cannot stand unless the limit sufficiently and specifically served a compelling government interest. A legacy and culmination of the Powell-led decisions in *Virginia Pharmacy*, *Bellotti*, and *Buckley*, *Citizens United* fundamentally changed American politics and, one could argue, society. The case was created by and at the same supercharged a self-reinforcing loop: corporate money leading to corporate-friendly laws leading to more money, ad infinitum.

The case was decided after Chief Justice Rehnquist, the lone dissenter in *Virginia Pharmacy* in 1976, who had warned of such an outcome, retired from the Court in 2005. Once a conservative Supreme Court majority was secured with John Roberts as chief justice, several right-wing dark money groups, including one representing Senator Mitch McConnell, filed lawsuits opposing limits on campaign funding. The Federalist Society–assembled court granted cert and heard arguments from Federalist Society star Ted Olson, who argued that the dark-money-funded nonprofit Citizens United was allowed to donate unlimited funds on behalf of candidates—or, more accurately, in opposition to presidential candidate Hillary Clinton—under the First Amendment. The Court overturned its own precedent imposing limits on this kind of spending; but more significantly, its overturned legislation passed by a bipartisan Congress just a few years earlier. This was not judicial restraint. Nor was it originalism—the Founders clearly intended to curb the influence of special interests on lawmaking (and, obviously, to leave lawmaking power exclusively in the hands of Congress). Without purse or sword, the Court reached beyond legislative intent and popular will to tip the balance of power toward unelected corporations. To do so, its conservative majority strained the First Amendment beyond anything the Founders could have imagined.

Federalist Society scholars also deserve credit for the decision. The principle of judicial restraint, ostensibly a central tenet of the Federalist Society, should have stayed the Court's hand. Yet legal scholars and judges in Federalist Society forums, in particular Randy Barnett and Richard Epstein, had been eroding this principle for years by articulating a unique interpretation of its requirements. Barnett, a Georgetown Law faculty member and Cato Institute fellow, is one of the most prominent scholars of originalism and among the most influential Federalist Society scholars; Epstein, who directs the Classical Liberal Institute at NYU, is a senior fellow at the Hoover Institution, an emeritus professor at the University of Chicago Law School, and a luminary in both the Federalist Society and the Law and Economics network. The Barnett-Epstein theory of judicial restraint, endorsed by Clarence Thomas, holds that if prior cases were not decided based on true originalist principles—that is, if they were the result of "judicial activism"—the doctrine of judicial restraint would compel a current court to overturn the prior rulings; as a corollary, *stare decisis*, or the idea that well-founded precedent should rarely be overturned, held only for cases decided using the "right" methodology. As Allison Hayward, the chairman of the Federalist Society's Free Speech and Election Law Practice Group, explained about the imperative of overruling precedent to allow corporate free speech, "Whatever appealing qualities might attach to a justice's respect for precedent and restraint in ordinary circumstances, none are found here. It is vitally important that future justices appreciate the position the Court is in, and the power the Court has to improve the law. Rather than decry judicial activism, principled Court watchers need to allow for space for future justices to repair the mistakes of the past."[21] The Federalist Society's definition of judicial restraint bears an uncanny resemblance to judicial activism.

In *Citizens United*, a majority of the court—Roberts, Scalia, Alito, Thomas, and Kennedy—accepted these arguments and overruled a slate of earlier cases, including the line of cases emanating from the Burger Court and a more recent Supreme Court decision, *Austin v. Michigan Chamber of Commerce* (1990), which had covered the exact same terrain.

The four liberal justices signed a dissent focused on the hypocrisy of their brethren. As he had done in *Heller*, Justice Stevens presented copious sources that undercut the majority's argument, using originalism and judicial restraint. His ninety-page dissent, joined by Justices Breyer, Ruth Bader Ginsburg, and Sonia Sotomayor, charged the majority with abandoning court precedent and deciding questions beyond the issue presented, a step Stevens called "contrary to the fundamental principle of judicial restraint." The majority had violated their own commitments and threatened the legitimacy of the Court by issuing a holding that operated like "a sledge hammer rather than a scalpel." The Federalist Society had failed to follow its own principles, once again interpreting the Constitution against its original meaning, breaking with precedent, and making a mockery of judicial restraint.

Justice Scalia felt the need to write an entirely separate originalist concurrence to rebut Stevens's bold claim that "there is not a scintilla of evidence to support the notion" that the First Amendment made no distinction between people and corporations. Apparently, Scalia had forgotten that his closest friend on the court, Chief Justice Rehnquist, had offered numerous scathing dissents, in the 1970s and 1980s, making just the opposite point. Stevens even cited Rehnquist's opinions a few times in his dissent.

In his majority opinion in *Citizens United*, John Roberts argued that, in fact, overturning prior cases was *more* faithful to the spirit of *stare decisis* than affirming them. *Stare decisis*, wrote Roberts, was not an "inexorable command . . . especially in constitutional cases." It is instead a "principle of policy," and though it "counsels deference to past mistakes," it "provides no justification for making new ones." Fidelity to cases that were "mistakes" is not only not required but serves only to "undermine the rule-of-law values that justify *stare decisis* in the first place." Unlike Scalia, Roberts was at least making the effort to legitimize the Court.

TEXTUALISM AND ORIGINALISM, undisciplined, inconsistent, and hypocritical, are now core theories of legal interpretation—if not *the* core theories to be reckoned with to make a constitutional argument.

Any lawyer arguing a constitutional case or any plaintiff pleading for constitutional cover must prove their case using dead men's words—always turning back the clock—a straitjacket on the judiciary, which likely would horrify the Founders.

In fact, nothing has done more to bolster the doctrines of textualism and originalism than their adoption by judges and regulators across the political spectrum. In her confirmation hearing in 2010, the liberal justice Elena Kagan proffered that "we are all textualists now." Ketanji Brown Jackson, another liberal justice, noted in her testimony in 2022 that she believed in "adherence to the text. I am focusing on the original public meaning because I'm constrained to interpret the text." When pushed on whether she believed in "living constitutionalism," Jackson gave the only acceptable answer: that she was not a proponent of that theory. She explained that while living constitutionalism "infuses" the Constitution "with my own policy or perspective" or "the policy perspective of the day," she would maintain a fidelity to the text because, as she accurately noted, "the prevailing interpretive frame for interpreting the Constitution is now very clearly looking back through history. That is now the way in which constitutional interpretation is done." Her comments were a measure of the Federalist Society's influence and success, a sign of Lewis Powell's foresight about the potential of a patient, long-term ideological campaign.

Due to their longevity and credibility in the academy and their dominance of the judiciary, challenging the validity of textualism and originalism would be a foolhardy errand for serious scholars and certainly for lawyers arguing a case. The federal judiciary is dominated by Federalist Society members who earned their place on the federal bench thanks to their allegiance to this foundational interpretive method. But textualism and originalism are threatening the legitimacy of the Court and the rule of law because they are pliable tools that have been bent to produce any outcome its practitioner wishes to reach. The Federalist Society promised neutrality and theoretical rigor, but in reality, Federalist Society judges have delivered consistently conservative votes. And yet law students, legal scholars, and lawyers learn the law based on the reigning legal theory of the highest courts, textualism, which often acts as an end run against justice using wordplay.

A neat, if horrifying, example was the torture memos written by two prominent Federalist Society members and Bush Department of Justice officials, John Yoo and Jay Bybee. The memos making the legal case for torture were leaked after an explosive report with graphic pictures revealed routine torture in the Iraqi prison Abu Ghraib. The laws against torture were ratified after World War II in U.N. charters and Geneva Conventions. These mandates were clearly written, prohibiting torture, defined clearly as any act "specifically intended to inflict severe physical or mental pain or suffering... upon another person with his custody or physical control." Through hairsplitting textual analysis, the torture memos authorize a wide variety of torture methods and justify what looked to be a clear moral wrong. A dictionary is cited over thirty times in one of the memos, which is fifty pages long, and another twenty-five times in a second, eighty-one-page memo. Each word in the simple sentence quoted above—including "suffering," "severe," "intend," and "pain"—is defined using definitions from several dictionaries, so that a text that seemed upon first blush to prohibit torture of prisoners does not indeed do that. The torture memos are emblematic of the dangers of pharisaical formalism turning the letter of the law against its spirit. Where ambiguity did not exist, it is manufactured. The memos conclude that there are plenty of options to inflict what might "constitute cruel, inhuman, or degrading treatment," but that did not technically qualify as torture. Like good textualists, the memo writers stuck to the text alone and found loopholes large enough to permit the worst human rights abuses that U.S. troops had committed, at least with legal backing, in this century.[22]

Yoo's career shows the power of the Federalist Society network. After graduating Yale Law School, he clerked for two prominent conservative justices, Laurence Silberman (an appellate court judge and former Nixon White House official) and Clarence Thomas. Yoo then served on the board of advisers of the right-wing Claremont Institute, took a fellowship at the Heritage Foundation, followed by a John M. Olin Foundation fellowship, after which he joined the UC Berkeley law faculty briefly until he served in the Bush administration. After the torture memos were leaked, he left the Justice Department for a fellowship at the American Enterprise Institute and returned to his position as a tenured law professor at Berkeley, where he remains, teaching constitutional law. The academic credibility endowed on textualism was made possible by Bork and other Federalist Society founders; and it was that academic credibility that enabled the memos, which were written in accordance with textualist precepts, as well as the torture of Iraqis—many of whom were ultimately found to be innocent.

What these carefully written memos by preeminent scholars of the right revealed was not lawlessness run amok, but *lawfulness*—quite literally the memos were chock-full of legal jargon—in defense of a clear wrong. "It is about who we are," said Arizona senator John McCain at the time, a former torture victim. "This is a moral debate." This was exactly the problem—the textualist legal formality of the memos purposefully evaded the moral debate. By considering only the text of the law, the moral issues are left off the table, the legal question hinging on the inherent ambiguity and flexibility of words and their contingent definitions. Doctrines like originalism and textualism in constitutional interpretation, as well as Law and Economics in market regulation, prioritize form over function, letter over spirit, text over meaning, and the law over justice. Though accepted as rigorous analysis by their many adherents and undoubtedly used as such by some, these formalist legal tools have made appeals to justice and *right* harder and harder to make in the Federalist Society–dominated judiciary and legal academy.

While the Supreme Court has unlimited power and autonomy to decide cases using whatever legal tools the justices might devise, including patently immoral or amoral ones, there is a natural check on their powers: the Court's legitimacy. "With neither purse no sword," noted *Federalist* 78, the Court's power derived solely from the public's trust—by commanding "the esteem and applause of all the virtuous and disinterested." Legitimacy, like "trust," is a key pillar of our democracy but impossible to measure. In *Planned Parenthood v. Casey*, the 1992 case that affirmed the ruling in *Roe v. Wade* (1973) that a woman had a right to have an abortion, Justice Sandra Day O'Connor, a moderate conservative and often the swing vote on the Court, argued that any other result would "seriously weaken the Court's capacity to exercise the judicial power and to function as the Supreme Court of a nation dedicated to the rule of law."[23] O'Connor reminded her conservative colleagues that the Court "cannot independently coerce obedience to its decrees. . . . The Court's power lies, rather, in its legitimacy, a product of substance and perception that shows itself in the people's acceptance of the judiciary as fit to determine what the nation's law means and to declare what it demands." Absent a "most compelling reason," the overturning of *Roe* would "subvert the Court's legitimacy beyond any serious question." O'Connor repeated the assertion several times: "The Court's legitimacy depends on making legally principled decisions" that can be "accepted by the nation."

Roe was finally overturned in 2022, once the bench was filled with six hard-liners from the Federalist Society. The originalism argument was an easy one: writing for the majority in *Dobbs v. Jackson Women's Health Organization*, Samuel Alito argued that "a constitutional right to abortion has [no] foundation . . . in this Nation's history and tradition." Indeed, according to Alito, women had *no* foundational rights at all, let alone abortion. *Stare decisis*, Alito believed—and an entire canon of Federalist Society scholarship proved—did not bind the Court if it viewed the precedent as wrongly decided.

During oral arguments, to drive this point home, the Court's conservatives cited previous landmark cases that ignored *stare decisis*. Alito referenced *Brown's* overturning of *Plessy* and *West Coast Hotel's* 1937 overturning of *Lochner*. "You know, we have *Plessy, Brown*. We have *Bowers versus Hardwick*, to *Lawrence*," said conservative Justice Amy Coney Barrett, invoking two gay rights cases as well as *Brown*. "*Brown v. Board* outlawed separate but equal," said Brett Kavanaugh; if the Court hadn't overturned *Plessy* "this country would be a much different place."

The irony was profound. The ruling in *Brown* had launched decades of conservative backlash, from which sprung originalism's retrograde approach to legal interpretation. Now, a Supreme Court steeped in originalism was marshaling the ruling in *Brown*—the case that catalyzed the right's revolt against judicial activism—in its argument to overturn *Roe*. This head-dizzying hypocrisy might make a publicly accountable, historically informed court blush, but the Federalist Society lifers who decided *Dobbs* clearly felt no shame.

Chief Justice Roberts did not join the majority to overturn *Roe*; instead, he pleaded with the majority to think about the Court's legitimacy. He asked the newly appointed zealots on the Court to take a "more measured course." Knowing what was on the line, Roberts wrote that the Court should not overturn all of *Roe* "out of adherence to a simple yet fundamental principle of judicial restraint," reiterating his dictum "If it is not necessary to decide more to dispose of a case, then it is necessary not to decide more."

Alito, quite rightly, threw Roberts's own end run around *stare decisis* in *Citizens United* back at him. Hadn't Roberts written that *stare decisis* was "a doctrine of preservation, not transformation" and that "we cannot embrace a narrow ground of decision simply because it is narrow; it must also be right"? Alito might have saved his breath and responded as Powell had once done: it was too late.

Back in the 1950s and 1960s, while the proto-originalists were coalescing around an effort to fight back against *Brown*, Aaron Director, a key figure in the Chicago School of economics, began to bring economic thinking to the university's law school. His first aim was to make Law and Economics, then a new theory, credible. Credibility would be measured through citation by other scholars. Director established *The Journal of Law and Economics* in 1958; he was joined by Ronald Coase, his fellow faculty member, who became codirector in 1964. The journal started publishing theoretical articles applying the models being created by Gary Becker, Milton Friedman, and other economists to legal interpretation. Law and Economics really took off after the 1971 Powell memo triggered the paranoia of billionaires, especially John Olin, that the Ivy League was being taken over by leftists and the courts by activists. Law and Economics, like the Federalist Society, was funded by the right to do battle over legal theory in elite corridors. It is a movement, not an organization, yet a relatively cohesive one that supports young scholars throughout their careers via grants, fellowships, and elite professorships at top schools.

The Manhattan Institute's James Pierson, who was involved in creating Law and Economics, reflected on the group's aims to *The New York Times* in 2005: "I saw it as a way into the law schools—I probably shouldn't confess that. . . . Economic analysis tends to have conservatizing effects."[24] As it turned out, law schools were much more amenable to establishing fellowships and endowed chairs in Law and Economics than in more obviously conservative legal theories, owing to the prestige and supposedly neutral politics of economics.

The long-term goal of Law and Economics is the same as that of the Federalist Society: to change laws. For Law and Economics, that ambition began with antitrust. The Chicago School's early obsession with antitrust laws (more specifically, with getting rid of them altogether) stemmed from its principal funder, Harold Luhnow. As president of the William Volker Fund, Luhnow supported Hayek, Mises, and the building of the MPS. He viewed antitrust laws as akin to socialism and urged Chicago scholars to build a case against it.

Robert Bork, who graduated from Chicago Law in 1953, studied under Director, who taught courses in antitrust using economic theory. Bork became, alongside Director, one of the movement's pioneering scholars. After law school, he worked at a prestigious Chicago law firm before joining the Nixon administration. Bork built on his mentor's antitrust model in a series of papers and a 1978 book, *The Antitrust Paradox*. Bork's argument was textualist and economics-based: using the text of the antitrust laws, he argued that their original intent was to protect consumers against price-fixing and not, as was commonly held, about breaking up powerful companies. Bork's book elaborated on Director's, Coase's, and George Stigler's models of market power to show that large firms were more efficient and benefited consumers more than small ones. The paradox was that legal interventions in the market to break up firms had led to less efficient firms and higher prices. Therefore, he argued that antitrust laws should be used only when there was evidence that companies were abusing their market power to raise prices unjustifiably—by which he meant hardly ever. Bork's synthesis of neoclassical market theory with originalist legal analysis was exactly the kind of fusionist thinking that Law and Economics was hoping to inspire.

Regardless of its dubious veracity, Bork's originalist theory took hold of antitrust enforcement. With Lewis Powell on the Supreme Court, the route from theory to market-shaping law was short. Beginning with 1977's *Continental Television Inc. v. GTE Sylvania* and continuing to the present, the Supreme Court has all but nullified our country's antitrust laws. Technically, those laws—hard-won Progressive Era reforms against market power—still exist on the books; in reality, their purpose and power, their guts and teeth, are gone. Law and Economics analysis would go far beyond antitrust, but antitrust remains its most stunning success.

ALTHOUGH IT was born as an adjunct to the Chicago economics department and would continue to wear its association with Chicago economists as a badge of honor, Law and Economics took off in the same way that the Federalist Society did—through money.

Beginning in 1974, the nascent movement was helmed by Henry Manne, a corporate lawyer turned law professor whose beliefs and practices were staunchly libertarian. Manne approached the Olin Foundation in 1982 to request funds to establish a center for Law and Economics. The foundation decided to fund the innovative entrepreneur who was selling exactly what they were looking for. John Olin wanted not only to save academia from Black activists, as we saw in chapter 3, but also to shift the law toward the free market in order to preserve the vast fortune bequeathed to him by his father.

The Olin Corporation's experience with environmental regulators had not been pleasant. After President Nixon created the Environmental Protection Agency in 1970, the Olin Corporation was sued for several violations, including dumping toxic waste at the Love Canal site and falsifying records in a cover-up, for which three officers of the company were convicted. Olin also got into trouble for dumping so much toxic waste in Saltville, Virginia, near its plant that the Appalachian town became uninhabitable. The Olin Foundation dared to dream of a world where corporations would no longer be victimized by a tyrannical state, and worked to make it so. Manne, who believed that no business regulations were justified and that both hostile takeovers and insider trading led to efficient market outcomes, was the perfect zealot to turn the law toward the Olin Foundation's interests. Manne first approached Olin for funds, intending to train a cadre of corporate lawyers in free market principles who would then fill positions as general counsels at big companies. But the mission expanded quickly.

After becoming a professor of law and producing several texts focused on law and economics, the free market, and securities regulation, Manne created the Law and Economics Center. It was founded in 1974—first at the University of Rochester, moving shortly thereafter to University of Miami, and eventually migrating to George Mason Law School. "A single generation of lawyers from one school dedicated to true liberal values," Manne wrote, "could turn the American legal system back into a productive and desirable channel." He proposed a wholesale revision of the law school curriculum toward Law and Economics because "no other social science discipline can begin to match the relevance and importance of economics for the training of modern lawyers.... The idea should be to infuse the entire curriculum with economic sophistication."[25]

It took decades, but by the 1980s, Law and Economics was ready to go mainstream. Manne's most influential innovation was Law and Economics "summer camps," which welcomed hundreds of state, local, and federal judges to exotic locations to participate in workshops designed to teach them the basics of economics. At these retreats, judges were told they were learning "cutting-edge" economics consecrated by mathematically sophisticated, Nobel Prize–winning theory. Among the guest speakers at these events were economics stars like Becker, Friedman, and Coase.

In 1976, Manne received funds from the Olin Foundation and a few other corporate donors to begin the Economics Institute for Judges, which would pay judges and professors to attend a mini-course designed, like the summer camps, to teach them basic economic ideas. Although these three-week seminars were subsidized by right-wing donors, there was no evidence in the promotional materials that they were in any way political, which is why so many judges attended. Each judge and professor who attended received a copy of *Economic Analysis of Law*—the canonical text of Law and Economics, written by Richard Posner—and each learned, in Manne's words, "the economics of property law."[26]

The seminars turned Manne into a star in the movement. By 1979, Manne's Law and Economics center was firmly ensconced at George Mason Law School. The funding for the school was provided almost entirely by the Charles Koch Foundation after Manne had a falling-out with the Olin Foundation. However, the Olin Foundation continued to fund other Law and Economics centers at some of the top law schools in the country—Berkeley, Georgetown, Columbia, Harvard—as well as academic fellowships for aspiring scholars. It stated clearly its reasons for supporting these programs: they were "an opportunity to shift the ideological balance" at universities and law schools.[27]

The Law and Economics seminars inaugurated by Manne have led to more scholarship in the subfield and more opportunities to raise funds. In some fields of legal scholarship, it is now a requirement to attend a seminar—if not specialize entirely—in Law and Economics. Seminar attendees often receive honoraria and comped travel and attendance.

Judges learn from eminent Nobel winners in the morning and lounge and socialize in the sun in the afternoon. An agenda for one such event today lists classes on "Coase theorem" (which refers to the theory that in the absence of transactional costs, parties will arrive at the most optimal decision), "Competition and Monopoly," and "Exchange Theory," followed by discussions, receptions, and dinner.[28] The institute's courses for judges steers away from overtly political topics. The website states that the purpose of the Judicial Education Program, as it is known, is to give judges "a basic knowledge of economics principles" in order to "help judges better understand the long-term implications of their decisions, thereby improving the development of the law and benefitting America's free enterprise system."[29] There are waiting lists each year to attend the popular seminars.

By 1990, 40 percent of all federal judges had attended the Judicial Education Program courses, including appellate court judges and Supreme Court justices. Even Ruth Bader Ginsburg was a fan, raving that "the instruction was far more intense than the sun." She expressed her "enduring appreciation" to Henry Manne for "lifting the veil on such mysteries as regression analyses, and for advancing both learning and collegial relationships among federal judges across the country."[30]

An analysis of more than a million judicial decisions over thirty years measured the effect of the summer camps on judicial rulings and found that "after attending economics training, participating judges use more economics language in their opinions, issue more conservative decisions in economics-related cases, rule against regulatory agencies more often, favor more lax enforcement in antitrust cases, and impose more/longer criminal sentences."[31] The group of "Manne-judges"—as the paper refers to summer camp attendees—imposed sentences that were 13 percent longer on certain crimes than nonattendees, a finding that holds regardless of political affiliation before attending the seminars. In fact, the courses were so influential that judges' rulings were shaped by who, in particular, taught the course. For example, judges who attended seminars run by Milton Friedman—who usually began his lectures by showing the economic benefits of legalizing drugs—did not increase penalties for drug-related crimes afterward.

Law and Economics spread with great efficiency. Thanks to Manne's seminars and robust funding by the Olin Foundation, Law and Economics has not been as controversial as the Federalist Society, which has enabled its ideologies and analytical tools to spread far more widely. While the Federalist Society is more famous, for its connections to presidents and Supreme Court justices, Law and Economics has arguably had a more profound, more generalized effect on the field of law—in the academy and beyond.

LAW AND ECONOMICS is distinct from economics. Economists use a variety of tools, such as empirical analysis or mathematical theory, to address a variety of questions. Law and Economics is a legal theory—a way of interpreting legal text. The questions economists ask and answer are related to market growth, inflation, competition, and so forth. The questions that Law and Economics attempts to answer are: How should a statute be interpreted? How should a case be decided? How should a criminal be sentenced?

Furthermore, whereas economics has developed along a variety of paths over the years, considering and discarding novel theories and analyzing new empirical data, Law and Economics has remained static in its fundamental assumptions. Thus, although the economic theories on which Law and Economics is built have been challenged, complicated, or debunked, they nevertheless remain the movement's underpinning. In other words, Law and Economics is the zombie through which neoliberal economics continues to self-propagate, continuing to influence law and policy. Without awareness by the public and most of the legal profession, the law has become a host for the spread of a viral ideology based on a fossilized economic paradigm.

Law and Economics' leading light today is Richard Posner, the Chicago Law professor turned federal appeals court judge. Posner is not just a legal theorist and textbook author but, according to a study in *The Journal of Legal Studies*, the most-cited legal scholar of all time by a "considerable margin," with a whopping 48,852 cites compared to runner-up Cass Sunstein's 35,584, as of 2021.[32] His opinions and legal theories became even more influential when he was appointed to the U.S. Court of Appeals by President Reagan in 1981.[33] Across the legal curriculum, but especially in the basic first-year law school courses like contracts, property, torts, and corporate law, Posner has reshaped how legal scholars and their students think. Any scholar writing about these areas must deal with a Posnerian analysis, even if they disagree with it. When I was in law school, I was taught to analyze each case through a Law and Economics lens, which my torts professor described in shorthand as "What would Posner say?" As a professor of contracts and property, I have yet to encounter a single textbook that doesn't integrate a Posnerian analysis of the law.

In his *Economic Analysis of Law*, the sacred text of Law and Economics, Posner proposes a method of legal analysis based on basic economic principles, in particular what he calls "efficiency" and "utility maximization." A key concept in law and economics is *utility*. In its classical definition, proposed by the eighteenth-century philosopher and lawyer Jeremy Bentham, utility is a measurement of happiness. For Law and Economics, utility is a flat and ambiguous measure synonymous with the equally vague ideal of "efficiency." As Posner explains, "The social goal most emphasized in modern economics is not happiness or utility but the efficient allocation of resources, in a somewhat special sense." Posnernian neo-utilitarianism dispenses with measuring happiness or any other social good, settling instead for valuing only what could be valued by the market.

According to Posner, utility maximization leads to certain "natural" and "unalienable" principles. Law and Economics does not take a position on whether the market's laws are inherently good or bad; rather, like nature's laws, they just are. Humans are rational decision makers and utility maximizers. The market rewards the efficient and punishes the inefficient. Prices reflect the true essential value of goods. The free market, and only the free market, allocates resources fairly. Government intervention disrupts the delicate yet natural orbit of the free market, leading to "unintended consequences." Unlike the actual laws of nature, which do not need reinforcement, economic laws must be protected by the courts. As was clear at the very first meeting of the MPS, the logic of neoliberalism—and so of Law and Economics—is circular. Although one is urged simply to have faith in the free market rather than state intervention, the free market requires a strong state with a particular set of laws to function. At least this is what Law and Economics convinced the nation's judges.

Judges trained in Law and Economics are to assume, per Posner's *Economic Analysis of the Law*, that a person always acts as "a rational utility maximizer in *all* areas of life, not just in 'economic' affairs." Posner urges judges and practitioners who are deciding cases or writing laws to consider, for example, "the law of demand; opportunity costs; the tendency of resources to gravitate toward their most valuable uses," and more.[34] When left to operate without government intrusion, the "natural" laws of the market would lead inevitably to "equilibrium."

Like textualism and originalism, Law and Economics is a formalist response to the threats posed by the legal realists of the Warren Court.

Legal realists made law on a case-by-case basis, looking at practical effects, differences in power, and the expectations of the parties. Law and Economics urged judges and practitioners to instead abstract away from the actual case and to make decisions based on their economic effects alone. Efficiency thus becomes a *proxy* for justice. As Posner notes in his book *The Economics of Justice,* "Because there is no common currency in which to compare happiness, sharing and protection of rights, it is unclear how to make the necessary trade-offs among these things in the design of a social system. Wealth maximization makes the trade-offs automatically."[35] In fact, in Law and Economics discourse, leaving the market alone is the highest-order aim because it is assumed that the market is the only fair allocator of resources. Thus, judges who go to the Law and Economics seminars to learn about economics, if they are paying attention, leave instead with an ideologically tainted view of what fairness requires.

Posner proposes that principles of wealth maximization and cost-benefit could and should be used across the legal spectrum. As he wrote in his introduction to *Economic Analysis of Law,* economic analysis is useful in cases as diverse as those involving "drug addiction, theft of art, sexual acts, surrogate motherhood, flag desecration, public international law, presidential pardons, democratic theory, terrorism, and religious observances."[36]

Posner is indeed a true believer, and to his credit, he applied these principles even when his position led to a politically unpopular position. For example, his efficient take on marriage led him to opine that it should be treated as a market because "marriages not undertaken for mutual advantage create inefficiency, just as in the market sector."[37] For Posner, if a breach of the marriage contract is "efficient"—that is, if it yields an increase in net wealth—the law should in fact encourage the breach and not get hung up on "moral qualms" about promise breaking. But even in arguing this controversial and seemingly nontraditional position, his hypotheticals and the unquestioned assumptions on which they are based reveal a dogmatic adherence to a fixed system of value unchanged since the days of Locke. "Suppose a woman is assigned the right to her person initially. What will she do? By assumption, it is her only asset. She has to exchange it for something in order to live.

Presumably she will marry some rich man. The only question is which one?" What if she marries a hateful man? Is that not inefficient? No, says Posner. Assuming, which he does, that woman's "product" is "household rather than market commodities." He goes on to argue:

> She will be less productive in some households than in others; if she hates her husband, or if he treats her like a chattel, she will be less productive, just as the slave will be less productive than the free man. This is an economic argument for having a "marriage market," formal or informal, rather than just randomly assigning poor women to rich men. But even if random assignment is used initially, the Coase Theorem implies that there will be a subsequent reassignment of women so as to maximize their household production, provided some form of marriage market is allowed to operate. The amount of reshuffling of marriage partners can be reduced, however, and resources thereby conserved, by giving women (or their families, in a society where women cannot enforce rights on their own behalf effectively) the exclusive right to their own person in the first place. The economic argument for this assignment of rights is compelling.[38]

Eric Posner, Richard's son, who is a Law and Economics scholar in his own right, writes in his book *Radical Markets* that Americans should use the "logic of the market" to fix "social problems" like immigration. He posits that liberalizing immigration would increase economic growth by enabling Americans to buy or rent immigrants to work for them. In a *Politico* article first titled "What If You Could Get Your Own Immigrant?," a title that was wisely changed because it was "offensive to readers," Posner arrives at the conclusion "Yes, Mary [the buying American] would be able to pay Sofia [the immigrant] less than the minimum wage, but even at $5 an hour, Sofia would earn many times what she earns on a farm in Paraguay."[39]

Curiously, the "logic of the market" allocated values based on racial and gender hierarchies similar to those proposed by "natural law," values that had justified colonialization. When Paraguay was colonized and the

Paraguayans deemed as labor, it was on account of fixed rights decreed by John Locke's imagined creator. The fact that Sofia from Paraguay would be desperate enough to leave her home country to earn a living as a bought immigrant for an unknown American making $5 an hour was just the law of the market. Like natural law theories, Law and Economics appeals to an authority outside the legal system to guide decisions inside of it. The Posners were not assigning these values; it just so happened that the "market," in all its allocative efficiency, determined marriage to be a woman's only asset and valued an immigrant's work at well below the minimum wage. Not an omniscient, omnipotent God blessing existing hierarchies of power but an omniscient, omnipotent market doing the same.

Yet while natural law derived its authority from "some brooding omnipresence in the sky" in Oliver Wendell Holmes's words, Law and Economics wraps itself in the authority of science. But look beyond its formal-appearing theories and it is clear that its foundational ideas are unfalsifiable and untestable, more like clever hypothetical and logic games than anything resembling science. Even those of its basic economic assumptions that can be rigorously tested have been falsified. The core ideas on which Law and Economics builds its entire apparatus—that markets are efficient and people are utility maximizers in all scenarios— are wrong. Research in psychology, sociology, anthropology, and even economics has shown that market failures are rampant and that human beings are quite regularly irrational. Yet the bankrupt principles that animate Law and Economics continue to be made into policy by the scholars, practitioners, and judges who have internalized its teachings.

Even when actual economic data has debunked Posner's assumptions about how economics should work, he has chosen to stick with the fossilized theories of law and economics.[40] For example, Posner's textbook builds on George Stigler's proposal that minimum wage laws led to fewer jobs, a theory concocted without any empirical data but for which he nonetheless won a Nobel Prize in Economics. Posner even built on wage theory with a few hypotheticals of his own, determining not only that raising the minimum wage reduced employment, but also that it did so for "marginal workers—middle-aged women, the young, and blacks." This thesis was based on the same empirical data Stigler used for his theory, which is to say: none. Posner's text included a sophisticated mathematical graph, which for the average law student or judge who is not a trained economist seemed like proof enough of his theory that raising the minimum wage harmed women and minorities. However, when economists David Card and Alan B. Krueger tested Stigler's theory using real-world data over a long period of time, they found that increases in minimum wage laws had in fact *increased* employment—in other words, the opposite of what Stigler theorized, and Posner hypotheticalized. The study was part of a momentous wave of empirical studies called the *credibility revolution*, in which microeconomists who work with data rather than theory have tested and debunked many long-standing theories in economics. Card and Krueger had to wait for a natural experiment and collect enough data over a long period of time to prove their case, which they were able to do in 1994, providing their volumes of rigorous data to be parsed through by other economists.[41] Still, Posner was not persuaded.

In the ninth edition of *Economic Analysis of Law* (2014), Posner continued to claim that minimum wage laws led to unemployment. In a lengthy footnote to the section, Posner included a long string of citations and noted that "a vast empirical literature on the economic effects of a minimum wage" supports his theory. He described Card and Krueger, the only economists who sought to verify the theory, as "the principal contrarians."[42] Posner would continue to stick with the old dead theories that justified their opposition to minimum wage rather than adapt with the field. So too would the neoliberal economist James Buchanan, discussed in chapter 8, in a 1996 article in *The Wall Street Journal* written in response to Card and Krueger's study. "Just as no physicist would claim that 'water runs uphill,' no self-respecting economist would claim that increases in the minimum wage increase employment," wrote Buchanan. "Fortunately, only a handful of economists are willing to throw over the teaching of two centuries; we have not yet become a bevy of camp-following whores." The Nobel committee sided with the "camp-following whores" and dedicated the 2021 Nobel Prize to Card and other microeconomists of the credibility revolution (Krueger had already passed away).

The ideological nature of Law and Economics is most evident when Law and Economics scholars refuse to change with the field of economics, aligning legal theory with a single strand of neoliberal economics. The danger is about not just the miseducation of jurists and law students, but rather law and economic theories have been shaping law for decades. For example, Richard Posner built on Stigler's wage work in his influential 1974 National Bureau or Economic Research working paper "Theories of Economic Regulation," which was used by the Reagan administration to oppose unions and minimum wage laws.[43] Posner's influence alone—as well-cited scholar, prolific writer, government official, and federal judge—is responsible for much of neoliberalism's legal coup, which goes to show the value of a single articulate defender of free enterprise.

The rise of Law and Economics was abetted by arguments from neoliberal economists that economics is a hard science. As cutting-edge economic modeling propelled the Chicago School's pretensions to scientific rigor, legal scholars imported the economists' methods into their scholarship. Neoliberal economists, famously, had and still have a case of "physics envy," which has led the field toward macroeconomic, math-heavy ideas. Likewise, Law and Economics scholars could be said to have a case of "economics envy"—the valorization of grand theory over case-by-case analysis.

In Friedrich Hayek's 1974 Nobel Prize speech (the one denouncing the Nobel Prize), he said that he opposed placing the mantle of "science" on a discipline that does not follow the scientific process because it "confers on an individual an authority which in economics no man ought to possess." It was dangerous "charlatanism," he warned, for economists to equate their understanding about a complex phenomenon like a market with the physical sciences that can isolate and measure variables. Markets operate in dynamic societies that do not permit precise prediction, nor can any economist gain sufficient knowledge to shape them. In 1974, the economics community was still dominated by Keynesians and it was clear Hayek's concerns were directed at them. He warned of the Communists who became "dizzy with success during the early stages" and insisted that Nobel winners take an oath of humility vowing "never to exceed in public pronouncements the limits of their competence."[44] Hayek's prescient warning went unheeded, especially by his colleagues.

IT WAS the Law and Economics movement, not neoliberal economists like Friedman, that made the neoliberal coup possible. While Chicago economics attracted the most attention for launching neoliberalism, the agent enabling viral spread was the *legal theory* of economics. It was through reshaping the law that free market ideologies became reality. In other words, the route to market freedom was through state power. Part of the appeal of the Law and Economics workshops and the framework as taught in law schools was the ease and consistency of its applications. It put structure back into the law, especially after the Warren Court's supposedly wild deviations from precedent. Economics was scientific and rigorous. It had theoretical frameworks, not to mention the glow of the Nobel Prize conferred on the Chicago economists on whose coattails the theory rode.

Yet the structure was a mirage. Law and Economics imported untested theories advanced in economics into the law as though they were settled orthodoxy. Indeed, when a Law and Economics scholar ventures a theoretical answer to a question of jurisprudence, they always start with simplistic hypothetical scenarios of a property or contract dispute and the likely behavior of rational actors within those disputes. Once they establish how person A and person B would act in the hypothetical, an explanatory theory is proposed and then a policy outcome derived from the hypothesis. These theories are rarely—if ever—based on simple observations of the world. They are based, rather, on economic ideas.

Even basic ideas like efficiency are premised on complex theoretical observations that are far from intuitive. For Law and Economics scholars like Posner, efficiency is "exploiting economic resources in such a way that 'value' . . . is maximized, with value standing in as an aggregate measure of wealth."[45] This concept of efficiency—or the "socially optimal allocation"—is drawn from the work of the Italian economist Vilfredo Pareto. As Posner describes it, "Pareto superiority is the principle that one allocation of resources is superior to another if at least one person is better off under the first allocation than under the second and no one is worse off."[46] A social policy that allocates resources is "Pareto efficient" or "Pareto optimal" if it increases net wealth. If some people—even a majority of people—lose but net gains are increased, Pareto efficiency is achieved. Nor does it matter *who* wins or loses in the transaction.

The theory is almost always explained using hypothetical situations. For example, if factory A wants to purchase factory B, the Pareto-minded jurist must calculate the net gain of the merger, which consists of increased company profits and market gains minus total losses like the loss of "duplicative" jobs and services. Unquantifiable losses to communities or ecosystems are simply left out of the equation. Another common example of Pareto optimality concerns taxes. If a law takes (or taxes) money from A and spreads it evenly to the benefit of B, C, and D, that is not Pareto optimal; but if B, C, and D each lose $100 while A gains $1,000, it *is* Pareto optimal. It's all about the net gain, which is $700.

Once one begins to fill out the hypotheticals with real terms, the shortcomings of "efficiency" quickly become apparent. If B, C, and D lose $100 each in the form of health insurance and A's gains come in the form of stock dividends, this is still a socially optimal allocation according to Law and Economics. In the real world, if an environmental rule costs oil producers $100 billion to be in compliance, but the reduction in emissions is worth only $10 billion—the value ascribed to the lives saved and injuries avoided—the regulation is not efficient. The principle, as Posner emphasizes, is wealth maximization; where or how that wealth is maximized is inconsequential. This means that redistributive measures are not only unnecessary but actively detrimental. As Posner argues, reducing poverty is a net positive, but doing so through redistribution would disincentivize those who are taxed more from productive work *and also* disincentivize the poor who would otherwise have to work—a net negative.[47] This is Law and Economics's basic theory of efficiency—efficiency being the sine qua non of all that follows.

Another favorite heuristic of Law and Economics is the Coase theorem, named after Ronald Coase, whom we met earlier, and who won the Nobel Prize in Economics in 1991.[48] He articulated his theorem in his 1960 article "The Problem of Social Costs," which paved the way for the application of economic principles across various fields of law. Its influence has been enormous: it remains the most cited legal article of all time. "The Problem of Social Costs" advances a theory of bargaining over property rights. Coase's thesis is that in a world "without transaction costs"—for example, search and information, negotiation and bargaining efforts, enforcement, coordination, and psychological efforts and doubts—people would bargain with one anther to produce the most efficient distribution of property rights, regardless of initial rights and without legal intervention. In fact, in Coase's view, allocations decided upon privately are superior to those decided by litigation because parties could better identify and price externalities and interests than courts could. In determining what was optimal, Coase relied on Pareto as well.

A popular example of the Coase theorem used in law textbooks is of two businesses that share a space: one a loud music store, the other a doctor's office that needs quiet to function. In a dispute by one property owner against the other, a judge would have to decide either to allocate rights to the doctor and order the music store owner to stop emitting noise, or allocate rights to the music store and make the doctor live with the noise. But, according to the Coase theorem, neither of these outcomes is optimal, because the courts do not know the relative value of both businesses. If the doctor's business is much more valuable than the music store owner's, the court's decision in favor of the latter would reduce efficiency. The Coase theorem assumes that the two business owners are in the best position to value their business and that if the court does not intervene, the parties will reach the most optimal solution—which, in this case, would be the doctor paying the music store owner to stop playing music.

The theory relies on some key assumptions: first, that both parties are rational utility maximizers; second, that both can accurately value their business as well as the cost of the nuisance; third, that they can reach a bargain; and finally, that a world exists "without transaction costs, time, efforts, and the finances put forth to reach an agreement or transaction." Such costs could include human emotions, power differentials, imperfect information, and the many other concerns and meanings with which property rights are imbued beyond monetary costs and benefits.

When discussing property rights and disputes, textbooks inflected with Law and Economics almost always refer to the American ecologist Garrett Hardin's "tragedy of the commons." Hardin's first articulation of the theory was in relation to human overpopulation, which he believed should be controlled through forced sterilizations and banning immigrants. When applied to property law, the tragedy of the commons shows that when a lake, a pond, or any natural space or resource is commonly owned, it leads to a "tragedy" driven by individual selfishness. Each person will seek to extract as much of a resource—whether fish or lumber or something else—at the expense of all others. The solution is to privatize property, which Hardin believes will prevent individuals who are motivated by their own self-interest from exploiting community-owned resources.

Despite the fact that the tragedy of the commons has been debunked by Elinor Ostrom, the first of only two female economists to win the Nobel Prize in Economics, I have not found a single property law textbook or law school that does not teach the tragedy of the commons as a foundational property law doctrine. Indeed, both the Coase theorem and the tragedy of the commons are taught alongside some early theories of natural law as articulated by John Locke—for instance, that the labor and use of the land by British colonists in the Americas entitled them to its ownership.

On its face, Law and Economics seems straightforward and nonideological, but the devil is in the details—or, more specifically, the details that are *omitted* when a decision maker seeks efficiency. In practice, the alternative to deciding cases based on *efficiency* was to determine the admittedly messy math of *justice.* By narrowing the legal *issue* as one of economic efficiency rather than *fairness,* for example, the debate is thereby limited. The virtue of textualism and efficiency analysis in legal arguments was to put on blinders to all other issues that might be relevant to determining a dispute. This narrowing was the whole point.

To illustrate each economic concept, Posner often uses hypotheticals rather than economic data to drive the point home. Often, his hypotheticals begin with a seemingly straightforward dispute—a landlord-tenant, an employer-employee, or a lender-borrower diagreement through which he proves in example after example that what might seem fair in a given case is in fact counterproductive. While it might be emotionally satisfying to a judge to take a low-income tenant's side against a slumlord refusing to make necessary repairs, an example in Posner's book based on a real case, doing so would in fact end up harming low-income tenants in general by reducing available apartments. These assertions are made with certainty but without empirical proof, and often haphazardly.

Law and Economics made up for its lack of scientific rigor with a consistency in outcomes. In almost every hypothetical case dealing with issues of equality, Law and Economics echoed Greenspan's letter to Nixon: do nothing! (but with graphs). That is because the structure and methodology of Law and Economics ignores histories of allocation, inequality, and power. Calculations of efficiency do not account for original allocations and the capital and property rights accumulated historically; the theft of indigenous lands, Jim Crow, coverture laws, and Euclidean zoning, for example, are extraneous factors that are irrelevant to present calculations about efficiency. The economic theories that ground Law and Economics took a snapshot of the present, created a hypothetical theorem based on rationality, and waved away things that could not be explained. What this amounted to was state discipline for the poor and "market discipline" for the wealthy. According to Posner, "The function of criminal sanction in a capitalist market economy, then, is to prevent individuals from bypassing the efficient market." Or, "the criminal law is designed primarily for the nonaffluent; the affluent are kept in line, for the most part, by tort law."[49]

Nor does the hypothesized market of Law and Economics factor in work performed outside of formal labor markets or the production of resources that are not monetized. The economist Katrine Marçal asks, "Who cooked Adam Smith's dinner?"[50] The answer was his mother, whose household labor was not included in his—or in any—neoclassical model of how the economy works and so wouldn't be relevant in a Law

and Economics judge's efficiency analysis. As the pre-neoliberal economist Paul Samuelson quipped in his textbook about the narrowness of
general economic measures: "If a man marries his maid, total economic
output decreases."[51] The joke, often enough, is on women.

Law and Economics theories professed to uncover the universal laws
of supply and demand and to render visible the invisible hand of the
market. Once accepted as neutral and scientific, these models jumped
from the realm of economic theory into politics and then subsequently
became infused into the fabric of the law. It was through reshaping the
law that free market ideologies became reality. In fact, Law and Economics has so thoroughly influenced legal thought that even progressive
law professors, in fields as diverse as criminal justice and voting rights,
must use the language of efficiency and wealth maximization. As with
originalism, so with Law and Economics: we are all originalists, and we
must all be utility maximizers.

That requirement gets instilled early. Although many American law
students come to law school with their minds set on practicing "public law"—that is, constitutional law, criminal law, family law, or social
policy—most, due to the financial pressure of loan debt, end up going
into some form of *private law*: tax law, corporate law, banking law, bankruptcy law, and contract law. It is in these areas of the law that Law and
Economics has become the default mode of legal analysis. The cohort
of private-law scholars at elite law schools—those who shape the field,
write textbooks and legal treatises, and mentor future corporate lawyers and regulators—are, almost without exception, Law and Economics scholars ideologically oriented around free markets. The field has
been so successful in passing itself as nonideological that most law students see Law and Economics theories of markets as synonymous with
market law.

Given the subject matter of private law, it stands to reason that its
scholars and practitioners would gravitate to economically informed
methods of legal analysis. But the marriage of the two isn't simply a
matter of elective affinity. Playing a prominent role, as ever, are those
well-funded—by right-wing organizations and corporations—Law and
Economics centers at prestigious law schools. These centers often pay

for fellowships for aspiring law professors who want to enter the field, and they bring together Law and Economics scholars across the elite law schools for conferences, awards, and publications. Because private law is hyperspecialized, in each field a small group of scholars and practitioners can help shape the law as it is practiced by bankruptcy courts or Delaware Chancery Courts, which handle all corporate law matters (more than 65 percent of Fortune 500 companies are incorporated in Delaware).[52]

The bifurcation of legal scholarship into private law and public law has meant that legal issues faced by minorities, women, and the poor are rarely addressed in market-related fields like corporate, tax, and contract law. Claims for gender equality or racial justice are often cast as "identity politics" or as "redistribution" that are external to the natural market order. That is because the key assumption of the entire Law and Economics enterprise is that the market's current distributions of property rights are "natural" and, therefore, right. According to Ronald Coase, any allocations of property rights by courts is an inefficient "intervention" in the market. The assumptions build on one another. The market is efficient, which means the values it assigns are correct, which means that any claims to alter those rights are against the market, and thus inefficient. It is circular logic, but it has proved surprisingly effective and durable.

This is the sleight of hand that made Law and Economics such a formidable tool of the reactionary right. Like textualism and originalism, Law and Economics proposes to be a race-neutral and nonpartisan legal theory that just happens to double as an excuse to do nothing about existing inequalities. Any group claiming remedies for past harm is now left to beseech the courts to "intervene" in markets or to engage in counterproductive "redistribution." To make the market fair was not redistribution, but justice.

Hypothetical scenarios are often used to describe how markets work, but the market on which Law and Economics is also hypothetical. In the real world, only white men were endowed with property rights. It was *that* system of identity politics that built the modern market and *that* history of exclusion that is obscured and hidden away by Law and Economics. And also that history of racial hierarchy embedded in market advantage and disadvantage that Law and Economics reproduced indefinitely.

DESPITE OMITTING important variables of race, gender, and power, Law and Economics theorists have tried their hand at the world's knottiest problems. The 1992 article "The Optimal Regulation of AIDS," written by Richard Posner and the economist Tomas Philipson, launched the field of "economic epidemiology" and influenced the U.S. government's response to the AIDS pandemic, both in America and worldwide. Posner and Philipson's ambition was to treat "risky sexual behavior as a market in which trading takes place under condition of uncertainty about quality." Thus, "a fatal disease can be spread by voluntary utility-maximizing conduct of rational persons."[53]

The article was followed a year later by *Private Choices and Public Health: The AIDS Epidemic in an Economic Perspective*, a book in which Posner and Philipson make a classic conservative "personal responsibility" argument, arguing that people who engage in unprotected sex and who know about the risks of HIV transmission have made a rational choice based on a cost-benefit analysis. Posner and Philipson averred that, as with any market governed by the rules of efficiency, government intervention would be "counterproductive." Smugly in possession of a "risk model for sex," the lawyer and the economist ignored the actual experts and argued against government action of any kind in curbing AIDS, either domestically or abroad.

Posner and Philipson's determinations were not the result of empirical study; rather, their "findings" were based solely on general economic principles, which led them to some baffling claims. Posner and Philipson advised, for example, against more testing for HIV/AIDS. Testing, they reasoned, would likely "increase the demand for risky sex and hence the likelihood that the disease will spread."[54]

It was not efficient, therefore, to do much about AIDS. Not only were the "negative externalities" of AIDS low, they were suffered by those who voluntarily engaged in unprotected sex—people who also happened to be poor, young, gay, of color, or otherwise already stigmatized.

The economic case for letting the virus proceed unmitigated was not just motivated by efficiency, but a notion of freedom. The state should not intervene "paternalistically" in a free sexual market governed by rational choices. To protect people through subsidies (that is, health insurance) from their own "perverse" risk-taking would result in "moral hazard," which would artificially lower the price of risk (that is, death) and lead to higher-risk choice-making (that is, sex). As Posner and Philipson wrote, "Anything that lowers the costs of sex will increase the amount of it."[55] The Law and Economics response to AIDS: do nothing.

Posner and Philipson were not outliers; again, Posner is the most cited legal scholar ever. And their claims about AIDS were tied to a broader neoliberal "family values" framework. As the historian Melinda Cooper has shown, that framework was promoted as a means of "forcing individual risk-takers to internalize the costs of their own actions," thus "transforming public risks into private responsibilities."[56] Neoliberal social policy thus "restores the private family and its legal obligations of care to a foundational role in the free market order," which is, according to Cooper, "contingent upon a moral philosophy of prudential risk management that leaves no excess costs to the state."[57]

Indeed, Law and Economics neoliberals were just as invested in imposing a patriarchal family structure as was the religious right, but they made their case on efficiency rather than on faith or morality. Using austerity economics rather than paternalistic moralism, they advocated policies that punished nonnormative family structures, especially single mothers and racial minorities. Neoliberals did not necessarily judge "fatherlessness" or "broken homes" as immoral but rather as costly, with negative externalities borne by the rest of society.

Law and Economics "family policies," including Posner and Philipson's recommendations on AIDS, were not merely academic thought experiments. They were taken up by politicians and bureaucrats. Posner and Philipson's unsupported conjectures, accredited by the seemingly "scientific" rigor of economics and the elite credentials of its purveyors, caused a great deal of damage. For one, they were directly adopted into the World Bank's report on AIDS in 1997, which became a basis for policy and international aid. "Do individuals also weigh costs, benefits, and risks when deciding whether and how to engage in these activities?" the report asked.[58] Yes, according to what they called "a substantial body of economic research" showing "that actual and perceived costs and benefits, some of which can be affected by government policies, significantly influence private decisions about marriage, childbearing, and contraceptive use."[59] The ideas proposed by Posner and Phillipson were all debunked by real science (and common sense), but only after they were used by policy makers across the world to ignore the devastation of the AIDS virus for many years and to stigmatize those infected with the virus as having engaged in "individual risk-taking" in accordance with rational choices.

Economic epidemiology reared its head again at the start of the COVID-19 pandemic, when the Law and Economics giant Richard Epstein wrote a study showing that the pandemic would lead to the deaths of approximately 500 people and concluded that "progressives" were "overreacting." This particular "do nothing" response was in March 2020. The pandemic took 500 lives before he even published the article, prompting Epstein to revise his estimate up to about 5,000 fatalities. By the end of March 2020, the CDC had reported that a total of 3,926 people in the United States had died of COVID-19. Despite its risible incorrectness, the report circulated in the Trump administration and likely influenced its feckless response to COVID-19.

When questioned by *The New Yorker*'s Isaac Chotiner about his failed theory, Epstein argued that his "model" was based on "Darwinian economics." While the model may have failed at prediction, Epstein still defended it as good economics: "I'm not an empiricist," but the "probability distribution" was accurate in applying "standard economic-evolutionary theory out of Darwin—and applying it to this particular case." Epstein dismissed letters from scientists debunking his theory. "What I don't get from anybody is a systematic refutation which looks at the points parameter by parameter." He then challenged Chotiner to "debate him" based on the model and belittled Chotiner's academic credentials. "I think everybody is wrong," said Epstein. Epstein's truculence was somewhat unusual but his hubristic belief in economic modeling over real-world data was not.[60]

Epstein, Posner, and other Law and Economics stalwarts have influenced policy and decision making for years. Practitioners of Law and Economics are assured of their abilities to "model" and reason through every social problem without even a rudimentary understanding of the fields to which they're applying those models. These self-described "experts" replaced the unpredictability of the law with pseudo-sophisticated "economics," the balancing scales of justice with a flattened numerical equation of costs versus benefits. Like the originalism advanced by the Federalist Society, Law and Economics has narrowed the purview of the courts and constrained the role of the legal system in achieving justice.

IT IS no coincidence that at the very moment when the Supreme Court began to right past wrongs and extend constitutional rights to racial and sexual minorities, new legal doctrines rose to prominence. Those who devised them persuaded the courts to ignore issues of rights and justice in favor of abstract theories of economic efficiency or the immutability of the Constitution. The Federalist Society and the Law and Economics movement successfully laundered ideology into neutral doctrine and abetted a slow methodological coup of the American government through the legal system. Those who subscribed to the new methods changed the rules of the game and bought the referees, securing a winning streak that has lasted several decades.

Neoliberal law is supposedly neutral, but it actually predetermines a set of outcomes. Even in cases where lawyers and scholars are challenging corporate power, they have been forced to argue their cause using the language of textualism/originalism or Law and Economics—for example, by claiming that capping environmental waste is justified by the law because it increases economic efficiency. By changing the terms of the debate, neoliberals have produced outcomes that are anti-government-regulation and pro-business. Every gay couple claiming equality and every woman arguing for bodily autonomy has to argue for their right based on what some Founding Father intended hundreds of years ago; every agency attempting to regulate an environmental toxin, a payday loan, or an unsafe drug must convince a judge steeped in Law and Economics that the market costs of the proposed rule will not outweigh the market benefits. These tests and measures themselves have no constitutional backing whatsoever—the Constitution has been interpreted and reinterpreted for hundreds of years through a shifting set of legal doctrines; and even Madison and Hamilton could not agree on which of those was more valid than the other. Yet thanks to the efforts of right-wing funders, the law has been so narrowed as to make actual justice often irrelevant to the resolution of a dispute. These tests have formed an obstacle that many well-meaning reforms have been unable to breach.

Neoliberals recognized from the beginning that their revolution could succeed only insofar as the legal system was co-opted—or, rather, "standardized"—on a global scale. Ludwig von Mises, MPS's éminence grise and Hayek's mentor, explained the threat of economic nationalism to international trade as early as 1943: "It is an illusion to believe that such conflicts could be settled by arbitration on the part of impartial courts. A court can administer justice only according to the articles of a code. But it is exactly these prescriptions and rules which are contested."[61]

Only when an ideology captures the mechanism of justice can it cease being an ideology and become the invisible structure of a social order. Neoliberalism transformed every level of the judicial process, from the courts to the way that laws are made in legislatures to agency rule-making. The result is the society we live in today.

PART III

Metamorphosis

CHAPTER 6

The Conscience of Capitalism

The highest laws of the land (America) are not only the constitution and constitutional laws, but also contracts.
—HANNAH ARENDT, *DENKTAGEBUCH* (1951)

SURVEY OF AMERICANS conducted in the 1990s by the Library of Congress found Ayn Rand's 1957 novel *Atlas Shrugged* to be "the most influential book in the US," second only to the Bible.[1] *Atlas Shrugged* and Rand's other most popular novel, *The Fountainhead* (1943), presented godlike heroes, invariably entrepreneurs and industrialists, triumphing over innumerable villains: government bureaucrats, indolent workers, and the mediocre masses of nonproducers, whose legal codes and parasitic taxes pilfered the wealth created by her protagonists. Akin to traditional folklore and fables, Rand's stories were morality plays of right and wrong, where the righteous prevailed and the wicked were punished.

Rand, perhaps because she was a popular novelist (or perhaps because she was a woman), has not been given her due as an early foundational theorist of neoliberalism. Yet her pathos-filled allegories were—and remain—much more resonant cultural touchstones than Friedrich Hayek's *Road to Serfdom* or Milton Friedman's *Capitalism and Freedom*.

Former Speaker of the House Paul Ryan, for example, gave each new staffer a copy of *Atlas Shrugged* when he was in office. Rather than offer arguments or theory, Rand's novels elaborate on the morality—the "soul"—of neoliberalism, even if she herself didn't use the term.

Rand herself would have rejected any quasi-theological references to morality or the soul. The philosophy she developed and espoused— "objectivism"—had as its foundational principle the renunciation of all ideology but self-interest, which she considered the only "objective" truth.[2] She came by her skepticism of ideology honestly. She was born in 1905 to a wealthy family in St. Petersburg during the twilight of the Russian Empire. After the Bolsheviks confiscated her father's business amid the October Revolution, she and her family fled to Crimea. She immigrated to America in 1926, specifically to Hollywood, and was at once smitten by capitalism, the movies, and the emphasis placed on freedom.[3] She was forthright in her pronouncements, blunt in her criticism, and quick to call out even her closest allies for any hint of heresy. In 1981, an elderly Rand ate out with her former acolyte Alan Greenspan, then the chair of the Federal Reserve, and accused him of selling out his principles on account of his support for social security. She "scolded him so furiously that other diners turned and stared—a diminutive seventy-six-year-old woman was berating a famous, square-shouldered economist," according to Greenspan biographer Sebastian Mallaby.[4] Hayek, too, found himself on the end of a Rand tirade: she was so enraged by the Austrian's moderation on the role of government in the market that when she saw him, she yelled "compromiser!" across a crowded room and called him "an abysmal fool" and "our most pernicious enemy."[5]

After reading Barry Goldwater's 1960 book *The Conscience of a Conservative,* which played a pivotal role in rejuvenating the American conservative movement and propelling the Arizona senator to political stardom, Rand took great care to write him a harsh and disapproving letter, in the course of which she explains the core of her philosophy and her objections to the morality of mainstream Christian America.[6] Rand supported Goldwater and even called him "the only hope of the anti-collectivist side on today's political scene," but she condemned his faith and his dangerous rhetoric about "the higher good" of spirituality. To Rand, a true capitalist could not worship any other God but the market.

The first chapter of Goldwater's book, about "the issue of religion," so disappointed Rand that she told him she suspected it wasn't even written by him but by his ghostwriter. She was correct: Goldwater's ghostwriters were William F. Buckley, the founder of *The National Review*, and his brother-in-law Brent Bozell, author of *The Warren Revolution* (a critique of the Warren Court) and coauthor (with Buckley) of *McCarthy and His Enemies*, a defense of Joseph McCarthy. Both were prominent conservatives, Yale graduates, and Catholics.

In 1960, when Rand was writing to Goldwater, the yoking of the religious right and the free market right—such an obvious feature of our national politics today—seemed impossible. Rand was a vociferous defender of abortion and a proud atheist who denounced religious thinking as "superstitious," "primitive," and "backwards"—the same labels she bestowed on the "inferior" peoples of the Global East and South, whose lack of capitalist industry she blamed on their underdeveloped capacity to reason. In her letter to Goldwater, she took him to task for writing that "the Conservative believes that man is, in part, an economic, an animal creature; but that he is also a spiritual creature with spiritual needs and spiritual desires. What is more, these needs and desires reflect the *superior* side of man's nature, and thus take precedence over his economic wants" (emphasis hers). She wondered aloud whether he had actually even read or enjoyed *Atlas Shrugged*—he had told her that he had—because he was "diametrically opposed to its main thesis," which was that "man's material, industrial production" is "his noblest spiritual [quality]." She rejected the "false, mythical doctrine" that regarded "spiritual interests as opposed and *superior* to his material interests." He must know, she writes, that America's enemies damn it as a "'materialistic' country"; "surely" the senator could not support such foreign ideas.

But he did support them. Unlikely though the marriage seemed, Goldwater was the first to fuse Christian fundamentalism with laissez-faire libertarianism. And although it would prove a losing combination in the presidential election of 1964, that fusion would soon become mainstream, accepted, even obvious. How it did so is key to understanding how neoliberalism succeeded.

THE STORY OF the religious right and its role in the rise of modern conservatism has been told many times before. It usually spans Billy Graham's mass rallies in the 1950s, the rise of abortion as a flashpoint in American politics in the 1970s, the self-professed Moral Majority led by Jerry Falwell, founded in 1979, and all the way to the Supreme Court's overturning of *Roe v. Wade* in 2022 and beyond. One of the central terms in this story is "fusionism," the idea, pioneered by right-wing intellectuals, that the modern right would incorporate libertarians, social conservatives, the religious right, and other groups that might otherwise be opposed to all the rest.

It is easy to see, in retrospect, how that alliance has benefited corporations, the wealthy, and the powerful, but what have been the spoils for the religious right? The obvious answer is power, insofar as power is defined as the recognition of and priority given to the Christian right's "moral concerns"—namely, the prohibition of abortion and the maintenance of firm boundaries regarding sex and gender. The conventional characterization of the religious right takes its leaders and spokespeople at their word.

Another, complementary reading is that the religious right embraced free market economics as a reactionary response to civil rights laws. The strategic alignment between Christian conservatives and libertarians in the aftermath of the *Brown v. Board of Education* ruling is suggestive. After the IRS began sending Christian schools questionnaires about the racial makeup of their student body—a consequence of the Court's ruling in *Green v. Connally* (1971), which stripped so-called segregation academies of their nonprofit tax exemptions—an irate Falwell publicly denounced the immorality of the government, fulminating that "in some states, it's easier to open a massage parlor than a Christian school." The free market ideas of "school choice," charter schools and vouchers, first proposed by Milton Friedman in *Capitalism and Freedom* and a post-*Brown* article, became a cause célèbre for the Christian right. It was *Brown,* in other words, that first turned the Christian right against government intervention.

In reality, the creation of a unified and politicized religious right out of multiple Christian sects took real work and intention. That work was done by the right's think tanks and nonprofits, which tried a variety of strategies to mobilize into a reliable voting bloc a previously disparate group of Christian denominations.[7] Soon enough, elites on the right hit on abortion as the perfect issue to persuade religious conservatives to support the plutocrats' preferred platform. All they had to do was promise to appoint an anti-*Roe* justice to the Supreme Court. The usual suspects—the Kochs, the Bradleys, the Wilks brothers, and the DeVos Foundation, endowed by the family of Betsy DeVos, Trump's education secretary—funded a slew of antiabortion nonprofits and Christian-values nonprofits starting in the 1970s. The Federalist Society, meanwhile, worked on merging these assorted issues into a coherent ideology. For example, Leonard Leo, the longtime vice president of the Federalist Society, is credited today with overturning both *Roe* and campaign finance restrictions. (His efforts to transform politics paid off in 2022, when he received a $1.6 billion tax-deductible donation from electronics manufacturer Barre Seid.)

Whereas the donors were motivated to act for financial gains—that is, to maximize their utility—most voters voted based on deeply held beliefs or moral values. As Paul Weyrich, then the president of the Heritage Foundation, wrote to donors about his hopes for the right in the mid-1970s: "The new political philosophy must be defined by us [conservatives] in moral terms, packaged in non-religious language, and propagated throughout the country by our new coalition."[8] Weyrich began calling the movement he envisioned "the moral majority," which sounded like Nixon's silent majority and immediately struck a chord with figures like the up-and-coming Republican radical Newt Gingrich and like Jerry Falwell, who cofounded a PAC by that name with Weyrich. Right-wing groups produced documentaries like *The Silent Scream*, which inaccurately depicted a full-grown infant in the womb "silently screaming" as an abortion doctor begins to tear it apart.

The fusion of religious right and neoliberalism yielded a formidable voting bloc that would dominate American politics and change the market as well. Ironically, the moral majority's legal code was not Christian, but Randian. What the moral myopia of the pro-life movement has wrought is the channeling of all values, ethics, and virtues into a select few social concerns, leaving the bulk of the law to the punitive calculus of market efficiency. The moral blinders of pro-life politics have obscured the social and democratic—one might even say Christian—values underlying policies like protections for the poor and weak as well as antitrust law. In a strange reversal, the fusion of church and state in the religious right's dogma has entailed a separation of morality and markets. Inside the Trojan horse of family values waited an army of neoliberal deregulatory judges, regulators, and congressmen, who have cut the moral constraints that curbed the market's worst instincts and the equitable principles required for social cohesion.

Now, after a fifty-year struggle to overturn *Roe v. Wade*, the religious right can claim victory on its core issue. But in that same period, the merger of God and mammon diluted key Christian principles about wealth, greed, and poverty. Instead of a benevolent being that punishes the greedy and protects the poor, the fusionists' state became the stern father, tightfisted and emotionally distant.

FOR NEOLIBERAL purists like Rand, any concession to the pious, no matter how small, was unacceptable. She had no patience whatsoever for the Christians and their superstitions and suffered many insults from other conservatives without backing down. Even as the *National Review* panned her books, she was adamant. "An embryo *has no rights*," she emphasized. "Abortion is a *moral* right—which should be left to the sole discretion of the woman involved"; "to equate a *potential* life with an *actual* life, is vicious; to advocate the sacrifice of the latter to the former, is unspeakable."[9] She called pro-lifers "hateful" people who were "against the mind, against reason, against ambition, against success, against love, against any value that brings happiness to human life."[10]

Republican party leaders and their donors did not share Rand's moral absolution and thus were happy to oppose abortion rights to take control of everything else. Conservative Christians, meanwhile, had to rewrite practically the entire Bible to justify the greed and immorality of some of the right's most successful leaders. The Bible is preoccupied with the dangers of greed and even excess wealth. Yet with the rise of the prosperity gospel starting in the 1950s, many Christians have not only excused wealth but transformed it into a sign of God's favor. Today, the most popular evangelical ministries promise practitioners that God wants them to be rich. The incursion of neoliberal ethics into Christian doctrine has surely done damage to communities of faith by tainting their doctrine as well as their moral authority. Yet the Christian embrace of neoliberalism has also harmed the market—ironically, by replacing actual biblical prohibitions (such as usury) with the morality of profits and entrepreneurship.

Historically, the charge to protect the poor and weak—a fundamental tenet of most major religions—has fueled America's most effective market reforms. The Progressive movement of the late nineteenth to early twentieth century was propelled in part, if not entirely, by Christian belief. Transcendentalists, Quakers, and Christian abolitionists fought for justice based on their understanding of biblical morality. Protestant revivalists and evangelicals like William Jennings Bryan merged religious conviction and radical politics. Bryan gave a sermon opposing the gold standard and advocating looser monetary policy at the Democratic National Convention in 1896, saying, famously, that "you cannot crucify mankind on a cross of gold." Decades later, the Christian core of Martin Luther King's Poor People's Campaign was manifest, and he followed in a long line of Black Christian reformers. Before neoliberalism, some Christian churches financed books by economists such as Howard Bowen, who argued in 1953 that free enterprise was acceptable only if it gave something to society. In other words, Christian groups believed—to paraphrase Jesus's edict about the sabbath—that the market was made for man, not man for the market. Although the alliance between free market fundamentalists and Christian fundamentalists seems "natural" now, it was not inevitable that the evangelical right would find common cause with nonbelievers like Hayek, Friedman, and Rand, for whom a concept like "do good unto others" was suspect.

It would be a mistake, however, to see neoliberals as mere economists led by reason (as they saw themselves) or amoral mercenaries interested only in maximizing returns on investment (as their detractors saw them). Neoliberalism encompassed a moral ideology whose zealotry matched the evangelicals'. Neoliberalism came to prominence because it proposed a compelling narrative of the triumph of good over evil.

In Rand's novels, "good" were the innovators who created beauty and power through efficient production and "evil" were the government bureaucrats whose senseless regulations and parasitic taxation revealed their immorality. And like any morality play, the good prevailed and the wicked were made to suffer. *The Fountainhead*'s Howard Roark, frustrated by government bureaucracy inhibiting a large housing complex he's designed, blows up the building at night. At the end of *Atlas Shrugged*, due to government overreach, a catastrophic train wreck kills hundreds of passengers riding on the heroine's railroad. Her descriptions of the passengers on the runaway train are telling: An elderly schoolteacher in car 3 "who had spent her life turning class after class of helpless children into miserable cowards, by teaching them that the will of the majority is the only standard of good and evil, that the majority may do anything it pleases, that they must not assert their own personalities, but must do what others were doing"; an economics professor in car 2 "who advocated the abolition of private property, explaining that intelligence plays no part in industrial production, that man's mind is conditioned by material tools, that anybody can run a factory or a railroad, and it's only a matter of seizing the machinery." The mother who dies with her children apparently earned her fate because she is married to a government employee who enforces job directives, and whom she defends by saying, "I don't care, it's only the rich that they hurt. After all, I must think of my children."

Although the priests and administrators of neoliberalism spoke in terms of rational economics, the prophet was clear in her righteous judgments. She explained at length in unsolicited letters and shouting matches that her philosophy was a coherent worldview that conflicted with the moral view of Christianity. It was either *Atlas Shrugged* or the Bible—subscribing to both was heresy. While the priests spoke in terms of rational economics, the prophet offered righteous judgments.

Rand meted out punitive justice and condemnation without subtlety. Even a conservative stalwart like Whittaker Chambers was struck by Rand's tone of "dogmatism without appeal"; writing in 1957 in the *National Review*, he observed that *Atlas Shrugged* "supposes itself to be the bringer of final revelation" and casts dissenters as "willfully wicked." Though Rand claimed she was just being "reasonable," in reality, any "resistance to the Message cannot be tolerated.... From almost any page of *Atlas Shrugged*," Whitaker observed, "a voice can be heard, from painful necessity, commanding: 'To a gas chamber—go!' "[11]

Despite protestations by neoliberals that they were simply espousing value-free science, they were, in fact, replacing one set of values with another. Shareholder primacy for social responsibility. Efficient markets for natural law. "Blessed are the entrepreneurs" for "Blessed are the poor." Capitalism for democracy.

The alliance with the religious right wasn't a fusion so much as a complete takeover by the morality of *Atlas Shrugged* of that in Chistianity.

To neoliberal heads of state like Margaret Thatcher and Ronald Reagan, whose faith in markets was akin to religious faith, free market economics was the whole of morality. Speaking of Jesus's parable, Thatcher counseled, "No one would remember the Good Samaritan if he'd only had good intentions; he had money, too."[12] Compare this interpretation with Martin Luther King's: "On the one hand we are called to play the Good Samaritan on life's roadside, but that will be only an initial act. One day we must come to see that the whole Jericho Road must be transformed so that men and women will not be constantly beaten and robbed as they make their journey on life's highway." To change the road would require a collective effort, which was anathema to the Gospel according to Thatcher. "True compassion," said King, "is more than flinging a coin to a beggar.... A true revolution of values will soon look uneasily on the glaring contrast of poverty and wealth."[13]

Like King, the neoliberals sought not only a revolution in policy and material conditions, but a revolution in values—despite their denunciations of both revolutions *and* values. What is required to achieve "growth, prosperity and, ultimately, human fulfillment," said Reagan in 1981 at the IMF, is a "willingness to believe in the magic of the marketplace."[14] And Thatcher said, "Economics are the method. The object is to change the heart and soul."

While Friedman and other theorists frequently characterized the movement as little more than modern economic liberalism or a revival of classical economics, what they actually enacted was as far from earlier iterations of capitalism as the mixed economy they sought to dismantle. The dogma of free markets as a moral good is one of the key distinctions between neoliberalism and classical economics. Adam Smith would have agreed with Martin Luther King: "No society can surely be flourishing and happy," wrote the intellectual father of capitalism, "of which the greater part of the members are poor and miserable." To Smith, helping the poor sat at the core of morality; he did not consider a market economy a basis upon which to build a moral code (much less to be the code itself).

In *The Theory of Moral Sentiments*, Smith argued that vast inequalities must be checked. "It is but equity, besides, that they who feed, clothe and lodge the whole body of the people, should have such a share of the produce of their own labour as to be themselves tolerably well fed, clothed and lodged." His later and better-known book, *The Wealth of Nations*, was itself a response to inequity: "Wherever there is great property," Smith wrote, "there is great inequality." Not only was it a person's moral responsibility to take care of the poor, but a society that did not treat the poor with respect was an immoral one.

If *The Wealth of Nations* was the bible of the neoliberals, they were heretics, violating the basic tenets of the Smithian laissez-faire creed. First, classical economists like Smith were suspicious of excessive market power—of firms, trade institutions, banks, and monopolies. Smith believed that dominant industries with excess market power were primarily to blame for restricting competition and imposing steep barriers to entry in any trade. "People of the same trade seldom meet together, even for merriment and diversion, but the conversation ends in a conspiracy against the public, or in some contrivance to raise prices." And where should the remedy come from, according to Smith? Not the market, but the law, which he believed could at least address the power of these merchants over others. Smith's *Wealth of Nations* was written in an era when guilds controlled each trade and when European nations refused to trade with one another, and much of the book is addressed to these powerful merchants who suppressed the freedom of the lower classes by their control of licensing. Smith was also writing in Scotland, a de facto British colony, in 1776, the same year the Americans were writing their own declarations of freedom. The book addresses British laws that imposed trade restrictions which prevented weaker nations and small traders from competing on fair terms. It is a book about corruption and abuse of power and echoes many of the concerns laid out by the American colonies—Smith was seeking freedom and equality of the people as well as the wealth of nations. In fact, when neoliberal foundations funded a reprinting of *The Wealth of Nations,* they chose only selected passages and left out others, thus misrepresenting the book's overarching message.[15]

Neoliberals, for their part, argued that only government regulation diminished market competition. Monopolies would be competed away; wages would be based on merit; and per Coase, knotty issues of legal rights would be handled through bargaining between rational individuals. There was a magic to it all, as Reagan suggested.

Second, classical economists kept market rules and market order separate from social mores and morality. While market actors were and should be governed by self-interest, men were only market actors *in markets*—that is, men were not to conduct themselves as market actors in every realm of life. For neoliberals, there was no place where the laws of market efficiency did not govern behavior. As we saw in the previous chapter, Law and Economics thinkers like Posner and Richard Epstein have applied the theory of efficiency to family law, crime, and even pandemic response.

Finally, for classical economists, market freedom was not total. Smith, David Ricardo, and other early boosters of laissez-faire still supported state control of banking and interest rates as well as rules prohibiting anticompetitive behavior. There are a surfeit of examples of classical liberals' own "heterodoxy," according to a neoliberal measure, but a few will suffice to illustrate the point. On taxes, because "the necessaries of life occasion the great expense of the poor" and the rich's principal expenses consist of "luxuries and vanities" and "magnificent house embellish[ments]," Smith advised that a levy should be implemented that fell "heaviest on the rich" and that should "contribute to the public expense, not only in proportion to their revenue, but something more than in that proportion." On minimum wage laws, Smith wrote, "Masters are always and everywhere in a sort of tacit, but constant and uniform, combination, not to raise the wages of labour above their actual rate . . . and sometimes . . . enter into particular combinations to sink the wages of labour even below this rate." These cabals, he said, were always "conducted with the utmost silence and secrecy till the moment of execution," which is why they rarely came in for public censure. In contrast, when workers combine, "the masters . . . never cease to call aloud for the assistance of the civil magistrate, and the rigorous execution of those laws which have been enacted with so much severity against the combination of servants, labourers, and journeymen." For neoliberals like Hayek, Lewis Powell, and Friedman, who compared unions to criminal syndicates that relied on the threat of violence, the bosses, not the laborers, were the victims.

While Smith believed that capitalism was the best system to meet the economic needs of society, neoliberals believed in capitalism as the one and only truth. For Smith, free markets would liberate merchants from the rigid feudal system that had concentrated power in the hands of too few. Capitalism was a means toward democracy and greater freedom. For neoliberals, however, capitalism was not just a means of shoring up morality, society, and democracy; it was an end unto itself, superseding, if need be, morality, society, and democracy. And the site of this revolution was, again, the law. Allied with the religious right, neoliberals stripped the law of its pursuit of justice and equity, subjugating it to the needs of the market. Neoliberal theory, in short, has resulted in the triumph of market ethics over social ethics.

EVIDENCE OF this triumph can be found in the quiet transformation of America's common law courts. The phrase "common law" refers to the law that was "common" across all the English king's courts, whose common law tradition was adopted by the United States. Common law is a law created by judges as they decide cases, with one case being binding on the ones that come after it. It didn't take long for Law and Economics to transform the common law—one case at a time. This transformation can perhaps most clearly be seen in contract law, which sits at the core of the economy. Indeed, if carbon is the basic element of the organic world, the contract is the basic element of the market.

Contracts are the basic building blocks of capitalism because they allow for free exchange between parties based on future expectations: *I will work for you now if you pay me later; I will loan you money if you promise to pay me back a portion every month with interest.* Most contracts do not need to be enforced by a court, but the promise and threat of legal enforcement are always in the background. The rest of the economy builds upon contracts between individuals, between individuals and firms, between firms and firms, between the state and firms, and on and on. Reliance on contracts is a necessary condition on which capitalism depends. Insofar as the contract was made willingly, without fraud or duress, the parties must perform their part or pay damages. This expectation is so entrenched in modern capitalism that it is background noise. In countries where the enforcement of contracts, or the "rule of law," has broken down, commerce also ceases to function.

Yet contract enforcement is not as straightforward as it appears. As the German sociologist Max Weber put it, "A legal order can indeed be characterized by the agreements which it does or does not enforce." The laws of contract, specifically their treatment of usury and "unconscionability," are also the moral laws of the economy—where mercy leavens justice, so to speak. It is this category of law that neoliberalism has eroded. Even if two people comply with the formal requirements of a contract—clear written terms, witnesses, and signatures—the court will not enforce a deal for, say, the purchase of a baby or an organ. A creditor cannot demand "a pound of flesh," and a bargain built on fraud will not stand. But what about a contract to work for eighty hours a week at a dollar an hour? Or a loan whose interest rate forces the borrower to pay back much more in interest than the amount borrowed? Economics cannot provide the answer for whether a court should *prioritize* or *value* efficiency over another value like equity or peace. These are questions of morality and ethics for which mathematical equations have no answer.

In the common law, the principle of fairness with the longest history is that of usury, prohibiting too much interest on loans. Usury laws are the place where laws most shape the market and thus where its values are reflected, like the tension between liberty and equality or the relative power of lenders versus borrowers. How much interest was considered too much reflected shifting social values as well as the relative strength of different segments of the population. Because of its potential to exploit and to discriminate, the debt contract has been regulated or banned across the world for most of human history. The amount of debt held in a given society, its nature, cost, fairness of terms, and the identity of borrowers and lenders, is a product of politics and can propel political movements.

Usury is one of the oldest and most consistent commands, dating back to the beginning of civilization, and reflects prevailing moral attitudes. The early Vedic texts prohibited usury, and the three Abrahamic religions have spoken directly about usury (or the very idea of interest), expressly prohibiting it at one point or another. In their beginning, all these religions forbade any interest-bearing loans—in other words, usury was synonymous with interest.[16] Trade still thrived in the Old World across the Silk Road, yielding innovative technologies and bustling markets. Usury was shunned because it allowed the rich to get richer and the poor to become ensnared in debt. Usury laws were a check against excessive inequality across society, but they were also a moral check against greed and exploitation.

Lending money at a profit—or too high a profit—was and is still against religious law, depending on the level of orthodoxy. The mandates against usury remain as religious doctrine, which is curious when reflecting on the fusion of religious fundamentalists with market fundamentalists. The King James Version of the Bible used today by most Protestant dominations denounces usury twenty-four times compared with the zero times it mentions abortion or homosexuality (according to biblical scholars, the Sodomites were in fact chastised for their sins of greed and inhospitality). Catholics have several papal encyclicals calling usury a grave sin, "heresy," "detestable," and "damned by God and man." The theological historian John Noonan explained that the doctrine of usury has been "enunciated by popes, expressed by three ecumenical councils, proclaimed by bishops, and taught unanimously by theologians."[17]

As Adam Smith explained it, state-imposed interest rate caps were required to prevent "the extortion of usury." Smith believed usury laws should always be set "to be somewhat above the lowest market price . . . though it ought not to be much above the lowest market rate."[18] He thought a rate of "eight or ten percent would be lent to prodigals and projectors, who alone would be willing to give this high interest."

Prodigals and projectors, in Smith's era, were speculators and schemers—a very different type of debtor than a productive borrower. Smith recognized that there was a distinction between market capitalism and the financialization of markets, creating complex financial products and prioritizing financial profit over a productive economy. Market capitalism was defined by investments toward production in the "real economy"—the building of railroads or oil derricks, for example. Financialization involves making bets on markets, speculating in currencies, or looking for "spread" between one financial product and another—unproductive activities because all profits stay within finance. Even when enforced effectively, interest rate caps do not prevent this kind of speculation, but they can confine it to certain high-risk domains like gambling establishments.

Smith's skepticism was bred from experience, as early capital markets suffered from booms and busts and collusion among financiers. At its best, capitalism channeled investment into productive industries, financing large-scale steel or agricultural projects as well as small-time shopkeepers, and creating shareholder dividends besides. But capitalism could also reward financial chicanery, asset bubbles, froth, and Ponzi schemes whose aim was not to channel investments toward productive use but to move money around to make a quick profit. In short, as Smith saw as early as 1776, not all debts were socially or economically productive, and those that weren't shouldn't be allowed. Without limits, Smith wrote, "sober people" would lose out to the risk-takers, and "a great part of the capital of the country would [be] thrown into those [hands] which were most likely to waste and destroy it."[19]

For all of U.S. history until the neoliberal coup, usury rates applied to all loans across the country. In each state, the strictest usury caps aimed to limit loan sharks and lenders who preyed on the poor and whose practices earned the most moral approbation. Some states were chartered as debtor havens and did not permit usury at all. The crime of usury could land a creditor in prison. Even as the nation grew and finance gained power, usury laws and strict barriers on out-of-state lending remained. Even as the robber barons' tentacles—Andrew Carnegie's steel, John D. Rockefeller's oil, Cornelius Vanderbilt's railroad, William Randolph Hearst's newspaper, and John Jacob Astor's real furs and real estate—took over the nation's industry, usury laws imposed maximum annual rates of 10 percent. As the Lochner court fostered laissez-faire in the face of massive unrest and as the magnates crushed labor uprisings with violence, usury laws still remained as a moral principle. There was no sense then that free markets were being hampered or constrained by usury caps. Financiers like J. P. Morgan and Jay Cooke were free to speculate and finance industries, but regular banks giving loans to regular people could not push interest rates higher than the law allowed just to make a profit. Railroad and finance magnate Russell Sage even dedicated his fortune to fighting the loan sharks that preyed on the poor through policy and through offering philanthropic small-dollar loans. Retail millionaire Edward A. Filene launched the credit-union movement, which gained a legal foothold thanks to his friend President Franklin D. Roosevelt. These magnates believed in market capitalism and laissez-faire, but that was a wholly different thing than playing financial games with people through interest.

Writing at the tail end of the most productive era of American capitalism—an era defined by state barriers on market capitalism and bans on financial speculation—Milton Friedman declaimed that usury laws were a prime example of government overreach and a drag on the economy. In an April 1970 *Newsweek* column, he attacked interest rate caps, stating that he knew of "no economist of any standing from [the time of Jeremy Bentham] to this who has favored a legal limit on the rate of interest that borrowers could pay or lenders receive—though there must have been some."[20]

Indeed there were. However, given that they were active before the rise of neoliberalism, it's unlikely Friedman considered them to have "standing." In fact, before neoliberalism's coup, most economists were Keynesians and before that, Smithians. Neither school opposed usury laws. Jeremy Bentham did want to debate the issue with his friend Adam Smith, articulating his case in a series of letters to Smith (later published as a 1787 pamphlet titled *Defence of Usury*). But Bentham, a utilitarian, was no free market radical. He advocated for expansionary monetary policies designed to achieve full employment. He was also an abolitionist who opposed capital punishment and the physical punishment of children and favored equal rights for women. He characterized his opposition to usury laws as part and parcel of his overall moral philosophy: "You know it is an old maxim of mine, that interest, as love and religion, and so many other pretty things, should be free."[21]

In the *Newsweek* column, Friedman claimed to be fighting usury on behalf of the people. He wrote that interest rate caps caused mischief to the "ordinary man," whose collective savings accounts made "the working class . . . the net lenders rather than borrowers." He denounced Wright Patman, a progressive representative from Texas who chaired the House Banking Committee, for his frequent advocacy of usury laws, blaming him "and his ilk" of "self-labeled defenders of 'the people'" for "keeping [ordinary men] from receiving the interest they are entitled to."

When Friedman began his war to free interest rates, there were many rate caps across every kind of loan. In fact, bankers were prohibited from competing with one another by offering more interest on deposits. (To attract depositors, many banks resorted to giveaways such as toasters and umbrellas.) Credit unions, savings and loans, and banks all had mandated rate caps based on the types of loans they offered. Savings and loans, which are financial institutions that specialize in taking savings deposits and providing mortgage loans, could only lend mortgages; credit unions could only bank the members of a single union; community banks could only serve a single community.

All these rules and regulations, Friedman believed, were inhibiting the free market. Lift the fetters imposed by the nanny state, he argued, and unleash the magic of the market. This left out half the story entirely. Most of the rate caps were just one side of a bargain with banks—call it a social contract—that began during the New Deal. The government would insure all mortgages, student loans, farm loans, and even consumer credit through large reserve funds tied to the U.S. Treasury. In exchange for this backstop, lenders complied with rate caps and limits on their activities.

The lending programs inaugurated and insured by the federal government created a (white) American middle class of homeowners, college-goers, social security recipients, car drivers, Sears, Roebuck customers, Montgomery Ward credit card holders, and credit-union members who received 3 percent on their deposits and paid at most 6 percent on their mortgage loans. In 1970, the highest interest rate caps on credit cards were around 8 percent (today, interest rates on credit cards run as high as 36 percent). Bankers enjoyed an automatic "spread" of 3 percent just by checking the boxes on the mortgage loan, and their bank or thrift was protected from competition thanks to various regulations. Of course, there were some bankers and nonbank lenders during this "golden era of banking" who pushed against the bounds of state laws so they could "beat the market" and enjoy more profits. And there were some who, like former president William Howard Taft, never liked the New Deal and would have preferred to go back to the days before deposit insurance, the secondary mortgage market, and all the rules and regulations; or those like the members of the John Birch Society, who saw communism behind every government benefit. But these contrarians could never convince the people that mattered most: voters.

ALTHOUGH USURY LAWS were prevalent, "prodigals and projectors" of the time were able to find other ways to turn high profits. Deprivation can often lead to exploitation, and Black Americans, having been largely excluded from both the New Deal and the war economy's largesse, were easy targets.

One method of making usuriouslike profits was the so-called contract sale. Predatory speculators bought properties for fire-sale prices after their white occupants fled to the suburbs, and those speculators then turned around and "sold" the (often dilapidated) home to a Black buyer for three to four times what they had paid. This contract sale, however, was a ruse. Although the contract held out the possibility of owning the home in the future, it was intentionally deceptive: the "buyer" was effectively a renter. As soon as the buyer missed a payment, they lost everything—house, down payment, and all the work they had put into the property.

It was this debt trap, in part, that turned hemmed-in urban communities into pressure cookers and fueled at first civil disobedience and legal action, then mass protest and rioting, contributing to economic pressures. Black families across all income levels were paying more in rent than suburban homeowners were paying on their mortgages. While one group was building equity, the other increased its debt load. As a result of the New Deal's racial exclusions, not to mention centuries of compounding injustice, Black families had more debt (and higher risk profiles) than white families across every income level.

Meanwhile, the bankers who refused to lend to black buyers directly were profiting circuitously from the sham contract sales. Banks gave loans to the speculators who purchased the homes and then used the home as bait to lure in Black buyers. The bankers and brokers defended their actions as a natural consequence of market pricing. "In a free economy a house is worth what anyone will pay for it," said one Chicago contract seller.

Credit became ubiquitous in American life in the 1950s, as department stores began offering revolving credit accounts and made it easier for consumers to make purchases on credit. Credit was marketed as a means to access the latest consumer goods without having to wait and save up money. Exploitative lenders started proliferating in redlined communities, and in response, activist groups, legal aid lawyers, and civil rights leaders and activists began to confront them. They did so in the legislature—by pushing for usury laws—and in common law courts through contract defenses like "unconscionability." Decades before the civil rights marches of the 1960s captured the nation's attention, residents of segregated Black neighborhoods in the North had already marched, protested, boycotted, and resisted the coercive debt market (in addition to dilapidated housing and police violence). In Harlem and in Chicago's South Side, groups of activists assembled to protest unjust evictions, putting the furniture back in the apartment even as the repo men were removing the goods. These organized, nonviolent acts of civil disobedience were supplemented by demonstrations, litigation, and advocacy at state legislatures.

In New York in the 1940s, a group called Mothers in Harlem effectively lobbied the state legislature to impose usury caps specifically targeted at installment lenders. As the late legal scholar Anne Fleming recounted in *City of Debtors,* the struggle continued over decades as lenders found loopholes and as legislatures and courts responded.[22] Groups of tenants sued slumlords. Squatters took up residency in blighted and run-down buildings, repairing them as they lived in them and fought in court for possession. In Chicago, lawyers aligned with the movement took these contracts to court to have them invalidated using different common law defenses of equity, with some notable successes. This was not a grand litigation strategy aimed at the Supreme Court, but a grassroots strategy accruing small wins that other lawyers could use to help their clients.

The rising awareness of the economic effects of racial segregation, highlighted by the civil rights movement, pushed many judges to strike down the most exploitative parts of many debt contracts. In *Williams v. Walker-Thomas Furniture Co.* (1965), for example, U.S. Court of Appeals Judge Skelly Wright struck down an installment contract under the theory of "unconscionability," which he defined as "an absence of meaningful choice" or as "terms which are unreasonably favorable to the other party." In the case, a single mother on public assistance bought goods on installment from Walker-Thomas, a rent-to-own type lender. After paying off most of her debt and the interest on the debt, she defaulted, and the store repossessed everything Williams had purchased during the previous five years. Evidence at trial revealed that the furniture store used repossession as part of their business—that it included complex and punitive terms in its contracts, routinely repossessed items, and brought suits against the majority of its borrowers. It won practically all these cases because the borrowers were undefended: most had little education—Williams herself could barely read—and either never received the court summons or, if they did, did not challenge the claims.

In his ruling invalidating the entire contract under the unconscionability doctrine, Judge Wright wrote that even if the terms had been transparently worded and revealed to the customer, they were still invalid because they were *unfair*. He acknowledged that the contract's flaws were tied to the legacy of racism and injustice outside the contract itself. The law must see the parties and their positions if it is to "mete out equity," rejecting formalist notions for a reality-based notion of justice. He described the unconscionability doctrine as a "growing area of the law—the law of the poor."

In a 1969 case in New York, one Ms. Jones purchased a refrigerator worth $300 on a $900 installment contract, and when she defaulted on a payment—after having already paid $600—the lender repossessed the appliance. The state Court of Appeals judge noted in his decision invalidating the installment contract that "the law is beginning to fight back against those who once took advantage of the poor and illiterate without risk of either exposure or interference."[23] The judge said that it was the role of the legal system to protect "the victim of gross inequality of bargaining power," who was usually among "the poorest members of the community," against "overreaching by the small but hardy breed of merchants who would prey on them."

Awareness of predatory lending was rising among legislators as well. Lawmakers in Washington, D.C., and Albany, New York, responded to the "Williams situation" by proposing legislation that curtailed coercive contracts. The District of Columbia lawmakers banned contracts like those from Walker-Thomas altogether, which forced lenders to shift to a rent-to-own model rather than repossession-after-default in order to comply with the new law. Although these reforms could not address the structural and historic outcomes of poverty and discrimination resulting from decades of racist policies, they did make a difference in people's lives.

While only a few courts invalidated predatory contract sales under the doctrine of unconscionability, the decisions nonetheless created a wave of panic in the business community. Inevitably, the judges were derided as "activist judges" by business groups—a label that, in this instance, fit. These judges took note of what the housing activists were saying. As one judge ruling for tenants in a 1970 case put it, "The continued vitality of the common law . . . depends upon its ability to reflect contemporary community values and ethics."[24]

The neoliberal backlash to the unconscionability rulings was led by some of the most esteemed figures in Law and Economics. In fact, Richard Epstein first rose to prominence by virtue of his work attacking judges' use of unconscionability, a practice he called "an assault upon private contracts" that caused great harm to the economy.[25] In his article "Unconscionability: A Critical Approach," published in *The Journal of Law and Economics* in 1975, he decried the *Walker-Thomas* case specifically as being misguided and likely to backfire. He argued these cases would end up *harming* the poor because lenders, uncertain of their contract rights, would refuse to sell poor people marked-up goods in the first place. Building on Ronald Coase's work, Epstein suggested that judicial intervention taking the place of free bargaining would disrupt the market, yielding even more exploitative pricing. Instead, the parties should be permitted to bargain, and a borrower should have the liberty to determine their rates and terms.

Richard Posner's analysis in *Economic Analysis of Law* is comparable. For Posner, intervening in an installment contract like the one at issue in *Walker-Thomas* distorts a market that is at "equilibrium." It's at equilibrium, says Posner, because the "windfall gains" from repossessing the good from a borrower who defaults late—that is, after the borrower has paid off most of the price of the good—are offset by the "windfall losses" for the lender from borrowers who default early. Intervening in this arrangement to protect the late-defaulting borrower would, Posner believed, "lead sellers to require larger down payments or higher initial installment payments, or charge higher prices, in order to protect themselves against windfall losses from early defaults."

The assumptions here are legion. First, that the sellers were not inflating prices (they were). Second, that the sellers were not reselling the same used furniture after each repossession—which, in fact, was precisely the installment lenders' business model. In real life— rather than the idealized economic model Posner used to analyze the case—a "windfall" loss for a lender meant not being paid back in full for an item they maybe had already sold to three different customers, whereas a windfall loss for a borrower might mean losing her refrigerator, falling short on her rent, or not having enough to eat. Lenders were repeat players who priced the risk and the windfall into a contract, buried under jargon, while the borrower had no choice but to purchase a necessity through a risky contract or live without. Assuming those realities away was not blind justice—but willful ignorance.

Posner pushed for the elimination of all equitable legal protections "like usury laws and pro-debtor provisions of bankruptcy law, [and] the broad interpretation of unconscionability"—and did so *on behalf of the people.* These laws, he said, actually harmed the poor because they made "it more difficult for poor people to borrow, thus harming them ex ante though benefiting some of them ex post." But he wasn't blaming the poor. Actually, for Posner, it was government intervention that had created the real problem—specifically, welfare. He argued that high-cost debt and installment contracts like the one in *Walker-Thomas* were "merely redressing an imbalance created by the welfare laws, which encourage risky borrowing by truncating the downside of the risk." Posner cited his son, Eric, for the idea that welfare laws distort incentives.

The neoliberal economists spoke abstractly of a future of pure market freedom and profit maximization; less law, they reasoned, led to more freedom. Posner and Epstein were lawyers whose targets were much more precise. They pushed for *more* law when it came to property rights, contract enforcement, and the creation of new categories of protected legal interests such as patents and trademarks. The laws they wanted to eliminate were market "distorting" laws, including usury, unconscionability, pro-debtor bankruptcy, rent control, minimum wage, and welfare. Their journal papers and efforts to train judges focused on the argument that although these laws *seemed* to be helping the poor, they were actually harming them. That was why it was so important for lawyers to really understand economics.

Despite relying on faults in logic and an utter detachment from reality, Epstein's and Posner's views on usury and unconscionability have become the standard framework in law-school pedagogy. In most current contracts law textbooks, Posner's analysis is included right alongside the *Walker-Thomas* case, as though the analysis correctly describes the decision's shortcomings. Law students and judges attending Law and Economics seminars are shown that judges who interfere in markets, however well intentioned they might be, are ultimately foolish and shortsighted. The lecturers wave off issues of poverty or social welfare by putting them under the rubric of redistribution, which legislatures, not courts, should handle. (Of course, when legislatures have tried to redistribute through taxation, neoliberal economists say that *legislators* who interfere in markets, however well intentioned they might be, are ultimately foolish and shortsighted.) Issues of historic inequality, the fact of different starting positions in the economy, and the lack of choice simply don't figure in the Law and Economics models.

While Posner, Epstein, and their fellow Law and Economics adherents spoke to courts and other lawyers, Friedman and other public intellectuals of the movement spoke to the masses. They promised various reforms cloaked in the rhetoric of freedom. While some of these reforms seemed appealing—"school choice," for example—Friedman's wish list also included loan choice, retirement choice, and student loan choice, policies that were strategically omitted from his snappy op-eds. What the neoliberals were proposing was the eradication of safeguards that had existed since the beginning of civilization. Let the sharks roam free. What could go wrong?

In 1978, the Supreme Court heard the case *Marquette Nat. Bank of Minneapolis v. First of Omaha Service Corp*, which posed a seemingly narrow question about whether a bank in Nebraska could mail credit card offers to residents of neighboring states. Banks and credit card companies had only just begun to offer credit cards across state lines in the 1970s, a practice made possible by the invention of the ATM in 1969. The case before the Court was about whether one state's laws could restrict direct-mail marketing by a bank chartered in another state.

During the oral argument, Justice Thurgood Marshall wondered whether this wasn't just an issue of a bank complaining about better marketing by a rival bank. In other words, he did not see the case as being about usury law. But the ramifications of the case were far broader than he perceived. One clue was that the bank arguing against the interstate enforcement of usury law was represented by Robert Bork, whose efforts to deregulate banking were well-known. At the time, however, banks were still heavily regulated from all sides, including by size and geographical market. For Marshall and the Court's other liberal, William Brennan, the case seemed to turn on a basic point of law.

The decision was unanimous: each bank was governed by the state's usury laws that chartered it. In the hearing as well as in his majority opinion, however, Brennan signaled that this was not an issue that the Court should be deciding and that he expected Congress to regulate the financial industry. He was right, in view of the Constitution's separation of powers, but his opinion was also a response to the recent and rapid evolution in credit-by-mail and other financial services. He wrote that "the protection of state usury laws is an issue of legislative policy, and any plea to alter [the law] to further that end is better addressed to the wisdom of Congress than to the judgment of this Court." In fact, Congress was about to enter its own deregulatory era and did not act to curb the pernicious innovations of the credit industry—and it has not acted since.

The case, like *Buckley v. Valeo* and *Virginia Pharmacy*, led to transformative legal changes even though almost no one quite saw that outcome at the time. In 1978, not only were banks heavily regulated, but there were an array of robust state usury laws and consumer protections. But the door had been opened.

In 1980, South Dakota's economy was in a slump, so the state government invited Citibank—which had recently lost one billion dollars on a credit card venture—to charter in the state. The state promised no usury laws, which, thanks to *Marquette Nat. Bank*, meant that one of the nation's largest banks would face no state usury caps if it moved to South Dakota. Citibank did just that, moving its credit card business to the state, bringing three thousand jobs and a healthy new source of tax revenue. Delaware, the home of corporate charters, was not about to cede ground to South Dakota, so it eliminated its usury laws, too. The race to the bottom had begun.

Over the following decades, as banking and credit were transformed through a surge of deregulatory legislation, interest rates would keep climbing and states that tried to enforce their usury laws would find that they had lost the power to do so. The Supreme Court in *Marquette Nat. Bank* had not altered the Constitution, nor had it deprived states of their historic right to impose usury laws. But unintentionally—or perhaps intentionally, for a few of the justices—it had enabled a lender anywhere to lend everywhere.

Today, there are essentially no barriers that prevent a credit card company from doing business across the country using one state's usury limits. And payday or title lending—that is, loan-sharking—which previously had been forced to operate in the black market, became a mainstream, profitable enterprise, doing immense harm. As Senator Elizabeth Warren has said, we "effectively engaged in the single biggest policy change in the credit area, the whole consumer credit area, through an obscure Supreme Court decision interpreting some ambiguous language." At the time, hardly anyone paid attention to *Marquette Nat. Bank*, and the definitive book on the Burger Court, by Linda Greenhouse and Michael Graetz, doesn't mention the decision once. But *Marquette* is one of the most consequential decisions in the modern history of the Court. It rendered moot usury laws that had existed for thousands of years, and it did so without public attention and fanfare—and, crucially, without a single vote by elected representatives.

*   *   *

THE *MARQUETTE* DECISION indeed marked a significant change in the history of usury law, but only thanks to the neoliberals' full-court press to change the common law of contracts. As with other parts of the neoliberal transformation, each legal change multiplied the effects of all the others until it was too late.

As the neoliberal coup progressed, usury caps were lifted while, at the same time, equitable defenses like unconscionability became extremely rare. These changes combined with others across the common law of contracts, torts, property, and corporate law. Many began in the courts and the legal academy after 1970, but their effects were latent, which is one reason many scholars date the rise of neoliberal economics to the Reagan and Clinton administrations. In fact, Reagan and Clinton were a culmination of legal changes that had increased the power of financial markets and diminished the power of courts and legislatures to tame them. Those changes made markets more efficient through the Coasian mandate of delegitimizing common law courts as the site of contract resolution or rights allocation.

Increasingly, practically all contractual arrangements between an individual and a large business became standardized, making unconscionability an impossible claim to litigate. Contracts began to include forced arbitration clauses—which require conflictual parties to resolve the issue with an arbitration attorney chosen by the business rather than filing suit—and the Supreme Court has also upheld provisions in contracts that ban class action suits, making it financially impractical for individuals who suffer fraud to seek relief in court.

The deleterious effects of this kind of contract provision can be seen in *AT&T Mobility LLC v. Concepcion* (2011), in which Vincent and Liza Concepcion wished to sue AT&T for false advertising but were prevented from doing so by clauses in the contract requiring arbitration and prohibiting class action. In his majority opinion, which was joined only by his fellow conservative justices, Justice Antonin Scalia wrote that federal arbitration mandates in the Federal Arbitration Act, enacted in 1925, preempted California state rules that prohibited "forced arbitration" clauses, and that the contract could both remove the right to a class action suit as well as the right to a trial. As the liberal justices wrote in their dissent, the practical effect of the decision was that these claims would be impossible to bring, which would mean that any contractual language, however unfair or unconscionable, would be left unchallenged. As Justice Stephen Breyer put it, "Only a lunatic or a fanatic sues for $30," and "what rational lawyer would [sign] on to represent the Concepcions in litigation for the possibility of fees stemming from a $30.22 claim?"

Implicit in the Law and Economics approach is that *law* should defer to *economics*—which means that *justice* is less important than *efficiency*. If there is a conflict, economic efficiency is preferable. One of the goals of the movement is to reduce litigation of all kinds, but especially litigation by individuals against corporations. Ostensibly, this is because litigation, according to theorists like Coase, is inefficient and therefore unnecessary. "The reasoning employed by the courts in determining legal rights," Coase writes in "The Problem of Social Costs," "will often seem strange to an economist because many of the factors on which the decision turns are, to an economist, irrelevant."[26] According to his famous theorem, courts should not be in the business of allocating legal rights because if "market transactions are costless, such a rearrangement of rights will always take place if it would lead to an increase in the value of production." Posner agrees: "The legal dispute-resolution machinery" imposed many costs, including "error costs," which he defined as "the social costs generated when a judicial system fails to carry out the allocative or other social functions assigned to it," as well as "direct costs," which included "lawyers', judges', and litigants' time." In a cost-benefit analysis of the legal system, Posner ruled the judiciary inefficient.[27]

Conservative Supreme Court justices have used this very rationale to swat down claims against corporations. Scalia opposed class action lawsuits because they "would undermine the informality, efficiency, and speed that are the raison d'être for arbitration in the first place." In a 2013 case, *Am. Express Co. v. Italian Colors Rest.*, in which the lower court had argued that the prohibitive costs of such small-dollar suits led to a loss of the right to sue, Scalia waved off the concern, stating,

"The fact that it is not worth the expense involved in proving a statutory remedy does not constitute the elimination of the right to pursue that remedy."[28]

Justice Elena Kagan wrote, in her dissent, that the effect of these decisions was that the "monopolist gets to use its monopoly power to insist on a contract effectively depriving its victims of all legal recourse." However, despite withering dissents from a succession of liberal justices, the left has lost most of the Supreme Court cases in the realm of forced arbitration clauses and class action bans. These decisions have deprived American consumers of the chance to pursue justice through the court system and have padded the coffers of corporations.

Closing the courthouse to average consumers was a major priority of the neoliberal agenda and one of the most successful transformations in American law engineered by Federalist Society judges and Law and Economics scholars.

As previously discussed, 1970 was the high-water mark for defenses of equity like unconscionability. After the Law and Economics transformation of common law courts, judges began to reject the unconscionability defense and reverse earlier decisions. In fact, several courts held that the defense was dead-letter law and should no longer be pursued in court. The courts decided that, as long as the terms are disclosed somewhere in the contract, the contract remains valid. Although the unconscionability doctrine is just one of the many common law defenses that was quietly taken away as neoliberalism became dominant, it reveals the process of wholesale revision that began in the academy, suffused the lower courts, and made its way back into the academy, where it became formal law.

In 2020, with funding from the American Bar Association, a group of law professors attempted to formalize the end of the unconscionability doctrine. Their assignment was to revise the *Restatement of Law* on the law of consumer contracts. The *Restatement of Law* is a series of volumes that serves as a guide for courts and lawyers on the state of the common law based on surveys of state and federal courts. Once the *Restatement* summarizes the law, that summary is cited by courts until it becomes precedent. The group, which included several Law and Economics professors, decided that unconscionability was, in fact, a dead-letter law. That was not entirely true, because some courts still consider unconscionability in contract claims, and plaintiffs still assert unconscionability claims. But the doctrine had been slowly snuffed out as Law and Economics came to replace law and equity. The professors were just nailing the coffin shut.

In this particular case, controversy quickly followed when one of the attendees of the private meeting leaked the draft *Restatement* to the public, which is how the broader legal community was made aware of the proposed change. A small collection of progressive law professors, including Senator Elizabeth Warren, herself a former professor, fought back by issuing letters, collecting data, and generally rebutting the group's presumption. The group won a pyrrhic victory and the formal law of unconscionability remains alive. But whether unconscionability dies gradually by a thousand cuts or suddenly through a committee vote, the thin reed of protection it offered plaintiffs battling unfair contract terms is no more.

ONE WAY to see the demise of equitable defenses is as yet another attack on the laws protecting the poor. Arbitration clauses are prevalent in employment contracts, especially in nonunionized workplaces and gig-worker arrangements. They are standard in "fringe lending" credit arrangements like payday loans, title loans, installment loans, and subprime loans. More than 90 percent of these debt contracts also include a ban on class action suits. Those most affected are low-income people of color, the same groups that employed the unconscionability doctrine to fight coercive credit during the civil rights era.

As avenues to justice or mercy have shut, the market freedom the fundamentalists promised has been achieved, although it hasn't quite felt as free as freedom should feel. Today, there is effectively no interest rate cap; it is up to the market. While middle-class mortgage and student loans face some oversight by regulators, when it comes to loans for the poor—that is, payday or title loans—the law has so many loopholes that there are virtually no constraints. Formal law benefits the market, and its sharp edges are felt by those who have the least access to legal remedies. Even the few doors of relief to the poor have been shut.

Contrary to Friedman's, Posner's, and Epstein's contentions that usury laws and unconscionability only hurt "ordinary men," lifting those restrictions has created a trillion-dollar lending sector. Payday lending, or modern-day loan-sharking, was virtually nonexistent in the 1980s; but thanks to the gospel of free markets, it has grown exponentially, from a total of 500 storefronts in 1990 to more than 20,000 in 2016, and over $40 billion in revenue annually.[29] Fringe lenders target mostly poor and minority communities, charging up to 600% APR (a geometric increase from the historic rates of around 6 to 8 percent permitted under usury law). Most borrowers spend an average of $520 in fees for a onetime loan of $375, according to Pew Research Center statistics. Each year, 12 million Americans spend $9 billion on loan fees.[30] The fringe lending market is dominated by a few large corporations that own a variety of pawn, payday, and title lending stores, which operate under different names and with different signage, giving the impression that these are community-based lenders when, in fact, they're simply branches of a corporation.

Payday lending is the free market's response to the inequalities created by the neoliberal era. The rates now charged routinely to poor communities used to be the primary domain of the mafia and other criminal lending syndicates. Not only do these lenders serve only the poor, but their stores are most prevalent in the formerly redlined communities where minorities live, still segregated from the wealthy enclaves whose debts are still federally subsidized and regulated.

Another illustration of the multiplying effects of neoliberal lawmaking, as decisions like *First National Bank of Boston v. Bellotti* increased corporate lobbying of state legislatures, more states began to lift their usury limits. State legislators in business-friendly states like Texas, Utah, and Idaho have welcomed payday lenders who exploit their citizens. The few states that have tried to drive these lenders out by imposing rate caps have been thwarted by the porous and loophole-laden federal preemptions, thanks to Court decisions like *Marquette Nat. Bank*. Banning usurious lending is a losing game of whack-a-mole where lenders can move faster than state legislators. Ban a payday loan and it changes into a title loan; try to impose fee limits and "fees" turn into insurance or "tips." Walmart, for instance, offers its employees "wage access," which gives workers a payday loan from their own future wage earnings, but with interest, or rather mandatory "tips," paid to the lender.[31]

Thanks to right-wing-funded groups like the American Legislative Exchange Council, statehouses are regularly supplied with form legislation funded and drafted by industry, making it easier to conduct their business in the state. There are no powerful counterlobbies with funds to protect marginalized and politically powerless communities from these laws, which legislatures can pass without controversy. Payday lenders even lobby against laws like minimum wage that have seemingly nothing to do with their business—unless of course their business is to prey on the poor. These lenders have even created their own research nonprofits, like the Consumer Credit Research Foundation (CCRF), which uses grants and data to "purchase" economic studies. For example, CCRF gave a grant and shared data with the Dartmouth economist Jonathan Zinman, whose research incidentally concluded that states like Oregon that managed to ban payday loans actually *harmed* consumers.[32] Harms included increased bank overdraft fees and late bill payment fees—that is, harms entailed by the condition of not having enough money.[33]

Because payday lenders thrive when people are flailing, rising inequality and job instability have been boons to the sector. In 2020, thanks to the economic and health devastations of the COVID crisis, payday lending profits soared, with a few public companies—such as Enova International, the largest player in the industry—recording record profits of over $250 million. As a Credit Suisse analysis told Bloomberg News, "Earnings were definitely higher than we would have expected because they benefited from an improvement in the credit environment." That environment was a product of the fact that "consumers tended to pay back debts with funds they were given by the government."[34] So much for market freedom.

Neoliberal economists and legal scholars have been the payday lenders' most effective defenders, arguing that the industry meets market demand. They are "increasing access to credit," "democratizing credit," and "diversifying credit options." These economists and scholars cannot say, like Alan Greenspan once claimed of installment lenders, that they were not making exorbitant profits—those were the days when usury laws were in effect. Today, the profit margins on loans are upward of 34 percent, which fulfills the dream of shareholder profit maximization that Friedman championed.[35]

As many would discover, the neoliberal nirvana of efficient free markets contained some fine print, which was that efficiency referred to capital growth and the freedom was for investors who could enjoy unprecedented capital growth without limit. The people, meanwhile, were free to choose their debts among an expanding array of exotic loans from fringe lenders. Indeed, capital's exponential buildup had a shadow: the explosive growth of debt.

Americans did not go willingly into the maws of the debt economy, but neoliberalism closed off all other routes to survival for the middle class. In neoliberal hypotheticals, each rational individual engaged in a Coasian bargain, weighing costs and benefits before choosing to borrow money at whatever interest rates the market chose to offer. In the real world, debt became a necessity for many Americans thanks to other neoliberal reforms, like wage and benefits cuts and job instability. Between 1950 and the present, private debt held by Americans has increased from 30 percent of the nation's GDP to over 170 percent. Debt is disproportionately held by the least well off, who, due to the removal of usury caps, are paying unprecedented interest rates of between 20 and 30% APR, on average. Payments on debt have, in turn, contributed to the accumulation of unprecedented sums of private wealth.

Under the guise of "cutting the deficit," neoliberals privatized public programs and eliminated benefits, even as they sought tax cuts and increased military spending. The political scientists Jacob Hacker and Paul Pierson have called this trend "the Great Risk Shift": the common risks of living—death, injury, or catastrophic losses—that were once publicly shared through federal programs were shifted onto each person and family. The emphasis on "austerity" turned employee pensions into 401(k)s. College endowments ballooned as student debt exploded. Government-subsidized fixed-rate mortgages were replaced by a hyperfinancialized mortgage market featuring adjustable rates, interest-only loans, and subprime loans based purely on a borrower's risk tolerance. Each person became an investor, a consumer, and an entrepreneur: improve your stock portfolio, watch your credit score, shop around for a mortgage, save up for education and health care, and plan for your retirement.

The Great Risk Shift meant that Americans, especially those who had been left out of New Deal–era credit subsidies, had to use high-cost debt to pursue homeownership or an education. In an ironic yet totally predictable twist, once debt was privatized and therefore profitable, banks that had long refused to lend to redlined and unsubsidized communities targeted these exact communities for their riskiest, highest-yielding loans. As economists and pundits explained, the irrevocable rules of the omnipotent market prevailed: the higher the risk, the higher the interest rate. No, Black communities were not being discriminated against, declared the hugely influential libertarian economist Thomas Sowell in his introductory economics textbook, *Basic Economics*; they are just riskier borrowers, and thus the high rates are in perfect accordance with the laws of supply and demand. What Sowell—a Hoover Institution fellow and a recipient of the Bradley Prize and the Hayek Book Prize who believes that "systemic racism" is a Nazi-like propaganda program pushed on Americans—does not account for are the laws and policies, as well as the history of exclusion and exploitation, that led to a population who can be defined as "risky borrowers." Sowell's explanation for racial disparities is simple: a gap in IQ between Black and white communities, an explanation that lands much closer to the Nazis' line of reasoning than those pointing to systemic racism. Ironically, systemic racism is now how some on the right describe American society. Charles Murray, the author of *The Bell Curve* and a notable proponent of the racial IQ thesis, lauded the man he dubbed "the Immortal Sowell" by noting that "in a reasonable world, Thomas Sowell's life would be celebrated in the same way we honor Frederick

Douglass, George Washington Carver, and Marian Anderson—as a black hero, born into a genuinely systemically racist America, who not only endured but prevailed."[36]

IN A RELIGION that renders the profiteer and the loan shark immune from divine judgment, someone has to be a sinner. Along with the risk shift in credit markets came a shame shift in conservative circles (and in American society writ large): from shaming usurious lenders to blaming the prodigal borrowers. High-interest loans lead to a vicious cycle of debt and then public shaming by "financial experts" who blame individuals for their profligate spending habits. High-cost debt itself is punitive and costly. Pouring salt on the wound, the modern right adds blame and shame, accusing debtors of bad decision making, ignorance, or inherent inferiority.

And on this issue, conservative Christian leaders were clear. They started castigating their flock for the immoral and irresponsible use of debt, even though the biblical prophets and Jesus himself reserved their judgmental scorn for the sinful usurious lender. Modern conservative Christians who shame debtors get the message exactly backward. According to biblical parables, Jesus instructed that mercy should go to the borrower whose "debts" should be forgiven. The pastors of the fusionist right turned their condemnation against debtors and heaped praise on the entrepreneurial lenders. Good Christians were rich Christians.

The public discourse on debt included rants on the floor of the stock market, head-shaking condemnations by the budgeting gurus, and moral diatribes from the evangelical right about personal responsibility and balanced-budget policy making. An entire industry of best-selling self-help guides, magazine advice guides, and TV and talk-radio programs grew to teach the habits, investments strategies, and self-discipline of the wealthy and successful to the American public. Popular cultural touchstones like Oprah's Debt Diet program exposed the profligate spending of "average" families with hundreds of thousands of dollars of debt. The audience at home watched as the mothers of these households, assumed to be the source of the excess, were chastised and punished through an austere "diet" of spending cuts and lessons on how to live on coupons and homemade meals. The scapegoats were publicly reformed as Wall Street got fat, consuming the unprecedented amount of yield on an ever-growing debt pile that could be manipulated and subdivided to release even more yield than the monthly checks from all of America's bad moms.

It was a religion and a nation turned upside down. Such was and is the power of neoliberalism, which was and remains a revolution not only in economics and law and politics, but in values.

CHAPTER 7

There Is No Such Thing as Society

Not ideas, but material and ideal interest, directly govern men's conduct. Yet very frequently the "world images" that have been created by "ideas" have, like switchmen, determined the tracks along which action has been pushed by the dynamic of interest.

—MAX WEBER.
"THE SOCIAL PSYCHOLOGY OF THE WORLD'S RELIGIONS" (1913)

I N A NOW infamous 1989 interview, as she railed against the demands made by her fellow Britons that the government help them—people "who have been given to understand 'I have a problem, it is the Government's job to cope with it!' or 'I am homeless, the Government must house me!'"—Margaret Thatcher raised the core tenet of neoliberalism: that notions of community and society are misleading. As Thatcher put it, people calling on their government to help them were "casting their problems on society and who is society? There is no such thing!"

In this, Thatcher was echoing Friedrich Hayek, whose ideas were central to the prime minister's policy agenda. Hayek was suspicious of the very concept of society, warning that behind attempts at bettering society lurked tyranny. To Hayek—and the politicians, economists, and legal scholars he inspired—any claims made by society were an unjustified intrusion into individual autonomy. Economic freedom trumped all other values.

The irony was that there *had* to be such a thing as a society—because without it, no economy could exist. Markets are a feature of states and the legitimacy and enforcement power of the laws of those states. Property laws assign value to the tangible and intangible and establish the reach of those rights. Contract law delineates the boundaries of market exchange. Corporate laws regulate the power of capital in society. Common law courts determine the parameters of these rights and police are sanctioned to punish violations. States create the legal scaffolding that enables investors and merchants to risk trading in modern markets. And that is just the bare minimum—government investments, subsidies, and joint ventures have been the fuel and engine of modern markets. Indeed, the market was not some magical creation spontaneously created out of nothing—without society, there would be no such thing as markets.

For all their libertarian rhetoric, neoliberals did in fact recognize this—which is why, rather than seek to eradicate the state, they worked to influence its regulatory apparatus to produce corporate profits at the expense of the people. The strategy was twofold: first, discredit democratic governance as rife with corruption and inefficiency; and second, secure the powerful levers of policy inside agencies impervious to public input and porous only to the revolving door of special interests. Democratic power wasn't lost in a smoke-filled room, but rather under the auspices of technical expertise.

As evidenced by the dim view members of the Mont Pelerin Society (MPS) had of anticolonial movements, critiques of democratic governance were commonplace among neoliberals. George Stigler attacked the regulatory state as captured by special interests. Milton Friedman fought state control of monetary policy. Richard Posner and other Law and Economics scholars provided the arguments for presenting a radical pro-market program as neutral.

As with other neoliberal "reforms," the campaign against democracy began post-*Brown*, when some elites felt victimized by courts and the voting public. Having been Court-mandated to share public schools with Black children, legislated by the 1964 Civil Rights Act to share social spaces, and by the 1965 Voting Rights Act to share representative democracy, neoliberals turned their backs on all of these institutions. There is no such thing as an integrated society, therefore there is no such thing as society. The piece-by-piece dismantlement of public institutions began as soon as the law applied equally to all people. Having lost a game they had always dominated, these men picked up their chips and upended the gameboard altogether.

THE MOST DOGGED critic of democracy in the neoliberal pantheon was James Buchanan, the Chicago-trained economist who would win the Economics Nobel in 1986. Buchanan's first major salvo against the government came in 1964. Coauthored with G. Warren Nutter, a libertarian economist and close adviser to Barry Goldwater, the article "The Economics of Universal Education" applied the economic argument against monopolies—that they reduce competition and consumer choice—to "government schools." The authors maintained that the public school "monopoly" should be broken up and privatized so that each parent could "cast his vote in the marketplace and have it count."[1]

The article was more or less a reprisal of Friedman's "The Role of Government in Education," which had been published the year after *Brown* and made similar arguments. But unlike Friedman, who usually tiptoed around race by pretending to speak on behalf of the market, Buchanan and Nutter were more blunt about the nature of their project: "We believe every individual should be free to associate with persons of his own choosing," they wrote in a 1959 article for the *Richmond Times-Dispatch*. "We therefore disapprove of both involuntary (or coercive) segregation and involuntary integration."[2]

Buchanan's major academic contribution, and the one that most helped animate the neoliberal revolution, appeared in a 1962 book called *The Calculus of Consent*, cowritten with Gordon Tullock, another University of Virginia professor. The background of the piece was a post-*Brown* federal government on the cusp of passing historic civil rights legislation. Using hypotheticals, theoreticals, and axioms about human behavior, the economists took aim at representative democracy, arguing that politicians were like self-interested businessmen trading votes for laws, driven by no principle other than reelection. Voters, likewise, acted purely out of self-interest, voting for politicians who promised them handouts. Behind every law for justice or government program claiming to be for "the common good" or "general welfare," Buchanan and Tullock saw a much more cynical enterprise of transactional deal making, which involved quid pro quo vote trading, or "logrolling." The book also rebutted the basic presumption underlying the political franchise, that of a citizenry shaping their governemnt by voting their values at the polls. Not so, it noted; voters formed cartel-like special interest groups for the purpose of rent seeking, or extracting more than their share from the government. If this was too dismal a description of government in 1962, it would not be after the neoliberal coup.

Typically, rent seeking in a political context referred to corporate lobbyists who sought changes in the law to boost business profits ("rents") that were paid for by the general public. Buchanan and Tullock's *public choice theory*—the moniker they chose for their central idea—turned the common understanding on its head. Actually, wrote the economists, it was the public organizing into groups (i.e., racial activists, labor unions, and consumer groups) who were extorting the political system for laws that helped their coalition. The political minority who were the victims of this conspiracy by the *demos*? The wealthy.

The cabal among voters, politicians, and bureaucrats in a majoritarian democracy, charged Buchanan and Tullock, always resulted in "discriminatory impact" on the taxpayers who did not vote for these programs but were forced, per the nature of democracy, to contribute anyway.[3] *The Calculus of Consent* used the example of property taxes levied for the use of programs benefiting the majority, calling such practices "discriminatory legislation." Voting majorities and the politicians who represented them, the authors reasoned, would always choose to spend other people's money for their own gain. Property owners and those who paid the highest rates of taxes, assuming a progressive tax system, would always be outnumbered.

Buchanan and Tullock's book is incredibly dense and practically unreadable for a nonacademic—it spans hundreds of pages and is replete with run-on sentences full of equivocations. What it amounts to, in the end, is a revolt of property owners against democracy. The "facts of history" reveal, the authors write, that "the constitutional rules that were 'optimal' in 1900 are probably not 'optimal' in 1960." They lament that, in the recent history of Western nations, there has been too much "collective intervention" in the economy. "As a result, legislative action may now produce severe capital losses or lucrative capital gains to separate individuals and groups." In other words, laws in the 1960s were taking from some and giving to others—the basic formula of taxation. Thus, for the "the rational individual . . . the imposition of some additional and renewed restraints on the exercise of such legislative power may be desirable." Translation: *Property owners, get out your pitchforks!* As for reform, the authors offer this: "The only means whereby the individual can ensure that the actions of others will never impose costs on him is through the strict application of the rule of unanimity for all decisions, public and private."[4] If the "optimal" structure of government was unanimous rule, then the optimal structure of government was not democracy, where the majority often rules and where not every voice has power. In fact, by Buchanan and Tullock's measure, *all* modern states were suboptimal—or illegitimate—because only a system where "the individual knows that he must approve *any* action before it is carried out" will suffice for optimal decision making. If there was no such thing as a society, no higher good to achieve, and social justice was a mirage, then asking anyone to give up something they did not want to give up amounted to tyranny.

Public choice theory was just that: a theory. It was a claim based on hypotheticals and conjectures rather than data or empirical analyses of observable fact. It built on the gamut of other neoliberal theories:

Pareto's theorem that an outcome which increased net gains was beneficial regardless of the distribution of those gains; the Coase theorem that law was unnecessary and rational property owners would bargain their way toward efficiency; and the even more foundational neoliberal assumption that all human beings were fundamentally out for nothing but self-interest: "every individual serves his own private interest," believed Friedman. "The great Saints of history have served their 'private interest' just as the most money-grubbing miser has served his interest."[5] Each idea built on a set of previous assumptions—none of which could be proved or disproved. Untested and unchallenged, these theories grew into more assumptions before they turned into state policy. The "heart of the economic approach," summarized Gary Becker, was a mix of beliefs, or a set of "combined assumptions of maximizing behavior, market equilibrium, and stable preferences, used relentlessly and unflinchingly."[6] Venturing another theory and waving away what did not fit into the model, Buchanan added another structure to neoliberalism's Potemkin village.

Like the theories on which it relied, public choice was an argument in support of a predetermined outcome, not a description of how the world actually worked. All one had to do was to press on any single assumption the authors made, with reference to practically any era in history, any experiment on a group of real humans, or any rigorous inquiry at all. First and foremost, people did *not* act rationally and in their self-interest all the time—not because they were altruists or saints, but because they were human and thus led by passions and emotion, not always or even usually pure logic. For a contemporaneous example, one could look at President Lyndon Johnson, who fought for the passage of civil rights bills despite recognizing that he and his party would likely never win the South again if they passed. And what "interest groups" or pressure groups twisted the arms of the justices with lifetime appointments on the Warren Court to secure the decision in *Brown*? In the nineteenth century, what explained the abolitionists who risked their lives to free another "special interest" group who did not even have the right to vote? And indeed, how had the southern slaveholder minority held such a powerful grip on the majority of the nation's voters, a grip that was loosened only after a long and bloody war? If actual recorded history had been consulted in good faith, Buchanan and Tullock would have been forced to admit that majorities without property or wealth rarely if ever had power over the elites who possessed both.

Buchanan's dystopia of elite property owners tyrannized by impoverished majorities and their captured politicians was the exact inverse of the southern political order of which he was a part. He resembled his fellow Virginian Thomas Jefferson, whose intimate familiarity with tyranny gave him "a special appreciation of freedom." In the words of the historian Edmund Morgan: "The presence of men and women who were, in law at least, almost totally subject to the will of other men gave to those in control of them an immediate experience of what it could mean to be at the mercy of a tyrant."[7] The Jim Crow South of Buchanan's era should have been Buchanan's primary example, as it was an instance of legislatures dominated by majorities to deprive the rights of minorities. But Jim Crow appeared nowhere in his writing on public choice. Perhaps what Buchanan actually feared was retribution.

Instead of facing America's dark shadow of racial exploitation through truth and justice, neoliberals chose denial and projection. Prefiguring Lewis Powell's memo calling businessmen "the real victims," Richard Nixon's private antisemitic tirades against his enemies in the media, and Robert Bork and the Federalist Society's self-description as a besieged minority, Buchanan flipped the charge of discrimination back on activist groups to argue that it was, in fact, the owners of property who were the real victims of society. The fact that these men believed in the racial inferiority of "lower races" was not unusual given the time and place, but it cannot be put aside when evaluating their scholarship. It is not necessarily the case that Buchanan's scholarship was *motivated* by his views on race. But given how much of Buchanan's scholarship focused on the threat democracy posed to individual liberty, the crumbling of the Jim Crow order is a necessary context for understanding it. Feeling forced to send your children to an integrated school, which you believed would defile your flesh and blood; forced to open up your government to people you felt in your gut to be undeserving of the same voice as you; forced to tolerate race mixing in social institutions, having been warned all your life of the inherent immorality or uncleanliness of the act—it was bound to leave one frustrated with the limits of one's power and inclined to resist.

Buchanan's status grew even as his vision got darker. In his 1975 book *The Limits of Liberty*, he concluded that "there are relatively few effective limits on the fiscal exploitation of minorities through orderly democratic procedures in the United States."[8] By "minorities," he didn't mean Black people; he meant men like himself and wealthy donors, like Charles Koch, who had become fans and funders of his scholarship. For Buchanan, the choice was between democracy or liberty. This most assuredly did not mean abolishing the state. As he said at an MPS meeting in 1986, "For most of our members, however, social order without a state is not readily imagined." Rather, "man is, and must remain, a slave to the state. But it is critically and vitally important to recognize that ten per cent slavery is different from fifty per cent slavery."[9]

The Limits of Liberty was a hit among those who favored the liberty side of the coin. Henry Manne invited Buchanan to give lectures on it at his Law and Economics Center at George Mason and even awarded the book a Law and Economics prize in 1977.[10] In 1978, the then president of MPS, George Stigler, dedicated the annual meeting to a discussion of Buchanan's book, under the banner "How Is the Leviathan to Be Chained?" In his introductory remarks, Stigler called the invitation-only participants, Koch among them, "a permanent minority" whose ideas were "widely . . . rejected." He asked the group, "If in fact we seek what many do not wish, will we not be more successful if we take this into account and seek political institutions and policies that allow us to pursue our goals?" Clarifying, in case it was not obvious, that this would include "non-democratic" ones, he suggested a "possible route" of restricting the "franchise to property owners, educated classes, employed persons, or some such group."

Buchanan tested some of these possibilities in Chile in the 1970s and 1980s. Alongside Friedman and the so-called Chicago Boys, he helped Augusto Pinochet create a new constitution that would lock in his own dictatorial power, limit majority rule, give the central bank absolute independence, and overrepresent the right-wing minority. The law also punished anyone advocating "class conflict," "Marxism," or anything "anti-family" with exile (or worse) without due process.[11] Chileans were given only a yes or no vote in an emergency election to ratify their new constitution, which was written so as to be practically unchangeable. Whether Buchanan was aware or not, activists who urged citizens to vote against the constitution were tortured or killed, giving new meaning to the creed "give me liberty or give me death."

Buchanan won the Nobel Prize in Economics for public choice theory in 1986. In giving Buchanan the prize, the Nobel committee celebrated his philosophical commitment to reforming constitutional rules so that "the political processes" would no longer be "a means for redistribution"—or as Assar Lindbeck, a committee member and Buchanan acolyte, described the franchise, "vote purchasing democracy." In his remarks accepting the prize, Buchanan "expressed disdain for the 'Eastern academic elite,'" reported Tom Redburn of the *Los Angeles Times,* who think of "themselves as enlightened advisers to 'a benevolent government for the rest of us.'" Having just been awarded academia's highest honor, Buchanan still saw himself as a mere commoner, noting "I'm proud to be a member of the great unwashed."

Buchanan, who appeared at a news conference in Fairfax, Virginia, after the Nobel announcement, was "dressed casually in a blue blazer, Hush Puppies and white socks" and was seated next to his wife, Ann. Asked how he felt about the $29,000 monetary award, the economist responded, "It won't make much difference in my life" because the couple were self-sufficient. They raised and grew all their food, he explained, and hadn't purchased anything canned or frozen in quite some time. A model of the kind of bootstrap self-sufficiency Buchanan expected of everyone, the economist had everything he needed on his four-hundred-acre farm.[12]

Buchanan's nihilistic theory of law and jurisprudence enabled the slow bankrupting of social institutions. Neoliberal orthodoxy became a self-fulfilling prophecy by imagining a world of self-interested actors and then making it so. By disempowering government regulators and regulations, it confirmed its own claims about ineffective regulators. By sowing mistrust of government, it hamstrung government and made it look untrustworthy.

WHAT BUCHANAN expressed in models and equations, Ronald Reagan and Margaret Thatcher voiced in political rhetoric. Reagan promised Americans that he would reduce the deficit while simultaneously cutting taxes, funding social security, and maintaining America's military might, all the while insinuating that the majority of government spending was going to Black welfare cheats who refused to find a job.

By the time Reagan won the presidency, the right's various outposts were already prepared to enact this slate of neoliberal programs across the government. Manne's Law and Economics seminars were teaching public choice theory to judges. The right-wing think tanks had been busy sanitizing the politics of backlash via various theories, including shareholder supremacy, market efficiency, and public choice. As Reagan romped in the 1980 presidential contest against Jimmy Carter, the party of Nixon's "southern strategy" was now dubbed "the party of ideas" by Newt Gingrich.

A key provider of those ideas was the Heritage Foundation. Heritage researchers worked closely with the House's conservative caucus, drafting detailed policy and selling it not only to legislators but to the media, at times bullying Republican lawmakers with various "scoring cards" and "indexes" that tracked their fealty to "conservative principles."

Heritage's influence on policy making reached a zenith with the publication of *Mandate for Leadership* in 1981. Comprising twenty volumes and thirty thousand pages, *Mandate* proposed more than two thousand reforms with varying degrees of specificity: from abolishing the Department of Energy to suggesting that leases for drilling stations "Nos. 53 and 68 in California and No. 68 in the Gulf of

Mexico . . . should be moved up in the schedule."[13] *Mandate* was well received within conservative circles.

By the end of that same year, its first in office, the Reagan administration had hired many of the report's authors and had implemented about 60 percent of the proposals.[14] It pursued significant tax cuts, aiming supposedly to stimulate economic growth and incentivize investment; sought to reduce government regulations and promote free market principles across various sectors; pushed for a substantial increase in defense spending, with a focus on modernizing the military and developing advanced weapon systems; aimed to reduce the size and scope of the federal government's civil rights programs; and supported efforts to increase local control over education. Thanks to the *Mandate*'s success, Heritage would earn the moniker the "Parthenon of the conservative metropolis."[15]

In fact, most of the Reagan administration's top deregulatory appointments came from the think tanks established by the right—not just Heritage, but the American Enterprise Institute, the Hoover Institution, and others. As a White House official told *The Atlantic* in 1986, "Without AEI, Reagan never would have been elected. . . . AEI made conservatism intellectually respectable." The think tanks put the academic sheen on free market ideas through their conferences, white papers, and the revolving door with conservative administrations. An AEI publication boasted that its "historic Pennsylvania Avenue location, Washington's corridor of power, will enable our scholars and fellows to interact more readily with key policy makers." The author of the *Atlantic* piece, Gregg Easterbrook, quipped that "aside from suggesting a picture of scholars poised on the roof, arms outstretched like antennae to receive emanations from Congress and the executive, this invocation of a large new building, and the commitment to the future that it represents, shows that AEI does not expect government to wither away." As Lewis Powell's 1971 memo had advised, ideological change would require "long range planning" and coordination. The payoff was now in view.[16]

The right's army of neoliberal wonks, having spent the prior decade railing against government bureaucracy, were now *in charge* of the bureaucracy. And, as it turned out, they were quite comfortable in the role. Though they had spent their careers plotting ways to shrink government, the federal bureaucracy *grew* under their leadership. As the *National Review* noted, federal spending increased from $591 billion in 1980 to over $2.4 trillion decades later. Heritage's budget rose in parallel: from $5.3 million in 1981 to more than $60 million in 2009.[17] In 2005, the Heritage Foundation released a short version of the *Mandate* as a book, noting that the manifesto now "serves a different purpose" than it had before conservative ideas were "well established in Washington, well accepted by American voters and well understood everywhere in terms of how they translate into policy."[18]

What is construed as the "deep state" by today's right is, ironically, the result of the takeover of state policy by right-wing antistatist actors. What Heritage wrought was a larger, more complex, and more technocratic federal bureaucracy that transparently served lobbyists—the *real* special interests—rather than the activist groups Pat Buchanan had labeled "special interests." Heritage's neoliberals chose to turn every program they had misperceived as a "handout" into just that—but for corporations. Convinced as they were that government programs were nothing but a shell game run by self-interested politicians diverting monies toward their minority constituents, they asked, "Why not do the same for our *own* constituents?" After all, weren't property owners and businessmen the real victims of government?

Although the era from the start of Reagan's time in office to the end of Bill Clinton's is often characterized as a time of "deregulatory" reforms, the claim has things almost exactly backward, if one separates rhetoric from action. Actually, the period saw *more* laws and regulations, requiring more lawyers, more compliance officers, and more lobbyists. Neoliberal elites increased their rent-seeking activities and thus their "rents." As corporate coffers grew, money flooded into politics. Corporations' increasing political sway then led to more profits through rent seeking. Buchanan's fears about special interest vote-trading had come to life, only in reverse.

From Reagan's tax and spending cuts to Clinton's tax and spending cuts, from Supreme Court decisions to Congress's embrace of Chicago School economics, neoliberalism became the software of the state. Trickle-down economics *was* economics; shareholder maximization *was* the point of corporate law; government benefits *were* socialism, but corporate benefits were capitalism. The acts of legislation that helped define the era included Reagan's 1986 Tax Reform Act; Clinton's signing of the North American Free Trade Agreement (NAFTA), which accelerated offshoring; Clinton's spending cuts in the Omnibus Budget Reconciliation Act of 1993; and his Personal Responsibility and Work Opportunity Act of 1996, cutting welfare.

Tax cuts, free trade deals, and financial deregulation—so-called Reaganomics (or "voodoo economics" according to critics)—were intended to spur economic expansion, create jobs, increase productivity, and restore confidence in the economy. Yet time and time again, these actions have failed spectacularly. The laws were not designed to free the magic of the market so that we would be collectively better off. The laws were designed to delegitimize democracy and law. They were designed to protect the privileged few against society's demands. They were designed to weaken federal power so that those who had amassed the most wealth could protect it from the claims of those on whose backs that wealth was made. In other words, the economic legislation and tax cuts were a Trojan horse for the dismantling of democracy and society. And they worked brilliantly.

IN MOST STUDIES of neoliberalism, tax cuts and deregulatory legislation are the main examples of neoliberal success in transforming American laws. But less remarked upon, although far more significant and long-lasting, were the many systematic changes to the administrative state. Most laws shaping markets are made by federal agencies, and most of these laws are made beyond the earshot of the legislature and without a public vote.

The administrative state comprises the alphabet soup of agencies that originated in the expertise-oriented Woodrow Wilson administration—which created the Federal Reserve and the Federal

Trade Commission—and was massively expanded by FDR, whose administration added sixty-nine new agencies, including a dozen or so just for credit and banking regulation. Progressive and New Deal reformers created agencies to foster a mixed economy, deploying experts and government resources to spur industrial development. The agencies developed expertise in their respective areas and held lawmaking power over everything from loan criteria and weight maximums on trucks to farming subsidies and airline routes.

Before neoliberals could transform these agencies in the 1980s and 1990s, they theorized about why the agencies should be transformed. That job was largely accomplished by George Stigler. According to his canonical 1971 article "The Theory of Economic Regulation," regulation, like electoral politics, was driven by special interests. In the case of regulation, special interests used the state's regulatory power to protect themselves from competition. He called the phenomenon *regulatory capture.*

Although Keynesian and progressive economists had recognized that not *all* regulatory rules on business were made in the public interest—the term "rent seeking" was coined to describe the problem of businesses influencing laws to their benefit—Stigler took this observation to the extreme. Rather than arguing that only *some* regulations were unwarranted or counterproductive, Stigler posited that, "*as a rule*, regulation is acquired by the industry and is designed and operated primarily for its benefit." By Stigler's lights, *all* regulation, from any quarter, was rent seeking by special interest groups colluding with self-interested politicians to promote their own interests.[19]

As scholars at the time noted, the paper had many methodological flaws. Most obviously, it relied on only two case studies: state trucking rules and state occupational licensing laws, both of which supposedly harmed free market competition. As many economists have since pointed out, Stigler could not even prove that these two examples had resulted from rent seeking. As one sympathetic scholar said at a celebration—held at the Stigler Center at the University of Chicago—to mark the fiftieth anniversary of the article: "Stigler was wrong. But . . . his errors were illuminating . . . [and] his influence is undeniable."[20] By discrediting market regulation, Stigler's model added another justification to shrinking government's power to contend with market power.

Buchanan's and Stigler's theories combined to paint a picture of state power as essentially a corrupt tool of special interests rather than a representative government acting on behalf of the people. They represented a stark rejection of the conventional view of market regulation as a necessary check on corporate power. In other words, neoliberalism was an exact inversion of how most economists and citizens viewed the interplay between government and corporations.

The new theory of how government worked was supplemented by their models of how the market, when freed from the tethers of the extractive state, was not only efficient and productive, but fair, rational, and self-governing. The government was run by flawed and fallen men while the market was scientific and precise. Understanding the market was like understanding the atom or the universe, a Nobel-worthy scientific endeavor. While microeconomists including Stigler and Buchanan highlighted examples of regulatory and legislative failures, and while legal scholars including Richard Posner and Richard Epstein hypothesized the many shortcomings of the courts, it was a group of macroeconomists who theorized the market as it might be—free of government, law, and of the same kinds of humans who ran governments and judiciaries.

The Chicago economist and Nobel Prize winner Eugene Fama's "efficient market hypothesis" held that market prices reflect all available information and that it was impossible to beat the market—impossible for mere mortals, that is. This theory credited the market with rationality, coherence, and accuracy that could not be matched. The way to know the true value of anything was to observe its market price, which held within it not just the predicted future but all the information about the company and its competition at any given time. The notion of "accurate" pricing assumed that markets were more science than psychology. Prices were bequeathed with an omniscience that no human—and certainly no government bureaucrat—could approach. The market would punish the weak and bless the strong. Market discipline would be meted out through declining stock prices. Despite having been debunked by other economists, such as Robert Shiller (who shared the 2013 Economics Nobel with Fama), the entire field of behavioral economics, and real-life events like asset bubbles and other such irrationalities, Fama's theory inspired many of the policies of the neoliberal era. It became the basis for getting rid of antitrust laws, for instance, because insofar as prices remained low, there could not be a monopoly. It also justified replacing government regulation of financial risk with market discipline, which would punish risks with lower prices.

A version of efficient market theory called *rational expectations theory*, proposed by another Chicago economist and Nobel Prize winner, Robert Lucas, came to essentially the same conclusion about the market's superior knowing without assuming that all information was reflected in all prices. Instead, it assumed that market actors generally or *mostly* held rational expectations about future market prices. Rational expectations theory is itself a companion to another theory, *rational choice theory*, which proved that individuals' choices were based in rational self-interest. Together, these theories portrayed the market as a well-ordered mechanism that moved predictably and logically even if its judgments were inscrutable to the untrained eye.

These theories were a result of a general scientific hubris of the post-war era that assumed that the problems which have long plagued mankind had been scientifically or technologically resolved or would be in a matter of time. Lucas was so confident in the market that he remarked in 2003, five years before the global financial crisis, that "the central problem of depression prevention has been solved, for all practical purposes, and has in fact been solved for many decades."[21] Idealism in scientific progress was not just the domain of neoliberals. It was shared, if not invented, by progressives at the turn of the twentieth century. The idealistic progressive view held that the state could be the fairest and most efficient allocator of rights, resources, and freedom, provided it was led by expertise and vision of an egalitarian society. This was obviously never achieved, if it was even possible.

Closer to reality and mainstream consensus were the legal realists, who saw abuses of power in markets and in governance, as well as economists like John Maynard Keynes, Joan Robinson, and

Gunnar Myrdal, who saw economics as a tool of statecraft, which at its best could make society a little fairer and even try to prevent further violence. Keynes's most famous line, "In the long run we are all dead," was uttered in response to the economic formalists, whose elegant theories modeled "long run" effects of things like stimulus spending. Keynes advocated fiscal stimulus and monetary flexibility *now* because now was all that could be observed—tomorrow would always present new challenges.

Neoliberal models were both dystopian and utopian, but regardless, they perceived the long run. Hayek denounced Keynesianism because it interfered with "the spontaneous order" of the market, but Hayek's faith in the market was not utopian like Friedman's or Rand's (or her heroes'). What Hayek saw "in the long run" was a road to serfdom: in every program promising "social justice" lay the seeds for collectivism and destruction. Hayek didn't oppose Keynes's policies with different policies but opposed the very idea of policies imposed on markets. Yet what links both Hayek's cynical dystopia of state tyranny and the market liberty of utopians like Friedman is an overconfidence in the ability to predict the long run. This is what makes neoliberalism an ideology, similar to religious fundamentalism, racism, communism, natural law, social Darwinism, or even the totalitarianism of the Nazis, all of which predict the future and, more crucially, attempt to hasten what is posited as inevitable. It hardly mattered that some of these ideologies were based on science and others on mystical forces.

When Stigler accepted his Nobel Prize in 1982, he extolled the virtue of theory in changing scientific understanding—"it takes a theory to beat a theory"—apparently even one with significant flaws.[22] The reason, he believed, that his "economic theory of regulation is achieving substantial scientific prosperity"—despite the fact that it was still "relatively primitive"—was that it was a strong theory.[23] But given the alternative ideas about the state and markets, it is more accurate to say that it took a strong theory to beat reality. And like its predecessor ideologies, neoliberalism *changed* reality. Neoliberalism attributed an inevitable knowing to the market that could neither be seen nor denied, but only obeyed without protest.

Neoliberal theories were metabolized into policy by the right's think tanks, which helped manufacture the enfeebled and corrupt state that had until then existed only in the neoliberal imagination. Based on the assumption of market rationality and government irrationality, more and more issues that had previously been decisions of policy were delegated to the market.

Ironically, in pursuit of shrinking the government and cutting costs, the neoliberal decades witnessed the creation of a large and complicated efficiency-industrial complex. A favorite tactic of right-wing think tanks was mandating "efficiency," "paperwork reduction," and "cost-benefit" measures across federal agencies to tilt the focus of the administrative state toward box-checking exercises that in fact changed the focus of each agency.

That model was another innovation of Richard Nixon's. The Nixon administration created the Office of Management and Budget (OMB) in 1970 with a mandate to oversee budgets for all the administrative agencies and evaluate each agency for efficiency. (The only government programs exempted from budgetary oversight are the Department of Defense and NASA.) A few years later, Nixon created another oversight agency, the Congressional Budget Office (CBO), to analyze (or "score") every act of legislation in terms of its effect on the national deficit. The OMB's inaugural pursuit was to ensure that regulations on business were reined in, especially those being created by the Environmental Protection Agency (EPA). The OMB and the EPA were founded at the same time—one to regulate environmental pollution and the other to make sure that those regulations did not cost businesses too much in profit. The OMB was Chicago economist George Shultz's idea; Shultz, the first director of the new agency, suggested that the OMB be used to determine the monetary costs as well as the monetary benefits of each regulation (called cost-benefit analysis, or CBA), environmental or otherwise, with the goal of promoting efficiency. While the OMB theoretically looked at most regulations, the EPA was clearly its main and often its only target. "In practice this requirement has been routinely imposed only on" EPA, noted the EPA's assistant director in a complaint to the OMB.[24]

A decade later, Congress created the Office of Information and Regulatory Affairs (OIRA) within the OMB through the 1980 Paperwork Reduction Act. In 1981, President Reagan issued Executive Order 12291, which empowered the OMB to formally review all federal lawmaking and oppose regulations that did not yield "net benefits to society," as measured in dollar costs. "Regulatory action shall not be undertaken unless the potential benefits to society from the regulation outweigh the potential costs to society."[25]

Far from reducing regulations, costs, or even paperwork, these mandates and the large bureaucratic agencies that were created to administer them have been used to delay and encumber market-curbing laws. By requiring any proposed reform to undergo an expensive and legally complex box-checking exercise, the quality of federal regulation has itself come to resemble a legally complex box-checking exercise for regulated industries. Instead of measuring the utility of any given regulation, often what makes a regulation viable is that it passes the bureaucratic gauntlet of other agency checks. These agencies are not seen as partisan—nor should they be, because they have been embraced by both left and right—but their cumulative effect has been to make it difficult to pass the kind of laws that increase public goods or that rein in the market for some social good: those kinds of regulations often cannot pass the cost-benefit test. The mission of the OMB and OIRA covered virtually the entire federal administrative state. However, it has had a particularly suppressive effect on the EPA's ability to impose environmental regulations on polluters because the costs of complying with these regulations (e.g., changes to waste disposal) are easy to measure while the benefits (in this case, cleaner streams) are often intangible, dispersed, and incalculable. The process of CBA shifts the burden onto regulators proposing the regulation to justify its costs on the industry they are regulating. The "scoring" exercise and OIRA's ever-expanding mandates made it harder to pass environmental laws, or, really, any regulation at all whose costs fall on corporate profits while its benefits fall outside of a balance sheet. Such is the norm of the neoliberal era: increases in the size and complexity of the administrative state alongside the curtailing of meaningful, positive changes across the economy. The checks on regulation are not themselves ideologically inflected, but the framework of cost-benefit analysis often yields, as it was always intended to do, outcomes constraining government action that might threaten corporate profits. Most neoliberal reforms likewise promised neutrality but delivered a consistent political agenda—one that benefited a well-connected minority of elites who could not pass their rent-seeking agendas at the polls.

The OMB and CBO were given more specific mandates with the passage of the Balanced Budget and Emergency Deficit Control Act (1985), which required automatic spending cuts and emergency sequestration of agency funding when certain budgetary thresholds were crossed. The bill was found to be unconstitutional a few years later, and was replaced by PAYGO (pay as you go) spending limits, which mandated new taxes to be included in every bill to achieve "budget neutrality." The mandates have done nothing to lower the deficit, but they have been used effectively to cut spending on social programs.

While the CBO and OMB are neutral organizations with bipartisan support, their mission of cost cutting and efficiency in government programs has resulted in laws that favor private markets rather than public programs. The CBA conducted by these agencies and the scoring of all legislation and regulation is tilted against bills that redistribute resources downward, but not against those that redistribute resources upward. Tax loopholes, for example, cost the government billions of dollars each year, but aren't scored because they don't involve spending. In contrast, the costs of every regulation aimed at reducing pollution is rigorously analyzed and challenged if it costs more than it benefits the economy. The entrenchment of CBO and OMB did nothing to reduce the size of government, but did end almost all poverty-aid programs.

In another ironic turn, regulatory capture—the threat identified by Stigler—became real only once the people warning against it came to power. Instead of eliminating the regulatory agencies, the neoliberals decided to capture them for their own goals. Rather than regulate the market or tame it, they rigged it. Instead of breaking up monopolies to protect the people, they protected monopolies *from* the people. All of this required more laws and regulations, which required more risk managers, compliance officers, and bigger firms.

THE NEOLIBERAL COUP led to a radical transformation of the American economy. The slow takeover of various domains of law—the triumph of Friedman's shareholder supremacy doctrine in corporate law; Bork's successful assault on antitrust laws; Stigler's delegitimizing of market regulation; Buchanan's projections abetting lawmaking by special interests, and Justice Lewis Powell's liberating of corporate dollars to affect elections—all began to bear fruit in the 1980s. Each of these changes was justified based on an idealized model of a free market economy that would essentially regulate itself. Firms would not monopolize markets because market competition would not enable it. Maximizing shareholder profits would supercharge the economy because shareholders were savvier and more knowledgeable than government bureaucrats.

In justifying each of these legal transformations, the cumulative effect of the others was out of sight and thus not factored into the model. Thus, for example, in urging lawmakers not to worry about monopoly power, Bork's argument focused narrowly on historic market prices to claim that monopoly power would not drive out competition because up until that point, monopolies had not skewed markets. But that was because a whole host of corporate and banking laws (and market norms besides) had kept corporate power in check. He did not acknowledge that if his friends, like Lewis Powell or James Buchanan, were successful in eradicating barriers limiting political spending by large corporations, dominant corporations would be able to suffocate their competition by buying laws, capturing regulators, or using the patent court system to drown their competitors in litigation. Nor did the assumption of efficient markets on which Friedman's shareholder supremacy model relied take into consideration that market prices would sometimes reflect not the inherent value of a company, but whether the Federal Reserve chairman would signal a market "put," giving investors confidence in future surging prices. In other words, most of these models ignored law and state power.

To be sure, the transformation of the market was not just led by ideas—there was plenty of lobbying money involved and a revolving door of industry insiders turned regulators and regulators turned industry insiders. But before our nation's capital could turn into a customer service department for corporate America, the ideology had to take hold. Neoliberal ideas had to move from the academy to the think tanks that big money donors built with the purpose of changing lawmaker's minds about what their job was. It is, contrary to neoliberal theory, difficult to corrupt lawmakers and to persuade them to serve the interests of the wealthy against voters. They had to be convinced—as the articulate true believers in the free market like Posner, Friedman, and Manne so convincingly did—that the free market would benefit the people. Not that it was the profitable thing to do, but that it was the *right* thing to do. As Reagan said, "Believe in the magic of the marketplace" and gain "growth, prosperity, and ultimately, human fulfillment." The neoliberals promised freedom through free markets but delivered neither. There was never such a thing as the free market—it was a decoy meant to persuade the rest of us to give up our power.

The hypocrisy was apparent from the start. In *The Great Transformation,* Karl Polanyi, a Hungarian American political economist whose brother Michael Polyani was a founding member of the MPS, calls the rise of the laissez-faire market economy in the nineteenth century "the product of deliberate State action."[26] That is, "the road to the free market was opened and kept open by an enormous increase in continuous, centrally organized and controlled interventionism."[27] Freeing the market required a string of legislative acts, draconian bureaucratic controls, market subsidies, and the centralization of authority, leading to more "control, regulation, and intervention."[28] Land enclosure laws, employment laws, and centralized monetary policy through strict enforcement of the international gold standard were all necessary for the delicate balance required to maintain the free market. Laws were needed to convert natural land into property, human activity into labor, and, most important, state power had to create money as a token of value without which the free market could not function. "Laissez-faire was not a method to achieve a thing, it was the thing to be achieved."[29] The same can be said of the second great transformation of the United States economy through financialization. Just as "laissez-faire was planned" through state intervention, so too was the magic of the market fostered and supported through legislation, regulation, and monetary policy.[30]

One of the most perfect expressions of the true character of neoliberalism is the Commodities Futures Modernization Act of 2000, which runs more than seven hundred pages and whose purpose is to *prevent* regulators from making laws regulating derivatives, or financial instruments whose value is derived from another underlying asset. Across the administrative state, fundamental provisions of long-standing laws and regulatory codes went from simple mandates to lengthy and complicated texts with loopholes and ambiguities requiring teams of lawyers to litigate them indefinitely. Regulatory agencies produced a glut of laws, subsidies, and special favors under the guise of getting the government out of the market.

In every sector, the neoliberal coup led to less freedom not only for average citizens but also for most corporations. Neoliberalism led not to competition but to consolidation: a winner-take-all competition with fewer companies competing for larger market share. Monopoly was the "natural" progression of markets uninhibited by regulation. A wave of mergers and consolidations led to fewer choices for consumers and higher profits for investors. In the airline industry, deregulation enabled mergers, pension cuts, and new equity structures, which resulted in reduced services and increased profit margins. In the electricity sector, power companies became more dominant monopolies, offering lower-quality services to customers and funneling the savings to equity holders in the form of dividends. Changes to bankruptcy laws made corporate bankruptcy much easier than personal or family bankruptcy. The effects of the neoliberal coup of the administrative state was an excess of procedure and red tape without any meaningful market regulation. All form and no substance.

CHAPTER 8

Barbarians at the Gate

What's the point of senators making laws now?
Once the barbarians are here, they'll do the legislating.

—C. P. CAVAFY,
"WAITING FOR THE BARBARIANS" (1904)

EATURING A PUBLIC decree in three languages—two ancient Egyptian scripts as well as ancient Greek—the Rosetta Stone has served as a codex for deciphering Egyptian hieroglyphics and is one of the most visited archaeological finds in the world. So significant has its discovery been to human knowledge that its name has become shorthand for anything that enables insight or understanding across cultures.

Less discussed is what is actually written on the stone: a proclamation of debt amnesty and the cancellation of back taxes. The laws of ancient Mesopotamia, which include religious laws and secular legal codes like Hammurabi's laws, reveal that financial contracts have existed since the creation of written laws. Centralized authorities with legal codes and common currencies enabled the citizens of those societies to enter debt contracts, to borrow money now for a promise to pay in the future. Then as now, the debt market that societies enabled created the very inequalities that threatened that society's continued legitimacy. This is why ancient societies periodically reset the scales through debt amnesty. Debt relief was used both routinely—typically every "sabbatical," or seventh year—and in response to specific hardships, such as climate-induced crop failure. Debt "jubilees" applied to society vertically (between rulers and subjects) and horizontally (among merchants and between individuals).

In antiquity, empires were under constant threat of invasion, plunder, revolution, and overthrow. Inequality and exploitation led to unrest and rebellion within, and opened the gates to so-called barbarians. Crushed by debt, the lower classes could at any point revolt against their masters—or, potentially, throw their lot in with foreign invaders. The jubilee was a rational act of self-preservation, shoring up legitimacy and goodwill, inoculating society against unrest and revolution. Power is never as stable as those who hold it would like it to be. Push too hard on a brittle system of power and it breaks. Better to protect the system by recalibrating its scales. "If the accretions of vested interest were to grow without mitigation for many generations," warned John Maynard Keynes, "half the population would be no better than slaves to the other half" because the "powers of uninterrupted usury are great."

Usury was forbidden in ancient societies because it accelerated the inequalities between debtors and creditors, but even without usury, debt had a cyclical quality that could indefinitely impoverish some while enriching others. Without intervention, the tendency of capital was to grow exponentially and confer power onto its holders, while the tendency of debt was to deprive a person of their liberty. In ancient societies, debtors could be sent to prison or enslaved. Or, more commonly, they would sell a daughter into slavery to satisfy their creditors. The forgiveness of debt meant freedom. As stated in Leviticus, "On the Day of Atonement you shall sound the trumpet throughout all your land . . . and proclaim liberty throughout the land to all its inhabitants . . . [the debtor] and his children are to be released in the Year of Jubilee." Not for nothing was this verse inscribed on the Liberty Bell, a symbol of the fledgling

United States' victory over tyranny and in subsequent centuries a rallying cry for abolitionists, suffragists, and civil rights leaders.

In neoliberal ideology, there is no need to balance power through debt jubilees because the market is seen as a self-regulating organism. Neoliberalism also redefined liberty from "freedom from debt" to "freedom from government and society." Debt was no longer a threat to liberty, but rather it was government intrusion into markets through debt forgiveness that was tyrannical. As debt exploded during the neoliberal era, so too did returns on capital—for one person's interest payment is another person's return on investment.

Backed by the full force of law, capital was granted the liberty to move across the globe, to expand endlessly, and to bend society to its demands. Once set free, it forged its way over and through the weak levies of the law, pushing against the tenuous guardrails that protected democracy from the ever present threat of dominion by the powerful.

The Reagan era was when the quiet coup became a big bang. By the time he took office, the Powell-memo-inspired long-range planning had been completed, the right-wing think tanks were positioned inside the administrative state, and Law and Economics had eroded common law contract protections. As such, neoliberalism transformed the world within a few short years in the 1980s—and it was done through finance. Finance refers to the market where abstract monetary values like debt contracts, insurance contracts, securities contracts, and all such future claims to money are exchanged. Before the neoliberal era, finance was a "sideshow to the real economy," which refers to industries that produce, distribute, build, or exchange tangible goods. The "age of greed" led by "the masters of the universe" (stockbrokers, junk bond traders, and vulture capitalists) changed the world economy and American culture in a relatively short amount of time and without much public backlash. It would take years for Americans to realize that Wall Street's gains had come at their expense. Monumental changes in monetary policy and banking regulation were hidden behind a curtain of complex laws and even more opaque financial products. The opacity and complexity of law and finance served a dual function: to insulate policy making from the general public and to make the Wall Street–Washington intersection a loop of insider experts. In a few years during the Reagan era, regulators and legislators transformed the economy by changing laws that had prohibited banks from doing exactly what was now legal: to take risks with other people's money.

Although the neoliberal revolution reshaped each industry, nowhere was the transformation more profound than in banking. Nowhere was the myth of a market free from government further from reality. What happened in banking is categorically different from what happened in the airline or electricity industry—different in fact from all other industries. The mammoth banks that the neoliberal era produced were not only larger than any banks previously; they were fundamentally different entities—a trend that has only accelerated in the aftermath of the financial crisis.

The roots of the neoliberal theory of finance had to do—like much else in the Reagan years—with the neoliberals' rejection of the state's role in shaping markets stemming from their denial of any "such thing as society." Their evasion of the role of society was most consequential as it related to banking because money and credit, the products of banks, are the nexus where the state and market connect. For much of U.S. history—that is, until the 1980s—banks were treated, in law and in practice, as quasi-public institutions.[1] The social contract between banks and the state sponsoring them has been recognized throughout federal banking legislation, which has referred to banks interchangeably as "federal instrumentalities," "a public franchise," and "akin to public utilities"—that is, stewards of "other people's money."[2]

This was not on account of theory or ideology. It was a recognition of undeniable reality: banks are different than other businesses for several interrelated reasons, including the fact that bank profits are derived from borrowing and lending "other people's money," making them prone to panics, runs, and crises that can be resolved only through government interventions like bailouts, which means banking is essentially a state-sponsored industry. These hard-earned lessons of crises past were baked into the banking laws of the era, which protected private banks in a cocoon of government subsidies and guarantees against default and, in turn, imposed limits on what banks could do as well as duties they had to the public. But neoliberals rejected public duties and constraints on banking based on their denial of society.

Neoliberals rejected the quasi-public role of banks, minimized concerns of concentrated power, and reoriented public focus on profitability and efficiency rather than safety and access. The transformation occurred over a decade and it included legislation and regulatory changes that would lift the regulations which had kept banks safe, small, and narrowly focused on essential banking services. But it all began with the foundational myth of market freedom as existing separate from state power. Neoliberals replaced long-standing banking laws, limiting bank risk and power with a practically absolute confidence in the self-regulatory power of the free market. In denying the importance, or even the very presence, of the state at the very heart of the market, neoliberals revoked the myriad protections developed to keep the banking system from overpowering the state either by size or risk. By eliminating safeguards around bank size and bank risk, neoliberalism created large and risky banks.

The outcome of ignoring history was to be doomed to repeat it.

RISK

Even before the era of global finance and complex derivatives, it was difficult to understand how banks functioned in an economy. In fact, neoliberal models often ignored the unique nature of banks in their models of the market, treating them like other corporations. Extending their scientific understanding of a mechanical market made up of rational decision makers, neoliberals had faith that the rules and governance regime that had kept banks small and stable for half a century were no longer necessary because modern technology and innovative mathematics had solved the problems of risk and crisis inherent in banking. Economistic hubris replaced the hard-earned lessons of banking history, which was marked by repeated crises and panics that could only be halted by the federal government. The mischaracterization of banks as entities distinct from society and the state flew in the face of history and common understanding at the time. Because the business of banking involves holding the deposits of the community, the "business of banking" is determined by its regulators. Banks' activities are heavily circumscribed and watched over, and unlike corporate charters, bank charters are hard to attain. "To [a bank] has been granted the exclusive privilege to do a specified business in a manner circumscribed by definite restrictions," noted an oft cited 1926 court decision. "It is wholly the creature of statute; and it does business by legislative grace."[3]

Neoliberal regulators not only ignored the inherent and ungovernable riskiness of banking but, more important, dismissed the unique threat bank power posed to democracy. While the history of banking regulation in the United States does not follow a single trajectory (indeed, it shows starts and stops, compromises, and heated disagreement), there has always persisted a fear, if not a paranoia, of the power of banks to surpass and overwhelm the power of the state. This fear was no mere delusion. European history held many examples of national power succumbing to speculative bubbles or to growing debt, and of revolutionary movements reacting to corruption and inequality. American leaders have thus recognized the political—and politically ruinous—nature of finance. In transforming banking, neoliberals did not cut the legal cord between banks and their regulators, but as was the case in other regulated industries, they made the connection between regulator and bank much more collaborative. Regulators went out of their way to show their friendliness to banks, for example, by staging a photo in which regulators held large scissors next to a stack of papers and red tape or a legislator who brought out a chainsaw to show he was serious about letting banks loose.[4] Regulators in the neoliberal era saw their role as promoting market competition and efficient profit making.

To understand the consequential changes to the financial sector during the neoliberal era, it is first important to understand a few key features of banks that distinguish them from all other firms. Banks are a mirror or a foil to other businesses and individuals in a market. Our assets—our money deposited at the bank—become bank *liabilities* because the bank must pay us back upon request. Counterintuitively, our liabilities—our debts—are the bank's long-term *assets*. Banks profit from the interest rate payments they accrue on lending, which is their compensation for taking on the risks of lending. A well-run banking system serves a useful function in an economy by enabling people to turn their expected future income into an asset like a home. Banks thus borrow short and lend long so we can borrow long and lend short. The role of banks in the market is thus to trade financial risks across various time horizons, which makes banking the most volatile business in an economy. These traits of banking illuminate the unique power of banks to augment both wealth and hazard.

These features make banks and banking difficult to understand and, indeed, confusions about banking abound from conspiracy theorists to notable neoliberal economists alike. For example, neoliberal economists minimized the role of banks to mere financial intermediaries, transmitting money in the economy between and among different parties. The truth is that banks don't just circulate the money in the economy, but rather they *create* money, a power that no other business can rival. Gold and silver, said Alexander Hamilton, "acquire life" and become "active and productive" only through the operation of a bank. The alchemical transformation through which banks multiply capital is lending and has been called *money multiplication*. The catalyst for this transformation is *leverage*, meaning the use of borrowed money (from depositors or investors) to augment more returns. The higher the leverage, the higher the risk, and the higher the revenue. Any institution that creates wealth, money, and capital through leverage is engaged in banking—even though it may not always identified as a bank per se. Investment banks, mortgage lenders, and shadow banks are also engaged in leveraged finance, sometimes called *maturity transformation*.

A simple model of money creation is called *fractional reserve lending*; in it, a bank holds a fraction of its customers' deposits at any given time and lends out the rest on interest. The customer deposits are multiplied through leverage each time the bank makes a loan. Banks thus create money through lending, a process referred to as the *money multiplier*. For example, when a bank issues a mortgage loan to a borrower, it does not drain the deposits it holds to do so—the depositors' bank statements still show the same amount as they deposited. If a bank decides to lend, it will credit the loan money to the borrower's account in exchange for a contract promising repayment. This has been called "fountain pen money" or, more accurately, "keystroke money."[5]

By lending the bulk of customer deposits, banks create new money on top of the old money. The loan amount does not come from a pile of money, because money is not a scarce resource like gold or even paper; rather, money is an abstract representation of debt enforceable by legal contract. The bank's depositors hold deposit slips, which are contractual promises by the bank to return their money upon demand (deposits are called *demand deposits*); the bank's borrowers hold a mortgage or note legally compelling them to pay the bank a certain amount of interest fees each month. Deposit slips, mortgages, and debt contracts are banknotes that are the equivalent of bank-created money in the economy. A bank charter thus endows banks with the magical power of money creation. Like Schrödinger's cat, both the new money and old money can exist simultaneously, but only if depositors know their money will be there should they need it.

But of course, there is a downside to creating money out of thin air, which is the second crucial feature of banks. Banks are inherently risky—even a small and conservative bank operates through leverage, keeping only a small fraction of customer deposits at the bank. Although all bank depositors have a right to their entire deposit at any time, in normal times, most depositors will only take out small sums, leaving the rest at the bank for safekeeping. Of course, the bank does not keep everyone's deposits on hand, relying on the probability that only a fraction of customers will demand them at any time. But probabilities are not certainties. Banks work if most bank depositors keep most of their money at the bank most of the time, but sometimes things can go very wrong.

If enough depositors are worried, a proper bank run occurs and it will not be long before the bank has run out of reserves (i.e., money in the vault to give to depositors). The fictional George Bailey in *It's a Wonderful Life* explained the very real risks of banking to the large group of depositors demanding their money from his building and loan: "You're thinking of this place all wrong. As if I had the money back in a safe. The money's not here. Your money's in Joe's house . . . right next to yours. And in the Kennedy house, and Mrs. Macklin's house, and a hundred others. Why, you're lending them the money to build, and then, they're going to pay it back to you as best they can. Now what are you going to do? Foreclose on them? . . . Now wait . . . now listen . . . now listen to me." But the depositors cannot listen to him because each depositor is acting rationally. If the bank is in trouble, each person's money is threatened and each will try to withdraw their money—and all of it—as soon as possible. The dilemma is this: if the bank is not in trouble, the mob demanding their money *is* the trouble. Once a bank run begins, even the most conservative and well-capitalized bank will be pushed to failure. Thus, the group is acting irrationally. If the entire group asks for their money, no one will get their money. Banking markets are governed in part by numbers and in part by mood.

A third feature of banks is that they operate together somewhat like an organism, an ecosystem, or a society. Each bank is a node in a broader network of other banks and companies—a run on one threatens a run on all. Like a game of musical chairs, the money multiplier works as long as customers keep their deposits in the bank so they can keep circulating. If the music stops, the entire system crumbles. Not just like an engine that stops the car until it can be started again, but more like an engine that when it stops, breaks the spell of the magic market.

Bank runs, being driven by panic, are usually contagious. Each bank is connected to the others through a web of loans, deposits, and joint investments. And bank customers cannot be discerning in a run, separating the good banks from the bad. The wisest, most rational thing to do is to get your money first and ask questions later. Historically, runs have not been isolated, and they have turned quickly into crisis. And when they have, the paper in everyone's hands is suddenly worth nothing. This paper, whether it is a deposit slip, a bond, or a banknote, is a legal right to some value. Where did the value go? It evaporated into thin air, including deposits and investments. What held a promise of money yesterday is just a piece of paper today when the magic is gone. What was real and tangible—a home, equipment, one's life savings—is repossessed by the same nameless and opaque financial system.

The music stopped during the Great Depression. "For so many months so many people had saved money and borrowed money and borrowed on their borrowings to possess themselves of the little pieces of paper by virtue of which they became partners in U. S. Industry," wrote *Time* on November 4, 1929, as the stock market was in free fall. "Now they were trying to get rid of them even more frantically than they had tried to get them."[6] When the newly inaugurated President Roosevelt addressed the country during an unprecedented bank holiday in the midst of the Great Depression, he denounced the greed and irresponsibility of banks: "There is an element in the readjustment of our financial system more important than currency, more important than gold, and that is the confidence of the people themselves. Confidence and courage are the essentials of success in carrying out our plan." Banks operate in a web of connection to other banks where a ripple or a failure in one bank affects all other banks. Banks run on trust and they fall on fear. Or as Roosevelt summarized the situation of the banks: "the only thing to fear is fear itself." Fear, like a contagious virus, would infect and destroy the healthiest banks.

This contagionlike susceptibility to failure is called *systemic risk* in the modern world. The only antidote to fear-induced bank runs is a credible promise of liquidity by a money issuer strong enough to keep funds flowing in crisis. Since the beginning of modern banking, the only entity capable of restoring trust has been a sovereign state because only a sovereign state has the power to create enough money to restore confidence. In other words, supporting the entire system from below is another web of support provided by the federal government. As Walter Bagehot, the first chronicler of the modern state's complex banking system amid a crisis, wrote in his 1873 classic *Lombard Street: A Description of the Money Market*, all the nation's banks and "all our credit system depends on the Bank [of England] for its security." He emphasized the point to ensure understanding: "This may seem too strong, but it's not. All banks depend on the Bank of England, and all Merchants depend on some banker."[7] Then and now, banks run on trust, meaning that credit markets operate well when they are trusted. And alternatively, a bank run is a panic induced by a lack of trust, which only a central bank can remedy. As Bagehot then observed, "credit is an opinion generated by circumstances and varying with those circumstances," so democratic legitimacy and social policy were required in order to uphold it; "no abstract argument and no mathematical computation will teach it to us." He wrote, "Credit in business is like loyalty in government. . . . [It] is a power which may grow, but cannot be constructed."[8] It is trust, not money, that is the currency of banking.

In addressing the crisis created by a private industry, Roosevelt concluded his March 1933 remarks by stating that it was the job of the public to remedy the failures of the banks: "It is your problem, my friends, your problem no less than it is mine. Together we cannot fail." The President meant that the crisis needed a coordinated societal response, the kind of response that only the federal government can muster in a panic. From then on, U.S. banks were insured by the "full faith and credit" of the Treasury.

The financial system is therefore a web of banks and banklike entities engaged in maturity transformation—a merry-go-round of risk that is underwritten by the public's trust of the system. Systemic risk is not just the downside of banking, but its upside too. Risk is the business of banking, which makes it all the more troubling that the entire sector is either explicitly or implicitly underwritten by the government treasury. There are two interrelated downsides to the umbilical connection between the government and its banks: first, the cost of risk and crises will always be borne by the government and the rest of society; second, and relatedly, banks and the governments that save them in a crisis have a conflict of interest. The higher the leverage, the higher the risk and the reward. The incentive of bankers is to increase their leverage to extract more profits—banks profit from the upside while the government (via taxpayers) pays for the downside. This perverse incentive is called *moral hazard*, referring to the tendency of insured parties to take more risks when they do not bear the full weight of the downside.

Banking is thus rife with conflicts of interest—between the state as both regulator and underwriter of the whole enterprise and the public, being both customer and unsuspecting victim. The reason so many conspiracies center around banks and central banks in particular is that the moneymaking power of banking verges on the occult, due to the somewhat "magical" properties of money—specifically, the here-one-minute-and-gone-the-next quality of banknotes in a crisis, as well as the magnitude of the disruption caused by the rippling effects of bank failures. The complex and paradoxical nature of money—in that its value is based on belief in its value—has led to scapegoating people or groups, as the history of antisemitism reveals.

Two years before taking his seat as an associate justice of the Supreme Court, Louis Brandeis explained the unique power of banks in a book called *Other People's Money and How the Bankers Use It*. Whereas the wealth of magnates like the fur-trading Astors was "static," "the wealth of the Morgan associates [was] dynamic," because the banker's wealth was generated through his control of "other people's money." John Jacob Astor could at most invest, but J. P. Morgan's wealth shaped markets; Morgan's wealth could lend. Morgan's monopoly was in credit, the supply of which was virtually limitless, whereas Astor's was in fur, the supply of which—beavers—could not be multiplied like money. Morgan and the so-called money trusts could make industries or crush them by deciding to lend or not. Save the market or let it fail. This also presented a conflict of interest because "experience shows that their judgment is warped" by the power of their alliances. J. P. Morgan himself held seventy-two directorships, forty-seven of them in the largest corporations in the country.[9]

The irony of the dynamic market-shaping power of the financial oligarchs was its circularity—for "the fetters which bind the people are forged *from the people's own gold*."[10] Brandeis said of the special power of the bankers that "if the bankers' power were commensurate only with their wealth, they would have relatively little influence on American business."[11] They held power over ordinary Americans because they were essentially holding the citizens' money hostage. "They control the people through the people's own money," which meant that they could easily convert their profits into outsized political influence.

To Brandeis, the solution was to make the banks akin to public utilities. He quoted Justice Oliver Wendell Holmes, who said, in a decision on an Oklahoma bank case, "We cannot say that the public interests to which we have adverted, and others, are not sufficient to warrant the State in taking the whole business of banking under its control."[12] But Brandeis and Holmes, legal realists as they were, recognized that full nationalization of banking would not be politically feasible. Brandeis concluded *Other People's Money* by proposing banking reforms to ensure that banks focus on people rather than profits, which he called "democratic banking."[13]

The New Deal was a major pivot in banking history. Not only did Roosevelt curtail bank power, he reconstructed the industry and created a mixed economy of credit allocation. So monumental were these reforms that they changed the nature of the entire economy. The New Deal created a powerful legal structure to both regulate and empower banks. The Glass-Steagall Act of 1933, for example, forced a separation of risky Wall Street trading from deposit taking. This "separation of banking and commerce" was a pillar of banking law until the neoliberal revolution. The 1956 Bank Holding Company Act prohibited banks from merging unless the merger was in the "best interest" of the community,[14] a high bar that prevented bank mergers until these barriers were knocked over by neoliberals who were more concerned with the best interest of shareholders. Banks were restricted from buying or trading stocks. They could not own other companies and could not themselves be owned by a corporation. In most states, banks couldn't even branch beyond a single location—a restriction intended to limit their reach, power, and risk. (Branching nationwide wasn't possible until the 1990s.) These laws erected dams and barriers that protected small banks against the ever present forces of conglomeration and power that accumulate in finance. Activity restrictions, capital controls, geographical limits, and interest rate caps—the risky magic of banking was carefully regulated. For a while, the only competition allowed between banks was who could give the best toaster!

In return for all the restrictions, banks were granted a monopoly franchise of safe and profitable lending funded by the federal government, including deposit insurance, loan guarantees, and other buffers and protections. The risks associated with banking were addressed through banking regulations while the risks associated with Wall Street speculation were addressed separately.

There were no banking crises between the New Deal reforms and their breach during the neoliberal era. These years coincided with a booming banking sector, unprecedented national and individual wealth, and a complete restoration of public confidence in the sector. But it was a little boring. And in a state of tranquility, the hard-won understanding of the causes and effects of a banking crisis were forgotten. So too were the fears about the unique ability of the financial sector to magnify its own power through the use of other people's money and the destructive power of irrational exuberance and panic.

In 1987, at the request of the Reagan administration, the Federal Deposit Insurance Corporation (FDIC) was asked to study "the need for major reform of the banking system." Its subsequent report, entitled *Mandate for Change: Restructuring the Banking Industry*, was not written by the Heritage Foundation like the *Mandate for Leadership*, but it had the same basic aims.[15] The FDIC's *Mandate* proposed that the Glass-Steagall restrictions and the Bank Holding Company Act "be abolished" in order to allow banks the "freedom to operate in the marketplace without undue regulatory influence."[16] The FDIC was sure that "systemic risks to the banking industry and potential losses to the FDIC will not be increased if activity restrictions and regulatory authority over bank affiliates are abolished." Market competition would also ensure that FDIC insurance would be priced more "efficiently" as banks became "subjected to greater market discipline through the refining of failure-resolution policies." The argument was that banks would not be incentivized to take risks because if they did, their failure would punish them.

As for excessive bank power? "There will [not] be fewer banks or less competition in any given market," assured the FDIC, because "while concentrations of political power may be undesirable, it is not clear that large organizations or highly concentrated industries are able to wield too much influence over government." Relying on the Chicago School model of antitrust, the FDIC believed that laws limiting bank size were outdated fears made irrelevant due to modern technology. They claimed, in line with Bork and Stigler, that "as excess profits develop in any market, they will be competed away." The FDIC also dismissed fears like those of Brandeis and FDR that money trusts like JP Morgan would have too much power compared to the state: "It is not clear that large organizations or highly concentrated industries are able to wield too much influence over government." That clarity would come soon enough.

Alan Greenspan, whom Reagan appointed as Fed chair in 1987, played a crucial role in justifying the legal transformation of finance, and in underwriting it as well through the nearly unlimited monetary power of his position. Testifying on behalf of bank deregulation soon after he took office, Greenspan urged Congress to leave banking to the market, noting that it was a "historic opportunity" to make the U.S. financial system "more responsive to consumer needs, more efficient, more competitive in the world economy, and equally important, more stable."[17] Those who fought against these repeals were by implication sacrificing the nation's ability to compete with other nations on account of naïveté or a lack of understanding.

What Greenspan meant by free markets was, however, not a market free of government intervention. In fact, the Fed's powerful yet murky monetary policy tools were always in the background, ensuring the smooth operation of a market. Greenspan's legacy as Fed chairman created financial markets so reliant on Federal Reserve support that it is near impossible today to delineate where government monetary policy ends and financial markets begin. Greenspan's conductorlike market interventions earned him the nickname "the Maestro." In crisis after crisis, Greenspan's policy "stabilized" the market through Fed support, which led banks to take risks with confidence that the Fed would step in. Each time a crisis loomed in the stock market, Greenspan plied banks with loans, bought distressed assets to place on the Fed's balance sheets, lowered interest rates, purchased Treasury bonds to boost bank profits, and promised any backstops necessary to return banks to profitability. The so-called Greenspan put covered up an inherently risky system with Fed funds, allowing risks to mount. Wall Street profits were insured against loss by American taxpayers, a transfer of wealth from the bottom of the population to the very top and an equal transfer of risk from the top to the bottom.

Slowly, banks and policy makers chipped away at the walls erected during the New Deal. Instead of a holistic revision of the social contract between banks and the American public, however, Congress passed a patchwork of reactionary legislation that undid the prior era's social contract without negotiating new terms. Between 1980 and 1999, Congress passed several deregulatory acts—from the 1980 Depository Institutions Deregulation and Monetary Control Act and the 1982 Garn–St. Germain Depository Institutions Act to the 1994 Riegle-Neal Interstate Banking and Branching Efficiency Act and the 1999 Gramm-Leach-Bliley Act—that collectively effectively deregulated the banking industry, enabling it to compete with other credit and investment options. Proving the bipartisan adoption of neoliberalism, both the Riegle-Neal Act and the Gramm-Leach-Bliley Act were passed during the Clinton administration. But by then it was already a formality. By 1983, John Shad, the chairman of the Securities and Exchange Commission, told Congress, capital was "thundering over, under, and around Glass-Steagall."[18]

In the battle between the forces of capital and those of regulation, capital has the advantage: through the powerful medium of compound interest, it can grow exponentially and unthinkingly, while the protective barriers around democracy must be perpetually, actively reinforced. Once capital began to grow on Wall Street, political power followed, making it even more difficult for regulators to stop it; the Clinton administration wasn't even trying. Treasury Secretary Robert Rubin, a former Goldman Sachs partner, and his successor, Lawrence Summers, knocked down the last of the legal barriers protecting the American public from the global empire of capital—all in the name of "efficiency."

The legal changes are usually referred to as *banking deregulation*, which is accurate insofar as the regulations and safeguards around banks were eradicated, but is a misnomer. In fact, what occurred was a shift in the regulatory framework. Before the 1980s, the rules for banks were simple. After neoliberalism, laws and regulations multiplied—where there had been two, now there were a dozen or so acts of legislation and a myriad of regulatory changes.

The "thou shalt nots" of Glass-Steagall were replaced with a heavy reliance on a firm's internal models of risk weights. Simple and blunt rules that prohibited banks from entering risky markets or becoming too large were replaced with a complex web of mathematical risk calculations, modeling market vulnerabilities, and ratings systems. JP Morgan's compliance department, for example, ballooned in comparison to the rest of the firm, as did its groups of mathematicians and quants modeling market risks. Company disclosures became longer and more complicated, employing even bigger teams of lawyers to draft them. There were more and more regulations placed on the firm even as the firm became more and more powerful.

Having done away with the blunt and outdated morality of the old economy, the neoliberals replaced it with *risk management*. Risk management brought data, science, and mathematical analysis to supposedly trade away the risks inherent in finance. These risk calculations were meant to compensate for the lack of opacity with complex math. At the large firms, risk management was handled by legions of quants from top schools using algorithms and highly sophisticated economic models. Algorithmic risk management paved the way for excessive risk-taking by providing seemingly exact calculations of each risk using "big data." Exact probabilities of the "value at risk" of each trade appeared to "solve" the uncertainty of risk through clever equations. Financial giants shrouded the ever-expanding pile of capital secured by legal contracts under a web of complexity. While parts of the financial risk system were observable to the naked eye, the various machinations of financial risks fell outside of the public's attention.

Greenspan even replaced the Fed's role of supervising the banking industry with the same risk management models used by the banks themselves. As he noted during a 2004 speech,

> The conduct of monetary policy in the United States has come to involve, at its core, crucial elements of risk management. This conceptual framework emphasizes understanding as much as possible the many sources of risk and uncertainty that policymakers face, quantifying those risks when possible, and assessing the costs associated with each of the risks. In essence, the risk

management approach to monetary policymaking is an application of Bayesian decision-making.[19]

Mathematical analysis as monetary policy replaced the simple and intuitive rules of the previous era. The new regulatory regime, according to Greenspan, involved regulators conducting "risk and cost-benefit analyses" relying "on forecasts of probabilities developed from large macro models, numerous sub models, and judgments based on less mathematically precise regimens."[20] The modeling and submodeling of risks by the Fed trickled down to the industry until finance became inscrutable to outsiders. Far from managing financial risks, all the effort put into creating such elegant statistical analyses provided false comfort, which in turn only increased risk-taking. And when the models failed to predict the unpredictable, the Greenspan put was available to lull the market back to profitablity.

No matter how sophisticated the risk analysis conducted by regulators, it was no substitute for basic trust in the integrity of the banking system. It was hard to understand each product or firm or risk model in the system—let alone trust in its soundness—so firms resorted to even more financial contracts to offset their risks and assuage their growing paranoia. Each new innovative product spawned a corresponding "hedge" that purported to neutralize risk, but instead added another layer of complexity and interconnection to the web. And regulators welcomed each financial innovation without thinking too hard about the fact that the same highly leveraged firms were insuring and hedging one another's risks, making it more than likely that a single failure would bring them all down. Risk models did not account for what bank analysts and regulators could not imagine. As financialization progressed, firms became more interconnected while their products became more obscure, turning finance into a shell game with each institutional node in the system trying to outrun the others to avoid disaster. The solution to each risk was another financial product attempting to impose order on chaos.

Risk management was the siren song of Wall Street, spinning the fantasy that risk could be limited if only the model was mathematically sophisticated enough. Even those who weren't beguiled by the tune participated because, if everyone believed in risk management, the system would continue to churn profits. "As long as the music is going, you have to dance," said Vikram Pandit, the CEO of Citigroup, after the music stopped. The sophistication of the models and the elegance of the mathematical proofs notwithstanding, it was smoke and mirrors. And all the theorizing and calculating and modeling and insuring and hedging and underwriting would be useless in a panic. Systemic risks cannot be managed with formulas because banks fail all at once. It is fear and panic—*distrust*—that makes banks vulnerable to risk.

Greenspan could change monetary policy by simply deciding it—such was the power and discretion of the Federal Reserve. In fact, most far-reaching transformations of banking laws were done well outside of typical democratic forums and thus outside of public purview. They were made within the highly specialized and complex process of regulatory review. Among the government agencies that oversee banks are the Fed itself, the FDIC, the Office of the Comptroller of the Currency (OCC), the Consumer Financial Protection Bureau, the Securities and Exchange Commission, and the Federal Trade Commission; financial markets are also shaped by state banking regulators, the various subagencies of the U.S. Treasury, and other regulatory bodies. Most large banks are also governed by international banking laws like the Basel Accord, an international capital regulatory framework that replaced the collapsed Bretton Woods system, and other complex trade and sanctions regimes. This regulatory network has grown larger and more complex even as banking has become riskier and more prone to crisis. Without a public vote or any public input, these agencies transformed not just finance but the global economy.

The overall effect of the changes was the financialization of the economy and the limitless growth of capital; both trends were mutually reinforcing. In other words, financialization was both cause and effect of capital's metastasis. One advantage of finance—at least from the point of view of corporate executives—is that, unlike production, there are no real limits to what it can touch. Finance joins with the law to create new asset classes, devise contracts for new forms of debt, and innovate until every last drop of yield is extracted from capital. The financialization of the economy unleashed the viral propagating force of capital to reorder society and the economy toward its needs. Capital grows by extracting yield or "rent." This usually involves taking some risk, either by lending capital at interest—debt—or investing in an equity. *Yield* measures the ratio of returns on investment, and is usually rendered as a percentage. After the neoliberal laws took effect, the strongest force shaping the global market was the velocity of capital's search for yield.

Wall Street, for its part, met the increased demand for yield by inventing an endless array of risks with which to improve yield ratios. A single home mortgage could be *securitized*—that is, turned into capital to be bought and sold. That security could be bundled with other securities and coded differently again to create new forms of risk at an added layer of remove from the original debt contract. Derivatives were called "synthetic" because they were engineered financial instruments built atop "real" assets, mortgages. One such innovation was the risk contract "derivative" of another risk. For example, if the original rent or interest payment on capital is the first-order yield with the lowest level of risk, the second-order, or derivative, level of risk is the securitization of that rental payment, which can be bundled with other rental payments. Each investor purchased a portion of that bundle and, as renters pay interest, yield is spread out. The higher the risk of default, the higher the interest required and the higher the yield.

As the mortgage-backed securities markets grew and as complex derivatives began to grow around them, banks kept extending past the former risk frontier. The law rode hand in hand with capital; as pressure mounted against the levies of regulation, regulators simply eradicated them. The narrative about Wall Street firms, their excess risks and the periodic financial crises they have caused, is that they are evading the rules, committing fraud, and/or breaking the law. However, these firms made the rules: their power, profits, and the high-stakes markets of risk and reward in which they operated are the direct result of decisions by lawmakers and regulators. When the banks regulated by the OCC asked that agency if they could engage in derivatives trading—an especially risky form of investing—the OCC agreed, stating that the "equity hedges enable the banks to protect against loss in banking transactions in the most efficient manner and therefore are convenient and useful to the banks' equity derivative business."[21]

Corporations can increase yield by lowering costs (e.g., layoffs, cutting "fat") or increasing revenue (higher costs, greater market dominance, reducing competition). Banks can do this, too. Banks met shareholder demands through increased size and market share, but that wasn't all. Being in the business of revenue generation through risk, banks have many other options available to them to increase revenue that are not available to regular corporations. Finance is a perpetual money generator, if one knows which levers to push. Those levers are the laws and regulations that had previously limited the types of risks banks could take with other people's money, and thus had capped their returns. After the neoliberal coup of the administrative state, those barriers were eradicated one by one until bank shareholders became among the most richly rewarded on the stock exchange.

The story of how the OCC allowed banks to engage in derivatives trading, the riskiest and most socially useless financial product of any era, is an illuminating window revealing the law's pivotal role in shaping markets. In 1863. during the Civil War, Congress passed the National Bank Act (NBA), which created a national banking charter and the OCC as its regulator. One of the key provisions of the NBA, which was modeled after state banking charters, prohibited banks from doing any business beyond the "business of banking," which was generally interpreted as deposit taking and lending. Over the course of the neoliberal revolution, and thanks to a crucial 1984 Supreme Court case *Chevron U.S.A., Inc. v. Natural Resources Defense Council, Inc.,* federal agencies were authorized to interpret any legislative language that was "ambiguous." In other words, the OCC could change the meaning of the NBA through regulatory decisions without ever having to go to Congress. Deeming the "business of banking" as an ambiguity on account of changing times, the OCC began to interpret the business of banking as essentially whatever was profitable for banks. This was in accordance with the free market mood of the era, but it enabled the OCC, in a short period of time and away from public oversight, to transform the historic business of banking.

The OCC did not need an act of Congress, a vote, or even a formal rule-making to determine whether to extend the business of banking to allow derivatives trading; it had the authority to interpret the NBA to deem it so. Through a series of interpretive letters issued during the neoliberal era, the OCC decided that the business of banking included much more than just deposit taking and lending, but also higher-risk activities like derivatives trading. How the OCC defined the "business of banking" *became* the business banks conducted, a direct line of influence between government and industry that looked nothing like the free market that neoliberals theorized.

While denouncing federal intervention in the market, neoliberals augmented the power of the government to create new markets that would transform the economy. They made sure, however, that the government transformed the market in close coordination with the banking industry. One of the most curious facets of financial regulation is that, at large banks, the designated regulator has offices and desks *within* the bank. Regulators attend social events, participate in office banter, and are often hired away from government by the bank itself at a much higher salary. (This form of capture might be called "capture by golf.")

The OCC's goal in blessing derivatives trading, according to these agency letters, was to "enable the banks to operate more efficiently, compete more effectively with entities that engage in similar optimal hedges ... and operate profitably." The upshot was that banks could now offset risks with derivatives contracts rather than the traditional means of risk mitigation like increasing capital ratios or avoiding the risks entirely. The OCC reasoned that derivatives trades would allow banks "to retain additional revenues ... and enjoy substantial cost savings." Shifting the focus to bank profitability allowed risky behavior that was lucrative in the short term but systematically destabilizing in the long term.[22]

As the financial industry grew riskier and more profitable, it also became more politically powerful, which only strengthened the industry's influence over their lawmakers.

No other industry has such a close nexus between law and profits. With a sweep of a hand or a thumbs-up through an interpretive letter, the OCC created a new asset class in derivatives and a trillion-dollar market to foster derivatives trading. Federal regulators and the bankers they supposedly supervised co-created the pileup of risk, but none of it would be possible without the lawyers who created the contracts and legal codes that were the tokens of value being traded. All representations of value, including fiat money, or paper currency issued by the government, are creations of the law—money is called "legal tender," but neoliberalism significantly expanded the types of legal claims that could be traded. Each time a regulator validated a new type of "hedge" or security, they created a new type of moneylike asset, which increased the velocity of capital growth. Obscure legal instruments like structured debt contract, stratified security interests, and risk hedges were counted as units of wealth with rights equal to any other store of wealth—such as company stock, banknotes, or a 401(k)—except these exotic products were typically only available to multiply the fortunes of the already wealthy, or "qualified investors."

Big law firms created the products that the big banks fed into a lucrative and fast-paced market, the scale of which remains opaque to even the most sophisticated of traders. There was simply no way to fully understand the entire world of finance, let alone predict its future, but that did not stop regulators, bankers, lawyers, and economists from pretending to. When I worked at a big law firm on Wall Street, I worked on many structured financial products. I scoured the derivatives contract, securities offering, or other such stack of papers looking for the one or two issues that it was my role as financial regulatory lawyer to oversee, and then I passed the papers on through the assembly line of other associates and partners, never wondering where my cog fit into the machine.

The derivatives market had no real use or utility to the larger market besides creating another opportunity for capital to grow. Warren Buffett called derivatives "weapons of mass destruction" when their detonation led to the 2008 financial crisis. By the time the public even became aware of the massive industry, the banks holding the liabilities demanded contract absolutism—that these contracts be backed by the full force of the law. The contracts were all fulfilled and the banks were made whole thanks to bailout money, another advantage of the incestuous link between law and finance—having deemed derivatives "efficient" and risk-neutral, federal regulators had their own reputation to protect.

There is no such thing as money and banking without the law, which creates the structure and the language of value. Courts and regulators determine which contracts are valid assets and what types of future claims banks can distribute. Being an outgrowth of law, finance is heavily invested in controlling the laws that shape its own enterprise. If a handful of banking regulators govern the very nature of value and the business of banking, it is obvious that the industry would seek to influence them. Banks are incentivized to see only the risks that their regulators see and invest in only the products those regulators approve, and that is exactly what happened during the neoliberal coup. The loop between regulation and bank profit is direct and circular— more "business-friendly" regulators, more business-friendly laws, more business-friendly profits, more money to dedicate to lobbying. Changes in law even changed the focus of banks from deposit taking and lending to proprietary trading and more investment-type activities. The very real wealth created in the shadow banking market was the ripe fruit harvested by lobbying.

Thus, for the big financial firms, lobbying toward certain outcomes is an *investment* that yields tangible returns. The wealth created by bank lobbying, including the trillion-dollar-derivatives market, is peak Posner-Pareto-Coasian "efficiency"—as in more net wealth created. It was efficient because the money exploding on Wall Street was a much higher sum than the lost jobs, pensions, and communities, at least according to the measuring scale Law and Economics imposed on regulations. Whether or not those were the right metrics for determining social value was not the purview of bank regulators. Those types of value judgments in any society, but especially in a democracy, should be made by the larger community, if not through robust debate, then by a fair and representative vote.

The neoliberal transformation also turned more institutions into banks—or into the banklike entities called *shadow banks*, a term that became ubiquitous after the crisis. Shadow banking refers to doing banklike activities—borrowing short and lending long—without a bank charter. However, the term is misleading because the nonbanks, the large Wall Street investment banks like Goldman Sachs, Morgan Stanley, and JP Morgan, were not operating in the shadows, but in close coordination with regulators; and those regulators were happy to exempt these large firms from the costly regulations imposed on chartered banks. Even the exotic legal products created by shadow banks in the shadow banking market were treated like bank deposits during the crisis.

For decades, armed with sophisticated math and bulletproof legal assurances, economists, regulators, and bankers had assured the market and one another that risks were modeled, priced, and hedged. It took just a few days of panic in 2008 to bring down the entire system, because basic trust has no substitute. Successful banking requires getting the numbers right, but banks are part of a web with other banks—they form a society of sorts where a loss of confidence can spread like a contagion. "Fear itself" is the disease and the primary risk of banking, and it cannot be modeled—only minimized.

Deregulating the banking sector was among the most consequential successes of the neoliberal movement—not just because it led to catastrophe, but because it required an absolute commitment to the theories of neoliberalism. To allow banks to regulate their own risks was based on unqualified faith in market discipline—or, as it were, the federal government's implicit promise to save the system when it failed. This was, in fact, the unspoken message, or dog whistle, that could only be heard by Wall Street.

The most obvious indicator of neoliberalism's turbocharging of capital is the incredible growth of the financial sector over the last several decades. In the 1950s, the financial industry made up less than 10 percent of all corporate profits; in 2015, it represented upward of 30 percent. Before neoliberalism, financial firms made up less than 10 percent of the total share of GDP; today it is over 20 percent. The number of employees in finance has tripled from the 1960s to the present. Nonfinancial companies have been "financialized" as private equity firms have pressed them to hold more debt and organize their business around the servicing of debt. Finance went from a support industry to the dominant power shaping the economy. Investment banks, private equity firms, and hedge funds—and the Wall Street law firms that supported and served them—grew in size and reach with every wave of deregulation.

It is in fact difficult to even compare the banking sector before the neoliberal transformation to what came after, but a few comparisons give the general picture. In 1970, the top ten bank holding companies had combined assets of around $154 billion.[23] In 2022, the top ten had combined assets of around $15 trillion. But more precisely, just six banks dominate the market: JP Morgan Chase ($3.8 trillion); Bank of America ($3.1 trillion); Citigroup ($2.4 trillion); Wells Fargo ($1.9 trillion); Goldman Sachs ($1.6 trillion); and Morgan Stanley ($1.1 trillion).[24] Total assets in the entire banking credit system were $953 billion in 1970 and are $40 trillion now. Meanwhile, the number of banks in the country has shrunk from over twenty thousand in 1970 to fewer than five thousand today, a reduction of more than 75 percent.[25] The assets of the top banks are growing at a much faster rate than other banks; they increased from 14 percent of GDP in 1970 to 63 percent of GDP in 2020, while the combined assets of the rest of the banks fell. Bank assets compared to the nation's GDP rose from around 80 percent of total GDP to over 185 percent, and these assets have grown substantially faster than the GDP.[26]

Government institutions supporting the banking sector grew alongside the banks on a similar or faster trajectory. For example, Fannie Mae, Freddie Mac, and Ginnie Mae are three government-sponsored enterprises (GSEs) that buy, insure, package, and generally enable the market to trade assets like mortgage-backed securities without fear of default. The supercharging of capital during the neoliberal era led to an expansion of GSEs' role in the market, with their assets growing from 3 percent of total GDP in 1970 to about 40 percent of GDP today. Although the GSEs were technically "privatized" to comply with

neoliberal mythmaking about free markets, they were quickly renationalized when they defaulted while holding their bloated portfolio of
toxic assets. Total assets held at the Federal Reserve also exploded from
hundreds of billions in the 1970s to more than $9 trillion—in fact, the
Fed held total assets of around $800 to $900 billion up until the financial crisis and grew 4,000 percent, to over $9 trillion, in just a few short
years, but the changes were more foundational than just doing much
more of the same. The Fed and the GSEs of the 1970s were market-
supporting industries. The Fed held bank reserves and stood ready to
offer liquidity should a bank have an emergency, a power the Fed rarely
used. As a report from the Treasury Department's Office of Financial
Research summarized the changes, "over the last 50 years, the Banking
Credit System grew vastly bigger relative to the economy, much more
consolidated, and much more dependent on both the government mortgage complex and the government's central bank, greatly increasing its
dependence on explicit and implicit government guarantees."

The case of two of the most profitable American companies in 1970,
General Motors and General Electric, is illustrative of the trends of the
era. Each firm dominated its respective market—GE in power and GM
in cars—on account of production, innovation, and government contracts. In other words, the federal government nurtured the success of
these companies, especially through major investments in their research
and development. Neoliberalism transformed these firms once again—
not just through changing leadership, like the much remarked-upon
transformation of GE's culture by the infamously cutthroat and highly
paid CEO Jack Welch (nicknamed "neutron Jack" for his deep job cuts).
But this focus on executives and cultural change misses the legal transformations of the era that dismantled the mixed economy and forced
institutional change. In other words, Jack Welch was a symptom, not a
cause, of the transformation.

Consistent with the era's ideology of shareholder maximization,
these firms were forced to go where profits are most maximized. They
had to become banks. Soon, GM and GE were selling not just cars and
energy but credit. They were aided by lawmakers who created a loophole in the historic pillar of banking law, "the separation of banking

and commerce" prohibiting commercial firms from owning a bank, in order to allow both firms to own a bank. Commerce and banking had been separated in the pre-neoliberal era to prevent excess power and to keep the special riskiness of banking from spreading beyond regulated banks. That is exactly what happened with GM's and GE's banks—their spectacular failure threatened to take down both companies, necessitating a government bailout. This is therefore not a story of regulated markets descending into deregulated markets over the course of the neoliberal decades. Rather, GE's and GM's rise and prominence was fostered by the New Deal's mixed economy containing subsidies and supports. The "deal" was that they would spread the wealth to workers through benefits, pensions, and stable salaries, even occasionally participating in important social programs—like Richard Nixon's affirmative action program. That deal changed during the neoliberal era, but not in the way that it was typically characterized: GM's deal with the government remained, including subsidies, contracts, and the like. But the deal these two corporations made with the American people, to share that wealth with workers and communities, was gone. Not because GE or GM changed or because the market changed but because laws did, which is to say that the government changed GE's and GM's duties and reneged on its deal with the people. It wasn't capitalism then and it was no more so capitalism after the bailouts.

CAPITAL

Capital itself, apart from the idea or structure of capitalism, is a self-propagating force. Like a virus, capital has only one aim: to augment itself. Just like water, capital becomes more forceful in larger quantities. Big pools of capital must be fed with ever more yield, which means more risk-taking. By removing barriers on the flow of capital across the globe, the forces of capital kept growing larger and larger, until capital's rate of growth could not be matched by any single economy. This of course increased the gap between the wealthy (i.e., the holders of capital) and everyone else, but it also distorted markets profoundly.

The unchecked growth of capital searching for yield combined with regulators' abdication of their duty to the public provided the perfect breeding ground for the premier predator of the neoliberal era: private equity—or leveraged buyout (LBO)—firms. LBO firms took advantage of readily available credit to acquire companies at extremely high debt-to-equity ratios (usually 90 percent debt to 10 percent equity). The debt was sold and traded in the junk bond market to yield more profit and raise the stakes of the purchase. The private equity firm then took over management of the company and, like an invasive parasite that changes the host's behavior to serve its own ends, twisted the company toward debt repayment. Often the purchased companies had been well capitalized by public investments but had to change their entire business model to service the debt. The result was frequently bankruptcy for the purchased company—and extraordinary profits for the LBO firm.

Private equity investors were called "corporate raiders," "pirates," or—in the case of the Nabisco LBO in 1988—"barbarians at the gate." Their strategy was to feed on the purchased firm until there was nothing left, or to force it to survive by cutting "fat": employees, pensions, unprofitable services, and inefficient products. Pension benefits, in particular, were a drag on balance sheets, which made companies with large pension liabilities ripe targets for buyout firms. The firms would force the company into bankruptcy, drop its pension obligations during restructuring, and reintroduce the more "efficient," more profitable company to the public.

The leveraged buyout craze led to a mass extinction event as many firms, large and small, failed or were merged into larger entities. Any firm that could be taken over and squeezed for more profits was prey in the eat-or-be-eaten world of hostile takeovers. For instance, a private equity firm that purchases a hospital, firing staff, cutting bed capacity, and reducing overhead costs is market discipline in action. Once the hospital is turned into a profitable venture, the disciplinarians can hold on to it or sell it to a new purchaser, who can enjoy the high yields. In the eat-or-be-eaten era of the "barbarians," even profitable corporations had to change their business model to extract more revenue to feed insatiable debt markets. David Roderick of U.S. Steel would declare in 1980 that the corporation was "no longer in the business of making steel; it was "in the business of making profits."[27]

When a private equity firm failed to keep a company viable and drove it to the brink of destruction, junk bond traders ("vultures") swept in to buy up the distressed remains to try to extract more payments. Sometimes the raiders and the vultures were one and the same. Wall Street's most iconic firms and traders made their billions through hostile takeovers and forced mergers. Speculators exploited the inefficiencies of currency markets, sending several countries into a tailspin and creating in 2007–2008 a crisis that took years (if not decades) of austerity to recover from. The magnates of the age were hailed as innovators even as they left mass layoffs, reduced pensions, and bankruptcies in their wake. Leveraged debt caused mayhem in markets and communities because the compounding pressure of debt reordered all other business priorities to its rapacious needs. If the barbarians at the gate were once the threat that pushed early societies to relieve debt, today debt itself is what governs—more precisely, what disciplines—society. To instill market discipline, neoliberals unleashed the market's predators, who promptly punished the weak through leveraged debt.

The private equity industry embodies the neoliberal movement's values while also revealing its inherent logic. The theory that the needs of a free economy should supersede the needs of a free society led to the idea that market actors did not have any social responsibilities besides making profits. Once that foundational notion was mainstreamed and market actors were exempt from social obligations, the dam that protected society from the potential energy of capital was removed, and capital was let loose to exploit and drown social trust under the demand for more yield. The private equity era has led to wide-scale job loss, wage cuts, reduced public services, a fraying social safety net, fewer services for the low-profit poor, and more for the high-yield wealthy.

The growth of private capital was linked to the hollowing-out of the middle class. As leveraged buyouts and new financial instruments turned firms into lean mean profit-making machines, employees and their benefits were the first to go. Employee benefits that were not cut were transformed into another source of yield production.

As employees lost pensions and benefits, they were offered a tax write-off through a 401(k) and were encouraged to invest toward retirement. Instead of a guaranteed pension, each worker tied their fate to the future of the stock market, whose periodic ups and downs became the only economic metric that mattered to the middle class. The innovation of the 401(k) bound Americans' retirement savings to the market well into the future thanks to a steep penalty of 40 percent for withdrawing money before the age of retirement. These golden fetters kept Americans tied to the bankers' fortunes not only in the present but indefinitely into the future. Let the banks fail and watch your retirement account disappear. This was the magic trick of the neoliberal economy.

Our golden fetters—the rise of 401(k)—created another large pool of capital that created more opportunities for Wall Street asset managers to extract fees and to shape the future of the market. These accounts hold stock in the same blue-chip banks, financial giants, and insurers that make up the financialized economy. The large asset portfolios are also managed by one of the many private equity firms who seeks yield in unconventional ways. The accumulated capital of middle-class retirement accounts became another tributary of capital flowing toward finance, accelerating capital's growth, augmenting Wall Street's power, and cannibalizing the nation's lifeblood. A worker's own retirement investment could be managed by an investment fund that made profits by buying, picking apart, and bankrupting the worker's employer.

After leaching power and profits from a decades-long feast of our wages, jobs, and health care, the financial sector fell along with the myths that sustained it. However, there's one basic truth that has yet to be fully absorbed: there was never any such thing as a free market. It was us—our laws, our democracy, our system of money derived from trust—that created the market; it was our investments, our labor, and our faith in our future that was the real source of value all along. And it was us—our Federal Reserve and our Congress—who saved the predators from their own gluttony.

*   *   *

CAPITAL'S RELENTLESS GROWTH was made possible by the law—for it is the law that converts things—land, labor, ideas, inventions—into property that can be rented, leveraged, exchanged, and invested. The law fuels capital's self-replicating engine, whose momentum drives the conversion of more things and ideas into capital and resists retrenchment. The legal system determines the type, nature, and limits of property rights and enforces those rights through its policing power—by punishing trespassing or copyright violations, enforcing rental payments on property use, and resolving disputes when property rights conflict. Once the law bestows its protection on an asset, it becomes durable and universally tradable capital that can yield both income and wealth for its owner. Karl Marx called the process whereby an object transforms into a tradable object of value "commodification"; the legal scholar Katarina Pistor calls the same process "coding capital." A thing—land, labor, or a banknote, for example—becomes capital by being placed on "legal steroids," she explains. The transformative alchemy that converts things into capital is the law. Contracts, deeds, notes, stock shares, patents, and credit are legal instruments blessed by either the legislature or the judiciary to encode capital.

With each subsequent historic change, new forms of property were added that came with their own legitimizing legal codes. Each, in turn, changed the economy in meaningful ways. Over time, more sources of value have been created, either through technological advance—as with the creation of copyright laws on the heels of the invention of the printing press—or political or societal change. So powerful is this process that one way to read political and social history is as an adjunct to the ever-expanding frontier of commodification. In the United States, once the Constitution recognized and protected "property in man," men and women became capital upon which future wealth could be built. Enslaved people could be securitized, traded, and used as collateral to secure credit. Likewise, in eighteenth-century England, the conversion of land from an "open" resource to a privately owned asset through the invention of the property deed spurred a series of other innovations, including insurance, exchangeable debts, and markets for risk—contracts reliant on the power of the legal system for enforcement.

And with them have come new markets for trade: with the transformation of land into tradable property, a mortgage market became possible; that market spawned mortgage-backed securities, which led to derivatives and insurance products that were each abstracted from an original asset but created more value with each turn. To push past the growth limits imposed by the natural world, abstractions had to be created. Whereas land is not subject to perpetual growth, the growth potential of derivatives is theoretically infinite. Not for nothing were these derivatives called "synthetic": they were engineered financial instruments built atop "real" assets.

The more unconstrained the growth of capital, the bigger the gap between the rich and the poor. Indeed, capital in the hands of the few can grow faster than when spread out for two primary reasons. First, because more of it is left idle in fewer hands—and left to grow by seeking yield. And second, because capital usually finds yield by imposing debt somewhere else in the capitalist system; in that respect, debt's imposition of interest is the other side of capital's drive for yield. The two cycles of virtuous capital growth and the vicious cycle of debt are mutually reinforcing: the powers of uninterrupted usury can go on indefinitely. Unless democratic institutions intervene, the world population will soon be made up of trillionaires on one end and a destitute supermajority on the other.

The growth of capital in the hands of the few has been unprecedented and unimaginable. There are countless online videos trying to explain the numerical reality of so much wealth—the *New York Times* website featured an infographic of nine ways to imagine Jeff Bezos's $172 billion in wealth compared to the median family's wealth of $118,200: a single white blood cell versus a finback whale, or a small triangular piece of Toblerone chocolate versus Mount Everest, and so on. To reach Bezos's wealth, an average worker would have needed to begin working 4.5 million years ago. But most stunning is the rapidity with which the Amazon founder's wealth can grow just through compounding interest ($500 per second); in the time it took the illustrator to create the infographic (ninety-five hours), Bezos would have made enough to buy a $169 million Park Avenue penthouse. Imagining this much wealth is stupefying. It is difficult to even contemplate trillions of dollars, so difficult that the number is necessarily an abstraction. In fact, money becomes more abstract the higher up the wealth ladder one climbs, whereas it becomes much more real and constraining the lower down one finds themself on the ladder. And just like virality leading to plague, it is society that can check the multiplying drive of capital.

Neoliberalism achieved the opposite. Not only did the neoliberal capture of the law abet the massive secondary and tertiary markets of risk built atop mortgages, but—by rescuing and insuring these privately created products during the financial crisis—it conferred new property rights backed by state power.

DEBT

The decision to end the Bretton Woods Agreement barriers on international capital flows, Richard Nixon had surmised, would allow the United States to tap into the world's savings, but that didn't actually happen until the Reagan era. The Reagan administration's fiscally irresponsible tax cuts and increased military spending led to massive deficits, but its liberalized financial policies converted U.S. debt into a financial product that could be bought and sold by other countries. An infusion of cash from foreign countries with a lot of savings, especially Japan, subsidized US spending. As the sociologist Greta Krippner explained, "What the Reagan policymakers discovered in the early 1980s, then, was that they lived in a world in which capital was available in a potentially limitless supply."[28]

Neoliberal financialization thus stretched beyond national borders to transform the world economy, binding not just American workers but national treasuries worldwide, became beholden to Wall Street finance. In turn, capital inflows from other nations strengthened the American economy and strengthened the dollar, which had a self-reinforcing effect. Because the U.S. economy had a more flush starting position than the rest of the world, capital liberalization tilted world-wide capital toward the coffers of the U.S. Treasury. This reinforced the country's position at the top of the hierarchy.

The Reagan administration pushed for more liberalization and deregulation of international markets and enjoyed the free lunch provided by foreign funds. In 1984, the Treasury Department initiated a foreign securities trading desk and earned itself the label of "the greatest bond salesman in history." Inflows of foreign capital benefited private and public borrowers alike. Financialization of the world economy provided a limitless supply of capital, which eliminated constraints on public spending; as an internal Reagan memo noted, capital inflows "helped finance an unprecedented domestic investment boom and a robust expansion that has dramatically improved our standard of living." Or as one historian recounts, Asia allowed the U.S. economy to drink "endless dollar cocktails." It was in this state of abundance that Reagan imposed austerity at home: welfare was cut, housing was not built, and redlined cities were deprived of funds.[29]

Once capital was unleashed by neoliberals' deregulatory agenda, its punitive side—debt—became the dominant force shaping not just the U.S. economy but the world economy. The borderless empire of capital extracted debt payments from across the world. The debt squeeze led to an explosion in corporate debt, sovereign debt, and family debt. The growth of debt was matched, contract by contract, by the growth of the financial industry; they were two sides of the same coin.

In the 1980s and 1990s, in addition to shaping the lives of families and businesses, debt's demands dominated the economies of developing nations. Nation-building loans from the IMF and development loans from the World Bank came with terms mandating austerity and limiting government involvement in private markets. The lending institutions rated countries based on measures like inflation and balanced budgets, instead of whether the governments were meeting the needs of the people. These loans often meant that much of a government's budget went first to repaying international creditors; only then did the government allocate funds to infrastructure, schools, or hospitals. Sovereign debt exploded during the 1980s and led governing regimes across the world to adopt neoliberal policies. Loans from the IMF were frequently accompanied by stringent conditions known as "structural adjustment programs," which advocated for neoliberal economic policies. Although countries had some level of decision-making power in accepting or rejecting these loans, the prevailing circumstances and power dynamics often left them with limited alternatives, compelling them to comply with the IMF's conditions in order to obtain crucial financial support.

U.S. common law courts and bankruptcy courts had jurisdiction over most of these debt contracts and often mandated loan repayment at all costs. Few countries have ever defaulted, even as protests demanding an end to austerity have erupted all over the world. Some of these protests have been profoundly destabilizing and helped clear the way for the rise of populist leaders, on both the left and the right, who have rejected globalization altogether (at least in their rhetoric). It's hard to blame them. Just as neoliberalism bound American citizens to the priorities of capital, so too have other nations been constrained by the workings of private equity firms.

For example, the neoliberal plan for Argentina in the 1990s was a $100 million loan from the IMF and an open trade policy aimed at reducing tariffs and eliminating trade barriers. Argentina pegged its local currency to the American dollar, and the scheme worked for about a decade (that is, if "worked" means enriching the Argentinian elite who could profit from Wall Street investments in local industries). After its trade partners suffered some economic disruptions, faith in the Argentinian economy collapsed, and the country sank into what's been called Argentina's great depression. Over half the population was pushed below the poverty line and a quarter of the population was indigent. After a decade of economic stagnation, suffered most acutely by the impoverished, Argentina paid its loans back to the IMF in full. Despite the hardships of the Argentinian people, no loan forgiveness was offered.

A portion of Argentina's debts was sold on the private market and purchased by Wall Street hedge funds and traders (today, a majority of sovereign debt is traded on private markets). In 2001, Paul Singer's Elliott Management, a hedge fund, purchased Argentina's distressed debt at a discount: $617 million worth of bonds for only $117 million. For the next fifteen years, Elliott Management sued the government of Argentina in New York bankruptcy court. Elliott was seeking full payment of the bonds plus accrued interest for the distressed debt it had purchased, which Argentina's government resisted paying. Demonstrations erupted in Argentina. Protesters called the country's creditors "vultures"—given that every dollar paid in hedge profits was a loss to teachers' salaries, public resources, and poverty aid. Still, Elliott Management sued on the contract.

At one point, Elliott Management persuaded the Ghanaian government to seize an Argentinian military vessel docked in a port east of Accra. The United Nations urged Elliot Management to release the vessel, but Elliott chose to pursue its claims and threaten further seizures of goods. The U.S. courts had jurisdiction over the conflict by contract— they sided with the hedge fund and demanded that Argentina pay its debt to Elliott before it paid other bondholders. In other words, until Argentina paid its old debts in full, it could not participate in private debt markets, which would mean that it would be shut out of the worldwide economy and deprived of the funds it needed to build its economy. Argentina's defaults had led to a devaluing of Argentina's bonds by the credit ratings agencies and forced Argentina to pay high interest due to its high credit risk.

Finally, in 2016, the case was settled. Private creditors led by Elliott met Argentinian ministers in a hotel room in New York, and Argentina paid them $9.3 billion. Elliott Management collected $2.4 billion in profits, which was a 1,270 percent rate of return on their investment. Currently, Elliott Management oversees $42 billion in assets, and Singer has amassed a personal fortune of over $4 billion.

The case of Argentina versus private equity was not an outlier. In fact, there is a substantial and expanding list of countries either in default or struggling to pay off their sovereign debt to private Wall Street investors, which often leads to severe austerity at home. What made this case unusual was how long Elliott Management was willing to hold on in order to extract its full payment. For his monomaniacal pursuit of repayment, Singer has been called one of "the most powerful, and most unyielding investors in the world," "the world's most feared investor," "aggressive, tenacious, and litigious to a fault," and "the doomsday investor."

However, the source of Singer's power was not necessarily his tenacity; rather, it was the law. Singer is a lawyer by training, and he demanded no more and no less than his legal rights under debt contracts. Along with the Kochs, Singer is among the largest donors to the major neoliberal legal institutions. He is one of the biggest donors to the GOP and former President Trump, and as a major donor of the Federalist Society, he even had a hand in choosing the Trump administration's list of judges, including for the Supreme Court. He is the chairman of the Manhattan Institute, a financial backer of several media, print, and research outlets. Singer defends his actions as furthering the aims of free market capitalism. As he argued in a *Wall Street Journal* opinion piece titled "Efficient Markets Need Guys Like Me," his firm's actions "maximize value" for the benefit of everyone. Everyone except the people of Argentina.

UNDERSTANDING THE WORLD of finance gives lie to the neoliberals' claims about the existence of a market free of society. The market is entirely a creation of the law, and law is the language of society. But in speaking on behalf of society, lawmakers must take care not to threaten the social foundations of the law's legitimacy. At a minimum, societies require a level of trust and social cohesion to survive. From Hammurabi to Gramm-Leach-Bliley, laws have both shaped and been shaped by social conventions, customs and beliefs, markets, and their inequalities. Inequality among citizens can exist but must be seen as legitimate. This is the work of ideology. Those with wealth and power can keep their status at the top of the hierarchy through their control of the law and its enforcement, but only insofar as their position is justified by a commonly held belief. But, as kings and other rulers have always understood, power can be slippery and ideologies tend to succumb to the pressures of reason and hypocrisy.

This dilemma plagued this nation's Founders: how to maintain democratic legitimacy based on the idea of equality while also benefiting from a market reliant on slavery. The hypocrisy, present from the beginning, would continue to threaten the union. Nearing the end of his long life, Thomas Jefferson grew anxious about the expansion of slavery, an institution he called "a hideous blot" and an "abominable crime." He wrote a fellow slaveholder, stating that "there is not a man on earth who would sacrifice more than I would, to relieve us from this heavy reproach [slavery] . . . we have the wolf by the ear, and we can neither hold him, nor safely let him go. Justice is in one scale, and self-preservation in the other." Justice versus self-preservation. Put another way, freedom for all or profits for the market. This paradox of power—the wolf held by the ear—was sustained not just by violence, but by mythologies that justified and legitimized the powerful. As both ancient civilizations and the American Founders understood, social tensions could be brought to a boil if the scales of justice tipped too far in either direction.

PART IV

The Virus

CHAPTER 9

Mistakes Were Made

Science progresses by trial and error, and when it is
forbidden to admit error there can be no progress.

—JOAN ROBINSON (1962)

BEFORE THE ELECTION of President Barack Obama on November 4, 2008, the financial sector was already in free fall, Congress had already authorized a $700 billion bailout, the Treasury had already rescued the FDIC insurance fund from default, and the money markets had already "broken the buck," causing global panic before the federal government promised to save them. Before the election, Washington Mutual, Wachovia, Countrywide, Lehman Brothers, IndyMac, and hundreds of community banks had failed, the GSEs had been nationalized, and about a dozen investment banks had been deemed too big to fail and were rescued by the Federal Reserve's legally dubious decision to purchase their toxic assets to prevent them from imploding. Before the election, federal regulators had been shocked to realize that despite their heroic efforts to save the banks, they had missed that the real problem was an insurance company, AIG, which had become the linchpin of the entire derivatives market and was now on the verge of defaulting on hundreds of billions of dollars of debts. After Obama was elected but before he took office, federal regulators decided to save AIG using $85 billion of public money and to take a 79.9 percent stake in the company (that is, to nationalize it). After Obama was inaugurated, the Fed and Treasury realized that AIG would need even more money to survive, so they provided it. AIG received a total of $182 billion.

In only his second month on the job, Obama found out that the same AIG executives who had driven the firm to bankruptcy had "negotiated" the terms of their rescue to include their typical multimillion-dollar bonuses to the executive suite and top employees. Obama was uncharacteristically angry when he found out, and as he reported in his postpresidential memoir, *A Promised Land,* he asked AIG executives to consider the optics of bonuses and eliminate them. The President was annoyed once again when the firm replied that the bonuses were written into employee contracts and so could not be waived—an excuse that hadn't been challenged by the federal regulators negotiating the deal, including Obama's new Treasury secretary, Timothy Geithner. Having run a nationwide grassroots campaign as an outsider candidate, Obama anticipated that Americans would bristle at the obvious unfairness of it all. After a series of unsuccessful negotiations, the President opted for a face-to-face meeting with the AIG executives. He came away from that meeting with the feeling that they were decent people, but also completely out of touch. "I tried to understand their perspective, but I couldn't," recalled Obama. "They couldn't understand why (as one would later tell me) their children were now asking them whether they were 'fat cats,' or why no one was impressed that they had reduced their annual compensation from $50 or $60 million to $2 million."[1]

Of all the chaotic events of Obama's first few months in office, the experience of speaking to the AIG executives at the White House was one of the more indelible; he spent a significant chunk of his 768-page memoir explaining how he felt about it. His main issue with these "fat cats" seemed to be their lack of decency. Obama's perspective was informed by his grandmother, Toot, who was a banker herself: in the early 1970s, she'd been a vice president at the Bank of Hawaii. Obama lamented the loss of what his grandmother had believed "a banker was supposed to be: Honest. Prudent. Exacting. Risk-averse. Someone who refused to cut corners, hated waste and extravagance, lived by the code of delayed gratification, and was perfectly content to be a little bit boring in how she did business." As Obama saw it, the financial crisis had been caused by a new breed of reckless and entitled bankers, "placing billion-dollar bets with other people's money on what they knew, or should have known, was a pile of bad loans." Banking had lost the defining trait of trustworthiness—what Toot had called "Kansas prairie character."[2]

In fact, those noble bankers of old were prudent and risk-averse not because of the Kansas prairie or their innate character but because *it was what the law required of them*. It was not "delayed gratification" that prevented them from making "billion-dollar bets with other people's money"[3]—it was the Glass-Steagall Act. The big banks' exposure to risk in 2008, wrought by executives gambling in the derivatives market with no federal oversight while being paid millions of dollars in bonuses, simply could not have happened in the 1970s. Not because the old bankers were better people, but because it would have been illegal.

Elected to the most powerful office in the country on the promise of "change," Obama shrugged off his disappointment with the audacity of the shameless bankers of his time. He recalled losing his cool momentarily and expressing his sense of injustice by letting out "something between a laugh and a snort" and giving the bankers a talking-to: " 'Let me explain something, gentlemen,' I said, careful not to raise my voice. 'People don't need my prompting to be angry. They've got that covered all on their own. The fact is, we're the only ones standing between you and the pitchforks.' " While his words had no impact on the bankers' decisions, lamented Obama, the image his words evoked—of a president protecting bankers from pitchforks—came to define his stance toward Wall Street. Obama felt misunderstood by his critics on the left who attacked his "general fecklessness and alleged chumminess with Wall Street" and "failure to hold the banks accountable during the crisis."[4] The critics had a point. It was hard not to compare Obama's response, unfavorably, with Franklin Roosevelt's line "I welcome their hatred."[5] The earlier Democratic president had publicly denounced the bankers as "the unscrupulous money changers [who] stand indicted in the court of public opinion, rejected by the hearts and minds of men."[6] FDR had not tried to reason with the bankers, but had sided with the pitchforks, demanding drastic changes. Not so for the Obama administration, whose slate of reforms after the crisis were cowritten by the bankers themselves. The bonuses got paid.

Yet presenting Obama as, effectively, an ally of the bankers is the wrong way to understand him and his administration's role. By the time Obama had a chance to try to convince the bankers to have some decency, the deal was already done. The bailouts were underway and all George W. Bush and his successor, Obama, could do was listen in on the briefings. Still, they had little idea what was happening. Few people did, even among the financiers. The financial system had grown so large and complex that it had become a risk merry-go-round of commercial paper, swaps, repo, and derivatives. With each turn, each increased in notional value even as they all came untethered from the "real economy." Neoliberalism had occasioned a collective forgetting of the downsides of financial risk and an overconfidence in the omnipotence of the market. As a result, the crisis was about more than whether the banks, or even the American economy, would survive. It was a crisis of faith. Too many choices that belonged to society and democracy had been deferred to the market, even as the market steadily drove up risk and leverage using savings accounts, pensions, mortgages, and investments. The people were the hedge that offset Wall Street's risk, and the bankers knew it. AIG's failure alone would have cost insured Americans billions of dollars. All the President could do was to give the bankers a lecture about bad behavior while his advisers bailed out the firm, gambling for resurrection. The problem was not Bush's ignorance or Obama's fecklessness; the problem was that it wasn't Bush or Obama who was in charge.

Neoliberalism's decades-long coup had been so successful that when the myths came crashing down, our democratically elected leaders had no choice but to quickly build them back up. With the neoliberal economy in free fall, this was no time for democracy. Both Presidents Bush and Obama handed off crisis management to "the experts"—industry insiders who had their own interest in keeping the system solvent. These men (and they were almost all men) had advanced via the inside lanes of banks, law firms, academia, or government. And when the system failed, they sprang into action to save the system. The only decisions to be made were tactical choices while in the "fog of war." The memoirs of the "experts"—*On the Brink* by Henry Paulson, Bush's Treasury secretary; *Stress Test* by Timothy Geithner, who was president of the New York Federal Reserve as Obama tapped him to succeed Paulson; and *The Courage to Act* by Ben Bernanke, the Federal Reserve chairman—reflected the state of mind at the time. These three top regulators described the crisis and its aftermath as an unpredictable war, which they fought with both "shock" and "awe," emerging in the end in apparent victory. Paulson quipped, when he asked Congress for a blank check, "If you've got a squirt-gun in your pocket, you may have to take it out. If you've got a bazooka, and people know you've got it, you may not have to take it out. . . . By increasing confidence, it will greatly reduce the likelihood it will ever be used."[7]

Who or what were they fighting for? It is too simplistic to say that they were fighting just to save the banks. It was, rather, a war to save the credibility of the market and to maintain the coherence of the myths that had guided so many for so long—to save the myth even as it was being debunked by reality. For these officials, having "the courage to act" often meant taking decisive action despite public backlash. Congress was dealt with on a need-to-know basis, but most of the Fed's controversial programs did not need congressional approval anyway. Instead of public debate or consensus, top Fed and Treasury officials deployed technical savvy, expertise, and the trillion-dollar "bazookas" to shock (and awe) the system back to life.

The 2008 financial crisis was not the nadir of neoliberalism, but its immortalization. It was proof that neoliberalism now dominated American policy and law—and that even a global crisis could not force a reconsideration of it. While there were plenty of bad actors involved, it is important not to personalize the crisis, not to make it a case of simple greed or malfeasance or of a wave of corporate corruption hitting American society all at once. Rather, the financial crisis was the product of thousands of changes to law and regulation carried out over a period of decades by acolytes—witting or not—of the idea that markets should be free from government regulation and intrusion. While the story of the crisis is, on one level, a dramatic one of major banks failing and of attempts by various policy makers to prevent the complete explosion of the American economy, it is, on another level, the story of the triumph of the ideology of neoliberalism despite itself.

AS THE STORY of the 2008 crisis is usually told, the trouble began that March with the failure of Bear Stearns, but turned into a true emergency with the default of Lehman Brothers in September. Or, more accurately, it became a full-blown crisis when it became clear that the Federal Reserve could not save Lehman Brothers or force another large bank to save it, as it had done with Bear Stearns.

The fate of Lehman Brothers—and, in turn, the financial markets in general—was negotiated over a tense weekend in September. In conference rooms near Wall Street, officials from the federal government and the CEOs of the top megabanks—Bank of America, Citigroup, Goldman Sachs, JP Morgan Chase, Wells Fargo, Merrill Lynch, Morgan Stanley, and State Street—met to work out what turned out to be a very generous bailout. As the economist Simon Johnson and the legal scholar James Kwak later described it, the deal "effectively meant that Treasury loaned the banks money, at an initial 5 percent annual interest rate (a rate that was not available in the market), that never had to be repaid." (The Treasury also received options to buy a small amount of common shares at a predetermined price.)[8] The deal was so good that upon seeing the terms, Citigroup CEO Vikram Pandit exclaimed, "This is very cheap capital!" John Mack, the CEO of Morgan Stanley, apparently signed the term sheet immediately without even speaking to his board of directors.[9] The government also agreed to guarantee the bad debt on the banks' books and to purchase and hold the banks' toxic assets in a newly created corporation, a special purpose vehicle (SPV)—a legal entity created for a narrow purpose like isolating risks. The Fed created three separate SPVs called Maiden Lane, Maiden Lane II, and Maiden Lane III, named after a narrow corridor in Manhattan's Financial District adjacent to the New York Fed and the New York Stock Exchange.

The bailout was not, as many have described it, a "taxpayer bailout." Ben Bernanke described the process when a *60 Minutes* reporter asked him whether the Fed had used taxpayer money to bail out the banks. No, explained Bernanke, it was not taxpayer money. Rather, because all the nation's banks have an account held at the Fed, all the government had to do was to add numbers to the banks' balance sheets.[10] Contrary to Milton Friedman's fixed money theories and the monetary austerity of the neoliberal era, money is a limitless legal contract issued by the federal government. Yet while it is true that the Fed can create money at any time without issuing taxes, the Fed is the people's authorized bank, and that money is still technically drawn from the American people's bank account. After decades of inflation fearmongering leading to monetary austerity was shouldered by Americans through lower salaries and higher debts, the Fed cranked up the money printer to restore a handful of Wall Street megabanks to profitability. The Federal Reserve had been created in 1913 to counter the power of J. P. Morgan over the economy—to protect the people from "the monopoly of big credit," in the words of President Woodrow Wilson. The postcrisis Federal Reserve reversed the principle, feeding the public's money into the monopoly of big credit.

After Lehman failed, the contagion spread quickly across the web of interconnected institutions, threatening to take down one bank after another. By all accounts, Merrill Lynch was next, so Treasury Secretary Paulson, Fed Chairman Bernanke, and New York Fed President Geithner turned their attention to rescuing that firm from a failure they believed would be cataclysmic. Over the weekend of Lehman's failure, the Fed and Treasury officials coordinated a forced merger between Merrill Lynch and Bank of America and an infusion of liquidity into the so-called too big to fail (TBTF) banks to stop the run from spreading. A relieved Paulson stood at a podium on Monday morning, September 15, 2008, to announce the bad news of Lehman's failure followed by the good news of the merger, hoping to assure the country that disaster had been averted. It had not been. The announcement that Lehman had failed and the Fed had not rescued it sent the market into a tailspin. Paulson had hoped that the market would stay calm upon hearing about their emergency interventions in saving the next domino from falling, but it was too late. Panic is immune to reason.

The next day, the panic spread to the Reserve Primary Fund, which broke the buck for the first time in history. The Reserve Fund was a large money market fund that promised customers the safety of a bank deposit but with stock market returns—what was too good to be true was in fact not true. The fund had invested $785 million in short-term commercial paper loans to Lehman, which it lost, meaning that the firm could no longer promise investors dollar for dollar redemption. Each investor could recover only 97 cents—a phenomenon called "breaking the buck," which set off a panic as anxious savers rushed to take their money out of all money market accounts. In other words, even a slight dip in the value of money market accounts caused an old-fashioned bank run, so destructive was the power of "fear itself." Paulson immediately assured investors that the Treasury would make depositors whole with government money, which prevented the collapse of those money market accounts.

The run on the money market with its $700 million in losses was nothing compared to the sinking titanic, AIG, with its hundreds of billions of dollars in defaults. AIG's failure—which, thanks to public intervention, was only a *near* failure, in the end—was a direct by-product of the market's magical thinking about risk in the era of deregulation. Banks believed that their internal algorithmic risk management system eliminated the downside of risks through the swaps contracts that hedged each pile of derivatives. AIG had insured all the banks against default in return for a steady flow of monthly premiums, assuming that all the bundled and structured and rated risks piled on top of the original risks had made them basically riskless. And the large investment banks, which should have known better, viewed their AIG insurance as a "hedge" against risk. The market also believed, or pretended to believe, in the evaluations by the credit-scoring companies—Moody's Investors Service, Standard & Poor's, and Fitch Rating—that turned what was formerly a junk bond into a triple-A investment worthy of a pension fund. No one was incentivized to look too closely because of the imperative to maximize shareholder profits and because they were always risking other people's money to make personal gains.

AIG had offered the fairy-tale free lunch: it allowed the banks to enjoy the upside of risk while it promised to protect them against the downside, all while making a pretty penny off the premiums. It was, of course, too good to be true. When the pile of mortgages, securities on those mortgages, and derivatives based on those securities began to default all at once, investment banks like Goldman Sachs and JP Morgan demanded that AIG fulfill its contractual promises to compensate them for their losses. AIG did not have the more than $600 billion it had pledged and the banks refused to take the losses. They had hedged against the risk of loss, and a contract was a contract, after all.

As with the money market's too-good-to-be-true promises, the fairy tale of risk hedges proved to be more neoliberal mythmaking. And just as with the money market, Fed officials covered up the the gaps between neoliberal myth and reality with real money—for the sake of the market. If forced to take losses, even small ones, insisted the TBTF banks, the market would collapse and the banks' shareholders would be scared and who knows what unforeseeable disaster would follow. Former Goldman Sachs partner Paulson and former Wall Street regulators Geithner and Bernanke repeated these claims, advising both Bush and Obama that making the banks take losses of any kind would be too risky and would cause market turmoil. There was some truth to this. FDR's bank holiday caused significant turbulence and Richard Nixon's dollar shocks and oil shocks did as well. The difference now was the power of the large institutions of the market compared to the power of the American president.

As the journalist James Stewart recounts in "Eight Days," his absorbing *New Yorker* account of the earliest days of the crisis, Geithner asked Treasury officials whether allowing AIG to fail was possible: "Can we let it go?" The answer, apparently, was no—or, at least, according to Bernanke, they couldn't let it fail "without sparking a global banking panic." Paulson took the news of the potential collapse to President Bush. The Treasury secretary informed Bush that "AIG is about to fail" and explained that the federal government needed to intervene.

A perplexed Bush wondered aloud, "How have we come to the point where we can't let an institution fail without affecting the whole economy?" The President had apparently believed in the neoliberal myths of free markets operating without "government intervention." The Fed and Treasury teams asked for the authority to rescue the firm, and Bush "gave his blessing." As the President rose to leave, he said, "Someday you guys are going to need to tell me how we ended up with a system like this. I know this is not the time to test them and put them through failure, but we're not doing something right if we're stuck with these miserable choices."[11]

For his part, Tony Blair, the British prime minister, expressed the same confusion; he said that the crisis was "the product of a whole new way that the financial and banking sector has been working in this past twenty or thirty years where you have got this deep integration of the global economy and where you have a lot of financial instruments that were created whose impact people didn't properly understand." When asked if his own party, Labour, understood, he replied "No, we didn't."[12] Even the "man who knew" was confounded by the crisis. When brought before Congress and asked to account for his role in the financial crisis, Greenspan admitted, "I made a mistake in presuming that the self-interests of organizations, specifically banks and others, were such that they were best capable of protecting their own shareholders and their equity in the firms." He said he was in a state of "shocked disbelief."[13] Having deferred the market's engineering to ideologues disguised as scientists, no one seemed to know to anything. Not Barack Obama; John McCain, the Republican candidate he defeated; or the general public. Margaret Thatcher's slogan "there is no alternative" had apparently been both a promise and a warning.

IT WAS INEVITABLE that in an era of deregulated banks, there would be large failures. What was surprising was that the market rules would be applied only when banks were making profits and not when they ultimately failed. Instead of allowing the market to enforce its discipline—as the policy makers had done routinely when it came to American families—the government stepped in and bailed out the banking industry. The Federal Reserve, its moneymaking powers having been hidden from view for decades, emerged from the shadows with unfathomable trillions to "infuse liquidity" into markets.

Policy makers were faced with a choice: they could let free markets take their course and allow a wide-scale failure of the financial sector, or they could use the considerable powers of the Federal Reserve to save the banks.

It is not clear, in hindsight, just how desperate this choice was. The experts' doomsaying notwithstanding, how would an AIG bankruptcy have affected the market outside of Wall Street? According to Geithner, "there would have been shantytowns." Perhaps. But even the Lehman failure, disruptive though it was, did not lead to catastrophe beyond shareholder losses and market dips. In the heat of the moment, there was indeed a pervasive and terrifying sense of apocalypse on Wall Street. However, not everyone was as fixated on Wall Street's survival as the men in the room. It is at least conceivable that Geithner (whose jurisdiction, as New York Fed president, was solely over the top investment banks), Paulson, Bernanke, and Lawrence Summers (a key economic decision maker in the Obama administration's response) could not make an objective determination about the havoc that a few bankrupt investment firms would cause. It certainly would have affected their lives and legacies—and their neighbors' and friends' livelihoods—but would it have doomed the average American? The evidence is ambiguous.

Nevertheless, by the time Obama was inaugurated in early 2009, the decision had been made. AIG, along with Fannie Mae and Freddie Mac and their combined $5 trillion in liabilities, had effectively been nationalized. Fed and Treasury officials had bailed out the thirteen top banks by spending billions on asset purchases and the Federal Reserve had begun the historically unprecedented tactic of reviving the market through money printing known formally as *quantitative easing* (QE). During the lame-duck period of a Republican administration that had been uninterested in federal spending, Bernanke and Paulson had decided to let the money flow. The crisis had a way of changing many a neoliberal mind about government intervention in markets. The Nobel laureate Robert Lucas, who had declared in 1980 that Keynesianism was not just dead but laughable, now admitted, "Well, I guess everyone is a Keynesian in a foxhole."[14]

The most shocking Keynesian in the foxhole was Richard Posner. In a September 2009 column in *The New Republic* titled "How I Became a Keynesian,"[15] Posner admitted that it was only "when the banking industry came crashing down and depression loomed for the first time in my lifetime" that he even thought to read Keynes's *The General Theory of Employment, Interest, and Money*. For someone who had a made a career out of debunking Keynesian economics, this was quite an admission. Having previously assumed that the book was outdated and debunked, Posner was surprised to find that despite the lack of heavy mathematics, Keynes's book was in fact "the best guide we have to the crisis."[16] He even called it "a masterpiece" for identifying what all the economists had missed: that markets are irrational, guided by "animal spirits" rather than perfect reason. It was apparently a revelation to Posner that the economy was "marked by uncertainty in the sense of risk that cannot be calculated." He wrote that Keynes "has wise words which Alan Greenspan and Ben Bernanke could, with profit, have heeded earlier in this decade." Posner believed that the Fed chairs should have done something about the irrationality of the market—they should have known that the assumptions about market rationality and efficiency were just theories. Of course, he offered this advice while ignoring his own crucial role in ensuring that efficient market theories were guiding not just markets, but also law and regulation.

Posner came close to offering a mea culpa for, effectively, his entire legacy.[17] "We have learned since September that the present generation of economists has not figured out how the economy works," he wrote. They "could not agree on what, if anything, the government should do to halt it and put the economy on the road to recovery." No one knew anything, inferred Posner. That same year, he published a book titled *A Failure of Capitalism: The Crisis of '08 and the Descent into Depression*. Posner called the crisis a disaster of capitalism and evidence that markets cannot self-regulate. The reformed Posner still believed that the deregulation of airlines and other industries was warranted and necessary, but that perhaps banks were not like other businesses and should not have been allowed to rack up so much risk. However, for all his public contrition, Posner was decidedly *not* abandoning neoliberalism. He did not suggest any regulations or reforms at the end of *A Failure of Capitalism*; in fact, he warned against acting in haste or even acting at all. Yes, the system had failed, but it would still be foolish to change it.

The postcrisis ninth edition of Posner's *Economic Analysis of Law* is an object lesson in neoliberals' perfunctory response to the failure of their ideology.[18] The moment of doubt and confusion has already passed, and Posner is once again certain about the market but with a slight caveat. The market is still divine, but now man has fallen. After the 2008 crisis debunked rational market theory and the economic assumptions underlying it, behavioral economics closed the cognitive dissonance between models and reality. Behavioral economics showed that the theory of rational *Homo economicus* had some "bugs" or irrationalities in reasoning that could be patched with simple awareness. Posner fits Keynes's insights into Law and Economics by pigeonholing his "masterpiece" as a comment on *psychology* and not economics: "The eclectic approach that does not draw a sharp boundary between economics and psychology (and is returning to favor today with the rise of behavioral economics) came naturally to Keynes," writes Posner, "because he was a great economist but not an academic economist in the twenty-first century understanding of the term." Posner adds that Keynes "had no degree in economics" and that "he was not a professor"; rather, he had been "an adviser and a high-level civil servant, and was also a speculator, polemicist and journalist." (Friedrich Hayek, as well as many other MPS luminaries, also did not have a PhD in economics. Neither did Posner.) The models did not need to be changed, only tweaked to account for blind spots. This crisis could be explained by psychology while leaving economics intact.

The 2008 crisis was a low point for the economics profession, and it could be argued—as some did—that perhaps it was time for a reckoning within the field that could lead to a new paradigm. The reigning paradigm, however, simply adapted itself. Calling themselves neo-Keynesians, devotees of neoliberalism invoked Keynes's name while following a neoliberal program of recovery, one that rescued the banks and left scores of Americans to fend for themselves. Apparently, the foxhole wasn't quite dangerous enough.

In Posner's reaction, and similar reactions by neoliberals, the deeper story of the crisis can be perceived. The year 2008 should have become a temporal bookend for the neoliberal era. Instead, the utter failure of neoliberal ideas only *accelerated* that era. The leading neoliberals resorted to Keynes not for understanding but for justification.

At the low point of the Great Depression, Keynes had suggested, rightly, that the central bank and the government should spend liberally to jump-start the economy out of a credit freeze. It was the correct response to that crisis: the New Deal's Keynesian spending on roads, bridges, parks, housing, and art not only revived the moribund economy and ended the depression, but also restored trust to state and market. Roosevelt used Keynesian spending to rebuild an economy based on what Americans needed and ensured, through heavy taxes on the wealthy, that economic gains would be spread widely.

By contrast, after 2008, what the so-called neo-Keynesians were advocating was fundamentally different. They wanted Keynesianism for Wall Street. Not roads or bridges but QE, which involved the Fed purchasing Treasury bonds and other financial assets from banks in order to increase the supply of money in the economy. That is, the Keynesian stimulus was aimed at bank balance sheets under the theory—still apparently taken seriously by American regulators—that the extra money would have no choice but to trickle down to things like roads and bridges rather floating up toward dividends for shareholders. The same economists who denounced Keynesianism for people were converted by Keynianism for finance. The conservative economist Greg Mankiw, one of President Bush's economic advisers, wrote in a November 2008 *New York Times* op-ed that, "if you were going to turn to only one economist to understand the problems facing the economy, there is little doubt that the economist would be John Maynard Keynes." Although none other than Richard Posner characterized Mankiw's op-ed as an about-face act of contrition, the piece in fact parrots the orthodox neoliberal approach. As Mankiw explains, he opposes deficit spending—which

Keynes explicitly recommended—because of its long-run risks to asset holders and social security recipients. Mankiw (along with fellow neo-liberal, though Democratic, economists like Summers and Bernanke) advocated not the New Deal–style fiscal spending that Keynes actually proposed but rather Federal Reserve "spending" in the form of QE and asset and debt purchases from banks.

In principle, stimulating the economy through monetary policy is not radically different from stimulating the economy through fiscal spending. But monetary policy is directed at the banks and the markets. The problem is that monetary policy is created in some instances based on two false assumptions: that saving the banks is akin to saving bank *customers*, and that financial firms are allocating their excess reserves and liquidity to their highest and best use—that is, that the market is efficient and that banks operate within that market. This was precisely the assumption that the financial crisis exposed as erroneous. There was no market discipline, and the Wall Street profit model was so tenuously related to road construction and bridge building that monetary stimulus was leagues distant from Keynesian spending. And yet, despite the evidence all around them, the free market fundamentalists at the Fed doubled down on their trickle-down assumptions, bailing out the banks because, supposedly, those funds would find their way into the rest of the economy (rather than wind up in shareholders' pockets).

Given the investment—intellectual, professional, personal—the officials in charge of the rescue had already made in neoliberalism, their opting to restore the status quo is not altogether surprising. What is curious, however, is that the "change" presidential candidate would choose to fill potholes rather than build a new road. Surprisingly, and perhaps without intending to, President Obama allowed neoliberalism to snatch victory from the jaws of defeat.

Of all the candidates vying for the presidency in 2008—Obama, Hillary Clinton, Joe Biden, John McCain, Mitt Romney—the eventual victor had the least personal or political stake in defending the old Wall Street–dominated regime. Whereas Obama's team of advisers was largely composed of academics somewhat outside the mainstream, all the other candidates were implicated personally or by association in the deregulatory agenda that had led to the financial crisis. Romney had received donations from private equity vulture Bain Capital, which he had cofounded, and, during the campaign, had infamously labeled 47 percent of Americans as vultures. As a senator, Biden had defeated bankruptcy and credit card reforms on behalf of the powerful corporations of his home state, Delaware. McCain had been investigated by the Senate Ethics Committee for helping save the thrift of a favored donor, Charles Keating. Clinton's spouse had deregulated Wall Street as president. Only Obama, it seemed, had escaped the ideology (or the money) of Wall Street. Yes, he received Wall Street donations, but he defeated the establishment candidates on the strength of small donations, rallies, volunteers, and inspired voters.

Obama was also the first presidential candidate to raise the alarm about a coming crisis. In a speech at the Nasdaq a full year before Lehman's failure, he warned that a recession might be possible, and blamed Wall Street for excessive risk-taking and malfeasance that could lead to millions of lost homes and billions in investor losses (projections that turned out to be exceedingly modest). "In this modern, interconnected economy, there is no dividing line between Main Street and Wall Street," Obama said. "Turning a blind eye to the cronyism in our midst can put us all in jeopardy. And we cannot accept that in the United States of America." Quoting FDR, he called for a "reappraisal of our values as a nation" and a "new social contract" that would "restore confidence" and "renew public trust in our markets." He alluded to various regulations and reforms directed at credit agencies, credit card companies, and mortgage issuers that "were met with millions in mortgage industry lobbying." He promised on behalf of the American people that "we will not tolerate a market that is fixed. We will not tolerate a market that is rigged by lobbyists who don't represent the interests of real Americans or most businesses."[19]

The Obama coalition—which would eventually give him the presidency—represented a political realignment from the Clinton era. Americans voted for the promising outsider who stood against the Democratic mainstream and, by extension, the Washington consensus. Obama voters took his rhetoric at face value, which led to further disillusionment and distrust when the alternative to the system seemed unwilling—or worse, unable—to do anything but shore up the system.

In his postpresidential memoir, Obama explained himself in his characteristic "on the one hand" and "on the other" deliberative style. On the one hand, his "very smart" insider advisers. On the other hand, his promise that "the time has come for change" in Washington. As the journalist Ron Suskind recounts in his book *Confidence Men: Wall Street, Washington, and the Education of a President*, Obama's campaign team urged him to reject neoliberalism altogether. The candidate admitted that he even considered framing the crisis as "a 'Bush-McCain' economic agenda that prioritized the wealthy and powerful over the middle class," but "on the other hand," it was too risky to do so. Obama had inexplicably made a promise to then Treasury Secretary Henry Paulson that he would not make any comments "that might jeopardize the Bush administration's chances at getting Congress to approve the rescue package."[20]

In his November 5, 2008, victory speech, Obama adopted a muted tone, keeping his remarks focused on unifying the country: "Let us remember that if this financial crisis taught us anything, it's that we cannot have a thriving Wall Street while Main Street suffers. In this country, we rise or fall as one nation—as one people." On the other hand, Obama was sent to Washington to fight corruption by a wary public choosing hope over cynicism and believing in the candidate's promise that reform was possible. But the fight for reform was over before candidate Obama was even inaugurated. Even after taking office, instead of calling the bluff like Roosevelt had, Obama chose to uphold the thin veneer of confidence in the system.

The Republicans' rancorous opposition to Obama notwithstanding, there was hardly any daylight between his administration and Bush's as it concerned their crisis response. A case in point was Obama's appointees: Geithner as Treasury secretary, and Summers as head of the National Economic Council.

Such appointments were a clear sign that the unity of Main Street and Wall Street would come at Main Street's expense. On the other hand, neoliberalism had so thoroughly transformed politics that even as the house it built was crumbling, there was "no alternative" but the house. Yet it was not the lack of alternatives that bred widespread anger that curdled into distrust; it was that the majority of American voters *had chosen the alternative.*

As Obama explained, "I loved the various up-and-comers who'd advised me throughout the campaign and felt a kinship with left-leaning economists and activists who saw the current crisis as the result of a bloated and out-of-control financial system in dire need of reform. But with the world economy in free fall, my number one task wasn't remaking the economic order. It was preventing further disaster."[21] Despite the fact that neoliberalism was collapsing under the weight of its own contradictions and its prophets were revealed as liars or fools, Obama had no choice but to restore it with the aid of those same defunct prophets. In his memoir, he writes that he "needed people who had managed crises before, people who could calm markets in the grip of panic—people who, by definition, might be tainted by the sins of the past." Such people were Geithner and Summers.

By the time Obama took office, gone were his group of campaign advisers, among them Paul Volcker, Austin Goolsbee, Warren Buffett, and other nonideologues. Thanks to Jason Furman, the economics policy director of the campaign and a Summers protégé, the economic decision making was streamlined through key figures, namely Summers himself. As Obama recounted, his team helped him understand "the nuts and bolts of the crisis" while also "scaring the heck out of [him]." Obama "felt confident that on the substance of the economy," he "knew what [he] was talking about."[22]

FOR THAT CONFIDENCE, Obama had Summers to thank. Summers's smarts were matched by his self-assurance, traits that appealed to Obama who, though similarly gifted, lacked the insider knowledge the economist so expertly wielded. For Treasury secretary, Obama considered only two candidates: Summers and Geithner. The latter, a Summers protégé himself, got the job because he was already involved in the ongoing bailout.

Nevertheless, Obama asked Summers to remain as White House economic counselor in exchange for a future appointment as Federal Reserve chairman. But, as Obama lamented in his memoir, Summers's "lack of interest in human niceties" and his "political incorrectness" harmed his reputation with the progressives who would eventually thwart his potential appointment.[23] The key members of the Senate Banking Committee—Jeff Merkley, Sherrod Brown, and Elizabeth Warren—had told Obama that Summers would not have their votes, which were essential for confirmation. Contrary to Obama's analysis, their opposition to Summers was not over style but rather his decades-long fealty to neoliberal orthodoxy: his role steering the Clinton administration's deregulatory agenda as Treasury secretary, including the repeal of the Glass-Steagall Act; his tenure at the World Bank, during which he exported neoliberalism globally; and his uncompromising stance against market regulation. To his critics, Summers was the epitome of the elite Washington–Ivy League nexus that had mainstreamed neoliberalism and caused the crisis itself.

These critics, including but not limited to the three Democratic senators, were not wrong. When the Financial Crisis Inquiry Commission, created by Congress to investigate the causes of the 2008 event, issued its report in 2011, it drew a direct line from the Commodities Futures Modernization Act of 2000—which exempted over-the-counter (OTC) derivatives trades between financial firms from routine regulation—to the financial crisis. Obama's earlier advisers, Volcker and Buffett—who had called derivatives "weapons of mass destruction"—had urged the candidate to reform the market and prohibit banks from derivatives trading. However, according to Ron Suskind, these advisers and other reformists were run out by the forceful intervention of Summers and his proxies after Obama won.

After the crash, which revealed his prognostications to have been utterly misguided, Summers never acknowledged that he had been wrong. And, having never acknowledged his mistakes, he kept making them. When the chairwoman of the Council of Economic Advisers, Christina Romer, tried to advise President Obama that the postcrisis fiscal stimulus should be twice the planned $700 billion, Summers simply cut her out of the discussion and crossed out her numbers. He never even presented Romer's counterargument to his plan to the President, leaving Obama with the impression that the council was in agreement on the bailout. Most economists believe now (as many did then) that the meager size of the stimulus, compared to the funds provided to the failing banks, was a mistake based in an austerity mindset of a previous era. That mindset, which Summers continues to cling to, tends to see the economy from the perspective of asset holders, viewing inflation, for example, as more destabilizing than unemployment and banks as more deserving of government money than homeowners.

In fact, Summers *himself* came around to the view that the stimulus was insufficient; mistakes were made, in other words, but not by him. In a 2012 *Washington Post* op-ed, he wrote that "economic forecasters divide into two groups: those who cannot know the future but think they can, and those who recognize their inability to know the future."[24] Unless he saw all the data and a model he liked more than his model, his model was presumed to be superior. Theory beats no theory. In 2021, he said "there was no question that the 2009 stimulus should have been bigger. . . . But was it too small by a factor of five? That's not an argument I've heard."[25] He may not have heard her, but Romer had made the argument.

The problem was Summers's absolute confidence in his ideology and Obama's absolute confidence in *him*, which allowed Summers to become the gatekeeper of possible economic responses to the crisis. By cutting off the opportunity to prove a real-life counternarrative to neoliberalism, Summers could continue to claim that his way was the only way that made sense. Like Milton Friedman, Summers attacked those he disagreed with as uninformed or worse. In a 2005 central bankers' summit full of praise for Fed Chair Greenspan and the state of the economy, the economist Raghuram Rajan presented a dissenting view that compared the U.S. economy to the irrationality of Asian markets before they crashed. Unwilling to let a single voice of dissent threaten the orthodoxy, Summers rose from his seat in the audience, unprompted, to the lectern to attack Rajan as a "Luddite" and his theory as "misguided." Summers defended Greenspan's Fed as having "evolved" the financial market through complexity and financial innovation over more "primitive" (Asian) markets. It wasn't that Summers was racist or sexist exactly (or at least not obviously so like his neoliberal predecessors), but his statements often revealed a belief in a fixed hierarchy of intelligence with the direction of evolution culminating toward the kind of knowledge possessed by someone—well—like him. Rajan was right, of course, but that hardly mattered.

While neoliberalism is far bigger than any one person, even American presidents, Summers is the rare example of how accumulated personal power can distort market competition. He dominated the agenda for two presidential administrations and assured his legacy by filling the most powerful posts with his followers and keeping his critics firmly on the outside. And once someone became a critic, they were automatically treated as an outsider. As Elizabeth Warren recounted, during a dinner she had with Summers in 2009, he leaned in and told her, "I had a choice. I could be an insider or I could be an outsider. Outsiders can say whatever they want. But people on the inside don't listen to them. Insiders, however, get lots of access and a chance to push their ideas. People—powerful people—listen to what they have to say. But insiders also understand one unbreakable rule: They don't criticize other insiders." Warren, for her part, took the advice as a cautionary tale. She continued to criticize the Wall Street–friendly course of the Treasury bailouts, a position that would earn her the ire of the Obama administration and cost her the directorship of the Consumer Financial Protection Bureau, the agency she fought to create.

When Summers became an outsider himself during the Biden administration, he ignored his own advice and publicly criticized the administration until they made him an insider once again. As an October 2022 *Washington Post* article put it, "The White House's initial distance from Summers emerged as a major public relations problem." The public relations problem was Summers himself, who was refusing to stay on the sidelines. "From his perch outside the administration," noted the *Post*, "Summers repeatedly slammed the [administration's policies] as reckless, and Republicans constantly pointed to criticism from a top Democratic economist. Biden officials worked to contain the damage as concerns about the fastest price hikes in four decades helped lower the president's approval rating." Even when Summers wasn't in the room, it was only his voice that mattered. "The president spoke to Summers over the summer, emphasizing that they were taking his counsel seriously." According to a White House official, President Biden spoke more often to Summers than he did his own Treasury secretary, Janet Yellen. When Summers and his proxies—Jason Furman, most conspicuously—loudly and repeatedly criticized Biden's student-loan forgiveness plan, the administration quietly walked back some of its most generous features. Aides say Biden enjoys talking to Summers, who conveys his worldview with authority."[26]

Summers, like neoliberalism itself, is a closed system of false prediction. His legacy of being wrong about the market earned him even more opportunities to make decisions. The consummate expert, Summers has stayed on top because his faith in the system only grows with each new crisis. Although Summers has distorted the market himself, he too is ultimately a creature of neoliberalism, not its master.

IN THE STORY of the 2008 crisis, ironies abound. A foolproof financial system falls to pieces. Neoliberal economists suddenly discover Keynes. But perhaps the most telling irony is the response of the billionaire defenders of free enterprise—including the Kochs, the Scaifes, Paul Singer of Elliott Management, Steven A. Cohen of SAC Capital, and Stephen Schwarzman of Blackstone Group—who should have been the most vocal opponents of the government bailout. That is, if it was free enterprise they had been defending.

During that year's election campaign, Charles Koch had called Obama a dangerous socialist and bemoaned his victory as "the greatest loss of liberty and prosperity since the 1930s." After the election, Koch assembled a group of other billionaires to fight Obama and defend the free market. "If not us, who? If not now, when?" he said to the cavalry.[27]

When the $700 billion bailout was being debated, one could be forgiven for assuming that the libertarians, those lovers of liberty and exalters of the free market, would oppose it. And indeed, as the journalist Jane Mayer has revealed, in the beginning the Kochs had "in fact taken what appeared to be a principled libertarian position against the bailouts. But the organization quickly and quietly reversed sides when the bottom began to fall out of the stock market, threatening the Kochs' vast investment portfolio." After Republicans in the House of Representatives voted against the Troubled Asset Relief Program (TARP), the bill authorizing the bank bailouts, "a list of conservative groups now supporting the bailouts was circulated behind the scenes to Republican legislators, in hopes of persuading them to vote for the bailouts." The coalition of rent-seeking billionaires led by Koch included Americans for Prosperity, Freedom Partners, Donor Trust, the Coors Foundation, and the Bradleys. Foxhole Keynesians all.[28]

The easy abandonment by billionaires of the free market reveals the hollowness of the entire neoliberal project. From the very beginning, liberty and market freedom were just theory—a fig leaf covering up a systematic takeover of the state by a group of wealthy reactionaries opposed to the just allocation of resources. So long as the ruthless blade of the market was pointed at the poor, it was the fixed and unchangeable will of God, nature, and the market; but when it was their money on the line, the billionaires ditched theory and took shelter in the nanny state and her abundant funds. That is, their devotion to the free market was never a principle to begin with—it was always a particular means to a particular end. Capitalism for thee but not for me.

And they won. The bailouts quickly returned banks and private equity firms to profitability and, before too long, capital resumed its exponential growth. Flush with funds, private equity firms even rushed to buy up all the homes lost through default. Homes they rented back to the people who had lost their mortgages when the banks had gone bust—a sort of trickle-down economics that tended, always, to point debt down and capital gains up. When Treasury Secretary Paulson asked Congress to authorize the $700 billion for TARP in October 2008, he pitched it as an "asset purchase." The "troubled assets," Congress was led to believe, were the underwater mortgages held by people. But it quickly became clear that the troubled assets were in fact bank assets. The Obama administration promised to carve out some TARP funds for mortgages, but their meager efforts to do so made it clear that the program was not designed for homeowners. Of the $700 billion for TARP, over $250 billion went to eight major banks, $182 billion to AIG, and the rest spread out to auto manufacturers and credit markets.[29] Included in TARP was the Home Affordable Modification Program (HAMP), which earmarked $46 billion that would still go to *banks,* but was to be used to modify underwater mortgages. The idea was that the banks, having been rescued by the government, would voluntarily work with homeowners defaulting on their debt so that they could avoid foreclosure. But without mandates on banks to voluntarily help customers and with Treasury officials apparently uninterested in enforcing HAMP, the program was roundly denounced as a failure. The banks whose debts were generously forgiven by the government were stubbornly opposed to paying it forward.[30] There was no place in the neoliberal ethical code for demanding that banks serve the public. Even after the free market's banks were essentially nationalized, the quasi-religious belief in the market as the sole arbiter of fair resource allocation stood in the way of routing bailout funds to help people. The market knew best even when it obviously didn't.

When grilled by Senator Warren about the program, Geithner defended the Treasury's actions by saying: "'We estimate that [the banks] can handle ten million foreclosures, over time. This program will help foam the runway for them."[31] Neil Barofsky, the inspector general of TARP, recalled this conversation as a lightbulb moment, a feeling shared by Warren. "Elizabeth had been challenging Geithner on how the program was going to help homeowners," wrote Barofsky, "and he had responded by citing how it would help the banks. Geithner apparently looked at HAMP as an aid to the banks, keeping the full flush of foreclosures from hitting the financial system all at the same time."[32] The ten million foreclosures that the banks had to suffer would certainly be a drag on profits, but they could manage it. As for those ten million families? Well, they could rest easy knowing that the market would soon be back to making record profits.

AFTER THE INITIAL bank rescues conducted by the Paulson-led Treasury, the Obama administration had to decide what to do with the rest of the failed or failing banks. The President apparently consulted only with Summers and Geithner, who presented him with three options: to have the Fed continue to purchase banks' "toxic assets"; to temporarily nationalize the banks, which would place the banks' assets and liabilities on the federal government's balance sheets; or to put the banks through a "stress test" to determine whether the bailout had strengthened them enough to withstand future downturns, an exercise that had the added benefit of reassuring the jittery market that the crisis was over.[33] Once the three options had been presented, Obama asked, "Anything else on the menu?" Summers and Geithner replied, "Not right now, Mr. President." Although Obama admitted that he wasn't enthusiastic about the options, he did not consult with any other people or consider other options, deciding instead that of the three, the stress-test idea was "the best way forward. Not because it was great," conceded Obama, "not even because it was good—but because the other approaches were worse."[34] That was conveniently what Summers and Geithner, in consultation with teams of bankers and their attorneys, had already concluded as the right path forward. Although I was not privy to any of these conversations while I worked on Wall Street, I know that the senior partners at my firm and others who represented the largest banks were in constant contact with Treasury officials throughout the crisis and the bailout. In fact, many of the experts that made up the Treasury's sophisticated team of crisis responders had come from the very industries in peril. The close relationship between the regulators and bank lawyers was ostensibly justified and indeed necessary because they were the only experts who understood the financial system that was failing, but that rationale begs the question of why the system they—we—built was being saved.

There were alternative paths out of the crisis, but the unquestioned destination was restoring trust in the market as quickly as possible. Geithner's memoir is the most aggressively defensive of the retrospectives and with good reason—as president of the New York Fed, the bailout began with him, and then, later, as Treasury secretary, it ended with him as well. Geithner viewed himself and his team as first responders with the singular goal and major achievement of rescuing the U.S. financial system. A crisis was no time to ask questions about why Wall Street needed to be saved. His narrative demands that we measure his success by his own metric, to which a counterfactual is impossible to imagine. He often derided his critics, including other regulators such as FDIC Chair Sheila Bair and Elizabeth Warren, as "populists," "moral hazard fundamentalists," and those who wanted "Old Testament Justice." Geithner had no time for such grandstanding and rhetoric. His mantra "plan beats no plan" was reminiscent of "it takes a theory to beat a theory." His other mantra, "no more Lehmans," led his team to ensure that no additional banks would enter bankruptcy. According to Geithner, Lehman Brothers failed because U.K. regulators dragged their feet on approving the British bank Barclays' hastily assembled purchase of the troubled firm over the hectic weekend of September 13–14. Had they acted as vigorously as U.S. regulators, the markets would have avoided the irrational panic that followed Lehman's failure.[35]

Although President Obama had utmost confidence in his advisers, what kept him up at night, by his own account, was his earlier promise to then Harvard Law Professor Elizabeth Warren to focus on reforming the economy. There were other options available than those presented to him by Summers and Geithner, among them saving homeowners, breaking up the banks, and allowing banks to fail. But, as Geithner recounts in his memoir, the President "felt constrained from making any rash moves while I still had so many fronts of the economic crisis to deal with."[36] Like his predecessor, Obama was trapped by the predicted catastrophe he was told would result from the cascading failures if just one more domino fell. As the nation had learned during the Great Depression, the financial system runs as much on public confidence as it does on money. When that trust evaporates, only the federal government has the power and the credibility to shore up the system, and thus a crisis for the banks quickly and routinely becomes a crisis for the people.

Once the Fed's capital purchases had restored the banks to profitability, the administration hastened to assure the public that the system was fine through the stress tests. Once he committed to restoration, Obama felt restrained in what he could demand from the banks—even that they forgo their annual bonuses. "By committing to the stress test and the roughly two-month wait for its preliminary results," Obama wrote, "I'd placed on hold whatever leverage I had over the banks."[37]

AFTER THE CRISIS, it became clear that the most sophisticated risk models created by the quants had not even taken into account the kinds of systemic risks that were routine historically, such as a bank run. The risk models had taken the theories of efficient markets to heart, it seemed, and ignored the types of risk that neoliberal theories assumed away—like human irrationality, asset bubbles, panic, and global crisis. As David Viniar, Goldman Sachs's CFO and its top risk analyst, said of the shock of the financial crisis, "We were seeing things that were twenty-five standard deviation moves, several days in a row."[38] Andy Haldane, chief economist at the Bank of England, said "a 25-sigma event would be expected to occur once every 6 × 10124 lives of the universe." He added wryly that when he tried to calculate the likelihood of such an event happening, "the lights visibly dimmed over London. . . . Even a 7.3 standard deviation event should occur only once every 13 billion years."[39] Put another way, the financial crisis was either an unpredictable event that could occur only once in the span of our planet's geological timeline, like the meteor that killed the dinosaurs, or the models were wrong. Yet those same models were being used, after, to predict the market's future through the stress tests. All neoliberalism's sacred principles and foundational assumptions had been undeniably debunked, but the administration chose to respond to that crisis with the *very same* risk management techniques the banks had used to assess their own risks.

The stress tests focused on *capital risk*—that is, a bank's leverage ratio. The question the stress tests was trying to answer was whether another crisis or "adverse scenario" would deplete bank capital so significantly that it would result in insolvency, or whether the bank could maintain a small buffer of capital given a run or other market downturn. The capital-ratio regime was supposed to allow "light touch" regulatory oversight. The capital ratios were part of the neoliberal era's turn toward mathematical modeling of risks and as with other regulatory changes during the era, it grew more complex and manipulable by banks. Even before the crisis, it was clear that banks were massaging numbers to reach their capital ratios without reducing their risk.

Instead of simplifying the regulatory scheme or changing the incentive structure for banks to take fewer risks, the Fed chose instead to double down on the models by adopting them. The stress tests would be conducted by teams of quants at the Fed, who remained in contact with compliance officers at the largest banks. The stress scenarios varied from a "baseline" scenario of the current economic conditions through a potential "adverse" scenario to an unlikely, "severely adverse" economy. The Fed released the results of the first-ever stress tests in May 2009, reporting that the banks had passed with flying colors. Yet real-life stresses soon surpassed even the test's worst-case scenario, as the eurozone crisis deepened. The "severely adverse" scenario modeled unemployment at around 8 percent—a few months later, it was over 9.4 percent. The main reason the banks passed the stress tests was that the Fed had purchased their toxic assets and was plying them with liquidity as the crisis boomeranged across the globe.

The tests were officially a fact-finding exercise meant to accurately gauge the vulnerabilities of the system; but internally, they were the chosen exit strategy from the crisis. What was obvious to everyone and vigorously denied by Obama officials was that the purpose of the stress tests was to reassure markets that everything was fine.

Even *Saturday Night Live* mocked the stress tests in a cold open with Geithner revealing that the only possible test grades were pass/pass and that some banks, GMAC specifically, had written "taxpayer bailout" to every open question on the test. Instead of restoring confidence in the banks through reforming the system, the Federal Reserve boosted confidence by saving the banks and essentially promising to stand behind them in the future. The regulators saw no option: the banks were too large and too risky to ever fail without taking the economy down with them. The Fed, having essentially purchased all the bank's toxic assets—which made them a major equity holder in the banks—had aligned their incentives with the banks. To paraphrase an old joke, when you owe the bank $100,000, it owns you, but when you owe it $600 billion, you own it. The banks now owed the Fed roughly the latter amount and thus they were in charge of the economy. If they failed, so too did the Fed.

However, the unavoidable suspicion that the tests were just an exercise in publicity did not diminish the effect of that publicity. It did not matter whether the banks were well capitalized or not—all that mattered was that the Fed believed them to be well capitalized. What the Fed believed, it made real.

Bank stress tests are the epitome of neoliberal regulation. They are so complicated as to surpass the understanding of anyone but a professional at a top bank or inside the Fed. They rely on the assumption that the only risk that matters is the risk that can be measured algorithmically at a given moment in time. They are an esoteric exercise conducted in private by a regulator in cooperation with the regulated industry. After more than a decade of stress testing, most of the top banks have passed their stress tests each year. When a bank is not cleared, the Fed issues an objection to deficiencies in the bank's *procedures* or *models* regarding the bank's management or stress-testing technique. Deficient banks have had to fix their procedures; a handful of banks have had to come up with more capital through a collaborative remedy. The stress tests keep bank compliance officers and bank regulators busy plugging numbers as the banks continue to grow larger, more powerful, and more likely to be considered TBTF the next time around.

Trust was restored to the banking system after the Great Depression via a social contract with banks—they would play it safe and serve the economy, and the government would save them in the case of a crisis.

After the financial crisis of 2008, trust was restored by ensuring business would continue as usual: public insurance, private profits.

And so what was formerly a social contract has turned into a hostage situation. The survival of the TBTF banks is a political imperative linked to the survival of the American economy. It is hard to fathom a future crisis being resolved any way other than through bailouts, and equally hard to imagine future regulators demanding anything in return, given the bloated balance sheets of the top firms. JP Morgan crossed the $3 trillion threshold in assets in 2020 and gained another trillion in 2022, virtually guaranteeing mutually assured destruction in the event of any real market stress. Today, stress tests notwithstanding, the banks cannot fail without taking us all down with them. Neoliberalism hasn't won because it's right. It has won by convincing policy makers that there is no alternative.

ACCORDING TO the Financial Crisis Inquiry Commission report, the crisis was caused, in the simplest terms, by banks taking too much risk in the pursuit of profit. Many neoliberals agreed, even if only temporarily. Not all did, however. Commission member Peter Wallison, a senior fellow at the conservative American Enterprise Institute, dissented from the report's central finding. He blamed the financial crisis on government policies like the Community Reinvestment Act (CRA), which requires the Fed and other federal banking regulators to encourage financial institutions to help meet the credit needs of the communities in which they do business—specifically, those of low-income minorities. Wallison believed that such policies pressure banks to lend to risky borrowers. His claim was that these government policies set the stage for the collapse of the housing market, and the financial system with it.

As farfetched as this claim was to anyone familiar with finance and the complex derivatives empires being built up on bank balance sheets, it held sway in some quarters and has since been parroted by politicians, pundits, and academics. Republican senators like Marco Rubio and Lindsey Graham, for example, pointed fingers at the CRA for causing the financial crisis. Republican congressman Scott Garrett said that "for years Congress has been pushing banks to make risky sub-prime loans.... Congress passed laws that said we're going to fine you and we're going to file lawsuits against you lenders if you don't make risky loans."[40] Stephen Moore, one of the Trump administration's chief economic advisers, blamed the CRA for pushing banks to lend unjustifiably into "credit-deprived areas."[41] One Fox News commentator remarked, "Look.... You go all the way back to the Community Reinvestment Act, under Jimmy Carter, expanded under Bill and Hillary Clinton—they put the guns to the banks' heads and said, 'You have got to do these subprime loans.'... That's what caused this mess."[42] Glenn Beck and other right-wing pundits connected Democratic congress-woman Maxine Waters, President Obama, and Black-owned banks in Chicago to the TARP legislation, just "asking questions," so to speak, without leveling precise allegations (which would have been preposterous if stated plainly).

Law and Economics scholars Charles Calomiris and Stephen Haber also got in on the act. In their book *Fragile by Design*, published in February 2014, they attributed the crisis to groups of activists coercing banks and government officials to lower underwriting standards in order to lend to more minorities. In their account, activist groups like the Association of Community Organizations for Reform Now (ACORN) used the mandate for "good citizenship" contained in the CRA to effectively extort banks to lend to minorities and the uncreditworthy. The banks struck deals because they needed approval from their regulators to merge, which is how "a coalition of urban activist groups espousing populist ideologies forged an alliance with too-big-to-fail banks and GSEs." The result was to "set in motion a process that undermined lending standards for all Americans and helped precipitate the subprime crisis of 2007."[43] Blaming the CRA and reckless government lending became yet another neoliberal dog whistle.

Black communities in cahoots with the federal government had not in fact coerced Wall Street to lower lending standards. In reality, the opposite was true. Decades of state-sanctioned exclusion, segregation, and redlining had created zones of low wealth and high-credit risk in

Black and brown neighborhoods. At the same time, decades of deregulation had glutted a financial sector with capital looking for higher returns on risk. Presidents Reagan and Clinton had both promised that entrepreneurs would come to the "enterprise zones" formerly known as the ghetto. And they were right—entrepreneurs *would* find profits in these newly minted enterprise zones. Flocks of mortgage originators incentivized by "yield spread premiums" that increased their profits whenever they sold borrowers higher-interest loans breached the perimeter of the redline, offering lower-class urban residents financial inclusion and "the democratization of credit." Lenders dispensed with laborious underwriting—and, in many cases, any scrutiny of documents related to mortgages altogether—because the mortgages were immediately fed into the insatiable derivatives market, where they could be sliced and diced and extracted for even more profit by the predators at the top of the food chain.

When the CDOs exploded, federal regulators contained the damage to capital markets but did nothing to protect affected communities from the fallout. Some called the catastrophic effect "the largest drain of wealth" ever to befall the Black community. Congressman Brad Miller described the crisis and the resulting loss of homes "an extinction event" for Black Americans. More than 240,000 Black families lost their homes, and by 2009, the median net worth of the Black household was 53 percent lower than it was in 2005, and 35 percent of black families had zero or negative wealth.

In 2010, Steve Bannon, cofounder of the right-wing news site Breitbart and not yet famous as Donald Trump's adviser, released a documentary about the financial crisis called *Generation Zero*. Described by the *Richmond Times-Dispatch* as a "a horror film about the U.S. economy," it presented a grand narrative that absolves free market capitalism for the financial crisis while blaming the right's favorite bugaboos: minorities, activists, and the Clintons. The first line of the film's promotional material revealed the thrust of the argument: "Deregulation is not the problem. The current economic crisis is not a failure of capitalism, but a failure of culture." The roots of the crisis can be traced to the 1960s, when hippies, protesters, and Black activists forced the government to spend money on social programs, including welfare, and on minority loans, which led to a rising deficit and a mountain of risk. Bannon, a former Goldman Sachs partner, was silent about Wall Street's role in the bailout. Most of the film's messaging about the crisis is represented visually. For example, it shows an image of Henry Paulson trying to save the bankers but then cuts to a Black Panther rally during the 1960s. Images of hippies and Black activists are shown alongside a money-printing Federal Reserve. The horror that was prophesied in the film was the inevitable inflation—and cultural destruction—that would come from social spending. The dog whistles were visceral but clear—it was "those people" who were to blame.

Capitalism had not failed; the government had failed capitalism by, apparently, using public money toward the undeserving poor. *Generation Zero* inadvertently revealed the truth of neoliberalism: that it was a means to evade forming a society with "those people." The type of capitalism neoliberalism hailed was not compatible with democracy. The type of unidirectional capitalism that increased property values, stocks, and assets for those who already held them. The type of capitalism that looked a lot like colonialism. It was the capitalism that stood ready to protect asset values from market disruption but did nothing at all to modify the initial allocation of those resources. The market was not wrong, and the hierarchy was fixed, natural, and scientific, and should not be altered. Any government intervention that disrupted the status quo of property was anticapitalist while market interventions like the unprecedented trillions outlined above was the law enforcing contracts and ensuring market stability. Bannon and Trump did not represent a rejection of neoliberalism, as many have claimed. They represented neoliberalism stripped of the sophisticated risk models and peer-reviewed journal articles. Neoliberalism was not a falsifiable economic science, as the crisis of 2008 showed. It had been proved wrong, but still persisted. It was, rather, a system to protect those who have always ruled.

Despite each of its economic principles being abandoned and debunked, neoliberalism still dominates the discourse. Why? Because it was never about the free market. While Trump's populist nationalism has been interpreted by many as a thorough rejection of neoliberalism, Trump is better seen as an avatar of neoliberalism. Race and racism—or more specifically, fears of an impending global "race war"— were the animating forces that led to the rise of neoliberalism in the 1960s and 1970s. Trump was not the antithesis of neoliberalism but rather the apotheosis of neoliberalism's core logic, though stripped of its social niceties.

CHAPTER 10

Stonks

For somehow this is tyranny's disease, to trust no friends.
—AESCHYLUS, *PROMETHEUS BOUND*

O N JANUARY 6, 2021, inflamed by President Trump, thousands of rioters attacked the U.S. Capitol building in an attempt to stop the counting of electoral votes and keep a president who had been voted out of office in power. Among the rioters were militia and paramilitary groups like the Oath Keepers and Proud Boys, whose members were outfitted in fatigues and body armor, toting guns and zip ties. The self-described "revolutionaries" came to the Capitol—many for the first time—unified only by their rage and their certainty that they were avenging a grave injustice. They believed that a group of domestic enemies—the "deep state," the media, Democrats, so-called RINOs (Republicans in Name Only)—had colluded to overthrow the lawfully elected leader. The irony of the situation was lost only on them.

Donald Trump and his followers' attempted coup was a fitting end to a shocking, chaotic, and unprecedented administration. It was a symptom of the same rifts in American culture that led in 2016 to Trump's election, among them unremedied legacies of racism, the conspiratorial turn arising from distrust in powerful institutions, and the economic inequalities caused by the neoliberal economy—rifts highlighted throughout this book.

Another factor in the insurrection was the rise of big tech. As the journalist Max Fisher explains in *The Chaos Machine,* Facebook founder and CEO Mark Zuckerberg rejected an offer of $1.2 billion for his company from Yahoo in 2006. But the offer was the impetus for a host of innovations to increase how much Facebook users used the platform. These innovations included the Like button and the newsfeed.[1] When Facebook's valuation surged over $1 billion within a year of the Yahoo offer, it attracted a $240 million investment from Microsoft; by the fourth quarter of 2007, Facebook's value stood at $15 billion.

In 2010, Facebook discovered the key to increasing user engagement exponentially: private or public groups that could be organized by any user on any topic. Groups allowed users to connect with one another based on interest, location, or activism. As more groups formed and arguments inevitably cropped up within those groups, Facebook discovered that such controversy led people to spend even more time on the site. Nothing drives more engagement than what sociologists call moral outrage, a feeling of anger typically directed at perceived violators of the norms of a particular in-group.[2]

Facebook's algorithm quickly learned how to stoke moral outrage based on preexisting fault lines in American society. The process can create an echo chamber effect, where individuals are exposed primarily to perspectives that validate their existing beliefs, fueling moral outrage, and exacerbating societal divisions.

By the end of 2010, Facebook was valued at upward of $41 billion. It kept growing, acquiring Instagram in 2012 and WhatsApp in 2014 (which, together with Facebook Messenger and Facebook itself, constituted the top four most downloaded apps of the 2010s[3]). By the time of its IPO in 2012, Facebook had more than one billion users worldwide and was worth over $100 billion.

Facebook's stratospheric rise in market value drew in even more investors expecting returns, which pushed the company to develop more ways to engage more users for longer. Groups proliferated, drawing in more eyeballs, users, and ads. The groups also became more controversial, leading to the creation of more conspiracy theories. Marjorie Taylor Greene's 2018 Facebook post drawing connections between the Rothschilds and the California wildfires—discussed in the Introduction—was one example of many.

In short, the spread online of the most divisive and least factual information is neither a coordinated, man-behind-the-curtain operation nor a random or organic development. Rather, it is the natural outgrowth of a perfectly efficient market. Outrage and emotion produce the greatest revenue, and so more is supplied to meet demand.

This is not just a problem caused by network design or the malfeasance of individual tech companies or their algorithmic manipulation; rather, it is the internal logic of capital extraction in a new form, same as the old but on the internet. In all epochs, money and capital create a force of self-accumulation that can grow exponentially unless checked by society. Capital's exponential spread is constantly in search of new sources of extraction. Just as the colonial powers turned land, people, and resources into commodities, forcing a wholesale replacement of preexisting cultures in the process, these firms created markets for extraction out of places that were not previously subject to market rule. We became resource-rich data exporters. Our desires and hopes were mined, as were our fears and resentments, all toward shareholder returns. Once our feelings and social ties became a market that could yield profits, the rest was inevitable.

The tech revolution amplified the rate of innovation, commodifying as it evolved; its dictates were generated more by financial pressure than technological innovation. Capital's new frontier transformed our identities and desires, known to us or not, into property and capital, compilations of data that could be sold and traded. Public forums for speech, community, identity, and self-expression were valuable precisely because they had not previously been subject to the vicissitudes of market forces. The frontier pushed the market into heretofore unfinancialized spheres of our minds and private lives, which became revenue-generating terrain to be extracted by capital's metastatic growth. Like a cancer, capital grew by consuming the ties that bound society, leaving polarization and distrust in its wake. The tech industry leeched our social ties, friendships, and group loyalties for gain and then profited one more time from the distrust and paranoia it sowed. Then again, because capital must keep growing, online spaces sold back to each consumer an effigy of "community" and a simulacrum of social connection.

One of the core neoliberal theories, Garrett Hardin's tragedy of the commons, held that selfish people would inevitably exploit and overuse resources on land that was commonly held. He was wrong about people and about common spaces, for it wasn't sharing that would deplete the planet but privatization and monetization. Once private gain trumped public interest, there would be no common space that would be protected from private profiteering, including public forums for speech, community, identity, romance, and self-expression. The real tragedy of the commons is that by controlling the commons, private firms could create renewable resources by stoking our fears. The tragedy in this case, though, is that rage, resentment, and distrust are, unlike natural resources, renewable and abundant. As we have learned over the past several years, hatred, bigotry, and paranoia can be monetized and sold to investors.

As disorienting and dangerous as the commodification of our social life is, it actually isn't the biggest threat the tech companies pose to society. Rather, the most pressing issue is the result of that commodification: their vast power. The big five—Microsoft, Amazon, Google, Apple, and Meta—have become so dominant because they own every facet of the ecosystem and are still pursuing growth. Amazon, for example, in addition to its seemingly infinite online marketplace, has an immensely profitable cloud computing division and also owns the wires and network infrastructure that connects each region of the world. Apple doesn't just make the most popular personal devices but also "hosts" the apps available on its exclusive platform. Microsoft owns the Office suite, a major gaming console in Xbox, and telecommunications companies including Nokia as well as LinkedIn, Skype, and GitHub, the dominant internet hosting service worldwide. Facebook, even before its recent and questionable venture into the metaverse, owned each of its near competitors and thus had neutralized many potential threats. And Google controls not just the most dominant search engine worldwide but also the dominant internet server, which syncs up an array of apps and services. The tech giants also buy up and hold almost all of the patent claims in their domains and use their teams of lawyers to crush competitors. Despite Bork's confident assurances to the contrary, the real antitrust paradox is the big five have been able not just to outcompete but to eliminate their competition.

The firms have also diversified. Google and its parent company, Alphabet, control several private equity firms and venture capital investment firms. Jeff Bezos, Amazon's founder, has ventured into media with his purchase of *The Washington Post*. Microsoft founder Bill Gates has invested in media, biotech, energy, rail, and freight shipping. He also owns three hundred thousand acres of farmland, an AI development firm, a think tank, research laboratories, and a satellite company, Earth-Now, that aims to "blanket the earth with live satellite video coverage" aimed at monitoring crops, the ocean, and war zones.

For years, neoliberals leveraged American fears of an overbearing state to garner support for the free market. Today, it is clear that neoliberalism has succeeded brilliantly. The neoliberal era's deregulatory prerogatives and permissive antitrust orthodoxy have led to concentrations of corporate power never before seen in our history, as well as the utter erosion of the so-called countervailing power of the state. Trapped in the myth that the free market was coextensive with freedom, the federal government ceded more of its power to private enterprise. And while neoliberalism convinced us to stay ever watchful against the tyranny of the state, our liberty and freedom were actually being looted by corporations driven by their own imperatives of perpetual growth and extraction. The quiet coup of neoliberalism made possible the very real coup attempt by Trump and his supporters.

AFTER THE FINANCIAL CRISIS, those controlling big pools of capital looking for exponential growth shifted away from the murky world of hedge funds and private equity firms toward the murkier but less regulated world of venture capital.

Instead of earning profits from modeling future risks and trading and hedging accordingly, venture capitalists seek to actively shape the future. Venture capitalists invest in start-ups, looking for so-called unicorns—unique, industry-disrupting start-ups that reach extremely high valuations. Venture capitalists value startups based on their future potential: whether they have a credible strategy for fast growth. However, once a start-up becomes venture-backed, its future growth is often more or less assured, thanks to the self-reinforcing magic of an insular market. What separates unicorns from the pack is that they promise not just profits but total market domination. Unicorn companies with billion-dollar valuations—Uber, Airbnb, Alibaba, Square, Slack, SpaceX, and ByteDance—set out to make markets where none existed previously, beyond the existing internet into Web 3.0, into novel forms of assets, and beyond earth altogether.

Tech's manifest destiny is led not just by innovative tech, but by charismatic leaders of unicorn companies with a plan for the future. These firms sell not a product but a community, a cause—even self-transformation. Their success lies in commodifying community membership along lines of identity and belonging. Their product is rarely the technology itself but rather the restoration of something lost.

Adam Neumann launched WeWork with the mission to "create community" and "raise consciousness." The latter was good for some laughs in the media, but the former hardly raised eyebrows: community has yet to be monetized, making it a frontier place beyond the commodified homeland of existing markets. Neumann insisted he was selling community and communal living and not just office space, identifying himself as a community-building expert, having been raised on a kibbutz. Neumann even tried to trademark the word "we," meaning that he would have a legally protected property interest in "we" for use across their enterprise. As a synopsis of neoliberal lawmaking, one could hardly ask for better satire. WeWork was adamantly *not* a real estate company, insisted Neumann, which is why the company earned a valuation of $47 billion while its competitor, the real estate giant Regus, was valued at $3 billion. (Regus's more modest mission: "Our global network of workspaces enable you to work wherever you need to be, in a productive, professional environment.") In 2019, within weeks of filing for an IPO, WeWork began to unravel, bursting the $47 billion dream. Neumann was dismissed as the company fell to a $3 billion valuation. What accounts for the gap between office space and community? Surely not just good marketing. Nothing in the business changed, but the market stopped believing in community and saw the company for what it was: nice office rentals. As a real estate company, WeWork was profitably extracting yield from rents, the tried and true means of capital growth historically.

The unicorn promises to do more: to financialize what Wall Street had not dreamed of financializing: not more asset classes, but *society* itself. The market has come full circle.

Our modern visionaries at the edge of the market frontier, however, reveal a rather grim and limited vision for humanity's future. The $154 billion Vision Fund, WeWork's angel investor, is illustrative. It was started by Masayoshi Son, the founder and CEO of the multinational conglomerate SoftBank. Vision Fund's mission, as stated in its marketing documents, is to spread "happiness to everyone" and to "increase people's joy." The initial $100 billion investment in the Vision Fund came from Mohammad bin Salman, the tech-friendly Saudi known as MBS who is the de facto ruler of one of the most unequal countries in the world and whose $1.4 trillion of oil wealth is invested in several tech unicorns. Although foreign migrants toil under coercive labor arrangements akin to debt slavery and live in slumlike conditions in Saudi Arabia, the royal family's wealth is converted into "joy-spreading" visions of humanity's future.

The Vision Fund's portfolio of happiness-spreading investments are made up of a variety of tech firms specializing in AI, fintech, or e-commerce whose business is profit making but whose marketing promises are much loftier. These include:

Kabbage, an AI-based lender with "core values" including Care Deeply, Inspire Innovation, Win, Stay Connected, Unconditional Commitment, and lastly, Create Holy Shit Moments

Uber, the golden egg, whose more modest mission is "We ignite opportunity by setting the world in motion"

DoorDash, which describes its delivery service app as "just the beginning of connecting people with possibility—easier evenings, happier days, bigger savings accounts, wider nets and stronger communities"

Opendoor, a real estate broker intending "to empower everyone with the freedom to move"

Zymergen, a biotech company that is "reimagining the world" through "a combination of Darwinian selection of genetically engineered microbes combined with machine learning, analysis and automation"

Not all of these start-ups will survive, but those that do will do so by prospecting new terrain for extraction.

Funds like SoftBank's or venture capitalist firms like Andreessen Horowitz control the largest pools of money and are seeking the highest returns, which means that they place bets on companies and founders based purely on potential and vision rather than demonstrated profits. A successful venture capitalist should be a visionary themselves with the ability to predict where the market will be in five to ten years rather than where it is now. In reality, these firms create winners by investing in them. WeWork's failure notwithstanding, most founders chosen by these angel investors become unicorns immediately—the signal of trust and the resources of the firm create a virtuous cycle of more investors and more market trust. Venture capital flows predominantly to white male founders—women get 2 percent of VC funding and Black founders receive 1 percent—and a similar lack of creativity exists in the types of ventures funded; AI and crypto tend to dominate funders' visions for the future economy.

Tech's leading lights often offer the bleakest visions for the future of humanity—Zuckerberg's Meta is betting on a future where people spend most of their time in virtual reality while Peter Thiel, the right-wing libertarian who founded PayPal, seems to see a future of Hobbesian, every-man-against-every-man disorder. The group of men at the top of the tech hierarchy can certainly dream big where it comes to technology's potential to transform society, but cannot seem to escape neoliberal assumptions about the direction of that transformation. For example, in January 2022, a few tech visionaries took to the modern public square, Twitter, to debate solutions to the problem of "population collapse." The debate was in response to a tweet by Elon Musk, who now controls X (formerly

Twitter), stating, "We should be much more worried about population collapse." Sahil Lavingia, a venture capitalist and successful tech founder, quickly responded with a solution: "We should be investing in technology that makes having kids much faster/easier/cheaper/more accessible: Synthetic wombs, etc." Vitalik Buterin, the founder of Ethereum, responded with an article with data revealing a likely cause of women having fewer babies, which is a vast disparity in pay between men and women who have children—a gap dubbed the "motherhood penalty." Yet instead of proposing ideas for closing the pay gap or that the gap *should* be closed, Buterin agreed that technology was the answer: "Synthetic wombs would remove the high burden of pregnancy, significantly reducing the inequality."

Balaji Srinivas, a founder of Coinbase and an Andreessen Horowitz partner, also agreed, retweeting Buterin with an article stating that people had doubted in vitro fertilization too before it became possible, insinuating that opposition to artificial wombs should be similarly dismissed as short-sighted Luddism. These influential men are the visionaries developing and investing in the economy of the future and their response to society's problems amounts to: more technology. To the fact that, as Buterin's cited source revealed, men make anywhere between 20 to 60 percent more than equally qualified women with children, artificial wombs. To a dying planet, colonize Mars. Instead of creating a fairer system or rectifying inequalities of historic dimensions or valuing raising children more than, say, mining cryptocurrency, tech's leading visionaries aspire to create a world of efficient baby making without women.

There are a few men richer than Musk, but none who so perfectly embody the ideals of neoliberalism. Musk is a pure Randian hero: a builder and a visionary whose only pursuit is more—more attention, money, and power. Musk decries federal taxation and regulation even while his businesses rely on subsidies. By 2015, Tesla had received around $4.9 billion in federal subsidies, all before his company turned a profit, a milestone he reached in 2020. SpaceX received an added $2.89 billion contract from NASA in 2021. Beginning in 2019, Musk's SpaceX began launching Starlink satellites into space every week—he controlled more than 4,500 by July 2023, according to *The New York Times,* making up the majority of all satellites currently in space and giving Musk control over internet access around the world.[4] Even robber barons like John D. Rockefeller and Cornelius Vanderbilt could not dream of dominating a market so quickly and thoroughly as Musk has done in space. Musk purchased Twitter in October 2022 and quickly drove away users by turning the platform into a private soapbox and an engine of ad revenue generation. His reputation as a visionary genius was not diminished even as his erratic decisions drove Twitter toward near failure.

Part of Musk's appeal is his lawlessness—he treats SEC rules as a joke, criticizes public officials, and flouts social norms. Modern capitalism's heroes seem so bored with winning that they have turned their energies toward socially destructive causes. Musk's political ideology is incoherent using standard categories, but clear in its emotional core: resentment verging on hostility at the entire system of governance. And his followers resonate because Musk, like Marjorie Taylor Greene, is another antibody pointing to the same disease. It is that resonant *feeling* of things being unfair that inspires many of his followers. And just like Greene, Musk can harness it to increase his own power while attempting to weaken society and democracy even further. If Musk is the visionary corporate leader of our era, his vision is not particularly appealing. Musk opposes social justice, which he calls "wokeism," and his vision for the future of democracy is cynical and nihilistic, seemingly set on escape to Mars or offshore rather than cooperation.

Charismatic leaders appeal to their followers on an emotional level, and few have as fervent a following as Musk. By simply tweeting about a stock or a company, Musk can increase valuations beyond any carefully executed, consultant-informed business plan. For example, after Musk tweeted an endorsement of the encrypted messaging app Signal ("Use Signal"), an entirely unrelated publicly traded stock, Signal Advance, Inc., rose by over 5,000 percent. Dogecoin, created in 2013 as the first combination of a meme and a cryptocurrency, had a value of next to nothing for much of its existence—until May 2021, when Musk tweeted that he was considering accepting Dogecoin for Tesla purchases. Dogecoin subsequently rose to a market cap of $70 billion.

Most Americans cannot own Tesla stock—or enough of it to make a real difference in their net worth—but they can buy proximity to

Musk. Shut out of traditional stocks and assets, they can find profits off the fumes emitted by the sputtering engines of the financialized economy. As the longtime financial journalist Matt Levine put it, "The way finance works now is that things are valuable not based on their cash flows but on their proximity to Elon Musk.... His tweets can endow arbitrary objects with *mana*."

Musk's ability to influence the market and boost valuations gives the lie to one of neoliberal's core assumptions and signal intellectual achievements: the efficient market hypothesis, discussed in chapter 7, which holds that stock prices are accurate reflections of value because they reflect all relevant information, including a company's products, executive teams, past revenues, and predictions for future profits. But it was difficult to take neoliberal theories, even Nobel-winning ones, any more seriously than a dog meme coin in 2021 when amid a shutdown of the U.S. economy, the stock market was booming largely due to Federal Reserve interventions and stimulus checks invested in the future of memes.

"It's hard to separate what's good for the United States and what's good for Bank of America," said its former chief executive, Ken Lewis, in 2009. That was hardly true at the time, but in the intervening years as asset values continued to grow, what was good for finance and what was good for America diverged even more starkly. The numbers and metrics that measure the health and wealth of our economy measure only what can be measured: things like asset prices, market rises and dips, and interest rates. What is hidden from "the market" are the nation's many abandoned communities, increasing homeless population, and the limited potentials of those outside of the market, which is a growing number of people. The wealthiest 10 percent of Americans own 89 percent of stocks, for example. Half of the U.S. population has zero or negative wealth, while the top 1 percent owns more than 30 percent of the nation's wealth and the top 20 percent owns 86 percent.[5] On one end of the economy, the wealthy compete for yield, pushing up home and stock prices, while the other end pays more in rent and interest. The COVID crisis and its aftermath worsened the chasm between the financial world and the real world. As inequality, unemployment, and evictions climbed, the Dow Jones surged right alongside them—one line a measure of compounding suffering, the other a measure of compounding returns for investors.

The competition for yield-producing investments has led to the generation of creative new forms of assets that manufacture scarcity out of thin air, such as the non-fungible token (NFT). An innovation made possible by the blockchain—the distributed ledger network underlying cryptocurrencies—NFTs are unique digital assets that use blockchain to prove ownership and scarcity, sort of like digital collectibles or artwork. The assets themselves are usually a JPEG or a meme of something funny or artistic or interesting. The "thing"—if one can even use such a traditional descriptor—being purchased is an exclusive right to a concept. The purchase of an NFT confers upon its owner a right to say "this thing on the blockchain is mine and no one else can own it but me." Anyone can look at the image or download it, but an NFT can have only one true owner, a feature that marks a property right. That is, it is the exclusivity in ownership that made NFTs valuable.

However, scarcity is not the true mark of an asset—it is social acceptability. Only society, speaking through the law, can confer property rights. Cryptocoins and NFTs are not recognized by the U.S. legal system as assets; rather, their value is conferred exclusively by the blockchain community, which created its own pseudo-legal enforcement mechanisms. An especially fervent community of NFT boosters hyped the new asset, pushing up its yield. As economist Hyman Minsky explained it: "Everyone can create money; the problem is to get it accepted." It worked so long as people believed it worked, which is also true of most forms of money and capital.

Their extralegal character notwithstanding, the market for NFTs hit over $23 billion in 2021. That year, the NFT for a digital collage created by the internet artist Beeple sold at Christie's for $69.3 million.

The hype led to more and weirder NFTs—so long as there was a community of buyer-believers, entrepreneurs kept innovating. In 2022, the TikTok star Stephanie Matto made $200,000 selling her farts in a jar. When the shipping and handling of the physical jars became too cumbersome, she decided to launch a line of NFTs: for 0.5 in the cryptocurrency Ethereum (or $191), buyers could purchase the underlying idea of a visual representation of a fart in a jar.[6] Many did, revealing the fundamental truth about value: that it is neither fixed nor scarce.

THE CRYPTO BOOM of recent years has been led by the young and disaffected. For many, the ownership of alternative assets is less about building equity or earning a return than signaling membership in a particular group. As the cryptoinfluencer Yano Yanowitz noted in a widely shared Twitter thread, people buy NFTs to join "a passionate community." Such is the case for thirty-year-old Glauber Contessoto, a high school graduate who poured his life savings—$188,000—into Dogecoin and became a multimillionaire after Musk's tweet. Even as he lost his millions in the subsequent months as the value of Dogecoin plummeted, Contessoto not only refused to sell but purchased more, posting a screenshot of his cryptocurrency trading app to Reddit and stating, "If I can hodl, you can HODL!" (The crypto and NFT communities embrace a dogmatic version of "buy and hold" encapsulated in the slogan "hold on for dear life" or "hodl.") In June 2022, Contessoto wrote that his investment was worth only $230,000, down from a high of $3 million, and still falling. Although he regretted not taking out some when he had the chance, he wrote that "the big thing was being a part of the Dogecoin community. The whole goal for Dogecoin has always been mass adoption; to be, eventually, legal tender. . . . For us to get there, we have to all believe in the same thing. So I still feel like I was doing the right thing by holding."

Among retail-investor communities, none is more infamous than the devotees of the Reddit subthread WallStreetBets (WSB). Days after the Capitol siege, and spurred on by a supportive tweet from Musk (who typed, simply, "Gamestonk"[7]), followers of WSB took advantage of the latest generation of trading apps, especially Robinhood, to pour capital into companies like AMC Entertainment Holdings and GameStop that hedge funds had bet would lose value, or *shorted*. The largely young investors' objective was twofold: to prop up companies for which they were nostalgic—and to stick it to the hedge funds.

Unlike most retail investors, who invest in the market to earn a return, investors in so-called meme stocks see the market as a "battleground on which they join forces to right perceived wrongs and fight the powerful."[8] In the heady days at the end of 2020 and the beginning of 2021, meme-stock warriors turned toward zealotry, calling their stock buys a "revolution." Small volume traders using Robinhood's accessible and easy platform described the GameStop event as a David and Goliath standoff where the Davids won through collective action. When Robinhood halted trading amid a massive demand for meme stocks, it was revealed that the app was profiting from customer trades by selling payments for order flow (essentially, a commission made by the broker for routing trade exchanges to a particular market to large traders, including hedge funds like Citadel Capital—incidentally one of the meme-stock investors' prime targets). It was hedge funds all the way down.

A year after the WSB revolt fizzled, Mat Bowen, a Dogecoin, AMC, and GameStop trader with a divinity degree from Princeton University, told *The New York Times* that he was willing to "ride these stocks to zero . . . for my fellow citizens." The traders saw stock purchases in moral terms. "The battle of good versus evil is not just limited to the walls of a church or a synagogue or a mosque," said Bowen. For the meme-stock investors, "evil" was Wall Street and the so-called experts manipulating the market. Even traders who were just looking to make a profit, like a twenty-five-year-old named Harrison Fritz, were enraged by Robinhood's sudden halt in trading during the price surge, which resulted in widespread losses. "It created a huge, deep-seated hatred and feeling of being robbed of what could have been life-changing money for many people," Fritz said. Jesus Gonzales, a twenty-two-year-old with a finance degree and a $220,000 portfolio that includes AMC and GameStop shares, believed that owning these stocks is not like regular market trading because their purpose is to remedy a power imbalance through the formation of "the largest, most powerful decentralized hedge fund in the world."[9]

In recent years, when American politics verged into the absurd, markets also became a joke. It was hard not to see the billions of real dollars that flowed into meme stocks, meme coins, and NFTs as a sign of the nihilism that gave Trump the presidency. If the system was rigged—or at least felt rigged—why not take down some short sellers for the "lulz" (deriving from LOL—laugh out loud—lulz is defined by the Urban

Dictionary as synonymous with schadenfreude, or an LOL derived from other's suffering)? "We're living in a system where there's no such thing as justice anymore and the entire world is falling apart," said one meme-stock trader to the *Times*. "Nothing really matters, so we might as well try to have fun while we're here." The cynicism of neoliberal mythmaking was not so well hidden after all.

The meme-stock craze repels attempts at finding meaning in it—its irony and incongruity are the point. But another way to see this event is as a form of resistance and protest whose assessment of the problem is more accurate than its aims or means. Meme stocks are an antibody response to an infection, a rot, somewhere in the nation's institutions and systems. The problem is that antibodies can sometimes attack the body itself, damaging healthy structures in a misguided attempt to kill the virus. But just because some of the antibodies have gone haywire doesn't mean that they're not responding to real harm.

THE CRYPTOCURRENCY INDUSTRY began as a backlash to neoliberal hypocrisy even as it doubled down on neoliberal myths about money and society. Bitcoin sought to create the monetary system of Hayek's and Friedman's dreams—rooted in scarcity and free of state control. The explosion of cryptocurrencies and the so-called blockchain revolution began with the launch of bitcoin, which began as a reaction to the bank bailouts. In 2009, Satoshi Nakamoto—a pseudonym for the actual creator—laid out the code and logic of bitcoin. Bitcoin was a new form of currency, "mined" by computer algorithm through end-to-end encryption that would be a fixed unit of exchange existing on the blockchain. Embedded in the genesis block of code upon which all bitcoin could be "mined" was a single line of text: "The Times 03/Jan/2009 Chancellor on brink of second bailout for banks."

Nakamoto's pitch was that the supply of bitcoin, unlike the U.S. dollar, would be finite; bitcoin's code makes it impossible to "mine" more bitcoin than what was initially written into the code. Bitcoin revived the dream of a fixed and unalterable money like gold. Called "digital gold" by its promoters, bitcoin drew money and attention claiming to be a new

asset, fixed and firm and unalterable, with the same value now and forever. But there is no such thing—the libertarian dream of a stable stateless forever asset is an illusion. The gold standard ended because it made
money more, not less stable; there was always more money in circulation
through bank and government notes than gold held in reserve, which
caused a run to gold and a crisis each time the market panicked. Whether
metallic, paper, or digital, money's present and future value is a matter of
trust and belief and keeping "fear itself" at bay. Despite so much protest
and denial, money is unavoidably a creation of the state; its relative value is
determined, more or less, by social conventions and *feelings,* more or less,
people have about the future. What neoliberalism did was to make money
undemocratic. In other words, the problem with the bailout was not the
creation of money, but its destination on the bank's portfolios. In terms
of the dollar itself, the bailout was a boon to its value, which rose after the
crisis, cementing its status as the world's reserve currency, not *in spite of*
but *because of* the money-printing power of the federal government.

Bitcoin's appeal was that it offered an alternative to the unjust economy neoliberalism had created. By presenting an accessible, transparent,
decentralized, and trustworthy alternative to traditional market mechanisms, bitcoin purports to level the playing field. However, ideologically,
bitcoin is little more than a newer, purer version of neoliberalism. Friedrich Hayek dreamed of a private, stateless currency that could move
around the globe free from any state's control; Milton Friedman, for his
part, proposed at the very first MPS meeting that the money-printing
power of states be revoked and henceforth controlled by algorithm.

With limited tokens available and no possibility for more at any time
in the future, bitcoin is a high-tech gold standard that manufactures
a scarce asset which takes great effort and energy to mine. It is a nice
story that enriches the first speculators and ensures that the more people believe in the myth, the more valuable the token. It is not surprising
that bitcoin began to take hold on the libertarian right wing drawn to
the utopian possibility of money free from state power. Later investors,
including major Wall Street firms, bought bitcoin as yet another source
of yield extraction. The holy grail of an asset without society continues
to seduce idealists and speculators alike.

The result has been what can only be described as a bubble. Bitcoin is no good as a currency because of its myriad operational issues but also because its price fluctuates drastically. Measured against the dollar, which is still the only measure of value that matters, bitcoin has climbed steadily, going from being worth a few hundred dollars a coin in 2012 to a few thousand in 2016 and to $11,000 a coin in 2019.

It was at this point that states got into the bitcoin mining games, with China leading the pack. Bitcoin mines, which are industrial farms with high-speed computers working faster (and consuming drastically more energy) than amateur outfits, work around the clock to "solve" the algorithms that mine additional bitcoin, which are then sold in the market for dollars. Once these state-run enterprises formed, bitcoin's price soared from $11,000 to a high of $68,000 in 2020. Bitcoin's skyrocketing price has led to a mining frenzy, speculation and fraud, and a volatile boom-and-bust cycle whose every turn further enriches the already wealthy holders of bitcoin ("the whales").

As the cryptocurrency community has drawn more talent and investment, it has moved beyond the utopia of digital gold and experimented with other ways of creating an economy outside of the law. Ironically, some of these experiments have ended with the community demanding more law and centralization. The trend in the industry is toward the creation of mechanisms to punish fraud, resolve ownership disputes, and even hold votes to establish governance mechanisms.

A recent illustration occurred on Ethereum. Second to bitcoin in value and popularity as of this writing, Ethereum isn't simply a cryptocurrency but a decentralized blockchain platform that allows other coins to use its protocol. If bitcoin dreamt of getting the state out of money creation, Ethereum sought to get the law out of the market. By making all exchanges irreversible and self-executing, the so-called smart contract would end litigation and regulation, replacing the bloated and burdensome legal system with code.

A smart contract is a collection of code embedded on the Ethereum network and self-executing based on a preset "if-then" scenario. For example, if a social media account owner successfully induces one hundred users to purchase a product, the contract is satisfied and the account owner is paid a certain amount. Rather than relying on an out-side party, smart contracts execute automatically and are enforced by every "node" (or individual computer) connected to the blockchain. No state, legal system, or law-enforcement entity would be required in a market run on smart contracts.

Doing business using smart contracts on a decentralized platform was an appealing alternative to the mainstream economy and its complex and corrupt legal maze. For nonprogrammers frustrated by the bureau-cratic gatekeeping and abuses of power by "legacy institutions," smart contracts translate into equality and democracy; they have the potential to solve poverty, inequality, racism, and corruption. In TED talks, pod-casts, books, and forums, boosters elaborate on how the blockchain will revolutionize the economy: more "democratization," more inclusion, and greater integration of people and countries.

The main advantage of smart contracts, at least to their greatest evan-gelists, was their immutability. Just as bitcoin could not be inflated by a central bank, a smart contract could not be contested by any court. A smart contract was irrevocable, indisputable, immutable. Once the coun-terparties set the terms into the code, it would be recorded on the ledger forever and would self-enforce without any way for outsiders to stop it.

Attempting to make contracts less flexible, like pining for fixed money, was was not a vision of the market's future but a renunciation of the long-dead past—not just a revival of the gold standard but of Lochner, too. Smart contracts were an extension of the contract absolutism that led to the bank bailouts and to Law and Economics' opposition to judicial meddling in any contract, no matter how unfair. According to the logic of Law and Economics, laws harm the market's natural efficiency. Smart contracts are the ne plus ultra: code *as* law achieves maximum efficiency by eliminating even the bare minimum of discretion. But contract law has evolved over centuries not just to ensure contract execution but to achieve fairness. The flexibility of a contract is a feature of the law and not a bug.

It did not take long for the Ethereum community to see the down-sides of smart contracts. In 2016, a team of coders created the first venture capital fund on the Ethereum network, which they called the decentralized autonomous organization (DAO) fund. The DAO was touted as a harbinger of the new egalitarian future that Web 3.0 would deliver: Decisions would be made by decentralized investors rather than managers or boards of directors, and operations would be executed by smart contracts. Ernesto Frontera, a journalist who describes his beat as "the intersection of blockchain technology and human liberation," hailed the DAO as "a revolutionary" technology, the first nonhierarchical organizational form in history and "the first truly decentralized, autonomous and community-run fund ever!"[10] With similar enthusiasm, *Wall Street Journal* and *Forbes* journalists characterized the DAO as a new kind of corporate structure that could replace traditional corporate structures (board, executives, shareholders) with direct shareholder democracy. The founders of the DAO, for their part, defined the fund ambitiously, stating in the prospectus that it was "a new breed of human organization never before attempted."[11]

The DAO launched on April 30, 2016. By the end of May, it had raised $150 million, thanks largely to the fanfare about its revolutionary potential to make corporate law and traditional private equity obsolete. Two weeks later, on June 18, a hacker found a bug in the code—or a provision written into the smart contracts—that they exploited to direct approximately $50 million from the fund to their private wallet.

According to any legal code, this was theft. But according to the DAO's own legal contract, the only "law" was the immutable code written into the smart contract. (As the DAO explained in its pitch materials, "The terms of the DAO Creation are set forth in the smart contract code" and could not be changed, modified, or altered under any circumstances because "the DAO is borne from immutable, unstoppable, and irrefutable computer code.") According to the DAO, the code *is* law. And because the hack was written into the legal code—albeit unintentionally—automaticity and decentralization meant that users had no recourse. As an Ethereum expert explained in a Medium post about the hack, "There is no such thing as theft and the intent is completely unimportant—the only important and relevant thing are the smart contracts themselves."

After the hack, a group of DAO stakeholders and Ethereum developers formed a group to counter the "bad" hack with a good hack to restore the funds to investors. Other Ethereum users and developers came together to try to stop the ongoing "theft" and claw back the money that had already been taken. The developers copied the hacker's technique and managed to recover about 70 percent of the funds, but the solution was only temporary: the method would remain viable on the smart contract and thus hackers would be able to steal again. The only way to stop it permanently was a "hard fork," which would split the blockchain into two parallel networks with the new blockchain run separately from the initial blockchain—essentially, a reset button that would restart the entire Ethereum blockchain anew.

Because Ethereum runs on a purely consensus model across all the nodes, users discussed what should be done. It was an existential struggle: to the DAO and Ethereum developers who favored the hard fork, the integrity of the entire network was on the line; to the "code is law" camp who opposed it, a hard fork would compromise the very theory on which the entire enterprise was based. As one commenter explained, "How would a hard fork be any different than standard central banking procedures like 'bail-outs'?"[12] A system without bailouts—without intervention at all—was one of crypto's principal attractions.

A vote of Ethereum users was taken—only 5.5 percent participated (so much for direct democracy)—and the hard fork was approved. The angry true believers decided to stay on the original Ethereum network (now called Ethereum classic, or ETC) and penned a statement they called their "Declaration of Independence," which reiterated their belief "in the original vision of Ethereum as a world computer that cannot be shut down, running irreversible smart contracts. . . . We believe in the original intent of building and maintaining a censorship-resistant, trust-less and immutable development platform."[13] Most users went to the new fork.

In 2019, the newly forked Ethereum network (ETC) suffered a potentially game-ending $600 million hack—the largest ever. The network's governance board quickly jumped to action to fix the bug—the decision to change the "unalterable" smart contracts that had led to the hack hardly needed to be debated. By then, blockchain purists were a minority. Many other supposedly "decentralized" networks have also developed top-down controls to deal with hacks. Like other societies, the blockchain community discovered the necessity of law and governance to ensure fair play.

The problem with the legal system is not that it has discretion and judgment, but—as this book has shown—that the neoliberal revolution created a tilt in legal judgment: toward large corporations and against regular people. This must be remedied—but the problem has no technological or mathematical solution.

But *code as law* reified the legal formalism embodied in textualism and Law and Economics. "Code as law" is "text as law" or economics as law, but there is no scientific endrun around justice. The crypto communities try to build an alternative economy to escape the rigged legacy market, but in building it atop neoliberal myths about money, society, and law, they inadvertently embed the legacy ideology that caused the rigging right into their initial design.

As the cryptocurrency community has continued to run up against the same dilemmas—lack of trust by the public, exploiters, scalability, and more—they have had to re-create more rules and legal structures. Which is to say, Web 3.0 has had the same sorts of problems facing earlier versions of the Web and indeed those confronted by all societies ancient and modern—problems to which law, democracy, and judicial discretion have been the solution. Yet, the community's faith in a technological, and therefore market, fix to the problems of governance has persisted. In fact, enthusiasts propose blockchain-enabled governance as a substitute to the legacy institutions that make up modern democracy. Proposals for imposing an alternative governance system on the blockchain abound, including "liquid democracy," direct per-share voting, committee voting, where users delegate voting power to trusted community representatives, or "quadratic voting," where votes are purchased and each additional vote costs twice as much as the first.

A creative governance protocol called "futarchy" proposed by Robin Hanson, a libertarian economist at George Mason University, seeks to impose an economic model on democracy. In futarchy, citizens "vote on values, but bet on beliefs." In futarchy, voters are asked to vote only on whether they approve or disprove of their government. All other choices, including all government policies related to taxation, crime, defense, are left to market speculators who bet on which policies will likely be most successful. The assumption, foundational to all neoliberal theories, is that the market's choices and predictions are right while the people are too ignorant or confused to be capable of self-government. Efficient market theory rises from the ashes of the financial crisis to take over democracy.

While some of the most robust and creative discussions about the tensions between democracy and freedom are happening among Web 3.0 enthusiasts, the tragedy is that they begin from the premise that the current system is irremediably broken. Rather than focus on governance and legal structures to curb greed, root out corruption, or otherwise reform the system, they envision a hack to get around democracy itself.[14] The utopias being built on the blockchain revealed a deep-seated nihilism. That is because they are steeped in the dystopian logic of neoliberalism, which can only envision a system of monetary value that rewards scarcity and accumulation. The market centrism of the last several decades has so constricted the public imagination that each revolution inevitably *doubles down on the same logic that created* that market centrism. To take down Wall Street speculators, buy stocks for the people. To defeat the tech giants commodifying user behavior, further commodify the web. Locked out of a system rigged toward the interests of asset holders? Create and trade novel assets. Frustrated that the rich and powerful can "buy" votes? Join a decentralized trading platform where votes go to the highest bidders.

And yet, it is these very communities that prove that, indeed, another monetary system is possible. They, too, are antibodies attacking the diseased system with misfires along the way. The fact that so many young people took all their chips and bought Dogecoin meme stocks, NFTs, and other abstract signals of group identity is a signal of their willingness to try something new. What these experiments in the crypto market frontier reveal is the magical properties of money, like the creation of value—something from nothing—a meme to an asset, which is a way to describe all currency creation. From bitcoin to DAO to NFTs, value was mined from a single unifying story or vision—an idea about the future that inspired many people to trade one currency for another. Hope and trust, not the green bills or digibits that symbolically represent them, are the true source of value. And they are abundant. They grow only to produce more, another lesson from the crypto frontier.

The only problem with some of the visions on offer is that they aren't nearly visionary enough. They cannot seem to escape the neoliberal ideals of fixed money, contract absolutism, and a market free of society. Even as the digital economy has eliminated traditional resource constraints, the market can still only be imagined as a zero-sum competition over scarce resources with property rights allocated based on the colonial logic that the one who "owns" an asset first captures all its rewards.

What is undeniable given recent trends is that the scarcest and most valuable commodity on the current market is hope: hope for a community of human beings to thrive together on this planet, create a market that is truly win-win, and to grow the pie for everyone. The transition from here to there is not more technology, but more trust; and the payoff, if done well, is more competition. Some of the brightest systems thinkers and coders of this generation are searching for liberation on the blockchain because they cannot imagine the possibility of reform. Our democracy actually promises one man, one vote. And our market laws promise to reward innovation. Neither do because they are corroded by bad ideas, ancient laws, and bullshit.

Revealing the high absurdity of both market and governance, a 2021 *SNL* cold open was appropriately titled "What Still Works?" Kate McKinnon interviewed Marjorie Taylor Greene (Cecily Strong) and asked her whether, in fact, Google would confirm the fact that "she's a real member of the U.S. government," concluding that the government no longer works. She next turns to the market. Asked to comment on market valuations relative to company earnings is a GameStop majority holder (Pete Davidson), who responds "the whole system is a joke." His market analysis is to hoot "Stonks!" The skit moves to vaccines, democracy, and the justice system, concluding, like many of us have, that indeed "nothing works." This realization is what drove many to the alternative money market that values jokes over sophisticated risk calculations—if the system is a joke, why not profit from the absurdity.

There is a silver lining, in other words, to nothing working: everything is possible, not just blockchain and NFTs, but also achieving economic justice, building thriving real-world communities, and more. Yet the escape offered by alternative currencies has only been an escape into another rigged game, built on zero-sum asset scarcities and a distrust of society buried at its foundation. Unless those assumptions too are examined, the system of abstract assets will continue to feed on absurdity until it exhausts itself. To actually reach for hope for a profitable future, justice cannot be avoided.

The root philosophy—the "genesis block"—of our economic theory is the myth of inherent hierarchy—of race, of gender, and of the kind of genius recognized as such. Neoliberal economic theory created a meritocracy of intelligence that was rooted in achieving its own ends: the masters of the universe were stockbrokers, and the geniuses of the market—Greenspan, Summers, Posner, and the rest—were not visionaries but, rather, articulate defenders of the status quo. A financial system that produces only zero-sum thinking can lead only to scarcity for most and obscene abundance for some—this is the road to serfdom. To step out of it, we must be innovative enough to challenge our basic ideas about genius and worth.

To see the value hierarchy hidden at the core of our modern economy, we must look at its fruits. To see what a system values, we must look at what it values in dollars and cents—or *who* it trusts with abundant credit.

One need look no further than Sam Bankman-Fried and FTX. Frustrated that, as a conventional quantitative trader in the mid-2010s, he could only ever achieve 1 percent spreads at most, Bankman-Fried began to explore cryptocurrencies, specifically bitcoin, in search of higher yield. He quickly discovered that he could make much more spread in a day trading in the Asian crypto market than he could make in years of high-frequency trading. Guided by the ambition to find the most efficient use of capital possible, he began buying crypto through an online exchange and selling it within a day. It was a classic "buy low, sell high" strategy that is the one consistent rule of wealth accumulation, no matter the market. To effect these trades, Bankman-Fried found a work-around to existing market laws that required some legwork; he withdrew cash from his bank, wired the money to Asia, flew across the world, and made trades across various trading platforms because the trading market in crypto was so inefficient. This was simple regulatory arbitrage—the inefficiencies were caused by the proliferation of market regulations. Closing these kinds of efficiency gaps through arbitrage is the secret to many a billionaire's wealth, including those of George Soros, Warren Buffett, and even Jeff Bezos. Wunderkind Bankman-Fried figured out how to make a 10 percent yield in one day of trading.

Using his gains and his knowledge, in 2019 Bankman-Fried created FTX, a platform where other traders like him could speculate in crypto markets and mine for more yield. Before its spectacular collapse in November 2022, FTX was the epitome of the venture- and crypto-captialists' dream of the future of money: decentralized finance (DeFi). In the world of DeFi, counterparties trade derivatives contracts—the same weapons of mass destruction that blew up during the financial crisis—but for cryptocurrencies. Much like the financiers of the early to mid-aughts, DeFi platform founders assure investors that it is nearly impossible to lose money in cryptotrading because of the "advanced statistical models" created by quants to slice and dice cryptoassets into various securities, including—yes—mortgage-backed cryptoassets.[15]

The types of trades on FTX ran the gamut: price speculation on cryptotokens, NFTs, and derivatives of NFTs, as well as variations on sports betting and speculation in the prediction markets. Market mayhem—and likely increased boredom during the pandemic—led to incredible rates of trading on the platform, and, in turn, skyrocketing revenues. In 2020 and 2021, FTX earned $85 million in trading fees; revenue grew by over 800 percent within a year. In 2021, the site reached a daily average trading volume of $993 million, a peak that surpassed prior peaks in derivatives trading. Sam Bankman-Fried had created another merry-go-round of risky bets even more abstract and socially useless than the derivatives empire that blew up the economy, and the market crowned him their king.

At its peak in October 2021, and before Bankman-Fried was convicted on several counts of fraud, FTX had a valuation of $32 billion, and the net worth of Bankman-Fried was $25 billion plus. For comparison, GM chairman and CEO James Roche's peak salary was $822,000, which was controversial at the time.[16] Bankman-Fried was a devotee of *effective altruism*, the philosophy developed by the Oxford philosopher Peter Singer and whose adherents made money in order to give it away. Effective altruism is the ultimate resignation to living in an unjust system. The process of making billions on Wall Street so you can donate billions to charities buying malaria nets enables an ethical bypassing of significant moral questions of justice: Is it just to live in a system where a twenty-year-old numbers guy is worth billions while half the world's population needs nets to avoid a curable disease? Or is it even efficient to keep plying money to the likes of Bankman-Fried, Adam Neumann, and Elizabeth Holmes, or would it be more efficient—not to mention *just*—to invest in creativity and smarts that are not born from privilege? I would wager that there are twenty-year-old women in Africa whose intelligence rivals if not surpasses Bankman-Fried's and who could fix the malaria net issue and much more if given $30 billion of market trust. Sam Bankman-Fried is very good with numbers and figured out an ingenious way of finding loopholes around the corroded legal maze of financial regulation to make trades across borders. That skill is incredibly valuable indeed in a market that no longer works, but he is no more a genius than the clever Black kid who figures out how to make a profit selling drugs while evading the random enforcement of drug laws. In addition, while it may be argued that drugs are bad for people, the regulatory arbitrage FTX did—even before it was all revealed to be a fraud—was an end run around the law that was much more socially destructive.

Effective altruism offers the winners of a rigged system a place to put their guilt—a mathematical equation in lieu of a much harder moral calculus—while allowing the public to avoid the harder questions of systemic justice. Bankman-Fried repeatedly pledged to donate 1 percent of FTX's crypto exchange fees to charities. It was because of this pledge that Bankman-Fried was comfortable with the disparate gains conferred by capitalism; his commitment to divest himself of his riches, as he put it, "softens the notion of wealth in some ways. . . . I think I feel more comfortable with [talking about wealth] in some senses than I otherwise would because of the donations."[17]

THIS IS INDEED a meager altruism. Meager, too, are the venture capitalists' techno-utopias and the unicorns' joy spreading, community-building ventures. The blockchain revolution was hardly comparable to the worldwide global revolts of the 1960s, a testament to neoliberalism's success. And so it bears asking: Have we in fact reached the end of history?

Conclusion: The Big
Dumb Machine

I WAS ON A flight across the country when I realized that the U.S. economy had become a big dumb self-cannibalizing machine. I was returning from a short trip to Florida, where I spoke at a TIAA-CREF convention about my work on the racial wealth gap. After my talk, lingering in the convention hall, I grabbed a cool water bottle and some souvenirs for my kids at the conference booths. I had some questions, as I often do for the organizations that I speak with, and I was grateful that an executive was kind enough to answer them. They were primarily about the structure of the firm and its capital holdings.

TIAA-CREF is the leading financial adviser for more than five million teachers, firefighters, police officers, hospital workers, college professors, and people who work across a variety of public sector jobs. They manage my benefits as a University of California–Irvine employee. The five million people TIAA-CREF advises are part of the disappearing middle class whose ranks have dwindled thanks to the efficiency-minded logic of the financialized neoliberal economy. TIAA-CREF is also one of the largest financial firms in the country, with over $1 trillion of assets.

What I wanted to know was how and where and in what it invested. More specifically, did TIAA-CREF use its big capital reservoir of middle-class pensions to protect those same pensions from the punishing force of finance? The answer, obvious yet still surprising, clicked everything into place for me. It was that they invested like any other Wall Street investor—in a portfolio of private equity investments, real estate, stocks, and bonds. TIAA-CREF's investments are managed by Nuveen, an asset manager wholly owned by the firm, which competes with rivals like BlackRock, Goldman Sachs, and State Street to grow its piles of money through a mix of strategies. In other words, workers' retirement savings were fed into the same financialized market that threatened their livelihoods.

Finance has become so stupefyingly complex and fragmented that the left hand can hardly see that the right is picking its pockets. The ironic tragedy of this investment strategy was hard to see from inside the firm, let alone address by a single company. While specialists on one side of the firm deal with the hospitals, government, or university employees whose benefits they manage, the financial specialists on the other side of the same firm focus on equities, bonds, and other yield-producing investments. Each person does their job to the best of their ability as measured by their department's particular metrics of performance. One hand serves their customers, while the other hand serves them up to the private equity firms slashing and burning their way through their jobs. As universities, hospitals, and school districts are besieged by the relentless demands of the hyperfinancialized economy, their employees' retirement accounts are the very barbarians pounding at their own gate. Would it not be better to take that trillion dollars and invest in affordable housing and alternative energy? I thought this, but didn't ask it.

TIAA-CREF is a perfect example of the self-cannibalizing machine that neoliberalism has built. The opacity of the financialized market has made us unwitting accomplices to the looting of our own society.

Once I could visualize the TIAA-CREF problem, I began looking for it everywhere: following the chain of money up from investors, big and small, to the investment portfolios of financial institutions at the top. I saw how the relentless search for yield acts like gravity, pulling assets into bigger pools of money. Follow the money to the apex of the financialized market, where reside the megabanks and private equity firms who securitize and insure and collateralize and financialize every institution for more yield. Then back down to the job cuts, student debts, and increased rents that feed the capital empire. Then see those firms employ hundreds of lobbyists who turn money into laws, tax loopholes, and political power.

"Believe in the magic of the marketplace," urged Ronald Reagan, because it would deliver "growth, prosperity and, ultimately, human fulfillment . . . created from the bottom up, not the government down." What neoliberalism delivered is the exact opposite. The money did not trickle down to "lift all boats" because unlike water, money doesn't flow down naturally. It has to be pulled down. Moreover, the market is not a bottom-up phenomenon (democracy is!). The natural flow of money is toward political power and then up and away, across borders, over taxation policies, and beyond public accountability altogether. The Wall Street risk merry-go-round knows only one kind of growth—the metastatic growth of capital into more capital.

Even based on its own terms, neoliberalism has been an utter failure. The premise and promise of liberal free markets were increased market competition, more opportunity for all, fewer taxes going to wasteful government spending, and more liberty to pursue our own dreams. In fact, the government is larger, small businesses have been decimated, and it's never been more difficult for a child born to a poor family to change her fate. A few companies write the rules in each market, our politics is a maze of complexity, big firms offshored jobs and taxes, generations of college graduates are buried in debt while a college degree became a necessary but not sufficient requirement for a middle-class salary. The generational asset divide grows with boomers dominating the political branches and the housing market, while millennials can't afford to buy homes in the cities and towns where they work. As the population of homeless grows, luxury condos and office buildings sit empty in big cities. What kind of market can't build houses for everyone who wants to buy one?

Neoliberalism's magic trick was a sleight of hand that enabled a privileged few to cheat the market, loot our shared resources, and seize the ladders of opportunity. The market is neither divine nor evil; it is an algorithm designed toward its own ends. And it should be clear by now that those ends are not *our* ends. Since the 1980s, the top 1 percent's net worth increased by $21 trillion while the bottom 50 percent lost $900 billion of its wealth. And that is only the wealth we can measure. Between $10 to $32 *trillion* is currently hiding offshore in tax havens, which leaves those of us with nonsheltered incomes paying most of the tax burden.[1] The majority of the federal government's revenue—over 83 percent, according to the Congressional Budget Office—comes from income and payroll taxes paid by working Americans, while only 8 percent comes from corporations.[2]

The rising tide has helped the wealthy escape the confines of national responsibility. Perhaps no industry boomed during the pandemic as much as the production and sale of megayachts for billionaires—megayachts being the only way a hundred-billionaire can distinguish himself from a mere ten-billionaire. "The market been absolutely roaring," said a market researcher for the industry, which was worth $10 billion in 2022.[3] That same year, the World Bank reported that 700 million people were living in extreme poverty, up 70 percent from prior years. Add to that the 108 million refugees of war and climate, also in 2022, according to the United Nations, many of whom died in lifeboats trying to escape their devastated homelands. Is that a fair allocation of the world's goods to the senses of anyone alive? Does this *feel* like justice to anyone? And, most important, how long can it last?

Neoliberalism taught us to distrust the state and one another. Any attempt to right historic wrongs through collective coordination would lead to serfdom and state tyranny, whereas the freedom to contract would deliver personal liberation. The lie was that we had a choice between one group of tyrants and another, for the reality is that we are tyrannized by both a bloated government bureaucracy and a cannibalizing capital market: the guys who buy the guns and the guys who sell them.

Over the course of this book, I have analogized the problem as a virus, a cancer, a parasite, a zombie. Each of these metaphors—from the real virus to the imagined zombie—references something that operates without heart or head, driven by a singular mission of self-replication. The dystopian future of AI overpowering humanity seems at hand and it looks like our 401(k)s. The fetters of our own gold binding us to the dumb, numb market. It is our collective investments that support and protect—and even ensure the longevity of—the zombie market. The self-replicating nature of the virus means that the pools of capital will keep growing exponentially: the billions of the top 0.1 percent will soon metastasize into trillions. And as the economic chasm between rich and poor grows, so too will our political divides.

In an earlier era, Supreme Court Justice Louis Brandeis blamed J. P. Morgan and his ilk for their excessive control over law and markets— the money trusts, as they were once called, controlled their customers' deposits and thus the flow of credit, which was the life force of the economy. Things are much more complex today. To attempt to identify a singular villain is to slip into Marjorie Taylor Greene territory. The capital markets during the neoliberal decades have become so overdetermined that it is practically impossible, except in egregious circumstances, to differentiate between outright fraud or corruption on the one hand and merely "dancing while the music is playing" investing on the other.

There is no conspiracy or coordinated group of bad guys. The blame lies, rather, at the heart of the neoliberal project: that we are better off trusting the market than one another. Law and Economics convinced judges and regulators that the rational market was a better allocator of rights than the unpredictable judgments of human beings. Meanwhile, neoliberal financialization turned the market into a yield-extracting algorithm—the big dumb machine.

Neoliberal theories all rest on a model of human beings as rational, self-interested decision makers: *Homo economicus*. There is a wealth of science debunking that presumption in all spheres, but, most important, in the field of anthropology. Our species' ancient history reveals that we humans are not *Homo economicus* but *Homo trust-icus*. We evolved as community builders, and our greatest feats have required groups of humans to work toward a common goal for long periods of time. Turning polarities into harmony—that is the magic of humanity. It is trust that is the vital force underlying both state and market. And corruption that is the death knell of both.

We are all under the boot of the big dumb machine, but it's hard to see the source of the pressure through the vast multitude of corporate entities and abstract financial products. Harder still to devise a policy or political agenda to decode a viral ideology or wage war against the metastatic growth of 0s and 1s in portfolio funds. It's much easier to feel the pressure and look around for a group of humans to blame. Nor can neoliberalism be defeated through repeated debunking because its free market theories were false advertising from the start. The coup resulted in a maze of complexity and the proliferation of agencies and laws that hide what is essentially an unfair market. Financialization is killing the market by sucking money out of the economy's circulatory system—and its fruits, money in the hands of a few, is killing democracy and our ability to do anything about it.

Neoliberalism did not emerge as an economic response against socialism, collectivism, or New Dealism—its purpose was to preserve an unjust world economic order. At a time of worldwide transformation, neoliberalism fused the interests of segregationists, wealthy heirs, and the corporate tentacles of the dying empires to keep the market rigged in their favor. It was hypocrisy from the start, because these would have been the losers of democracy and truly free markets. Neoliberal economics thwarted the pursuit of justice—racial justice, first and foremost, but over time, neoliberal policies would capture the entire judicial system because the worm of hypocrisy only grows. The "spirit" of the civil rights laws and United Nations declarations of cooperation were replaced by their cold and dead "letter." Without the spirit of justice, the law is an empty and manipulable set of codes. That gap between what is legal and what is fair is where pharisaical doctrines like textualism and Law and Economics have been silently at work. The result is widespread social distrust, which has already grown into political resentment and, if left unchecked, can lead to a breakdown of rule of law. Once trust in rule of law is gone, the dictator is not far behind.

To get out from under the boot of an unthinking and unfeeling zombie, the law must be made to *feel* and the market to *think*. Neoliberalism in law is a set of formulas and textual analysis that works hard to keep feelings and intuitions out of judgments. But justice is a shared feeling that cannot be faked—it either exists or doesn't. To achieve justice, the legal system must be recalibrated to measure what is *just* rather than what is profitable. Likewise, to restore trust in our institutions, they must become trustworthy. This includes the market, which must be freed from corrupt lawmaking. Thanks to fossil fuel lobbying, for example, banks are not allowed to consider the risk of climate change in their risk management calculations. That is a market tethered to losers. Markets must be flexible and adaptable enough to pivot to new industries and have the patience to build transitional technologies, but the big dumb machine is too subservient to the demands of financialization to think beyond immediate yield-seeking.

The metabolism of our economy is off-kilter. It can't consume away the bad and dead ideologies because they made their way into the law, halting the engine of forward motion—of creative destruction and competition. We have billionaires on one end—a glut of 0s and 1s metastasizing faster than anyone can spend—while on the other end, poverty, despair, violence, with both poles stuck in mutual stagnancy when we need forward motion.

The market cannot deliver its magic unless it is competitive, dynamic, and free—to all people regardless of starting position and to all good ideas, even when they threaten an established way of doing things. Adam Smith's radical notion in *The Wealth of Nations* was that a nation's prosperity suffered when trade groups created cartels to protect their market share, yet that is the economy that neoliberalism's legal regime created. As businesses merged to profit from efficient economies of scale, our culture and politics have gone in the opposite direction—toward polarization, segregation, and atomization. This is exactly backward. Our democracy should be moving us toward merger and integration of the collective "we the people," while our market should be constantly rewarding new and innovative ideas to solve our myriad ecological and sociological problems. The wealth of tomorrow's nations will be built on solving economic chokepoints like the climate crisis, racial segregation, and rampant inequality. And neoliberalism purposefully took away the state's powers to confront each of these.

We do not need to create new programs and policies or laws and regulations—we just need a wholesale enlivening of the values that our laws claim to uphold. We must clean the hypocrisy out of the system to recover what we've lost. Understanding what ails our market and democracy amid a deluge of misinformation, myths, and outright fabrications will require precision in naming each node of disease in the system—no captured agency or harmful idea can be spared. Many of our current models of fighting corruption or excess power in one arena rely on the essential soundness of another part of the system. We expect to fix a corrupt legislature through the court system or to pass laws against election fraud, but these assumptions may not hold true once corruption becomes more rampant. Rule of law is a web of norms and expectations. So much has changed in such a short time that even the most foundational assumptions must be probed again to see if they still hold true. We cannot naïvely hold on to optimism that the bridge to justice retains its structural integrity because in fact it has already been corroded from the inside.

In 1947, Winston Churchill described democracy as "the worst form of government except for all those other forms that have been tried from time to time."[4] The famous line, which is the one most quoted by democracy's modern defenders, is both uninspiring and untrue. Untrue because no nation has yet to try democracy. The British controlled eighty-one colonies or territories at the time—the British were then dominating over 700 million people with violence. On the virtues of democracy, it was Churchill's contemporary W. E. B. Du Bois who said it best: "Our democracy is indeed pitiful in its accomplishment, but that is chiefly because we have not tried it, and not because human equality is not a defensible concept."[5] This is the challenge of our time—to save democracy, we must first and foremost try it. We do not need to tear our systems down and rebuild them from the ashes. The only radical notion that we must be willing to fully embody is the simple and obvious fact that all are equal.

As distrust and polarization have grown, our societies have become more fragmented and our governments more gridlocked. Meanwhile, the market has tied us all to one another. Capital's all-consuming spread has overcome national borders just as the COVID virus did. Just as human societies and markets have become larger and more complex, so too did the nature of risks like viruses. Technology has drawn ever larger groups of people together such that the "en-" of the endemic became the "epi" of the "epidemic," until finally, we have entered the era of "pandemics." As reflected in the terms "pan-African" and "pan-Asian," the "pan" (meaning "all") is meant to extend the *demos* to all people. The risks that humanity will confront in the future, whether viral COVID or viral capital, will be of the pan variety. And yet with risks come opportunities. The COVID-19 virus was also the first time many of us began to see the veins and sinews of the economy, the supply chain of which we were but just one consuming node. While money and viruses travel the globe through high-speed trading networks, so too do ideas, videos, dances, songs, and protests, stretching our moral imagination and empathy. It is almost as if the virus had to show us humans, the last to know, that our globe has been operating as a single panhuman organism.

THIS BOOK was very difficult for me to finish—I spent too much time reading too much material and then writing thousands of words that never made it into the final draft. I got especially obsessed with chapter 2, about colonial revolts around the world. I had to step away from the draft when I finally realized that I was doing the thing you are not supposed to do as an academic: "Me-search." I was trying to figure out why what happened to me had happened to me.

I was born in April 1978 in a free Iran on the verge of collective democracy. Before I learned to walk, the impossible occurred. The fundamentalist fascists took power and began executing, torturing, and imprisoning regular Iranians. Before the revolution, Western leaders, especially Kissinger and Nixon, had allied with the Shah and heralded Iran as a lodestar of secular modernity and free markets. By 1979, it was the example that other extremists would follow. While many still see the Middle East as a place prone to violence and fundamentalism, the truth is that Iranians were no more murderous or hateful than any other group of people. No more righteous either, but they had been, one and all, sick of their corrupt government.

The 1978 revolution was the third nonviolent mass revolution in twentieth-century Iran—the earlier attempts at sovereignty had been violently vetoed by foreign oil interests. This third revolution succeeded in removing the tentacles sucking out Iran's oil and vitality, but through violence and systematic terror. To maintain control over the Iranian population, the newly formed Islamic Republic of Iran murdered hundreds of thousands of people in mass executions. Another hundred thousand boys were sent to martyrdom during the eight-year war with Iraq that spanned my entire childhood in Tehran. The fascists repressed millions into silence in their homes while every Iranian not already in prison lived in terror that they were next. In fact, when my mother was taken one night from our home during a family dinner, a bag placed over her head, her body put in the back of a truck in the cold winter, and driven to certain torture or death, she recalls feeling an overwhelming feeling of relief that finally, the terror she had been trying to keep at bay had come for her. My mother served three and a half years for joining with other Iranian mothers to protest the war. My mother is a saint and a hero, but she was no revolutionary leader—just an average young mother of two who had, like the vast majority of Iranians, joined the revolution to oust the Shah and stayed faithful to the principles of democracy that it had sought.

The mullahs jailed, raped, and murdered until the dissent stopped and then continued to anyway. They tortured each prisoner until they divulged more names. My mother did not give up a single name, which is why she was not released like the other mothers. My mother no longer recognized these men—who had been regular Iranians but had become zombies with guns. The long struggle for democracy and free speech that she had given up everything to pursue had, in many of the men and women of the newly formed Islamic Republic of Iran, hardened into resentment and kept hardening until it signaled only murder in their dead eyes. In prison, hundreds of women slept on crowded and cold floors squeezed side by side and listened each night to the executions in the yard counting one bullet after another into an Iranian head that had dared to dream of freedom. My mom was shocked by the murders only one particular night, when a girl of twelve was taken out to the yard.

So why did the fascists persuade a group of Iranians to murder their way to power? The short answer is that decades of festering corruption and injustice turned some of my people's righteous anger into resentment and then cynical, murderous rage. Iran was the first nation taken over by Islamic terrorists and they have yet to loosen their grip. For forty-five years, they have ruled by no ideology but power and violence. And no one has suffered more than Iranian girls—many of whom are taken into custody for infractions like showing their hair. Once arrested, they are raped or killed, as in the case of Mahsa Amini in September 2022. Her death launched the fourth mass protest of Iranians for self-rule and independence. The mass protests had no leaders and no agenda, just a slogan: "Women, life, freedom!" More than five hundred people have been murdered in the nonviolent nationwide protest, and thousands have been injured. The bravery of Iranians taking the streets to protest while facing certain death was truly something to behold. With prison or death hanging over them, these girls danced in the streets and burned their mandatory hijabs. Whole communities marched, as soldiers fired metal pellets blinding hundreds of protesters. A popular protest chant urged, "Don't be afraid, we are all together!" Power like hope, trust, and money, is not a scarce resource. As the king-toppling American Revolution also proved, power shrinks when hoarded and multiplies when shared.

I was desperate and despondent during the protests—the girls being killed looked just like my own teenage daughters. And as a refugee from the same corrupt regime, I felt a sense of survivor's guilt and helplessness. And worst of all, I felt complicit. The reason I had asked the TIAA-CREF executive about their investments during that trip to Florida was because I had seen it in my own life. In early 2021, when I was being vetted by the incoming Biden administration for the job of the nation's top banking regulator, I had to list out every single stock I owned. I had never purchased stock myself but I had signed a paper at each of my jobs to have some portion of my salary go into a 401(k), which would be placed in some sort of fund. But now I needed to go into my 401(k) and see what the actual stocks were that made up that diversified portfolio. And they were what you might expect—blue-chip stocks that make good returns. Still, it was quite something to see that all this time I had been writing about a system that I invest in: Exxon, Raytheon, JP Morgan Chase, and so on. My own gold had been feeding the big dumb machine that I was writing about all this time. That same big dumb machine that I knew, based on historical research, personal experience, and gut feeling, would continue to strangle democracy until a committed group of fascists won enough support to take over.

I did not become the nation's top banking regulator—not because I wasn't qualified, but because the Democrats didn't have fifty-one votes to confirm anyone for the position. I would have been the first woman, the first minority, and according to the Treasury officials I worked with on my disclosures, the first nominee who had a mortgage on their house. I would also have been the first comptroller in a few decades who wouldn't be coming in or going out of the government through the revolving door. After eight months of vetting and waiting, my nomination was dropped without explanation. In fact, the seat was ultimately filled by an acting comptroller without Senate confirmation, likely because the administration knew that no nominee would probably pass muster. The President could not—or did not—appoint a reformer to one of the most powerful executive positions in his government. Why? For all the reasons covered in the preceding pages of this book—but in short, because the party and the industry could not agree on a nominee. The close-up encounter with the gears and levers of policy making was discouraging and somewhat surprising. I was not naïve about politics, but I thought we still had time.

The reason to consider the enduring power of neoliberalism and to attempt to fight it is that the fascists are coming, and we have already lost access to at least some of the levers of reform. We cannot predict whether the loss of our rights will occur slowly or suddenly and from which election cycle, but we can be sure that when the felt sense of injustice is pervasive and the political system keeps delivering more of the same, the people will reach for a remedy in revolution. This is surely where the Trump-Greene rhetoric will end—the warning shots have already been fired. And even if we voters continue to reject their scapegoating and racism, the political system may already be too corrupted to deliver justice.

Political revolution is an appealing response to perceived corruption—*"Que se vayan todos"* (Get rid of all of them) is a common rallying cry in Latin American nations, and similar sentiments have been voiced elsewhere. Yet political revolution is a dangerous answer to corruption because the resulting chaos can deliver power to the most power-hungry or violent revolutionaries. The Iranian mass revolution did just that: the fascists took over, quickly jailed and killed the rest of the revolutionaries, and began a decade of war and martial law. As a refugee of that violence and suppression, I am as worried about what could go wrong after the revolution as I am about the dangers of merely hoping for change. Not seeing a way out of this mess was one of the reasons this book was so difficult for me to finish. Finding hope and solutions came eventually, but only after I shifted my focus away from the government and toward the free market. I now believe that for those of us fighting for economic justice, it is time to look toward the market for solutions, if only because money now has more rights than voters and corporations more than governments.

It may seem counterintuitive to conclude that the way to defeat free market dogma is through the market, but it is only so because neoliberal myths have sold us a lie about markets as zero-sum competition over scarce resources. Neoliberalism was not the triumph of capitalism over state power, but the corruption of both for the sake of a minority of interested parties. The neoliberal coalition did not want trade on fair terms, so they rigged the game.

I have spent my career thinking of ways to unrig it, joining my progressive friends in government or nonprofits to push for legal change, assuming that the government was a better vehicle for change and progress than the market. Researching and writing this book changed my mind. The silver lining of a political system where money controls politics is just that—money can change politics. Perhaps faster than the government can while it is being held hostage by the angriest members of society.

WE CAN and must revive that market magic which invests in the future through the currency of trust. As this book goes to press, I am at work designing investment vehicles that could invest in people and communities using simple structures and complete transparency. I am convinced that without a truly innovative and adaptive free market, we cannot adequately face the risks and challenges which humanity will face in the coming years.

I am equally certain that we cannot have a free market without true equality of opportunity, which means remedying historic injustices—we must level the playing field before we can even start to play. We need not wait for politicians to do this necessary work, nor should we give up on democracy or our political leaders.

There is nothing inherent in the institutions of government— the Senate or judiciary—or the institutions of the market— corporations—that ensure morality or trustworthiness. Corporations and governments are made up of people and laws that can be either followed or distorted. And in fact, most people distrust both equally. That is the dilemma: bullshit on the one hand, leading to fascism on the other.

My hunch is that a smart market can achieve justice faster than the government because of what I know about the people that neoliberalism got so wrong. I believe that investing equally in all people and in all communities is not only right but profitable. Not profitable in the short term like a derivative or cryptocurrency, but profitable in the long term like a bond, treasury note, or a 401(k). So long as our savings accounts are locked up and out of reach until we're ready to retire, why not forgo immediate profits now for long-term returns—instead of safe investments like oil and weapons, why not take a chance on housing and education? Instead of efficient yield extraction, why not a slow investment with a large upside? I am confident that if we invest now in the "riskiest" neighborhoods, least capitalized industries, and most overlooked groups of people, our portfolios will see greater gains in the next twenty years. Is it risky? Yes, because the future is always unknowable.

Investors must compare the risks themselves, doing the math and investing their long-term savings accounts into companies building a future they would be happy to inhabit. The big dumb machine has stopped investing in the future, which is bad news for us. The shortsighted math of risk management that guides most investors pegs our future investments to present conditions; even so-called futures markets can see only as far into the future as the Fed's next rate cuts. And visionary venture capital funds, the supposed "smart money," are betting on a future that is the same as the past—but with rockets. The same tech investors who promised that the blockchain would solve all our problems and invested accordingly are now all-in on AI. The current market cannot even imagine, let alone invest in, a future different from today. Maintaining the status quo of broken markets and broken democracies means that there are no institutions capable of mounting a coordinated response to present risks, let alone future risks.

Investors must be able to assess risks holistically and in the long term and put their money into the future they choose. Voters and consumers must be able to metabolize bad ideas faster than our corroded and formalized legal system allows. And the market must bet on a future of growth and prosperity if it is to achieve it. Take guns, for example. Some of the highest earning corporations are large gun manufacturers and military suppliers. In fact, military spending is the U.S. government's biggest expense. Half of the federal discretionary budget goes toward military spending—and if we are invested in typical blue-chip stocks, our retirement accounts are also invested in the suppliers of the military. Imagine what Boeing and Lockheed Martin could build if they weren't supplying the government with weapons, and imagine what the government could spend on without so much going to weapons, many of which are now in the hands of former enemies like the Taliban. Endless war is not only immoral and destructive, it is inefficient. Our collective scientific knowledge is too far advanced, our technology too developed, and our markets too interconnected for so much capital invested in a future of more guns.

The current market is wrong about the nature of value. Value is not a resource to be mined, extracted, and hoarded. Value is flexible, co-created, and plentiful. We can all be better off if we aim for equality—we have the resources, talent, and technology to achieve justice without sacrifice, but that is not where the big dumb machine is taking us. The neoliberal market has been a failure because it was based on fear of change. Its driving motive was to halt the progress that the majority of the world's people supported, dooming it from the start. Doomed because racism is not only harmful and hurtful but wasteful and unproductive. Neoliberalism was doomed by the closed-mindedness of its progenitors who built scarcity and rigidity into the system itself. A fearful market will invest in guns over schools, and it will not thrive. Fear drives scarcity, which leads to corruption as a few interest groups divide up a shrinking pie. We can change it by seeing the reality of money and markets—it's always been us all along. Our trust is what makes the system run—take that away and the system falls. It is falling as trust becomes the market's scarcest resource. We can restore trust only by making our society just. But Americans do not need to wait on a Supreme Court opinion, a congressional bill, or an election—we can start with our investments. The way to show trust in people is to invest in them. We must start with the people at the margins—the communities written off by myths about an inherent hierarchy of human value corresponding exactly to a history of colonialism.

Of all the mistaken beliefs of neoliberals, the one that stood out most starkly was their blind faith in quantification—of everything from risk to genius. Knowing just a little bit about the world, these men used their measurements to dismiss whole populations and people as incapable of trade and innovation. IQ tests are a good example. The idea that such a thing as human intelligence could be captured on one test originated not with someone endowed with genius themselves, like Einstein or Du Bois, but with Francis Galton, Darwin's less gifted cousin, who wanted to understand how and why his cousin succeeded in tests while he struggled. That idea—which became social Darwinism, was picked up by American eugenicists as well as by the Nazis, and has since evolved into Charles Murray's bell curve—serves as the basis of many standardized tests. Contrast that with Middle Eastern ideas about genius, which was ascribed to the *jinn*, the muse, or even the genie, which exists as a source of knowing that can be accessed by any human being. This rings truer than saying that all genius can be reduced to a multiple choice test—and that these tests happen to reveal that white men are disproportionately endowed with genius compared to other races. Yet this idea of quantifiability and inherent value underlies so many neoliberal theories and programs that justify the historic allocation of resources. And the arrogant reliance in the neoliberals' own tests and metrics to quantify such complex human mysteries as creativity and genius has made the market blind to new ideas and values.

Neoliberals looked at the world's nations and saw commodities—copper in Chile, oil in the Middle East, and so on. People were either field hands, factory hands, or a drain on public resources. How can those views coexist with a free market? They cannot. The market has reached the end point of commodities extraction and the end point as well of a certain form of white mathematical genius (for example, Lawrence Summers or Sam Bankman-Fried). It is time to actually consider investing in different sources of value—who knows what kind of genius will emerge out of the educated women of Afghanistan, or the children of rural Appalachia and Ferguson, Missouri? Any venture capitalist or angel investor looking to invest in "outside the box" innovations or disruptive unicorns must themselves be able to look for talent outside the standard pipelines and their self-reproducing metrics. Having marinated for so long in racist mythology and political corruption, the market will continue to heap future rewards on past winners. Growing future geniuses requires investing in exactly those communities and people who have been least invested in, thanks to the mistaken nations of past regimes beholden to dogmas, old and dead.

Historically, the federal government was best suited to dedicate the resources required to make long-term investments in people and technologies. But the government's power to make bold investments has diminished due to corruption and distrust. Yet the power remains where it has always resided: in us, our choices, our investments, our shared vision, which have always been the force that created nations and corporations. That power, the magic that enlivens the market, is still alive. It resides outside the big dumb machine, in teenage girls launching spontaneous mass protests—and in each of us willing the future into being by investing in it. Each of us who owns stock can start by rethinking where to invest our money. And those lucky few of us who are asset managers, private equity managers, or the children of billionaires can decide if we want to use our power to keep the big dumb machine going and take our chances with the fascists, or to invest in actual returns on our equity.

The revolutions that rippled across the globe in the 1960s—in the interregnum between the era of empire and the global order to follow—coalesced, more or less, around a demand for freedom, political and economic. Neoliberalism suppressed these movements by co-opting their cause and weaponizing their language. Freedom, under neoliberalism, was narrowed to mean market freedom, which amounted to no more than freedom for shareholders to demand maximum profits. The global revolutions failed, and freedom remains as elusive as ever. And wherever we live on the spectrum of free nations on earth, we can all sense that our freedom is tied, umbilically, across the spectrum of human experiences such that none of us can be totally free insofar as we inhabit a world where to fall outside of a wall or document or home mortgage is to be subjected to violence, destitution, and tyranny. We have become too interconnected as a species to comfortably look away from such wide-scale injustices. Making things fair is the only way to enjoy the benefits of free trade; so, too, is justice, the necessary prerequisite to freedom and liberty. When there is a scarcity of freedom across the globe, freedom will continue to be a fragile commodity always under threat.

Milton Friedman was right that freedom is tied to capitalism—you need one to have the other—but it is not capitalism that can yield freedom, but the other way around. Free markets do not exist without the freedom to trade. This is what the 1776 revolutionary tracts, Jefferson's declaration, and Smith's *Wealth of Nations* were after. The problem with the free market is the same as the one with democracy: it must be tried.

To Thomas Paine, it was "common sense" that "all men being originally equals, no one by birth could have a right to set up his own family in perpetual preference to all others forever."[6] But it wasn't yet common sense that women or other races were equal, and so the 1960s Civil Rights Acts, the international charters, "nonaligned" pacts, and treatises of coexistence had to say it again. And again, new ideologies took hold to re-create the old order of empire.

But time rends. We are again at this precipice—justice and freedom and peace, or guns and fear and separation.

What is undeniable is that our global humanity—because the most commonsensical truth is that we are already a connected whole—will tip in one direction or another. And soon. Because the current state of precarious inequality is unsustainable.

My bet is that we make it. And we make it by betting on it—by investing in the future we want instead of the future being created by the big dumb war machine. Tear down all the walls and begin building and trading together, or continue on with the yachts and lifeboats.

We have no scarcity of resources, land, or genius to create abundance for all, but rather, we have a scarcity, a meagerness, a usury of trust. Until we expand the net of freedom over all people, we will continue to fight over imaginary scarcities while one side of humanity hides from the other. The growth of our economies, our technologies, and our markets depend on a stitching together of the artificially rent fabric of humanity. The market requires trust. Free markets require individual liberty. But once combined, they can produce so much more, like the money-multiplying power of good faith and credit. The free market can multiply prosperity indefinitely, but its denominator must be justice. Or put another way, to orchestrate the melody of free enterprise, we must begin with the harmonizing power of justice. Opportunity for all must mean opportunity *for all* if we are to see the best humanity has to offer. We are nowhere close to the potential of global free trade—not when children everywhere must study under the threat of war and the trauma of poverty in an era of plenty.

In other words, we can all have justice, freedom, and even market magic, but only if we have them in fact and not in theory. We must clean out these principles of their historic hypocrisy and go after each and all without sacrificing any group of people.

Acknowledgments

I AM DEEPLY GRATEFUL to so many people for making this book possible, especially to my agent, Amy Berkower, for trusting me and making this book possible, and my editor, Daniel Gerstle, for his deep and substantive engagement with each draft of this book. Thank you to the Hewlett Foundation (and Larry Kramer and Brian Kettering in particular), for your visionary commitment to this project through a grant that gave me the time to write.

I wrote and rewrote this book so many times and I am profoundly grateful for the thoughtful editorial help from Asia Meana, Jed Cohen, Trent Duffy, and Rebecca Homiski, as well as to Daniel Gerstle again, for your help revising, shaping, outlining, and trimming so many words. Thank you, Sol Solis, for paying meticulous attention to the manuscript in its final editing stage. I am grateful for the help of my talented and hardworking research assistants, Adriana Perera, Nasser Khateeb, Jake Hermansen, Adrienne Pham, Alex Mayeda, Joanna Yam, and Talha Muhammad, for researching, fact-checking, sourcing, footnoting, and bettering the project. Thank you to my heroes, the UCI law librarians, for sending me so many articles, books, and random documents over several years, especially Christina Tsou, Amy Atchison, and Ellen Augustiniak. Thank you, Stacy Tran, for organizing chaos into order for this project and more.

Thank you to my UCI Law and Northwestern Law students,

especially those in my Race, Law and Capitalism class—your insightful comments, research papers, and presentations inspired many of the ideas and connections in this book. Thank you to friends and colleagues who read and commented on this project at various workshops, faculty talks, and roundtables, including at UCI, UGA, Northwestern, Columbia, Wharton, and Harvard law schools—I am grateful for your attention and thoughtful engagement with my work. Thank you to my family: Madar and Baba, for bringing joy and strawberries to my door every Sunday; Cyra, Lucia, Ramona, Shima, Hediyeh, Darius, Pete, Ryan, Jared Bybee, thank you for reading every word and listening to me rant about Nixon, for your encouragement, support, consultation on naming the book, and for tolerating my assorted obsessions.

Notes

INTRODUCTION

1. Katherine Blunt, "Inside the Investigation That Secured a Guilty Plea for 84 Wildfire Deaths," *Wall Street Journal*, August 25, 2022.
2. Alex Wigglesworth, "PG&E to Pay More than $55 Million to Avoid Criminal Prosecution for Starting Two Wildfires," *Los Angeles Times*, April 11, 2022.
3. Brandon Rittiman, "ABC10 Investigation: PG&E Knew Old Power Line Parts Had 'Severe Wear' Months Before Deadly Camp Fire," abc10.com, February 16, 2021.
4. "Fundraising Totals: Who Raised the Most?" OpenSecrets, accessed July 8, 2023.
5. William Coleman, "John Maynard Keynes," *Quadrant* 30, no. 3 (1986): 44–48.
6. John Maynard Keynes, *The Economic Consequences of the Peace* (London: Macmillan, 1919), 268.
7. Ivan Penn, "PG&E Ordered to Pay $3.5 Million Fine for Causing Deadly Fire," *New York Times*, June 18, 2020; "Corporation's Revenue 2022," Statista, April 12, 2023 (yearly revenues are calculated at $201.68 billion).
8. Penn, "PG&E Ordered to Pay $3.5 Million Fine."
9. Anita Chabria and Taryn Luna, "PG&E Power Outages Bring Darkness, Stress and Debt to California's Poor and Elderly," *Los Angeles Times*, October 11, 2019.
10. Mark Specht, "California Utilities Shut Off Power for Fewer People, but Too Many Are Still in the Dark," *Equation*, February 2, 2022.
11. The CPUC has a mandate to "serve the public interest by protecting consumers and ensuring the provision of safe, reliable utility service and infrastructure at reasonable rates": "Consumer Affairs Branch," California Public Utilities Commission, accessed July 8, 2023.

12. Katherine Blunt and Russell Gold, "'Safety Is Not a Glamorous Thing': How PG&E Regulators Failed to Stop Wildfire Crisis," *Wall Street Journal*, December 9, 2019.

13. Blunt and Gold, "'Safety Is Not a Glamorous Thing.'"

14. Lily Jamali, "Hedge Funds Cash Out Billions in PG&E Stock; Fire Survivors Suffer and Wait," KQED, October 11, 2021.

15. Matthew D. Kearney, Shawn C. Chiang, and Philip M. Massey, "The Twitter Origins and Evolution of the COVID-19 'Plandemic' Conspiracy Theory," *Harvard Kennedy School Misinformation Review* 1, no. 3 (2020).

16. "Protestors Criticized for Looting Businesses Without Forming Private Equity Firm First," *Onion*, May 28, 2020.

17. "Mobile Homes," *Last Week Tonight with John Oliver*, HBOMax, April 7, 2009, 15:38.

18. Barbara Jeanne Fields, "Slavery, Race and Ideology in the United States of America," *New Left Review* 1, no. 181 (May–June 1990).

19. "John Adams to Thomas Jefferson, with Postscript by Abigail Adams, 20 June 1815," Founders Online, National Archives and Records Administration.

A NOTE ON TERMINOLOGY

1. Milton Friedman, "Neo-liberalism and Its Prospects," *Farmand*, February 17, 1951, 89–93.

2. Friedman, "Neo-liberalism and Its Prospects." Friedman wrote that "neo-liberalism would accept the nineteenth-century liberal emphasis on the fundamental importance of the individual, but it would substitute for the nineteenth century goal of laissez-faire as a means to this end, the goal of the competitive order," which he believed required limited state intervention, including stable money, police power, limited social services to prevent abject poverty, and the prevention of monopolies in order to foster competition.

3. Sean Illing, "Neoliberalism and Its Discontents," *The Gray Area*, Vox, Apple Podcasts, October 24, 2019.

4. John Maynard Keynes, *The General Theory of Employment, Interest and Money* (London: Macmillan, 1936).

CHAPTER 1: THE STRANGE CAREER OF NEOLIBERALISM

1. Alan Greenspan to Richard Nixon, "Subject: The Urban Riots of the 1960s," September 26, 1967, Campaign Files, Richard Nixon Presidential Library, Yorba Linda, California (copy on file with author).

2. Sebastian Mallaby, *The Man Who Knew: The Life and Times of Alan Greenspan* (New York: Penguin, 2016).

3. Mallaby, *Man Who Knew*, 93.

4. He had come recommended by Columbia professor Marty Anderson, Greenspan's

mentor and a close friend of Rand and Goldwater. Anderson, though little known, has been credited as the intellectual father of various Republican economic initiatives, from Nixon's Black capitalism program to so-called Reaganomics.

5. Mallaby, *Man Who Knew.*

6. Farrell Evans, "1967 Summer Riots in Detroit and Newark: The Kerner Commission," History.com, last updated June 21, 2021.

7. James Ridgeway and Jean Casella, "Newark, New Orleans, and the Myth of the Black Sniper," *Mother Jones,* July 2007.

8. Michael Newton and Judy A. Newton, *Racial and Religious Violence in America: A Chronology* (New York: Garland, 1991).

9. Joshua Bloom and Waldo E. Martin, *Black Against Empire: The History and Politics of the Black Panther Party* (Berkeley: University of California Press, 2013), especially Introduction, pt. 5, and accompanying notes; Kenneth O'Reilly, *Racial Matters: The FBI's Secret File on Black Americans, 1960–1972* (New York: Free Press, 1989).

10. U.S. Congress, Senate, Committee on the Judiciary, *Hearing on Nomination of Thurgood Marshall of New York to Be Associate Justice of the Supreme Court of the United States*, 90th Cong., 1st sess., 1967, vol. 261 (Washington: GPO, 1967).

11. *Report of the National Advisory Commission on Civil Disorders* (Kerner Commission Report, 1968); see also Julian E. Zelizer, "Fifty Years Ago, the Government Said Black Lives Matter: The Radical Conclusions of the 1968 Kerner Report," *Boston Review,* May 2016.

12. *Report of the National Advisory Commission on Civil Disorders*; Julian Zelizer, *The Kerner Report* (Princeton, NJ: Princeton University Press, 2016), Introduction.

13. Ronald Reagan, "April 29, 1967 Speech by Governor Ronald Reagan Before the University of Southern California Law Day Luncheon, Los Angeles," Ronald Reagan Presidential Library, Simi Valley, California.

14. Fred Powledge, "Polls Show Whites in City Resent Civil Rights Drive: Majority Queried in Times Survey Say Negro Movement Has Gone Too Far, but Few Intend to Change Votes," *New York Times,* September 21, 1964.

15. Mallaby, *Man Who Knew.*

16. Undoubtedly, Greenspan would have recoiled at Buchanan's antisemitism. In fact, Greenspan recalled being "absolutely devastated" when he heard Nixon rant about "the blacks" and "the jews" being "out to get him." See Mallaby, *Man Who Knew*, 121.

17. See, generally, Nicole Hemmer, *Partisans: The Conservative Revolutionaries Who Remade American Politics in the 1990s* (New York: Basic Books, 2022). Hemmer describes Buchanan as a precursor to Trump.

18. J. Christopher Schutz, *Jackie Robinson: An Integrated Life* (Lanham, MD: Rowman & Littlefield, 2016).

19. Mallaby, *Man Who Knew*, 107–8.

20. Ayn Rand and Nathaniel Branden, *The Virtue of Selfishness: A New Concept of Egoism* (New York: New American Library, 1964).

21. Greenspan to Nixon, "Subject: The Urban Riots of the 1960s," September 26, 1967.

22. Greenspan to Nixon, "Subject: The Urban Riots of the 1960s," September 26, 1967.

23. David Caplovitz, *The Poor Pay More: Consumer Practices of Low-Income Families* (New York: Free Press, 1967), xxvi.

24. Donald J. Harris, "The Black Ghetto as Colony: A Theoretical Critique and Alternative Formulation," *The Review of Black Political Economy* 2, no. 4 (1972): 3–33.

25. Mallaby, *Man Who Knew*, 108.

26. Greta R. Krippner, *Capitalizing on Crisis: The Political Origins of the Rise of Finance* (Cambridge, MA: Harvard University Press, 2011), 70.

27. Dan Baum, "Report: Legalize It All: How to Win the War on Drugs," *Harper's Magazine*, June 2013.

28. Milton Friedman, *Capitalism and Freedom* (Chicago: University of Chicago Press, 1962), 109–15.

29. Brad DeLong, "Weekend Reading: George Stigler in 1962 on 'The Problem of the Negro,'" *Grasping Reality on TypePad*, May 2019.

30. Mallaby, *Man Who Knew*, 123.

31. John A. Farrell, "Nixon's Vietnam Treachery," *New York Times*, December 31, 2016.

32. Richard Nixon, "Address Accepting the Presidential Nomination at the Republican National Convention in Miami Beach, Florida," August 8, 1968, Nixon Library.

33. Draft speech, Human Dignity, 4/6/68, labeled RN's Copy, File 8, ARRA 24, Nixon Library (copy on file with author).

34. Nixon campaign ad, "The Wrong Road" (on file with author).

35. Arthur I. Blaustein and Geoffrey P. Faux, *Star-Spangled Hustle* (Garden City, NY: Doubleday, 1972).

36. William F. Buckley Jr., "On Black Capitalism," *National Review*, March 25, 1969; Dean Kotlowski, "Black Power Nixon Style: The Nixon Administration and Minority Business Enterprise," *The Business History Review* 72 (1998): 418; Gerald S. Strober and Deborah H. Strober, *Nixon: An Oral History of His Presidency* (New York: HarperCollins, 1994), 110.

37. William F. Buckley Jr., "Why the South Must Prevail," *National Review*, August 24, 1957.

38. Buckley, "On Black Capitalism."

39. Dean J. Kotlowski, *Nixon's Civil Rights: Politics, Principle, and Policy* (Cambridge, MA: Harvard University Press, 2002), 135–36.

40. Robert E. Weems and Lewis A. Randolph, *Business in Black and White: American Presidents and Black Entrepreneurs in the Twentieth Century* (New York: New York University Press, 2009), 105n57, citing a memorandum from Howard J. Samuels to Matthew Nimetz, dated September 27, 1968.

41. Mallaby, *Man Who Knew*, 125.

CHAPTER 2: EMPIRE'S NEW CLOTHES

1. William J. Barber, *Gunnar Myrdal: An Intellectual Biography* (Basingstoke, Eng.: Palgrave Macmillan, 2008).

2. Leonard Silk, "Nobel Award in Economics: Should Prize Be Abolished?" *New York Times*, March 31, 1977; Friedrich August von Hayek, Speech at Nobel Banquet, December 10, 1974.

3. Avner Offer and Gabriel Söderberg, *The Nobel Factor* (Princeton, NJ: Princeton University Press, 2019), 102.

4. "Nixon Reportedly Says He Is Now a Keynesian," *New York Times*, January 7, 1971.

5. Aimé Césaire, *Discourse on Colonialism* (New York: Monthly Review Press, 2001).

6. Hannah Arendt, *The Origins of Totalitarianism* (New York: Harcourt Brace Jovanovich, 1973).

7. John Locke, "Second Treatise," Chap. V, On Property, *Two Treatises on Government* (London: Phoenix, 2010), §§ 25–51, 123–26.

8. Friedrich A. von Hayek, *The Road to Serfdom* (Chicago: University of Chicago Press, 1944), 53.

9. Clayborne Carson, ed., *The Autobiography of Martin Luther King, Jr.* (New York: Warner/Hachette, 1998), 301.

10. David Lewis, *W. E. B. Du Bois: A Biography, 1868–1963* (New York: Henry Holt, 2009), 687.

11. Thomas Paine, *Common Sense: And Other Writings* (New York: Modern Library, 2003), 11.

12. Frantz Fanon, *The Wretched of the Earth* (New York: Grove, 1968).

13. Paine, *Common Sense*, 15.

14. "Speech by President Sukarno of Indonesia at the Opening of the Conference," *Asia-Africa Speaks from Bandung* (Jakarta: Ministry of Foreign Affairs, Republic of Indonesia, 1955), 23; see also Louis Menand, *The Free World: Art and Thought in the Cold War* (New York: Farrar, Straus and Giroux, 2021), 781.

15. Mont Pelerin Society, "Statement of Aims," MontPelerin.org, accessed July 7, 2023.

16. Jamie Peck, *Constructions of Neoliberal Reason* (New York: Oxford University Press, 2010), 279–80.

17. "The Sveriges Riksbank Prize in Economic Sciences in Memory of Alfred Nobel 1974," NobelPrize.org, accessed July 7, 2023.

18. Christopher R. Dietrich, "Mossadegh Madness: Oil and Sovereignty in the Anticolonial Community," *Journal of Human Rights, Humanitarianism, and Development* 6, no. 1 (Spring 2015): 63–78.

19. Mohamed Abdul Khalek Hassouna, *The First Asian-African Conference Held at Bandung Indonesia* (Cairo: League of Arab States, 1955), 42.

20. Quinn Slobodian, *Globalists: The End of Empire and the Birth of Neoliberalism* (Cambridge, MA: Harvard University Press, 2018); Erich Streissler, ed., *Roads to Freedom: Essays in Honour of Friedrich A. von Hayek* (London: Routledge, 1969), 146–47.

21. Slobodian, *Globalists*, 22.

22. Carson, *Autobiography of Martin Luther King, Jr.*, 340.

23. Wilhelm Röpke, *Economic Order and International Law* (Leyde: A. W. Sijthoff, 1955), 250.

24. Slobodian, *Globalists*, 2.

25. Slobodian, *Globalists*, 10, citing Carl Schmitt, *The Nomos of the Earth in the International Law of the Jus Publicum Europaeum* (New York: Telos Press, 2003), 235.

26. William Harold Hutt, *The Economics of the Colour Bar* (London: Ludwig von Mises Institute, 1964), 7.

27. Hutt, *Economics of the Colour Bar*, 51, 11.

28. Hutt, *Economics of the Colour Bar*, 178.

29. Hutt, *Economics of the Colour Bar*, 180.

30. Hutt, *Economics of the Colour Bar*, 174, 3, 28.

31. Scott Shane, "Robert Dallek on Nixon and Kissinger," *New York Times*, April 18, 2007.

32. Karin Fischer, "The Influence of Neoliberals in Chile Before, During, and After Pinochet," in *The Road from Mont Pèlerin: The Making of the Neoliberal Thought Collective*, ed. Philip Mirowski and Dieter Plehwe (Cambridge, MA: Harvard University Press, 2015), 309.

33. James Burnham, *Suicide of the West: An Essay on the Meaning and Destiny of Liberalism* (New York: Encounter Books, 2014).

34. Enoch Powell, speech to Conservative Association meeting in Birmingham, April 20, 1968.

35. Kojo Karam, *Uncommon Wealth: Britain and the Aftermath of Empire* (London: John Murray, 2022), 102.

36. Enoch Powell, "Fixed Exchange and Dirigisme," September 4, 1968, John Enoch Powell Speech Archives, EnochPowell.info, accessed July 7, 2023.

37. Jeffrey E. Garten, *Three Days at Camp David: How a Secret Meeting in 1971 Transformed the Global Economy* (New York: Harper, 2021).

38. Milton Friedman, "Should There Be an Independent Monetary Authority?" in *In Search of a Monetary Constitution*, ed L. B. Yeager (Cambridge, MA: Harvard University Press, 1962), 224.

39. Milton Friedman, "Nobel Lecture: Inflation and Unemployment," *Journal of Political Economy* 85, no. 3 (June 1977): 451–72.

40. Nicholas Wapshott, *Samuelson Friedman: The Battle over the Free Market* (New York: Norton, 2021), 193, 200.

41. Hayek, Speech at Nobel Banquet, December 10, 1974.

42. William Greider, *Secrets of the Temple* (New York: Simon & Schuster, 1987), 543, citing an interview with Friedman on July 19, 1984.

43. Wapshott, *Samuelson Friedman*, 213.

44. Karam, *Uncommon Wealth*, 78.

CHAPTER 3: CORPORATE GUERRILLA WARFARE

1. Jerry M. Flint, "GM Reports a Rise in Hiring of Workers in Minority Groups," *New York Times*, February 7, 1970.

2. The term preceded Nixon—it first appeared in President John F. Kennedy's 1961

Executive Order 10925, which mandated that the government "take affirmative action to ensure that applicants are employed, and that employees are treated during employment, without regard to their race, creed, color or national origin." Lyndon Johnson had also endorsed equal hiring, but neither Democratic president had proposed specific targets. Section 706(g) of the Civil Rights Act of 1964 also allowed courts to order "affirmative action" as a remedy in cases where employers were intentionally discriminating based on race. Specifically, Title VII of this law mandated, "It shall be an unlawful employment practice for an employer . . . to fail or refuse to hire or to discharge an individual . . . because of such individual's race, color, religion, sex, or national origin."

3. Hugh Davis Graham, "Richard Nixon and Civil Rights: Explaining an Enigma," *Presidential Studies Quarterly* 26, no. 1 (1996): 93–106; David Frum, *How We Got Here: The 70's; The Decade That Brought You Modern Life (For Better or Worse)* (New York: Basic Books, 2008); John D. Skrentny, "Inventing Race," *Public Interest* 146 (2002): 121–22, 125, 142.

4. Graham, "Richard Nixon and Civil Rights," citing John D. Ehrlichman, *Witness to Power* (New York: Simon & Schuster, 1982).

5. Ernest Holsendolph, "Report Urges End of Minority Unit," *New York Times*, June 1, 1975.

6. Holsendolph, "Report Urges End of Minority Unit."

7. Paul Delaney, "Presidential Panel Ponders Minority Capitalism," *New York Times*, October 4, 1970.

8. A.J. Baime, "U.S. Auto Industry Came to the Rescue During WWII," *Car and Driver*, March 31, 2020.

9. Justin Hyde, "GM's 'Engine Charlie' Wilson Learned to Live with a Misquote," *Detroit Free Press*, September 14, 2008.

10. Ed Cray, *Chrome Colossus: General Motors and Its Times* (New York: McGraw-Hill, 1980); Tom Mahoney, *The Story of George Romney: Builder, Salesman, Crusader* (New York: Harper & Brothers, 1958).

11. Donald E. Schwartz, "The Public-Interest Proxy Contest: Reflections on Campaign GM," *Michigan Law Review* 69, no. 3 (1971): 422.

12. Saul Friedman, "Campaign GM: The Leaders and Their Battle Plan," *Detroit Free Press*, May 17, 1970.

13. Agis Salpukas, "Critics Dominate Meeting of GM," *New York Times*, May 23, 1970.

14. Richard Halloran, "Nader to Press for GM Reform," *New York Times*, February 8, 1970.

15. Campaign GM lawyers included Philip Moore, of Businessmen for the Public Interest; Geoffrey Gowan of the Center for Law and Social Policy; Joseph Onek, counsel for the Senate Subcommittee on Administrative Law; and John Esposito, another young DC lawyer.

16. Donald E. Schwartz, "Proxy Power and Social Goals—How Campaign GM Succeeded," *St. John's Law Review* 45, no. 4 (May 1971): 765.

17. Jerry M. Flint, "G.M. Will Win Proxy Battle with Nader, but the War May Just Be Starting," *New York Times*, May 22, 1970.

18. Schwartz, "Proxy Power," 764.

19. Schwartz, "Public-Interest Proxy Contest," 505, citing a letter from a college investment committee to James M. Roche, May 1, 1970.

20. Morton Mintz, "Campaign GM Likely to Stir New Conflict on Campus," *Washington Post*, May 24, 1970, A3.

21. Flint, "G.M. Will Win Proxy Battle."

22. Adolf A. Berle and Gardiner Coit Means, *The Modern Corporation and Private Property* (1932; repr., New Brunswick, NJ: Transaction Publishers, 1991).

23. Schwartz, "Public-Interest Proxy Contest," 419, citing Address of Manuel F. Cohen, Chairman, SEC, Before the Economic Club of Detroit, January 27, 1969.

24. Schwartz, "Public-Interest Proxy Contest," citing Ill N.J. at 154, 98 A.2d at 586.

25. Andrew Smith, Kevin D. Tennent, and Jason Russell, "Berle and Means's 'The Modern Corporation and Private Property': The Military Roots of a Stakeholder Model of Corporate Governance," *Seattle University Law Review* 42 (2019): 535–63.

26. Jeff D. Clements, *Corporations Are Not People* (San Francisco: Berrett-Koehler, 2014).

27. Lewis Powell, "Attack on American Free Enterprise System" (memorandum to Eugene Sydnor Jr., Chairman, Education Committee, U.S. Chamber of Commerce), August 23, 1971, Washington and Lee University School of Law: Scholarly Commons.

28. Kim Phillips-Fein, *Invisible Hands: The Making of the Conservative Movement from the New Deal to Reagan* (New York: Norton, 2009), ch. 7.

29. Reece Jones, *White Borders: The History of Race and Immigration in the United States* (Boston: Beacon, 2021), 118.

30. Jane Mayer, *Dark Money: The Hidden History of the Billionaires Behind the Rise of the Radical Right* (New York: Doubleday, 2016), 77–78.

31. Powell, "Attack on the Free Enterprise System."

32. Phillips-Fein, *Invisible Hands,* ch. 3, 7, and 9.

33. Mayer, *Dark Money*, 114.

34. Mayer, *Dark Money*, 112.

35. Jane Mayer, "How Right-Wing Billionaires Infiltrated Higher Education," *Chronicle of Higher Education,* February 12, 2016.

36. Mayer, "How Right-Wing Billionaires."

37. Mayer, "How Right-Wing Billionaires."

38. "William E. Simon Foundation Donations Made" (Donations Recorded by Vipul Naik), https://donations.vipulnaik.com/donor.php?donor=William+E.+Simon+Foundation, accessed August 26, 2023.

39. Angus Burgin, *The Great Persuasion: Reinventing Free Markets Since the Depression* (Cambridge, MA: Harvard University Press, 2012), 100–102.

40. Julia Smith et al., "The Atlas Network: A 'Strategic Ally' of the Tobacco Industry," *The International Journal of Health Planning and Management* 32, no. 4 (2017): 433–48.

CHAPTER 4: BLIND JUSTICE

1. Alexander Hamilton, "The Judiciary Department," *The Federalist* 78 (1788): 14.
2. KC Johnson, "Nixon and the Powell/Rehnquist Nominations," February 8, 2009, https://kc-johnson.com/nixon-and-the-powellrehnquist-nominations.
3. Johnson, "Nixon and the Powell/Rehnquist Nominations."
4. Rick Perlstein, "The Coven," in *Nixonland: The Rise of a President and the Fracturing of America* (New York: Scribner, 2009).
5. Kevin J. McMahon, *Nixon's Court: His Challenge to Judicial Liberalism and Its Political Consequences* (Chicago: University of Chicago Press, 2011).
6. Tinsley E. Yarbrough, *The Rehnquist Court and the Constitution* (New York: Oxford University Press, 2000), 2–3.
7. William Rehnquist, "A Random Thought on the Segregation Cases," https://www.govinfo.gov/content/pkg/GPO-CHRG-REHNQUIST/pdf/GPO-CHRG-REHNQUIST-4-16-6.pdf.
8. Robert L. Hale, "Coercion and Distribution in a Supposedly Non-coercive State," *Political Science Quarterly* 38, no. 3 (1923): 473.
9. Robert L. Hale, "Bargaining, Duress, and Economic Liberty," *Columbia Law Review* 43 (1943): 625.
10. Jedediah Purdy, "Neoliberal Constitutionalism: Lochnerism for a New Economy," *Law and Contemporary Problems* 77, no. 4 (2014): 197.
11. *West Coast Hotel Co. v. Parrish*, 300 U.S. 379, 391 (1937).
12. Richard Nixon, telephone conversation with John Mitchell, October 20, 1971, American RadioWorks.
13. John Jeffries, *Justice Lewis F. Powell* (New York: Fordham University Press, 2020), 234.
14. Michael J. Graetz and Linda Greenhouse, *The Burger Court and the Rise of the Judicial Right* (New York: Simon & Schuster, 2016), 85.
15. Anders Walker, "A Lawyer Looks at Civil Disobedience: Why Lewis F. Powell Jr. Divorced Diversity from Affirmative Action." *University of Colorado Law Review* 86 (2015): 5.
16. Walker, "A Lawyer Looks at Civil Disobedience," 6.
17. Nixon, telephone conversation with Mitchell.
18. Nixon, telephone conversation with Mitchell.
19. Nixon, telephone conversation with Mitchell.
20. Nixon, telephone conversation with Mitchell.
21. Lewis F. Powell Jr., "Reception and Dinner Honoring Lewis Franklin Powell, Jr., 1971," Washington and Lee University School of Law: Scholarly Commons, https://scholarlycommons.law.wlu.edu/powellspeeches/?utm_source=scholarly commons.law.wlu.edu%2Fpowellspeeches%2F21&utm_medium=PDF&utm_campaign=PDFCoverPages.
22. Jefferson Decker, *The Other Rights Revolution: Conservative Lawyers and the Remaking of American Government* (New York: Oxford University Press, 2016), 41.

23. *Va. State Bd. of Pharmacy v. Virginia Citizens Consumer Council, Inc.*, 425 U.S. 784 (Rehnquist, J., dissenting).

24. *Sorrell v. IMS Health, Inc.*, 564 U.S. 552 (2011).

25. *Final Report of the Senate Select Committee on Presidential Campaign Activities* (Senate Report 93–981), at 10 (1974), quoted in Brief for Appellees Center for Public Financing of Elections, Common Cause, League of Women Voters of the United States, et al., *Buckley v. Valeo*, 424 U.S. 1 (1976) (nos. 75–436, 75–437).

26. *Buckley v. Valeo*, 424 U.S. 1 (1976).

27. *First National Bank of Boston v. Bellotti*, 435 U.S. 765, 810 (1978).

28. Graetz and Greenhouse, *Burger Court*, 263.

29. Graetz and Greenhouse, *Burger Court*, 264.

30. Graetz and Greenhouse, *Burger Court*, 250.

31. *Central Hudson Gas and Electric Co. v. Public Service Commission*, 447 U.S. 557, 591 (1980).

32. Lewis Powell, "Attack on American Free Enterprise System" (memorandum to Eugene Sydnor Jr., Chairman, Education Committee, U.S. Chamber of Commerce), August 23, 1971, Washington and Lee University School of Law: Scholarly Commons.

33. Hamilton, "Judiciary Department," 14.

34. Karl Evers-Hillstrom, "Most Expensive Ever: 2020 Election Cost $14.4 Billion," OpenSecrets News, February 11, 2021; "Campaign Spending Data 1960–2008," Elections 101, https://elections101.iowa.gov/wp-content/uploads/2019/08/Campaign -Spending-Data–1960–2008updated.docx, accessed July 7, 2023; Anu Naranyanswamy, Darla Cameron, and Matea Gold, "How Much Money Is Behind Each Campaign?" *Washington Post*, February 1, 2017.

35. Elliot Zaret, "Commercial Speech and the Evolution of the First Amendment." Constitutional Accountability Center, September 1, 2015.

36. John C. Coates IV, "Corporate Speech and the First Amendment: History, Data, and Implications," *SSRN Electronic Journal*, February 27, 2015, 36, https://doi.org/10 .2139/ssrn.2566785.

37. Powell, "Attack on American Free Enterprise System."

38. *Griggs v. Duke Power Co.*, 401 U.S. 424 (1971).

39. Graetz and Greenhouse, *Burger Court*, 288.

40. Graetz and Greenhouse, *Burger Court*, 290.

41. *Milliken v. Bradley*, 418 U.S. 717 (1974).

42. Graetz and Greenhouse, *Burger Court*, 89.

43. Graetz and Greenhouse, *Burger Court*, 98.

44. Graetz and Greenhouse, *Burger Court*, 98.

45. The village of Euclid, Ohio, had subdivided the municipality into industrial areas, single family homes, business districts, and apartment buildings. A property owner took his case all the way to the Supreme Court, arguing that the restrictions on the use of his land were a violation of his property rights. Given the Lochner court's legacy, this should have been an easy case for the Court in favor of property rights. One of the so-called four horsemen, George Sutherland, broke with his fellow conser-

vatives, proving that property rights were not as sacrosanct as they seemed. Sutherland was more concerned with protecting property owners from the nuisances of apartment buildings—or, really, the people who resided in them—than he was with protecting property rights from state power. The existence of low-income neighborhoods was "detracting from their safety and depriving children of the privilege of quiet and open spaces for play, enjoyed by those in more favored localities—until, finally, the residential character of the neighborhood and its desirability as a place of detached residences are utterly destroyed." He called apartment buildings a "nuisance . . . like a pig in the parlor instead of the barnyard." The lower court in the Euclid case had put it more bluntly: "The blighting of property values and the congesting of population, whenever the colored or certain foreign races invade a residential section, are so well known as to be within the judicial cognizance." Sutherland added that "very often the apartment house is a mere parasite, constructed to take advantage of the open spaces and attractive surroundings created by the residential character of the district . . . interfering by their height and bulk with the free circulation of air and monopolizing the rays of the sun which otherwise would fall upon the smaller homes." *Village of Euclid v. Ambler Realty Co.*, 272 U.S. 365 (1926).
46. Graetz and Greenhouse, *Burger Court*, 98.
47. *San Antonio Independent School District v. Rodriguez*, 411 U.S. 1, 49–50 (1973).
48. *Regents of the University of California v. Bakke*, 438 U.S. 265, 274, 279, 316, 317 (1978).
49. Graetz and Greenhouse, *Burger Court*, 121.
50. *Regents of the University of California v. Bakke*, 297.
51. *Regents of the University of California v. Bakke*, 265.

CHAPTER 5: THE LEGAL COUP

1. James Q. Whitman, *Hitler's American Model: The United States and the Making of Nazi Race Law* (Princeton, NJ: Princeton University Press, 2018).
2. *Conroy v. Aniskoff*, 507 U.S. 519 (1993) (Scalia, J., concurring).
3. Antonin Scalia and Bryan A. Garner, *Reading Law: The Interpretation of Legal Texts* (St. Paul, MN: Thomson/West, 2012).
4. Richard A. Posner, *Economic Analysis of Law*, 9th ed. (New York: Wolters Kluwer Law & Business, 2014), 737.
5. Amanda Hollis-Brusky, *Ideas with Consequences: The Federalist Society and the Conservative Counterrevolution* (New York: Oxford University Press, 2019).
6. Marcia Chambers, "Yale Is a Host to Two Meetings About Politics," *New York Times*, May 2, 1982, 53.
7. "About Us," Federalist Society, accessed September 26, 2023.
8. Robert Bork, "Civil Rights—A Challenge," *New Republic* 31 (1963): 21.
9. Stuart Taylor Jr., "Bork at Yale: Colleagues Recall a Friend but a Philosophical Foe," *New York Times*, July 27, 1987.
10. *Dronenburg v. Zech*, 741 F.2d 1388 (D.C. Cir. August 17, 1984).

11. George J. Stigler, "Nobel Memorial Lecture: The Process and Progress of Economics," December 8, 1982, NobelPrize.org, 67.

12. The aphorism is supposedly borrowed from Thomas Kuhn's idea that scientific revolutions occur when new theories subvert and replace old theories—and that idea is true in certain theoretical sciences, like quantum physics, in which grand theories like Einstein's theory of relativity dominate the field because of their explanatory power and elegance, only to be proved or disproved later as observation and rigorous empirical analysis advances. Yet as Daniel Farber has noted, although "physics presents a breathtaking example of mathematical elegance combined with fantastically accurate predictions," physics is not the paradigm of science. He offers biology as a counterexample: "Biology does have a central paradigm (evolution) and an understanding of its molecular basis. But organisms, because they are the products of evolution rather than design, are extremely complex, and no one seems to think that their features can be predicted in any detail on the basis of a deductive theory." Daniel A. Farber, "Toward a New Legal Realism." *University of Chicago Law Review* 68 (2001): 279, 295.

13. U.S. Congress, Senate, Committee on the Judiciary, *Hearing on Nomination of Robert H. Bork to Be Associate Justice of the Supreme Court of the United States,* 100th Cong., 1st sess., 1987, 33 (statement of Sen. Kennedy).

14. "Federal Judicial Caseload Statistics 2020," United States Courts, accessed July 8, 2023.

15. Steven Teles, a historian of the movement, describes the Federalist Society's strategy as having chosen to pursue "an indirect approach to legal change, one that operates as a focal point for discussion and as a safe harbor for individuals who feel isolated from the mainstream of American legal culture." Steven M. Teles, *The Rise of the Conservative Legal Movement: The Battle for Control of the Law* (Princeton, NJ: Princeton University Press, 2008), 137.

16. Calvin TerBeek, " 'Clocks Must Always Be Turned Back': Brown v. Board of Education and the Racial Origins of Constitutional Originalism," *American Political Science Review* 115, no. 3 (2021): 821–34.

17. TerBeek, " 'Clocks Must Always Be Turned Back.' "

18. Hollis-Brusky, *Ideas with Consequences,* 19.

19. *District of Columbia v. Heller,* 554 U.S. 570 (2008).

20. Hollis-Brusky, *Ideas with Consequences,* 21.

21. Hollis-Brusky, *Ideas with Consequences,* 75.

22. Jay S. Bybee, "Memorandum for Albert R. Gonzales, Counsel to the President Re: Standards of Conduct for Interrogation Under 18 U.S.C. §§ 2340–2340A," August 1, 2002, available at National Security Archive, George Washington University, Washington, DC; John C. Yoo, "Memorandum for William J. Haynes II; Application of Treaties and Laws to al Qaeda and Taliban Detainees," January 9, 2002, available at National Security Archive, George Washington University, both accessed September 26, 2023.

23. *Planned Parenthood of Southeastern Pennsylvania. v. Casey* (91–744), 505 U.S. 833 (1992).

24. Jason Deparle, "Goals Reached, Donor on Right Closes Up Shop," *New York Times*, May 29, 2005.

25. Teles, *Rise of the Conservative Legal Movement*, 103.

26. Teles, *Rise of the Conservative Legal Movement*, 105.

27. Teles, *Rise of the Conservative Legal Movement*.

28. Dylan Matthews and Byrd Pinkerton, "How a Resort Weekend for Judges Made Courts More Conservative," *Vox*, June 1, 2019.

29. "Mason Judicial Education Program," Law and Economics Center, Antonin Scalia Law School, accessed July 7, 2023.

30. Elliott Ash, Daniel L. Chen, and Suresh Naidu, "Ideas Have Consequences: The Impact of Law and Economics on American Justice," National Bureau of Economic Research, Working Paper 29788, 2022, 11. See also Teles, *Rise of the Conservative Legal Movement*.

31. Ash, Chen, and Naidu, "Ideas Have Consequences," 1.

32. Fred R. Shapiro, "The Most-Cited Legal Scholars Revisited," *University of Chicago Law Review* 88 (2021): 1595.

33. Richard A. Posner, "Theories of Economic Regulation," National Bureau of Economic Research, Working Paper 41, May 1974.

34. Posner, *Economic Analysis of Law*, 9th ed., 3–4.

35. Richard A. Posner, *The Economics of Justice* (Cambridge, MA: Harvard University Press, 1981), 112.

36. Posner, *Economic Analysis of Law*, 9th ed., xxii.

37. Posner, *Economic Analysis of Law*, 9th ed., 63.

38. Richard A. Posner, "A Reply to Some Recent Criticisms of the Efficiency Theory of the Common Law," *Hofstra Law Review* 9 (1980): 792.

39. Eric Posner and Glen Weyl, "Sponsor an Immigrant Yourself," *Politico*, February 13, 2018.

40. George J. Stigler, "The Economics of Minimum Wage Legislation," *American Economic Review* 36, no. 3 (June 1946): 358–65.

41. David Card and Alan B. Krueger, "Minimum Wages and Employment: A Case Study of the Fast-Food Industry in New Jersey and Pennsylvania," *American Economic Review* 84, no. 4 (1994): 772–93.

42. Posner, *Economic Analysis of Law*, 9th ed., 444–45.

43. Posner, "Theories of Economic Regulation."

44. Friedrich Hayek, "Banquet Speech," 1974, www.nobelprize.org/prizes/economic -sciences/1974/hayek/speech/.

45. Richard A. Posner, *Economic Analysis of Law*, 2nd ed. (Boston: Little, Brown, 1977), 10.

46. Richard A. Posner, "The Ethical and Political Basis of the Efficiency Norm in Common Law Adjudication," *Hofstra Law Review* 8 (1979): 488.

47. Posner, *Economics of Justice*, 9th ed. For a critical but fair account of Posner's views on race, see Jerome McCristal Culp Jr., "Posner on Duncan Kennedy and Racial Difference: White Authority in the Legal Academy," *Duke Law Journal* 41 (1991): 1095–1114.

48. Robert Hahn, "Ronald Harry Coase (1910–2013)," *Nature* 502, no. 7472 (2013): 449.

49. Richard A. Posner, "An Economic Theory of the Criminal Law," *Columbia Law Review* 85 (1985): 1195, 1205.

50. Katrine Marçal, *Who Cooked Adam Smith's Dinner?* (New York: Simon & Schuster, 2016).

51. Paul A. Samuelson, "Economics: An Introductory Analysis," *Harvard Law Review* 65, no. 3 (1952): 542.

52. "Annual Report Statistics," Division of Corporations, State of Delaware, https://corp .delaware.gov/stats/, accessed June 27, 2023.

53. Tomas J. Philipson and Richard A. Posner, *Private Choices and Public Health: The AIDS Epidemic in an Economic Perspective* (Cambridge, MA: Harvard University Press, 1993), 38.

54. Tomas J. Philipson and Richard A. Posner, "A Theoretical and Empirical Investigation of the Effects of Public Health Subsidies for STD Testing," *Quarterly Journal of Economics* 110, no. 2 (1995): 445–74.

55. Posner and Philipson, *Private Choices and Public Health*, 5–6.

56. Melinda Cooper, *Family Values: Between Neoliberalism and the New Social Conservatism* (New York: Zone Books, 2017), 174.

57. Cooper, *Family Values*, 170–72.

58. Martha Ainsworth and A. Mead Over, "Confronting AIDS: Public Priorities in a Global Epidemic," World Bank, 1997, 106.

59. Ainsworth and Over, "Confronting AIDS," 105–6.

60. Isaac Chotiner, "The Contrarian Coronavirus Theory That Informed the Trump Administration," *New Yorker*, March 30, 2020.

61. Ludwig von Mises, "Economic Nationalism and Peaceful Economic Cooperation," in *Money, Method, and the Market Process: Essays by Ludwig von Mises*, ed. Richard M. Ebeling (Norwell, MA: Kluwer Academic, 1990).

CHAPTER 6: THE CONSCIENCE OF CAPITALISM

1. Tom Geoghegan, "Ayn Rand: Why Is She So Popular?" BBC, August 17, 2012.

2. Lisa Duggan, *Mean Girl: Ayn Rand and the Culture of Greed* (Berkeley: University of California Press, 2019).

3. Anne C. Heller, *Ayn Rand and the World She Made* (New York: Nan A. Talese/Doubleday, 2009).

4. Sebastian Mallaby, *The Man Who Knew: The Life and Times of Alan Greenspan* (New York: Penguin, 2016), 274.

5. James B. Murphy, "Friedrich Hayek: Not Exactly the Libertarian Darling He's Claimed As," *Literary Hub*, September 25, 2019.

6. Ayn Rand to Senator Barry Goldwater, June 4, 1960, Ayn Rand Institute, Irvine, CA, Archive Item Ref. Code: 043_05A_011_001.

7. The activists who devised and tried these strategies include Paul Weyrich of the Heritage Foundation, the direct mail strategist Richard Viguerie, Howard Phillips of the Conservative Caucus, Terry Dolan of the National Conservative Political Action Committee, and representatives from the Alliance Defending Freedom and the National Right to Life Committee.

8. Randall Balmer, "The Real Origins of the Religious Right," *Politico*, May 27, 2014.

9. Ayn Rand, *The Ayn Rand Lexicon: Objectivism from A to Z*, ed. Harry Binswanger (New York: NAL, 1988).

10. Rand, *Ayn Rand Lexicon*.

11. David Mills, "Ayn Rand's 'To a Gas Chamber—Go!'" *Patheos*, June 22, 2014.

12. Margaret Thatcher, interview for *Weekend World*, London Weekend Television, January 6, 1980.

13. Clayborne Carson, ed., *The Autobiography of Martin Luther King, Jr.* (New York: Warner/Hachette, 1998), 340.

14. Ronald Reagan, "Remarks at the Annual Meeting of the Boards of Governors of the World Bank Group and International Monetary Fund," September 29, 1981, American Presidency Project, University of California–Santa Barbara.

15. Adam Smith, *Selections from The Wealth of Nations*, ed. George J. Stigler (New York: Appleton-Century-Crofts, 1957); see also Adam Smith, *An Inquiry into the Nature and Causes of the Wealth of Nations*, ed. Edwin Cannon (Chicago: University of Chicago Press, 1976).

16. In the years 2000 to 1400 BCE, usury is mentioned in the Vedic texts of ancient India; in 700–100 BCE the Sutra texts prohibit usury, as do the Buddhist Jatakas of 600–400 BCE. Vasishtha, a well-known Hindu lawmaker of that time, forbade usury and disparaged the practice, saying that only "hypocritical ascetics are accused of practicing it." See L. C. Jain, *Indigenous Banking in India* (London: Macmillan, 1929), 6. Vasishtha made a special law that forbade the higher castes of Brahmanas (priests) and Kshatriyas (warriors) from being usurers or lenders at interest. See Jain, *Indigenous Banking in India*, and David Graeber, *Debt: The First 5000 Years* (Brooklyn: Melville House, 2011), 10–11.

17. John T. Noonan Jr., *A Church That Can and Cannot Change: The Development of Catholic Moral Teaching* (Notre Dame, Ind.: University of Notre Dame Press, 2005).

18. Adam Smith, "Book II: On the Nature, Accumulation, and Employment of Stock," in *The Wealth of Nations* (London: W. Strahan and T. Cadell, 1776).

19. Smith, *Wealth of Nations*, 340.

20. Milton Friedman, "Defense of Usury," *Newsweek*, April 6, 1970.

21. Jeremy Bentham, *Defence of Usury* (London: Payne and Foss, 1787).

22. Anne Fleming, *City of Debtors: A Century of Fringe Finance* (Cambridge, MA: Harvard University Press, 2018).

23. *Jones v. Star Credit Corp.*, 59 Misc. 2d 189 (Sup. Ct. Nassau Cty. 1969).

24. *Javins v. First National Realty Corporation*, 428 F.2d 1071 (D.C. Cir. 1970).

25. Anne Fleming, "The Rise and Fall of Unconscionability as the 'Law of the Poor,'" *Georgetown Law Journal* 102 (2014): 1383–1441; Richard A. Epstein, "Unconscionability: A Critical Reappraisal," *Journal of Law and Economics* 18 (1975): 293, 307, 315.

26. Ronald H. Coase, "The Problem of Social Costs," *Journal of Law and Economics* 3 (1960): 15.

27. Richard A. Posner, "An Economic Approach to Legal Procedure and Judicial Administration," *Journal of Legal Studies* 2, no. 2 (1973): 399–458.

28. *Am. Express Co. v. Italian Colors Rest.*, 570 U.S. 228 (2013).

29. "Payday Lending in America: Who Borrows, Where They Borrow, and Why," Pew Charitable Trusts, 2012.

30. "Payday Loan Facts and the CFPB's Impact," Pew Charitable Trusts, January 14, 2016.

31. Nakita Cuttino, "The Rise of 'Fringetech': Regulatory Risks in Earned Wage Access," *Northwestern University Law Review* 115, no. 6 (2020): 1505.

32. Stephen J. Dubner, "Are Payday Loans Really as Evil as People Say?" Freakonomics.com, April 6, 2016.

33. Joe Valenti and Eliza Schultz, "How Predatory Debt Traps Threaten Vulnerable Families," Center for American Progress, October 6, 2016.

34. Davide Scigliuzzo, "Charging 589% Interest in the Pandemic Is a Booming Business," Bloomberg.com, May 17, 2021.

35. "Fact v. Fiction: The Truth About Payday Lending Industry Claims," Center for Responsible Lending, January 1, 2001.

36. Charles Murray, "The Immortal Sowell," *Claremont Review of Books,* March 3, 2022.

CHAPTER 7: THERE IS NO SUCH THING AS SOCIETY

1. Sam Tanenhaus, "The Architect of the Radical Right," *The Atlantic*, July–August 2017.

2. G. Warren Nutter and James M. Buchanan, "Different School Systems Are Reviewed," *Richmond Times-Dispatch,* April 12, 1959, D3.

3. James Buchanan and Gordon Tullock, *The Calculus of Consent: Logical Foundations of Constitutional Democracy* (1962; repr., Indianapolis: Liberty Fund, 1999).

4. Buchanan and Tullock, *Calculus of Consent.*

5. Milton Friedman, "The Line We Dare Not Cross," *Encounter*, November 1976.

6. Gary S. Becker, *The Economic Approach to Human Behavior* (Chicago: University of Chicago Press, 1976), 5.

7. Edmund S. Morgan, *American Slavery, American Freedom: The Ordeal of Colonial Virginia* (New York: Norton, 2003), 376.

8. James M. Buchanan, *The Limits of Liberty: Between Anarchy and Leviathan* (Chicago: University of Chicago Press, 1975), 188–91.

9. Philip Murowski, *Never Let a Serious Crisis Go to Waste: How Neoliberalism Survived the Financial Meltdown* (London: Verso, 2014), 41, citing Buchanan's "presidential talk" at the Mont Pelerin Society, San Vincenzo, Italy, August 31, 1986.

10. Nancy MacLean, *Democracy in Chains: The Deep History of the Radical Right's Stealth Plan for America* (New York: Viking, 2017), 152.

11. MacLean, *Democracy in Chains*, 158–60.

12. Tom Redburn, "Economist Theorist of 'Public Choice' School: James M. Buchanan Wins Nobel Prize," *Los Angeles Times*, October 17, 1986.

13. John J. Miller, "The Heritage Mandate: Government Grows, but a Famous Book Shrinks," Wayback Machine, January 20, 2005, accessed September 26, 2023.

14. Richard Holwill, *The First Year* (Washington, DC: Heritage Foundation, 1981), 1; Kathy Sawyer, "Heritage Foundation Gives Reagan Passing Grade," *Washington Post*, November 22, 1981.

15. Matt Bai, "Newt Again," *New York Times*, February 25, 2009.

16. Gregg Easterbrook, "'Ideas Move Nations': How Conservative Think Tanks Have Helped to Transform the Terms of Political Debate," *The Atlantic*, January 1986, 66–80.

17. Bai, "Newt Again."

18. "New 'Mandate for Leadership' Will Help Citizens Keep Politicians Honest" (press release), Heritage Foundation, January 10, 2005, accessed July 9, 2023.

19. George Stigler, "The Theory of Economic Regulation," *Bell Journal of Economics and Management Science* 4, no. 2 (1971): 3–18.

20. Daniel Carpenter, "George Stigler's Errors and Their Virtues," *ProMarket* (Stigler Center for the Study of the Economy and the State), July 6, 2021.

21. Adair Turner, *Between Debt and the Devil: Money, Credit, and Fixing Global Finance* (Princeton, NJ: Princeton University Press, 2016), 2.

22. George J. Stigler, "The Process and Progress of Economics" (Nobel Memorial Lecture), December 8, 1982.

23. Stigler, "Process and Progress of Economics."

24. Andrew Rudalevige, "Beyond Structure and Process: The Early Institutionalization of Regulatory Review," *Journal of Policy History* 30, no. 4 (2018): 577–608.

25. Rudalevige, "Beyond Structure and Process."

26. Karl Polanyi, *The Great Transformation* (1944; repr., Boston: Beacon Press, 2001), 38–62.

27. Polanyi, *Great Transformation*, 38–62.

28. Polanyi, *Great Transformation*, 38–62.

29. Polanyi, *Great Transformation*, 38–62.

30. Polanyi, *Great Transformation*, 38–62.

CHAPTER 8: BARBARIANS AT THE GATE

1. Bray Hammond, a leading historian of early American banking, had described the relationship of early American society with its banks in these terms: the community "adapted private initiative and wealth to public purposes, granting privileges and exacting duties in return. . . There persisted a strong conviction that a charter was a

covenant." Bray Hammond, *Banks and Politics in America, from the Revolution to the Civil War* (Princeton, NJ: Princeton University Press, 1957), 67.

2. *McCulloch v. Maryland*, 17 U.S. 316 (1819) at 436 (holding that the Second Bank was an "instrument employed by the government"); Louis D. Brandeis, *Other People's Money and How the Bankers Use It* (New York: Frederick A. Stokes, 1914), 18–19, 46; Warren L. Dennis, *The Community Reinvestment Act of 1977: Its Legislative History and Its Impact on Applications for Changes in Structure Made by Depository Institutions to the Four Federal Financial Supervisory Agencies*, Department of Housing and Urban Development, Working Paper No. 24, 1978, http://faculty.msb.edu/prog/ CRC/pdf/wp24.pdf. Senator William Proxmire compared a bank charter to "a franchise to serve local convenience and needs" and suggested that "it is fair for the public to ask something in return."

3. *Divide County v. Baird*, 55 N.D. 45, 212 N.W. 236 (N.D. 1926).

4. Simon Johnson and James Kwak, *Thirteen Bankers: The Wall Street Takeover and the Next Financial Meltdown* (New York: Vintage, 2011), 105.

5. Michael McLeay, Amar Radia, and Ryland Thomas, "Money Creation in the Modern Economy," *Bank of England Quarterly Bulletin* 54 (2014): 14, 20–21.

6. *Time*, November 4, 1929, 46.

7. Walter Bagehot, *Lombard Street: A Description of the Money Market* (London: Henry S. King, 1873), 17–18.

8. Bagehot, *Lombard Street*, 17–18.

9. Brandeis, *Other People's Money*, 18, 49. JP Morgan & Co., along with two New York banks, National City and First National, constituted the so-called money trusts.

10. Brandeis, *Other People's Money*, 18–19. Emphasis added.

11. Johnson and Kwak, *Thirteen Bankers*, 105.

12. Johnson and Kwak, *Thirteen Bankers*, 66.

13. Brandeis, *Other People's Money*, 214.

14. Bank Holding Company Act of 1956 (Pub. L. No. 84–511, 70 Stat. 133); Banking Act of 1933 (Pub. L. No. 73–66, 48 Stat. 162) (also known as the Glass-Steagall Act).

15. Federal Deposit Insurance Corporation, *1987 Annual Report* (Washington, DC: Federal Deposit Insurance Corporation, 1988), 22.

16. Federal Deposit Insurance Corporation, *Mandate for Change: Restructuring the Banking Industry* (Washington, DC: Federal Deposit Insurance Corporation, 1987). The report included this assertion: "If banking companies are to maintain the earnings potential fundamental to their continued viability, they must have the opportunity to offer the products and services necessary to compete on even terms with their new competitors."

17. U.S. Congress, Senate, Committee on Banking, Housing, and Urban Affairs, statement of Alan Greenspan, chairman, Board of Governors of the Federal Reserve System, 100th Cong., 1st sess., December 1, 1987.

18. Jonathan Levy, *Ages of American Capitalism* (New York: Random House, 2021), 606.

19. Alan Greenspan, Chairman, Board of Governors of the Federal Reserve System,

remarks at the Meetings of the American Economic Association, January 3, 2004, "Speeches of Federal Reserve Officials," federalreserve.org.

20. Greenspan, American Economic Association remarks.

21. Saule T. Omarova, "The Quiet Metamorphosis: How Derivatives Changed the 'Business of Banking,'" *Cornell Law Faculty Publications* (2009): 1021.

22. Office of the Comptroller, interpretive letter #892, Re: 12 USC 24 (7), September 13, 2000, p. 9.

23. Federal Deposit Insurance Corporation, *1970 Annual Report*, 194–95 (table 105); Robert Adams and John Driscoll, "How the Largest Bank Holding Companies Grew: Organic Growth or Acquisitions?" Board of Governors of the Federal Reserve System, December 21, 2018 (estimates today are between $14 and $19 trillion); Alex J. Pollock, Hasim Hamandi, Ruth Leung, and OFR, "Banking Credit System, 1970–2020," Office of Financial Research, January 6, 2021, https://www.financialresearch.gov/the-ofr-blog/2021/01/06/banking-credit-system–1970–2020/.

24. "Large Holding Companies," Federal Financial Institutions Examination Council, National Information Center, 2019, accessed September 20, 2023.

25. "Large Holding Companies."

26. "Large Holding Companies."

27. Levy, *Ages of American Capitalism*, 608.

28. Greta R. Krippner, *Capitalizing on Crisis: The Political Origins of the Rise of Finance* (Cambridge, MA: Harvard University Press, 2011), 101. A Treasury report concluded that "the capital inflows to the United States . . . will permit interest rates to be lower here than they otherwise would be, preserving jobs in interest rate sensitive industries, and [allowing] more capital formation than would otherwise be the case."

29. Krippner, *Capitalizing on Crisis*, 71, 101.

CHAPTER 9: MISTAKES WERE MADE

1. Barack Obama, *A Promised Land* (New York: Crown, 2020), 165.

2. Obama, *A Promised Land*, 165.

3. Obama, *A Promised Land*, 165.

4. Obama, *A Promised Land*, 165–66.

5. Franklin D. Roosevelt, "Address at Madison Square Garden," October 31, 1936, American Presidency Project, University of California–Santa Barbara.

6. William J. Clinton, "First Inaugural Address," January 20, 1993, Avalon Project at Yale Law School, New Haven.

7. Andrew Ross Sorkin, "Paulson's Itchy Finger, on the Trigger of a Bazooka," *New York Times,* September 8, 2008.

8. Simon Johnson and James Kwak, *Thirteen Bankers: The Wall Street Takeover and the Next Financial Meltdown* (New York: Vintage, 2011), 154.

9. Johnson and Kwak, *Thirteen Bankers*, 153.

10. "The Chairman/Alice Waters," *60 Minutes*, CBS News, https://www.youtube.com/watch?v=hiCs_YHlKSI.

11. James B. Stewart, "Eight Days: The Battle to Save the American Financial System," *New Yorker*, September 14, 2009.

12. Rajeev Syal, "Tony Blair Admits Labour Didn't Fully Understand Complex Financial Sector," *Guardian*, July 22, 2012.

13. U.S. Congress, House, Committee on Oversight and Government Reform, testimony of Alan Greenspan, October 23, 2008.

14. Justin Fox, "Bob Lucas on the Comeback of Keynesianism," *Time*, October 28, 2008.

15. Richard A. Posner, "How I Became a Keynesian," *New Republic*, September 22, 2009.

16. Economists may have forgotten *The General Theory of Employment, Interest, and Money* and moved on, but economics has not outgrown it, or the informal mode of argument that it exemplifies, which can illuminate nooks and crannies that are closed to mathematics. Keynes's masterpiece is many things, but "outdated" it is not.

17. Posner, "How I Became a Keynesian."

18. Richard A. Posner, *Economic Analysis of Law*, 9th ed. (New York: Wolters Kluwer Law & Business, 2014).

19. "Barack Obama's Speech at Nasdaq," *New York Times*, September 17, 2007.

20. Ron Suskind, *Confidence Men: Wall Street, Washington, and the Education of a President* (New York: Harper, 2011).

21. Obama, *A Promised Land*, 211.

22. Obama, *A Promised Land*, 182.

23. Obama, *A Promised Land*, 211–12.

24. Lawrence H. Summers, "Promoting the Economic Rebound," *Washington Post*, March 25, 2012.

25. Benjamin Wallace-Wells, "Larry Summers Versus the Stimulus," *New Yorker*, March 18, 2021.

26. Jeff Stein and Tyler Pager, "Larry Summers Has President Biden's Ear—But Not Always His Support," *Washington Post,* October 3, 2022.

27. Jane Mayer, *Dark Money: The Hidden History of the Billionaires Behind the Rise of the Radical Right* (New York: Doubleday, 2016), 6.

28. Mayer, *Dark Money,* 21.

29. Department of the Treasury, "Treasury Announces TARP Capital Purchase Program Description" (press release), October 14, 2008, https://home.treasury.gov/news/press-releases/hp1207#:~:text=Treasury%20Announces%20TARP%20Capital%20Purchase%20Program%20Description,-October%2014%2C%202008&text=Washington%20%2D%20Treasury%20today%20announced%20a,to%20support%20the%20U.S.%20economy, accessed September 21, 2023; Department of the Treasury, "Troubled Assets Relief Program (TARP)," accessed September 26, 2023.

30. "Report Raises Concerns About U.S. Housing Aid Program," Reuters, July 24, 2013.

31. Neil Barofsky, *Bailout: How Washington Abandoned Main Street While Rescuing Wall Street* (New York: Free Press, 2013), 157.

32. Barofsky, *Bailout*, 157.

33. Barofsky, *Bailout*, 123.

34. Obama. *A Promised Land*, 158.

35. Timothy F. Geithner, *Stress Test: Reflections on Financial Crises* (New York: Crown, 2015).

36. Obama, *A Promised Land*, 297.

37. Obama, *A Promised Land*, 297.

38. P. T. Larsen, "Goldman Pays the Price of Being Big," *Financial Times*, August 13, 2007.

39. Sam Jones, "Failing the Stress Test; or, in the Long Run, We're All Dead," *Financial Times*, February 13, 2009.

40. Mark Thoma, "Low-Income Loans Didn't Cause the Financial Crisis," CBS News, January 21, 2015.

41. Mark Thoma, "Here's What Really Caused the Housing Crisis," CBS News, January 10, 2017.

42. Sven Beckert, *Empire of Cotton* (New York: Vintage, 2015), 281.

43. Charles W. Calomiris and Stephen H. Haber, *Fragile by Design: The Political Origins of Banking Crises and Scarce Credit* (Princeton, NJ: Princeton University Press, 2015), 497–98.

CHAPTER 10: STONKS

1. Max Fisher, *The Chaos Machine: The Inside Story of How Social Media Rewired Our Minds and Our World* (New York: Little, Brown, 2022).

2. William J. Brady, Killian McLoughlin, Tuan N. Doan, and Molly J. Crockett, "How Social Learning Amplifies Moral Outrage Expression in Online Social Networks," *Science Advances* 7, no. 33 (August 2021).

3. Sam Shead, "Facebook Owns the Four Most Downloaded Apps of the Decade," BBC News, December 18, 2019.

4. Adam Saratariano, Scott Reinhard, Cade Metz, Sheera Frenkel, and Malika Khurana, "Elon Musk's Unmatched Power in the Stars," *New York Times,* July 28, 2023.

5. Robert Frank, "The Wealthiest 10% of Americans Own a Record 89% of U.S. Stocks," CNBC.com, October 18, 2021; Alexandre Tanzi and Mike Dorning, "Top 1% of U.S. Earners Now Hold More Wealth Than All of the Middle Class," *Bloomberg,* October 8, 2021.

6. Matt Novak, "Reality Star Who Sells Her Farts in Jars Pivots to Selling Fart NFTs," Gizmodo, January 5, 2022.

7. Musk's tweet referenced a viral meme depicting a self-serious trader, prognosticating with hand on chin, standing in front of a PowerPoint chart showing a rising stock price called "Stonks."

8. Tara Siegel Bernard, Emily Flitter, and Anupreeta Das, "Buy GameStop, Fight Injustice. Just Don't Sell," *New York Times*, January 29, 2022.

9. Bernard, Flitter, and Das, "Buy GameStop."

10. Ernesto Frontera, "A History of 'The DAO' Hack," CoinMarketCap, June 2021.

11. Edmund Lee, "Why Blockchains Can Be Really Bad. Or: How Techno-Futurists Can Ruin Things," *Vox*, June 19, 2016.

12. Frontera, "History."

13. "The Ethereum Classic Declaration of Independence," Ethereum Classic, August 13, 2016.

14. Gilad Edelman, "Paradise at the Crypto Arcade: Inside the Web3 Revolution," *Wired*, May 10, 2022.

15. Edelman, "Paradise at the Crypto Arcade."

16. Clare M. Reckert, "Executive Pay Still Rising," *New York Times*, April 30, 1972.

17. Theodore Schleifer, "How a Crypto Billionaire Decided to Become One of Biden's Biggest Donors," *Vox*, March 20, 2021.

CONCLUSION: THE BIG DUMB MACHINE

1. Robert Frank, "The Wealthiest 10% of Americans Own a Record 89% of All U.S. Stocks," CNBC.com, October 18, 2021.

2. Congressional Budget Office, "The Federal Budget in Fiscal Year 2022: An Infographic," March 28, 2023.

3. Max Matza, "Jeff Bezos and the Secretive World of Superyachts," BBC.com, May 14, 2022; Insight Partners Industry Report, "Luxury Yacht Market Forecast to 2028—COVID-19 Impact and Global Analysis by Type, Material, and Size," February 2023; Evan Osnos, "The Haves and the Have-Yachts," *New Yorker*, July 18, 2022.

4. Winston Churchill, speech in the House of Commons, November 11, 1947.

5. W. E. B. Du Bois, review of *Is Man Free?*, by Richard M. Weaver, *Scientific Monthly* 66, no. 5 (1948): 432–33.

6. Thomas Paine, *Common Sense: The Call to Independence* (Woodbury, NY: Barron's, 1975).

Index

Page numbers after 368 refer to endnotes.